Asbury Theological Seminary Series in World Christian Revitalization Movements

This volume is published in cooperation with the Center for the Study of World Christian Revitalization Movements at Asbury Theological Seminary. Building on the work of the previous Wesleyan/Holiness Studies Center at the Seminary, the Center provides a focus for research in the history and practice of revitalization movements within the Christian tradition. The purpose of this project is to sponsor interdisciplinary, international, and interdenominational research on the relationship between religious revivals and socio-cultural change. The research includes the impact of revivals and revival movements on the formation of revitalized societies. It seeks to develop analytical models of these movements, including their biblical and theological assessment, and it bridges relevant discourses in several disciplines in order to gain insights for effective Christian mission globally. The Center recognizes the need for conducting research that combines insights from the history of evangelical renewal and revival movements with anthropological and religious studies literature on revitalization movements. It also networks with similar or related research and study centers around the world, in addition to sponsoring its own research projects.

Professor Crutcher's study of John Wesley's understanding of experience takes that discussion to new depths and clarity, and in so doing he serves to advance the concern for revitalization within Christianity that cannot be meaningfully articulated without attention to this foundational issue.

J. Steven O'Malley
Director, Center for the Study of World Christian Revitalization Movements
Editor, The Asbury Theological Seminary Series in Pietist and Wesleyan Studies

The Crucible of Life

The Role of Experience in John Wesley's Theological Method

Timothy J. Crutcher

EMETH PRESS
www.emethpress.com

The Crucible of Life
The Role of Experience in John Wesley's Theological Method

Library of Congress Cataloging-in-Publication Data

Crutcher, Timothy J.
 The crucible of life : the role of experience in John Wesley's theological method / by Timothy J. Crutcher.
    p. cm. -- (Asbury Theological Seminary series in world Christian revitalization movements. Pietist/Wesleyan studies)
 Includes bibliographical references (p.   ) and index.
 ISBN 978-0-9819582-7-9 (alk. paper)
 1. Wesley, John, 1703-1791. 2. Experience (Religion) 3. Theology--Methodology. I. Title.
 BR110.C78 2010
 230'.7092--dc22   2009048557

To Brint, for the priceless gift of an intelligent friendship

Table of Contents

Note on Citing Wesley 9
Foreword 11
Acknowledgements 13
Introduction 15

Part One

1. Cultural and Philosophical Background 21
2. Wesley and Aristotelian Logic 27
3. Wesley and Scientific Materialism 37
4. Wesley and British Empiricism 45
5. Wesley and the Rationalist Tradition 61

Part Two

6. The Epistemic Role of Experience 75
7. The A Priori Role of Logic 89
8. The A Priori Role of Scripture 97
9. The Dynamics of Experience 115
10. The Spiritual Senses 125

Part Three

11. From Experience to Scripture 141
12. From Scripture to Experience 155
13. Wesley's Sources for Religious Experience 185
14. Wesley's Theological Method 203

Part Four

15. Implications of Wesley's Experiential Theology 215
16. Experiential Theology as Relational Theology 219
17. Experiential Theology as Ecumenical Theology 231
18. Experiential Theology as Interdisciplinary Theology 243
19. Experiential Theology as *Overly Pragmatic* Theology 247
20. Retrospect and Prospect 259
Works Cited 265
Index 271

Note on Citing Wesley

All citations in this work are from John Wesley unless otherwise noted. In citing Wesley, one faces the difficulty of citing him in the way most accessible to readers. On the one hand, the publication of the new Bicentennial edition of Wesley's works will hopefully standardize the process. But that edition is neither complete nor widely available outside of North America. For most students of Wesley in the world, the Third Edition of his works (John Wesley, *The Works of John Wesley*, 14 vols., ed. Thomas Jackson [1872; reprint, Kansas City: Beacon Hill Press of Kansas City, 1986]), in English and in its various translations, both print and on-line, remains the most accessible edition of his works. In this work, we have chosen to make that our general standard. We will cite that edition as *Jackson* followed by the volume number and page number (*e.g. Jackson* 9:134). Supplemental information from the Standard edition of Wesley's *Journal* (such as complete names where the Third Edition only gives, e.g., "Miss L—") has been added without notation. There will be occasions when we must refer to the Standard edition of the letters for material not in Jackson (John Wesley, *The Letters of the Rev. John Wesley, A.M.*, 8 vols., ed. John Telford [London: Epworth Press, 1931]), and those will be cited as *Telford* and follow the conventions of the Jackson edition outlined above.

In addition to this information, however, and to assist those who do have access to other editions (including non-English ones), we have also included enough information about the citation to be able to find it exactly in any other edition of Wesley's work. All citations from the *Journal* and from Wesley's letters, therefore, will include the date. Citations from sermons and other works divided into sections and subsections will include that information (*e.g.* Sermon #55 "On the Trinity" §23 or Sermon #50 The Use of Money §II.5); sections clearly implied but not expressed will be indicated by square brackets (e.g. The Doctrine of Original Sin—Part II §[II].20). Few editions of Wesley's Explanatory Notes upon the New Testament have page numbers, and so those notes will be cited merely by referring the reader to the appropriate biblical reference. While this does make the citations of Wesley in this work somewhat longer, it will hopefully enable any reader in any language to find the appropriate passages in Wesley quickly and easily.

Foreword

It is a delight to welcome this new volume on the place of experience in the theology of John Wesley. Much recent work has been at pains to expound the place of the quadrilateral of scripture, tradition, reason, and experience in the Wesley's epistemology. Timothy Crutcher provides a valuable corrective to this discussion by exploring in detail the place of experience in Wesley's thinking and by showing the subtle and complicated connection between the appeal to experience and the appeal to scripture. Yet he does this without ignoring the place of reason and tradition in Wesley. Thus we have a fresh and illuminating foray into Wesley that moves the discussion forward in a constructive fashion.

Crutcher's scholarship is marked by careful attention to Wesley's manifold writings and to the historical context in which Wesley operated. This is vital if we are not to remake Wesley in our image and use him as a convenient cipher for our own interests and prejudices. To be sure, our historical work is driven by interests. However, our secondary interests should be resolutely governed by an interest of the first degree, that is, the desire to find out what Wesley himself held. In the end we have to face the evidence that we encounter in the sources and let that evidence lead us wherever it will. Crutcher is no impartial student. He has deep affection for Wesley, and he is convinced that Wesley has much to teach us in the present. Yet the outcomes these interests evoke are not allowed to cook the historical books in advance; he attends systematically to relevant considerations in his interpretation of Wesley. It is particularly important in this regard that he dismantles the popular view that Wesley was a Lockean empiricist by showing that Wesley was an aggressive Aristotelian in his vision of the place of experience in his empiricism.

Crutcher also shows that Wesley can speak in a helpful way to the current debate about the move from modernity to postmodernity. The shift is at heart an epistemological shift, so it cannot be resolved without serious engagement with epistemological issues in their own right. Yet our engagement, if it is to be fruitful, requires that we bring to the table the density and diversity of historical investigation. In Crutcher's nimble hands Wesley turns out to be a valuable site of historical investigation in this regard. There is a pleasing combination of rigor and modesty in the work at this point.

An important feature of this work is that it was originally done at the margins of European scholarship and away from the more polemical impulses that have marred some scholarship on Wesley in the United States of America. It represents a fresh and independent perspective that injects fresh insight and vigor into the discussion. It also represents the work of a new generation of scholars who continue to find insight and inspiration in the theology of John Wesley. Clearly Wesley is in good hands in the transition to this new world.

William J. Abraham
Southern Methodist University

Acknowledgements

In the academic journey that has led to the production of work, I have had the good fortune to be guided by wonderful people and embedded in great institutions. I wish to thank Prof. Jacques Haers of the Catholic University of Louvain, under whose direction this project first set out. The Department of Religion at Africa Nazarene University, especially the Dr. Rodney Reed and University Vice-Chancellor Leah Marangu, generously gave me all the space they could for me to finish my research and writing. I have also benefited the support of my current institution, Southern Nazarene University, and from the dialogue and insights of my students in various courses on John Wesley that I have taught over the years. I am grateful for the encouragement given me by Dr. William Abraham, and for his gracious willingness to write the foreword for this book. I am also appreciative of the work of my student assistant, Allison Beaty, particularly in the tedious business of compiling the index for this book. Finally, I must acknowledge the faithful support of my wife Rhonda, and the wonderful distraction of my children: Andrew, Alexander, and Elizabeth. Without them this project may have been completed much more quickly than it was, but it would then have been a poorer piece for all that.

Introduction

The connection between theology and experience is both important and dangerous to the task of theology. It is important because, divorced from human experience, theology becomes dry and bookish, an objective confession of orthodoxy with little connection to the way believers live their lives. It is dangerous because, in unreservedly embracing human experience, theology becomes anthropology, a subjective rationalization of religious feelings and not a discourse about God. Any theologian who might wish to craft a theology that is both objectively true and subjectively relevant must live in the tension between these two extremes.

Although this tension has proven itself notoriously difficult to maintain, one theologian and evangelist who seems to have struck the balance well is the Eighteenth Century British church planter John Wesley. Depending on whether or not one approves of his movement, John Wesley was anything from a demagogue who propounded an irrational, enthusiastic and fundamentally damaging religion[1] to a religious reformer of the first rank who almost single-handedly saved England from revolution and civil war.[2] Reading such reports, it is hard to believe they are discussing the same person.

In emphasizing the role that experience plays in theology, Wesley was often charged with enthusiasm by his critics, who felt that the risks involved in speaking of or seeking out an "experience of God" were too great. Here the Bishop of Bristol, in a conversation recorded by Wesley very early in his ministry, speaks for a great number of Anglican clerics and leaders. "Sir," he told Wesley, "the pretending to extraordinary revelations and gifts of the Holy Ghost is a horrid thing, a very horrid thing!"[3] At the same time, Wesley's enduring influence (however much some overstate it) cannot be ignored, and that influence may be traced in large measure to his ability to balance objective truth claims and their subjective appropriation. He was, as we shall see, very aware of the dangers of using experience in theology, but he felt that to avoid it was also to avoid Christianity, and so he sought to use experience in a responsible way. The recovery of the insights that guided him in his approach is the primary purpose of our investigation.

Given that one can hardly open a book on Wesley's theology without seeing some mention of experience (often joined with Scripture, Reason and Tradition in something called the Wesleyan or Methodist Quadrilateral), one might legitimately ask why another such book is needed. However, while a good deal of productive thought and insight have come to the surface in the last century of studying Wesley's understanding of experience, there is yet work to be done and critical problems to be addressed.

First, despite broad recognition of the importance of experience to Wesley, there has not been any comprehensive survey of his use of experience in the way that his use of other theological sources has been studied, sources such as Scripture, tradition, or reason.[4] This book is intended to help fill that gap.

Second, it seems that most in-depth treatments of experience in Wesley have tended to place him at the extremes mentioned above rather than place him in the middle, where—or so we will contend—he belongs. Early in the twentieth century, there was a whole spate of literature emphasizing the priority of experience in Wesley, painting him in almost Schleiermacherian tones and drawing clear parallels between his use of experience in theology and the use of experiment in science.[5] In response and in reaction to that, the literature of the late twentieth century has tended to emphasize the priority of Scripture in Wesley's thought, leaving to experience a more confirmatory than constructive role.[6] That correction, while understandable, seems to have obscured the irreplaceable role that experience plays as a source for theological reflection in Wesley. This book is an attempt to elucidate the balance that Wesley achieved between Scripture and experience, a balance we believe worthy of emulation.

Finally, there is the significant and ongoing question of Wesley's own epistemological orientation and its relationship (or lack thereof) to his theology. No affirmations of knowledge—religious or otherwise—come in a vacuum. One's general understanding of knowledge will always, if only implicitly, inform one's approach to the knowledge of God. Almost all the studies that deal explicitly with Wesley's understanding and use of experience begin with a crucial assumption: that Wesley finds his philosophical home in British Empiricism—whether directly from Locke or mediated through Peter Browne.[7] However, this association demands that one either ignore the *foundational* role experience played in that tradition or concede that Wesley's explicit epistemology has little to do with his theological method, in which God's revelation as presented in Scripture is given a clear priority over experience. This book will challenge that assumption by showing how an understanding of Wesley as an Aristotelian empiricist (as opposed to a British one) allows Wesley to function with epistemological integrity, giving a priority to the truths of Scripture but relying on experience to determine how those truths are to be understood.

We will begin our investigation of the interrelationship between Wesley's theological method and his religious epistemology by situating Wesley within the philosophical context of Eighteenth Century England. By reflecting on how Wesley saw himself fitting (and not fitting) into his own intellectual milieu, the problems of classifying him as a British Empiricist become evident and his explicit association with the Aristotelian tradition become clearer. This is comprise Part One of our investigation.

Given this contextualization, we will move on in Part Two to explore the way in which experience actually functions as an authority in Wesley. We will first explore the way Wesley uses the idea of experience as a public and active concern (as opposed to a private and passive one). We will then note the importance of the way Wesley's a priori authorities, namely Scripture and logic, interact with experience. From here we will demonstrate the dynamic that this interaction creates as a new way of conceptualizing the central features of Wesleyan theological method. As one test case of this, we will finish Part Two by exploring the way understanding this dynamic shapes our approach to Wesley's doctrine of the spiritual senses.

In Part Three, we will move beyond religious epistemology to the way that epistemology grounds Wesley's theological method. We will offer a model of theological understanding which seems to fit Wesley's implicit epistemology and which can then be used to understand his theology, which holds both Scripture and Experience in such creative tension.

This study will conclude in Part Four by outlining the broad promises (and pitfalls) of a theology founded on this tension, and so indicate the ways in which Wesley's theology and his theological method remain useful even today.

Notes

1. So the shockingly memorable opinion of Edward P. Thompson, who called Methodism "a ritualized form of psychic masturbation" (*The Making of the English Working Class* [New York: Pantheon, 1966], 368).

2. E.g., J. Wesley Bready, *This Freedom Whence* (New York: American Tract Society, 1942), 340-41.

3. "Conversation with the Bishop of Bristol" (*Jackson* 13:500).

4. Scott J. Jones, *John Wesley's Conception and Use of Scripture* (Nashville: Kingswood, 1995); Ted A. Campbell, *John Wesley and Christian Antiquity. Religious Vision and Cultural Change* (Nashville: Kingswood, 1991); and Rex Dale Matthews, "'Reason and Religion Joined': A Study in the Theology of John Wesley" (Th.D. diss., Harvard University, 1986).

5. This approach can be seen in William J. Townsend, Herbert B. Workman, and George Eayrs, eds., *A New History of Methodism*, vol. 1 (London: Hodder and Stoughten, 1909), 27; Arthur C. McGiffert, *Protestant Thought before Kant* (London: Charles Scribner's Sons, 1919), 170; Henry Bett, *The Spirit of Methodism* (London: Epworth, 1937), 131; George Eayrs, *John Wesley: Christian Philosopher and Church Founder* (London: Epworth, 1926), 181-82; John E. Rattenbury, *Wesley's Legacy to the World: Six Studies in the Permanent Values of the Evangelical Revival* (Nashville: Cokesbury, 1928), 84; and George Croft Cell, *The Rediscovery of John Wesley* (New York: Holt, 1935), 72, among many others. Of course, there are early, more balanced approaches, such as those of Sydney G. Dymond, *The Psychology of the Methodist Revival* (Oxford: Oxford Univ. Press, 1926), 234 and Umphrey Lee, *John Wesley and Modern Religion* (Nashville: Cokesbury, 1936), 143. Still, once the idea of the primacy of experience in Wesley was planted, it would not go away. And so, even a decade after Lee's book, one can find Harald Lindstrom generally agreeing with the categorization of Wesley's as a "theology of experience" and his affirmation of experience as his main characteristic (*Wesley and Sanctification: A Study in the Doctrine of Salvation* [Grand Rapids, MI:

Zondervan, 1980], 2).

6. Examples here include the work of Colin W. Williams, *John Wesley's Theology Today* (Nashville: Abingdon, 1960), 33; Dale W. Brown, "The Wesleyan Revival from a Pietist Perspective," *Wesleyan Theological Journal* 24 (1989): 7-17; Wallace Gray, "The Place of Reason in the Theology of John Wesley" (Ph.D. diss., Vanderbilt University, 1958), 167-69; Jones, *John Wesley's Conception,* 94-101, 179-183; Randy L. Maddox, *Responsible Grace* (Nashville: Kingswood, 1994), 44-46; Jerry L. Mercer, "Toward a Wesleyan Understanding of Christian Experience," *Wesleyan Theological Journal* 20 (1985): 78-93; R. Larry Shelton, "The Trajectory of Wesleyan Theology," *Wesleyan Theological Journal* 21 (1986): 159-75; and Donald A. D. Thorsen, *The Wesleyan Quadrilateral* (Lexington, KY: Emeth, 1990), 201-225. This idea is also reflected in contemporary theologies of those who own the Wesleyan tradition such as H. Ray Dunning, *Grace, Faith and Holiness* (Kansas City: Beacon Hill Press of Kansas City, 1988), 88-93; and Michael Lodahl, *The Story of God* (Kansas City: Beacon Hill Press of Kansas City, 1994), 40-48, 50.

7. The exceptions to this are found in those who make much of the link between Wesley and the Rationalist tradition, such as Robert Tuttle, *John Wesley: His Life and Theology* (Grand Rapids: Zondervan, 1978), 69-77, 143-155, 215-229; and Mitsuo Shimuzu, "Epistemology in the Thought of John Wesley" (Ph.D. diss., Drew University, 1980).

Part One

1

Cultural and Philosophical Background

Before we look directly at John Wesley's understanding and use of the concept of experience in his religious epistemology and theological method, we need to examine the general cultural, scientific and philosophical background against which he worked. Wesley was an avid reader and an intellectual as well as a preacher. Because he deliberately interacted with the academic environment of his time and did so in writing, listening in on this contextual conversation gives us the opportunity to hear his philosophical concerns as he felt them. It is too easy for modern readers to import our contemporary issues and concerns too quickly, and allowing Wesley the first move in contextualizing himself philosophically is the best way to avoid that.

The task of laying out all the features of intellectual life in eighteenth century Britain that could have affected Wesley is too large for us to tackle here, nor could we do that as well as it has already been done.[1] We will, therefore, confine ourselves to the important issues being debated in Wesley's day—especially as they related to the meaning and use of experience. Since our aim is to understand Wesley himself, and not necessarily to trace all the influences that weighed upon his thought, this should provide us with context enough to guard us away from readings of him that would either make him too medieval or too modern.

In tracing these influences, we will focus on Wesley's explicit interaction with them. Wesley was, no doubt, influenced by the various schools of Eighteenth Century British thought in ways that he did not or would not acknowledge or did not understand. However, an investigation of this kind is a speculative affair and depends as much on one's assumptions about Wesley as on one's reading of his work. In fact, attributing to Wesley a particular Eighteenth Century philosophical cast—and then reading his work in light of that assumption—may be one reason why his doctrine of experience often seems at odds with other explicit commitments he holds (such as the priority of Scripture). At this stage, then, we will allow Wesley to contextualize himself within his intellectual milieu and save any necessary speculation for our engagement with Wesley's own thought on the issues of experience, knowledge and theology.

We will begin our contextualization in this chapter with an important cultural-linguistic issue, an ordinary language perspective on the way in which the word *experience* and its cognates were understood and used in Wesley's Britain. We will bring out the main features of the word's meaning and then show how Wesley's use of the word accords with this general understanding. This is important because, as we will see, Wesley has often been (mis)read as if he had been writing in contemporary English instead of the English of the 1700s.

From this cultural-linguistic issue we will turn, in the other chapters in Part One, to a more extended survey of the philosophical and scientific background against which Wesley formed his understanding of experience and the ways in which he interacted with that background. Through this investigation, we will concentrate on two main issues. The first is the basic epistemological approach to experience found in each school of thought, the second being the specifically religious or theological implications of such an approach to experience. Since the philosophical milieu of Eighteenth Century England was vast and deep, we cannot lay out all of the issues at stake, and the reader is referred to the standard works on the various philosophers for those matters. Our task will be to outline the main ideas at work and then investigate how Wesley explicitly interacted with those ideas. At the end, we will tie together these various threads as a way to orient us toward Wesley's own religious epistemology.

Cultural-Linguistic Background

Given how much our language shapes our thought, we begin with the pre-understanding of the word *experience* that Wesley would have imbibed merely by learning its meaning the meaning of the words associated with it. Given that language tends to shift, we cannot assume that Wesley used his words in the same manner that we use them today, separated as we are by more than two-hundred years. We must, therefore, see how words like experience were used in Wesley's time in order to understand him. Also, since he wanted to write *ad populum*, for common people, and not merely for the philosophically learned,[2] he tended to rely on the ordinary, as opposed to the technical, meanings of words, and there are several ways in which his understanding of those words vary from the way we use them today.

First of all, the word experience has today a predominantly internal and passive connotation, especially in philosophical or psychological circles. We think of *experiences* as things that happen to us or things that we create in our minds. They are internal realities which we usually distinguish from *experiments*, scientifically ordered observations of external reality. This understanding can be traced to the psychological revolution of the late nineteenth century, and contemporary post-modern ways of thinking have only reinforced it. This was not the case in Wesley's day. Although experiment had already acquired some scientific connotation in Wesley's Britain, an experiment was not yet wholly distinguished from an experience.

A second potentially misleading facet of our understanding of experience is that we tend to use the word to refer to a discreet event. We can have *an experience* of something, and we refer to a train of such events as experiences. These discreet and quantifiable entities then reside in our memory and can be called up, recounted, and individually referred to. As we shall see, this usage does not wholly match the usage of the word in Wesley's day.

Perhaps the easiest place in which to see the ordinary uses of the word experience and its cognates in Eighteenth Century English is in Samuel Johnson's well-known and respected dictionary, published for the last time in 1785. There, the following relevant definitions are given:

> Experience (n.s.)—1. Practice, frequent trial; 2. Knowledge gained by trial and practice
> To Experience (v.a.)—1. To try; to practice; 2. To know by practice
> Experiment—Trial of any thing; something done in order to discover an uncertain or unknown effect
> To Experiment—1. To try; to search out by trial; 2. To know by experience
> Experimental—1. Pertaining to experiment; 2. Built upon experiment; formed by observation; 3. Known by experiment or trial
> Experimentally—1. By experience; by trial; by experiment; by observation[3]

The first thing we see from these definitions is that these cognates are to some extent interchangeable and are used to define each other. So, where there are adjectival and adverbial forms of the word experiment, the respective forms of experience are not yet current. This means that where we today might speak of things as *experiential* or of knowing things *experientially*, speakers of English in Wesley's day would have more naturally used the words *experimental* and *experimentally* respectively. Recognizing this is important for interpreting Wesley's understanding of experience.[4]

In addition to this blending of cognates, there are three other specific implications of these definitions that alert us to some interesting possibilities for Wesley's use of these words. First, experience and experiment are clearly active words with external orientations, not passive ones focused inwardly. The other words used to define them (*try, practice, search*) are performative and often require objects. They refer to something that persons do, not to things that happen to them. Second, there is at least one clear distinction between experience and experiment, and that is whether or not it can be quantified. One could talk of an experiment as "a trial of a thing" or refer to experiments as discreet trials in order to obtain knowledge. However, if experience is defined as "practice or frequent trial," then it refers more to the end result of an ongoing process, and that could only be quantified if there are multiple processes or if the process is completed. Third, there is an important connection in almost all of the words listed above between experience or experiment and knowledge. In the section on the philosophical background below, we will examine this connection more closely, but it is interesting to see this empiricist bias even in ordinary uses of the word.

These ideas come only from the isolated placement of a word in a dictionary, but they do alert us to some interesting features of Wesley's own use of these words, which bears out all four of the observations noted above. In first place,

Wesley uses, as we would expect, the adjectival and adverbial forms of experiment to refer to experience. In his favorite quote from the Marquis de Renty, he translates that author as saying "I bear with me an experimental verity, and a plenitude of the presence of the ever-blessed Trinity."[5] Here experimental means "known by experience" in the non-scientific sense. In the prefaces to the second and third volumes of his *Arminian Magazine,* Wesley speaks of his inclusion in that magazine of "experimental letters,"[6] referring to letters that relate people's experience and not letters designed to "discover an uncertain or unknown effect." He also uses the adverb *experimentally* in a way that means "by experience," particularly in his sermons. And so we have him employing phrases like "experimentally knowing"[7] or "experimentally acquainted,"[8] which in their contexts have to do with ordinary experience and not scientific experiments.

The active and external shape of the idea of experience in Wesley is somewhat difficult to track through his use of words, though, as we shall see, it is evident in the content of his thought. At this juncture we need only note that Wesley rarely uses the verb *experience* in the passive voice and that the active construction always takes an object. He relies on the idea that experience is experience of something external to the one who experiences and so is potentially accessibility to everyone. So he will refer to something like "daily experience" or "universal experience" in defense of doctrines like original sin[9] and in pointing to things like the restlessness of life without God,[10] the absurdity of romantically extolling rural life,[11] and the difficulty of having both charity and zeal for certain doctrinal opinions.[12] We will return to this point in more detail when we look at the substance of Wesley's thought.

In terms of one's ability to quantify experiences and experiments, we notice something very interesting in Wesley. In all his works, Wesley never refers to "an experience," and thus never talks about "having an experience." The few times he uses the word *experiences* in the plural, it always refers to the experiences of a group of people and not to the successive experiences of one particular person.[13] As we might expect, his use of experience is consistently singular and seems to point to that collective body of knowledge or the point of reference one has simply by living, or in the words of Johnson, "by trial and practice." This means that Wesley could not have used the word to refer to a psychological event, and that becomes very important as we explore his thought on the role experience plays in theology.

When we come to the question of the relationship between experience and knowledge in Wesley, we begin to tread on more philosophical ground. As we saw in his use of phrases like "experimentally knowing" or "experimentally acquainted," Wesley combines the ideas often,[14] but we can better understand their relationship in Wesley if we will move beyond the philological and into the philosophical, which brings us to our next section.

Philosophical Background

It has become standard in works on Wesley's thought to rehearse the various philosophical influences upon him, and as we noted in the first chapter, there is a broad acceptance of the idea that Wesley was a Lockean. However, a careful examination of how Wesley interacts with his philosophical sources— particularly when it comes to the question of experience—reveals that all might not be as easily categorized as is commonly assumed. In this section, we will challenge some of those common assumptions, in the hope that removing them will allow us to hear Wesley more authentically.

The eighteenth century in England has been styled "The Age of Reason," but it might be better labeled "The Age of Reason and Experience," as ideas about experience played just as crucial a role. Reason was valued during this time mostly because of the way it helped to shape experience, as witnessed by the great interest in medical and experimental science. When people debated the meaning of reason, they were usually debating the relationship between reason and experience, particularly the empirical experience of the material world. If reason was King, experience was its Chancellor. As is often the case, however, the relationship between the two could be rather contentious.

Wesley's intellectual milieu contained many different perspectives on reason and experience, but we will concentrate on the four most important for our study: Oxford Aristotelian Logic, Scientific Materialism, British Empiricism and Continental Rationalism. Matthews has already made a convincing case that the foremost philosophical influence on Wesley's thought is the Oxford Aristotelian Logic in which he studied and taught,[15] so we will cover that tradition first in Chapter Two. The influence of the empirical tradition on Wesley has been widely assumed, and so we shall cover that next, but we will split our investigation into two parts. The first we will call Scientific Materialism, which centers on the figures of Francis Bacon and Thomas Hobbes and which will be the subject of Chapter Three. The second part is the culmination of this tradition in British Empiricism. Formulated by John Locke but continued in George Berkeley and David Hume, this school would eventually become the most intellectually pervasive of all the philosophical schools at which we will look, and we will cover that in Chapter Four. Finally, in Chapter Five we will come to the rationalist tradition, represented chiefly by the so-called Cambridge Platonists but also by Continental rationalists such as Nicolas Malebranche and his English interpreter John Norris. All four of these traditions help to shape British thought during the eighteenth century in general, but they come together in Wesley in a unique way.

We will begin each of the following chapters by briefly explaining the issues at stake in each school of thought, particularly concerning ideas about experience and their implications for religion and theology. We will then examine Wesley's own interaction with that tradition and the way in which evidences of that tradition can be found in his writing. In Chapter Five, after all four traditions have been explored, we will conclude with some thoughts on how understanding their interaction in Wesley offers the appropriate background for Wesley's own doctrine of experience.

Notes

1. Cf. Leslie Stephen, *History of English Thought in the Eighteenth Century*, 2 vols. (1881; reprint, Boston: Adamant Media Corporation, 2007); and Gerald R. Cragg, *The Church and the Age of Reason 1648-1789*, Pelican History of the Church, vol. 4 (Grand Rapids: Eerdmans, 1960).

2. "Preface" to *Sermons on Several Occasions* §2 (*Jackson* 5:1).

3. S. Johnson, *A Dictionary of the English Language*, 2 vols. London, 6th ed. (London: Richard Bentley, 1785), quoted in Matthews, "Reason and Religion," 380. These usages are also supported in the corresponding articles by the historically oriented *Oxford English Dictionary*, ed. John A. Simpson and Edmund S. C. Weiner, vol. 5 (Oxford: Oxford University Press, 1989), 563-566 *passim*.

4. Thus, Donald Thorsen's contention (*Wesleyan Quadrilateral*, 202) that Wesley was scientifically oriented (not merely scientifically influenced) in his theology seems to stem at least partially from a twentieth century reading of the word *experimental* in Wesley's phrase "experimental religion" (cf. "Preface" to *Sermons on Several Occasions* §6 [*Jackson* 5:4] and Wesley's second *Letter to Bishop Lavington* [27 November 1750] [*Jackson* 9:17, 28]). If Wesley was using *experimental* where a contemporary writer would more naturally use *experiential*, then the meaning of that phrase changes significantly and calls into question a strong distinction between the *empirical* and *experiential*.

5. Cf. *Journal* 1 March 1786 (*Jackson* 4:327); Sermon #55 "On the Trinity" §17 (*Jackson* 6:205); and "Letter To Miss Ritchie" [August 2, 1777] (*Jackson* 13:59).

6. "Preface" to volume 2 of *The Arminian Magazine* §4 (*Jackson* 14:282).

7. Cf. Sermon #14 "The Repentance of Believers" §18 (*Jackson* 5:164); Sermon #32 "Sermon on the Mount—Discourse 12" §III.8 (*Jackson* 5:420); and Sermon #86 "A Call to Backsliders" §II.2.2 (*Jackson* 6:517).

8. Sermon #16 "The Means of Grace" §I.4 (*Jackson* 5:186).

9. Sermon #8 "The First Fruits of the Spirit" §II.5 (*Jackson* 5:91); Sermon #44 "Original Sin" §II.2 (*Jackson* 6:58); and *The Doctrine of Original Sin—Parts II, III & IV* (*Jackson* 9:295, 318, 338, 361)

10. Sermon #78 "Spiritual Idolatry" §II.2 (*Jackson* 6:442)

11. *Journal* 3 November 1766 (*Jackson* 3:268)

12. *Journal* 19 April 1761 (*Jackson* 3:173).

13. The one possible exception to this may be found in "A Letter to a Gentlemen at Bristol" (*Jackson* 10:311). However, here *experiences* appears as part of a list of other things, also listed in the plural, and so may be explained by purely stylistic reasons.

14. Cf. especially his Sermons (cf. *Jackson* 5:474; 6:101; 7:221), tracts (cf. *Jackson* 8:177, 391; 11:73), and controversial letters (cf. *Jackson* 9:51, 505; 10:68)

15. Matthews, "Reason and Religion." Matthews' study focuses on how Wesley understood "reason" more than on the various philosophical influences that impacted his thought, but these two are, obviously, very closely related.

2

Wesley and Aristotelian Logic

Understanding Wesley as an Aristotelian and a logician is the key to understanding his doctrine of experience. While a certain form of Aristotelianism had been in use in the church since the Middle Ages, Wesley seems to have acquired his brand from his days at Oxford, where, since the 1615 publication of Robert Sanderson's *Logicae Artis Compendium,* there had been a strong tradition of asserting Aristotle's logic and metaphysic over against other systems, particularly Ramist logic.[1] By Wesley's time, this tradition had crystallized into Henry Aldrich's 1691 work *Artis Logicae Compendium.* This text, which Wesley himself translated from the Latin in 1750, remained a standard logic textbook at Oxford until 1843.

The Logic of Aristotle

Aristotle's approach to logic and metaphysics wedded reason to experience. Reason was understood as a processing faculty of the mind, and logic represented the proper rules by which that processing was done. Reason includes three functions: *apprehension* (in which the mind forms ideas based on sensory experience), *judgment* (in which the mind compares an apprehension with previous apprehensions to verify or falsify it), and *discourse* (in which the mind strings judgments together to make arguments). Thus, reason is valued for its ability to process information, but it is completely dependent upon experience for its raw material. Argumentation is important, but it is based on prior judgments and apprehensions, which are themselves products of experience. A cornerstone of this tradition was the well established paraphrase of Aristotle's ideas, which Wesley even quotes himself: *Nihil est in intellectu quod non fait prius in sensu* ("There is nothing in the understanding which was not first in the senses").[2]

Aristotle's system is thus an empirical one, but it represents a naïve form of empiricism. Aristotle rejected Plato's Rationalism, in which knowledge comes from Reason's immediate contact with ideal forms, but in its place he simply posits the veracity of our sense data, which only needs the proper ordering of logic to make it match with reality as it is. In contrast to Modern philosophical systems like Cartesian Rationalism or Lockean Empiricism, Aristotle's system is not driven by epistemology. It is relatively unconcerned with the reliability of our sensory experience and feels no need to resolve with absolute certainty the question of how we know what we know. He begins with an implicit trust in both our senses and in the ability of the mind to organize the data of the senses in the same way that reality itself is organized. Deductions made from experienced premises are taken to be as certain as the premises themselves; the rules of proper thinking are assumed to be the rules of reality.

Given this assumed correspondence, logic has a more important place in Aristotle's system than in the more skeptical modern ones. If the data we get from our sense is given and reliable, then the only real work of thinking comes from putting that data together in the right way. It is in logic that truth is separated from error as one draws the appropriate distinctions between apprehensions and discovers the ways they do and do not fit together. The correspondence between reality and thought also means that logic can be investigational as well as organizational. Thus it can have an a priori function helping the mind to explore new data as well as the a posteriori function of organizing data already given. Logic is, in Robert Sanderson's words, "an instrumental art directing our minds in the knowing of all things knowable."[3]

By way of contrast, Ramist logic eschewed any metaphysical assumptions and merged logic into rhetoric.[4] Logic became, for Peter Ramus, "the art of disputing well," concerned more with organizing words than organizing reality. Ramus developed his approach in direct opposition to Aristotle,[5] and he gained a disproportionate influence among Protestants, especially Puritans, because he himself was a Protestant convert and martyr, having perished in the Saint Bartholomew's Day Massacre.[6] He was also influential on Wesley's theological forbearer Jacob Arminius.[7] Wesley, however, would have considered himself a pure Aristotelian, despite his sympathies with some of the concerns that drove Ramist logic.[8] Time and again, he explicitly owned both Aristotle's logic and the metaphysical assumptions behind it. As we shall see, he was unconcerned with the epistemological questions that drove British Empiricism during his lifetime, and he assumed without question the correspondence between logic and reality, so much so that his use of logic could extend beyond sensory experience and even deal with the reality of God, much as Aristotle did in developing his "proof" for an "Unmoved Mover."[9]

Wesley the Aristotelian Logician

Wesley's reception of the tradition of Aristotelian logic was positive and strong. In all of his writings, one will find nothing but praise and defense of logic. It is his primary tool in defending himself against his critics, and he considered it to be foundational to all other learning. It even forms the perspective from which he examines and critiques most other philosophy that he reads. In one place, Wesley virtually equates the whole idea of reason with Aristotelian logic by defining it in the Aristotelian terms of apprehension, judgment and discourse.[10]

Wesley's absorption of the metaphysical assumptions behind that logic is not as overt but seems equally clear.[11] He explicitly affirms Aristotle's empirical stance, and his own naïve empiricism lines up much better with Aristotle's than it does with the more sophisticated empirical positions of Locke or Hume.

background

Wesley's training in his tradition began when he was a young undergraduate at Oxford, where he began his study at Christ Church College in 1720. There he pursued his undergraduate studies and trained for ordination in the Anglican church, which began with his deacon's orders in 1725. In 1726, Lincoln College made him a Fellow of the College and, later that year, a lecturer in Greek and Logic and moderator of the daily collegiate disputations. As a moderator, he served as an expert in logic, ensuring that the arguments made during the disputations followed acceptable and valid forms. Wesley took his Master of Arts from Lincoln in 1727 and then left to serve two years in pastoral ministry with his father. Returning to Oxford in 1729, he remained there until sailing to become a missionary in Georgia, in the American colonies, in 1735. [12]

These thirteen years at Oxford were very influential on Wesley. The learning and practice he received in logic was something of which he was very proud, and in his tract cumbersomely entitled "Some Remarks on 'A Defence of the Preface to the Edinburgh Edition of Aspasio Vindicated'," he had this to say about it:

> For several years I was Moderator in the disputations which were held six times a week at Lincoln College, in Oxford. I could not avoid acquiring hereby some degree of expertness in arguing; and especially in discerning and pointing out well-covered and plausible fallacies. I have since found abundant reason to praise God for giving me this honest art. By this, when men have hedged me in by what they called demonstrations, I have been many times able to dash them in pieces; in spite of all its covers, to touch the very point where the fallacy lay; and it flew open in a moment. This is the art which I have used with Bishop Warburton, as well as in the preceding pages. When Dr. E. twisted truth and falsehood together, in many of his propositions, it was by this art I untwisted the one from the other, and showed just how far each was true. At doing this, I bless God, I am expert; as those will find who attack me without rhyme or reason.[13]

Wesley is not shy about extolling his skill in logic, but this is not mere boasting on Wesley's part. His high esteem for logic stems from the way he sees it as interconnected with truth, which would have been a natural assumption for a good Aristotelian. He knew that learning how to think properly was hard work, something most people would not do unless on principle or for reason of conscience,[14] and not something one could even teach oneself.[15] Nevertheless, Wesley saw logic as the key to all other matters that have to do with the pursuit of truth and clear thinking. He places it at the top of his list of academic subjects, "even necessary next, and in order to, the knowledge of the Scripture itself."[16] If all one needed were proper bits of sense data in order to find truth, none of this would be necessary. But Wesley believes that sense data on its own is not enough; truth can only be found by learning how to think properly.[17]

This was not just an attitude that shaped Wesley's self-understanding; it also shaped the way he performed his own ministerial duties and the way he encouraged others in that work. Wesley himself tutored some of his preachers in Logic using Aldrich in 1749[18] and made Aldrich's and Wallis' textbooks required reading in the curriculum at his school in Kingswood.[19] When asking the clergy of England to evaluate their fitness for ministry, he has them ask themselves, "Am I a tolerable master of the sciences? Have I gone through the very gate of them, logic? If not, I am not likely to go much farther, when I stumble at the threshold."[20] Logic, for Wesley, was the beginning of knowledge, the "gate" or "threshold" of all the other sciences. This would be an odd statement for someone standing in the tradition of Bacon or Locke, but it is a comfortable one to a good Aristotelian. In a letter giving some study advice to Margaret Lewin, after discussing such subjects as grammar, math and geography, Wesley states "Logic naturally follows; and I really think it is worth all the rest put together."[21] He also criticizes those who deprecate logic (as we will see in Wesley's critique of Locke later) or who fail to give it its proper place.[22]

One sees Wesley's supreme devotion to logic not only in how he talked about it, but even more in how he used it himself. It is here that Aristotle's metaphysical commitments show themselves in Wesley most clearly. To begin with, Wesley explicitly affirms the connection between logic and metaphysics in his *Address to the Clergy*, already cited, where he discusses metaphysics as "the second part" of logic. There he states that it is useful, "In order to clear our apprehension, (without which it is impossible either to judge correctly, or to reason closely or conclusively,) by ranging our ideas under general heads?"[23] In other words, despite the basic empirical assumption—that knowledge comes through apprehension of (i.e., experience of) physical reality—there is a properly *meta*physical pre-understanding that enables proper apprehension, which is tied to logic. Wesley allows these "general heads" (in a way similar to Kant's categories) to clear and guide our perception. Of course, this is no innovation on Wesley's part, merely his faithful adherence to the empirical tradition of Aristotle. It is also clear that Wesley's metaphysical pre-understandings were assumed to reflect the nature of reality itself. Metaphysics helps the mind perceive that which is actually there. The assumption in Wesley that Truth and Reality were inherently logical can be discerned by looking at the way he used logic to confront his critics, just as he claimed to do in the long quote above.

When Wesley encountered an opinion that he sought to challenge or faced an accusation from an opponent, it was typical for him to deal with it as a logical problem. He would place his opponent's statements or accusations in the form of syllogisms and then dispute the terms used, the conclusions drawn, or point out a logical fallacy. In so doing, he was confident that he had won his case, regardless of whether or not his opponent was convinced by his arguments, indicating that it was truth, not rhetoric, which was his main concern. We see this kind of argumentation throughout Wesley's writings, but a few examples are enough to give one a sense of how much Wesley relied on both logic (academic Aristotelian logic at that) and the metaphysical presumptions that lay behind it.

First, we see that Wesley will employ logic to assert his own theological stances. In his sermon on "Justification by Faith," Wesley maintains that good works cannot save because there can be no truly good works prior to salvation. To prove his case, he offers these remarks:

> Perhaps those who doubt of this have not duly considered the weighty reason which is here assigned, why no works done before justification can be truly and properly good. The argument plainly runs thus: — [P$_1$] No works are good, which are not done as God hath willed and commanded them to be done: [P$_2$] But no works done before justification are done as God hath willed and commanded them to be done: [C] Therefore, no works done before justification are good. The first proposition is self-evident; and the second, [P$_2$, C'] that no works done before justification are done as God hath willed and commanded them to be done, will appear equally plain and undeniable, if we only consider, [P'$_1$] God hath willed and commanded that all our works should be done in charity...[P'$_2$] But none of our works can be done in this love, while the love of the Father (of God as our Father) is not in us; and [P'$_3$] this love cannot be in us till we receive the 'Spirit of Adoption, crying in our hearts, Abba, Father.'"[24]

One can see that Wesley does not cite texts from Scripture for his conclusion, but he seems to think that his conclusion is still undeniably true because it is a formal conclusion to scriptural premises. Wesley has no doubt that a proper syllogism, or a set of them in this case, establishes the truth of the doctrine. If people continue to disbelieve it, it is only because they have not "duly considered the weighty reason," i.e., the logic, that supports it. This is Wesley's final word on that subject in this sermon, further evidence that he considers its veracity sufficiently established.

Wesley also uses logic to defend himself when attacked. In defending his practice of field preaching in the *Farther Appeal To Men of Reason and Religion*, he puts the argument against him in the following logical form: "[P$_1$] That preaching which is contrary to the laws of the land is worse than not preaching at all: [P$_2$] But field-preaching is contrary to the laws of the land: [C] Therefore, it is worse than not preaching at all."[25] He then proceeds to attack the logic of that argument.

> The first proposition is not self-evident, nor, indeed, universally true: For the preaching of all the primitive Christians was contrary to the whole tenor of the Roman law; the worship of the devil-gods being established by the strongest laws then in being. Nor is it ever true, but on supposition that the preaching in question is an indifferent thing. But waving this, I deny the second proposition; I deny that field-preaching is contrary to the laws of our land.[26]

Upon which follows a meticulous interpretation of the Act of Toleration that would have made a barrister proud.

The easy way in which Wesley reduces his opponents' arguments to a syllogism that he can attack reveals his deep faith in logic and its metaphysical link with truth. He assumes that any argument can be put into logical form and that this form is the true form of the argument. He assumes that truth is logical and that the rules of logic are also the rules of truth.

The clearest example of this line of argumentation comes from Wesley's controversial exchange with Mr. Church over whether or not Wesley was an enthusiast. Wesley begins his defense by citing Church's remarks and putting them in syllogistic form:

> You add, 'I shall give but one account more, and this is what you give of yourself.' The sum whereof is, 'At two several times, being ill and in violent pain, I prayed to God, and found immediate ease.' I did so. I assert the fact still. 'Now, if these,' you say, 'are not miraculous cures, all this is rank enthusiasm.' I will put your argument in form:—[P$_1$] He that believes those are miraculous cures which are not so is a rank enthusiast: [P$_2$] But you believe those to be miraculous cures which are not so: [C] Therefore, you are a rank enthusiast.[27]

Here Wesley's a priori logical assumptions are very clear. Taking what is a rhetorical argument from Church, Wesley recasts it into the form of a syllogism. Yet he appears to do so without thinking he has misrepresented his opponent, assuming that the language of truth assertions must be inherently logical, even if one has to do some work to fill in the hidden premises. Having properly defined his opponent's attack, he then responds as the quintessential Aristotelian logician, talking of the definition of terms and the propriety of propositions:

> Before I answer, I must know what you mean by miraculous. If you term everything so, which is not strictly accountable for by the ordinary course of natural causes, then I deny the latter part of the minor proposition [P$_2$]. And unless you can make this good, unless you can prove the effects in question are strictly accountable for by the ordinary course of natural causes, your argument is nothing worth.[28]

Wesley points to Church's hidden premise that the cures in question were not, indeed, miraculous, and says that until that assumption can be proven, the argument is worthless. Church is obviously uncomfortable with being forced into a logical mode and is not himself convinced by Wesley's presentation. He writes back with a clarification, putting his own argument into logical form, but Wesley simply demolishes that one as he did the first, deleting the rhetorical touches and pointing out that the same hidden premise which drove the first argument was still in play.[29] Here again, Wesley is playing a different game than his opponent. Whereas Church is clearly using rhetoric to persuade readers, Wesley is using logic to establish truth, which would stand whether or not his opponents recognized and were persuaded by his logic.

We turn to one last example to show the difference between Wesley's Aristotelian (i.e., logical) empiricism and the other empirical traditions to which we shall turn shortly. It concerns the very foundation of science and modern empiricism as an inductive rather than deductive system, arguing from particulars to generals instead of the other way around. Here, Wesley confronts those who do not share his belief in the possibility of holiness because they will not admit to degrees of holiness, and he explicitly employs the rules of syllogisms to establish his case.

> This whole argument, 'If he is clean, he is clean;' 'If he is holy, he is holy;' (and twenty more expressions of the same kind may easily be heaped together;) is really no better than playing upon words: It is the fallacy of arguing from a *particular* to a *general*; of inferring a general conclusion from particular premises. Propose the sentence entire, and it runs thus: 'If he is holy *at all*, he is holy *altogether*.' That does not follow.[30]

By accepting the rules of Aristotelian logic, Wesley rejects the exclusively inductive empiricism of the British tradition. Further examples are legion, but these are sufficient to establish the point. Wesley was a thoroughgoing Aristotelian logician. When ridiculed for this by his opponents, he himself records these detractions and even glories in them, as if they showed that it was his opponents, instead of him, who did not understand how things really were.[31] That kind of attitude can only be understood if Wesley's faith in the a priori and metaphysical truth of logic was unimpeachable.

Of course, logic was not everything to Wesley, and he was well aware of its inherent limitations. He believed that the appropriate use of logic was irreplaceable, but it could not fix everything. In that same *Address to the Clergy* cited above, Wesley notes the following: "It [logic] is good for this at least, (wherever it is understood,) to make people talk less; by showing them both what is, and what is not, to the point; and how extremely hard it is to prove anything."[32] Nevertheless, Aristotle's logic and its metaphysical implications were deeply imbedded in Wesley's thought. He saw experience as necessary for knowledge, but not sufficient without logic to guide it. This necessary-but-not-sufficient stance on experience becomes even clearer when we see Wesley's reaction to the other two empirical traditions on offer in Eighteenth Century Britain.

Notes

1. Wilbur S. Howell, *Eighteenth Century British Logic and Rhetoric* (Princeton, NJ: Princeton University Press, 1971), 16. For a fuller treatment of this Ramist-Aristotelian debate at Oxford, cf. W. S. Howell, *Logic and Rhetoric in England 1500-1700* (Princeton NJ: Princeton University Press, 1956), 299-309. For a good summary of this tradition and Wesley's reaction to it, cf. Matthews, "Reason and Religion," 143-157.

2. Wesley quotes the phrase in a couple of sermons in 1788 (Sermon #110 "On the Discoveries of Faith" ¶1 [Jackson 7:231] and Sermon # 113 "Walking by Sight, Walking by Faith" ¶7 [Jackson 7:258]). The phrase, which is often misattributed to Locke, was current at least as early as the 13th century, showing up, in one form or another, in the work of Aquinas and Duns Scotus, and it may have originated in the Latin translation of Arabic Aristotelian sources (cf. Paul F. Cranefield, "On the Origin of the Phrase *Nihil est in intellectu quod non prius fuerit in sensu*," *Journal of the History of Medicine and Allied Sciences*, 25 [1970]: 77-80).

3.Quoted in Matthews, "Reason and Religion," 18. There is, thus, an analogous relationship between logic in Aristotle and modern scientific theories or paradigms, which guide the exploration of the unknown on the basis of the way the known is organized.

4. Norman E. Nelson, *Peter Ramus and the Confusion of Logic, Rhetoric and Poetry*, Contributions in Modern Philology 2 (Ann Arbor MI: University of Michigan Press, 1947), 14.

5. William Kneale and Martha Kneale, *The Development of Logic* (Oxford: Oxford University Press, 1962), 301.

6. Ibid., 302. This point is, naturally, much in debate. For a more positive spin on Ramus' life and thought, cf. Frank P. Graves, *Peter Ramus and the Educational Reformation of the Sixteenth Century* (1912; reprint, Charleston, SC: Bibliobazaar, 2009).

7. Richard Müller, *God, Creation, and Providence in the Thought of Jacob Arminius* (Grand Rapids: Baker, 1991), 16, 20, 63-65; and Carl Bangs, *Arminius: A Study in the Dutch Reformation* (Grand Rapids: Zondervan, 1985), 56-63.

8. Contra Walter J. Ong, S. J., *Ramus. Method, and the Decay of Dialogue* (Chicago: University of Chicago Press, 1958), 15, and Albert C. Outler, "The Wesleyan Quadrilateral in Wesley," *Wesleyan Theological Journal* 20 (1985): 15. Cf. also Matthews, "Reason and Religion," 149.

9. Aristotle, *Physics*, Book 8.

10. *Journal* 15 June 1741 (*Jackson* 1:315). As Rex Matthews has demonstrated, this equation holds true throughout Wesley's life and thought (Matthews, "Reason and Religion," 121-83, even entitling the chapter "Wesley's Consistent Concept of Reason").

11. They only place where Wesley disparages Aristotle's metaphysics comes in the introduction to his *Compendium of Natural Philosophy* ¶3 (*Jackson* 13:482). There Wesley's concern seems to be that of allowing Aristotle's assertions about science to simply stand *ipse dixit*, independently of experimental verification (see also Sermon #68 "The Wisdom of God's Counsels," ¶9 [*Jackson* 6:329]).

12. For further information about Wesley's life at Oxford, cf. Vivian H. H. Green, *The Young Mr. Wesley. A Study of John Wesley at Oxford* (London: Edward Arnold, 1961); and R. P. Heitzenrater, *John Wesley and the Oxford Methodists* (Ph.D. diss., Duke University, 1972).

13. *Some Remarks on 'A Defence of the Preface to the Edinburgh Edition of Aspasio Vindicated'* §9 (*Jackson* 10:353). Wesley's skill in logic was also acknowledged by others, with one Samuel Badcock describing the twenty-one year old Wesley as "the very sensible and acute collegian, baffling every man by his subtleties of logic, and laughing at them for being so easily routed" (*Telford* 1:7).

14. Cf. Wesley's remarks on this in his *Journal* 13 March 1747 (*Jackson* 2:49).

15. "Letter to Mrs. Lewin" [n.d.] (*Jackson* 12:261). See also a similar sentiment expressed in "A Letter to Mr. Joseph Benson" [7 November 1768] (*Jackson* 12:409) and "A Letter to a Member of the Society" [1 July 1772] (*Jackson* 12:294).

16. *An Address to the Clergy* §I.2 (*Jackson* 10:483).

17. Wesley is even suspicious of other traditions in logic besides Aristotle's. He critiques the famous *Port Royal Logic* (*The Art of Thinking* by Antoine Arnauld and Pierre Nicole), calling the Arnauld "a poor tool" ("Letter to Samuel Furley" [14 March 1756] (*Telford* 3:173).), and he says of Isaac Watt's popular logic textbook, "Watts' *Logic* is not a very good one" ("Letter to Sarah Wesley" [8 September 1781] (*Telford* 7:82).)

18. *Journal* 23 February 1749 (*Jackson* 2:129).

19. *A Short Account of the School at Kingswood* (*Jackson* 13:287).

20. Ibid. §II.1.5 (*Jackson* 10:491).

21. "A Letter to Miss Lewin" [n.d.] §9 (*Jackson* 12:261). Cf. similar sentiments expressed in *A Farther Appeal to Men of Reason and Religion—Part III* §III.8 (*Jackson* 8:219) [hereinafter cited as *Farther Appeal*].

22. Cf. Wesley note about Dr. Alexander Gerard's "Essay on Taste" (*Journal* 1 November 1787 [*Jackson* 4:403]).

23. *An Address to the Clergy* §I.2 (*Jackson* 10:483)

24. Sermon #5 "Justification by Faith" §III.6 (*Jackson* 5:60). The numbers in brackets have been added, here and elsewhere, to make the various parts of the syllogism clearer. [P₁] and [P₂] are the premises, [C] the conclusion. One should also note that Wesley supports [P₂] by making it the conclusion [C'] of a second syllogism (with premises [P'₁], [P'₂], and [P'₃]). Thus the whole argument is steeped in formal logic.

25. *A Farther Appeal—Part I* §VI.4 (*Jackson* 8:113).

26. Ibid.

27. *An Answer to the Rev. Mr. Church's Remarks on the Rev. Mr. John Wesley's Last Journal* §III.12 (*Jackson* 8:412).

28. Ibid. Wesley must have liked this argument because he used it verbatim to counter the same accusation in his second *Letter to Bishop Lavington* [27 November 1750] (*Jackson* 9:25).

29. *The Principles of a Methodist Farther Explained* §IV.11 (*Jackson* 8:459).

30. Sermon #13 "On Sin in Believers" §IV.3 (*Jackson* 5:151).

31. See *Journal* 16 September 1760 (*Jackson* 3:18-19) and *Some Remarks on Mr. Hill's 'Farrago Double Distilled'* §36, 44 (*Jackson* 10:436, 440).

32. *An Address to the Clergy* §II.5 (*Jackson* 10:492).

3

Wesley and Scientific Materialism

The development of science is one of the chief hallmarks of the Modern Age, eventually affecting every arena of human thought and practice. Along with new knowledge about the world and its workings came a new worldview, and an anti-metaphysical one at that. As science progressed, more and more people began to favor materialist or naturalist views of the world that could only affirm physical realities and left little place for spiritual or supernatural ones. In Britain, the development of a scientific worldview and its attendant epistemological convictions, was given its primary impetus by Francis Bacon. His thought was developed by his junior colleague Thomas Hobbes, and by Wesley's day it was being worked out in various ways and forms by such men as Joseph Priestley, George Cheyne and David Hartley. A brief examination of this worldview will give us sufficient background against which to understand Wesley's interaction with it, particularly as that interaction sheds light on his naïve empiricism and his view of experience.

The Scientific Worldview

In deliberate reaction to the metaphysical implications of Aristotle's logic, Lord Francis Bacon asserted a more scientific and materialist worldview. Born in 1561 of an aristocratic family, Bacon's career was more political than purely scientific, and his work ought to be understood more as philosophy of science than as science itself,[1] but he nevertheless was far more influential and effective at popularizing this nascent scientific worldview than anyone in his time or previously.

Bacon had a very utilitarian view of knowledge. "Human Knowledge and human power meet in one,"[2] he claimed, and the reason one acquired knowledge was to control the physical world. Bacon felt that the primary obstacle to knowledge, which was by its nature oriented toward the material and physical, was the *meta*physical constructs of knowledge that held sway in intellectual circles. He writes, "There are and can be only two ways of searching into and discovering truth. The one flies from the senses and particulars to the most general axioms…this way is now in fashion. The other derives axioms from the senses and particulars…This is the true way, but as yet untried."[3]

Bacon therefore considered it his primary task to overturn the deductive, metaphysical way of thinking prevalent in the West since the ancient Greeks and replace it with an inductive, observation-oriented way of thinking. There can be, for Bacon, no a priori knowledge of anything. All knowledge comes a posteriori through experimentation on the world, and Bacon labels any metaphysical system that would substitute for sensory experience in gaining knowledge an "idol of the mind." One of the worst of such systems for Bacon was the logic of Aristotle, which he cited as the worst of the "idols of the theatre," those grand systems of thought which purported to replace direct observation.[4] It is clear from Bacon's whole criticism of the various idols of the mind that he believes the mind to function best when it is allowed to function as a completely unbiased observer of sensory phenomenon. The best experimenter, he feels, is one of "ripe age, unimpaired senses and *well-purged* mind."[5]

The assumption that knowledge deals with sensory experience of the material world leaves little place in Bacon's thought for religious truth. While he himself publicly held to the late scholastic idea of "double truth," in which faith is at its best when it affirms a matter that is downright absurd from the standpoint of reason, his junior colleague Thomas Hobbes was not so shy in working out the full, anti-religious implications of this purely empirical worldview.

Thomas Hobbes, the sometime secretary of Bacon,[6] is known chiefly as a political philosopher, but the implications of his thought were much farther reaching. To begin with, Hobbes, like Bacon and Aristotle, is clear that knowledge only comes from the sensory experience. In *Leviathan*, he writes, "Concerning the thoughts of man…The origin of them all is that which we call *sense*, for there is no conception in a man's mind which hath not at first, totally or by parts, been begotten upon the organs of sense. The rest are derived from that original."[7] Unlike Aristotle, however, Hobbes will strengthen the materialist implications of this position. In claiming that all thoughts result from sensations, he emphasizes the fact that sensations result from our experience of physical bodies, which means that we can only know that which has substance (i.e., extension and magnitude). This makes Hobbes' position even more explicitly materialist than Bacon's. He even affirms that we cannot talk about God meaningfully unless God has a body.[8] Otherwise, says Hobbes, people speak of God "not *Dogmatically*, with the intention to make the Divine Nature understood; but *Piously*, to honour him with attributes, of significations, as remote as they can from the grossenesse of Bodies Visible."[9] In other words, any talk about God which would transcend Hobbes' view of language is only emotive and devoid of any truth content.

Hobbes is best remembered for bringing out the implications of the new scientific materialist worldview for political thought, but the broader tradition of scientific materialism endorsed by both Bacon and Hobbes had a profound and wide ranging affect on eighteenth century British intellectual life. On one hand, many of Wesley's contemporaries enthusiastically endorsed the scientific outlook and method, often called natural philosophy, and scientific experiments became an accepted pursuit of the cultured and well-to-do. On the other hand, however, this outlook caused much consternation about anything transcendent, raising doubts with some as to the efficacy of religion[10] and ire with others who saw religion as under attack. As we shall see, Wesley himself embodies both of these reactions at the same time, particularly as he interacts with some of those contemporaries, such as Joseph Priestly, who wrote an influential work on electricity; David Hartley, who worked out a materialist and determinist view of human psychology; and George Cheyne, a physician who promoted vegetarianism.

Wesley the Scientist

Throughout much of the eighteenth and nineteenth centuries, Wesley was portrayed as anti-intellectual and anti-scientific. Most of these accusations, however, were made by people who only quoted snippets of Wesley's work and who assumed an inherent opposition between Christianity and science.[11] A more careful reading of Wesley, however, shows that he held science in high esteem—although he was always careful to point out how limited it was. Examining his approach to empirical science gives us great insight into his overall approach to experience, as we shall see through his interaction with philosophers of science and his own scientific engagement.

Wesley's direct interaction with Bacon and Hobbes is slight, although it is enough to show Wesley's awareness of their general approach and how it differs from his own. Bacon appears in Wesley's work as the chief representative of the discipline of science. Despite Bacon's clear distaste for Aristotle and the negative implications of his epistemology for religion, Wesley seemed to hold the man in high respect. He always referred to him as "Lord Bacon," ranked him as a universal genius on par with Aristotle,[12] and gave him full credit for spurring on the process of scientific inquiry in triumph over the scholastic philosophers.[13] At age eighty-three, Wesley was still interested enough in him to read Bacon's *Ten Centuries of Experiments* while journeying about on a preaching tour, pronouncing much of what was related there as "useful."[14]

Wesley's evaluation of science in terms of its utility is a hallmark of his interaction with it, and it helps to explain his positive endorsement of Bacon. Wesley, as we shall see, does not go along with the epistemological shift that Bacon introduced, but he does seem to have imbibed from his culture an interest in experimental science and a respect for the one he saw as its founder in Britain.

Wesley's opinion of Hobbes is more guarded, as Wesley does not share Hobbes's political views[15] nor his nominalist view of language,[16] something that he saw at odds with his own Aristotelian and realist approach. In fact Wesley uses Hobbes's own dying words to comment on the inadequacy of a materialist epistemology, particularly when it comes to spiritual realities. Wesley notes: "His [Hobbes's] dying words ought never to be forgotten. 'Where are you going, Sir?' said one of his friends. He answered, 'I am taking a leap in the dark!' and died. Just such an evidence of the invisible world can bare reason give to the wisest of men!"[17] Here we can see that Wesley's concern with Hobbes's thought is *only* for its spiritual value, or lack thereof, and not at all with his ideas themselves.

These interactions reveal two important features of Wesley's approach to science, which help explain his complete *lack* of interaction with the epistemological issues that Bacon and Hobbes raised. Those features are Wesley's purely practical view of science and his a priori commitment to contextualize science within a theistic worldview, features which are also borne out in Wesley's interaction with other scientists and philosophers of science.

Wesley read Dr. Joseph Priestley's "ingenious book on Electricity"[18] soon after it came out, and his comments reveal his practical bent. Concerning electricity he notes, "Indeed the use of it we know; at least, in some good degree. We know it is a thousand medicines in one…But if we aim at theory, we know nothing. We are soon 'Lost and bewilder'd in the fruitless search.'"[19] Wesley is not against the idea of scientific theory here, but he does point out that very little was actually known. As we've noted before, he sees science as good because it is useful, but it is limited. It is the usefulness of his dietary advice that causes Wesley to cite George Cheyne several times as a authority on moderate eating (which also fits in well with Wesley's ascetic bent),[20] but of Matthew Bolton's meticulous biological experiments Wesley can only say, "If faith and love dwell here, then there maybe happiness too. Otherwise all these beautiful things are as unsatisfactory as straws and feathers."[21]

This bent to interpret science within the framework of theology is most clear in Wesley's comments on the writings of the explorer Henry Wilson and the philosopher and early psychologist David Hartley. Wesley cannot believe Wilson's account of the virtuous natives of the Palau islands on account of his own conviction of the truth of original sin,[22] and he cannot accept Hartley's determinist and materials account of human thought on the basis of his belief in freedom as a gift from God. In commenting on Hartley's *Observations on Man*, Wesley says:

> I care not one pin for all Dr. Hartley can say of his vibrations. Allowing the whole which he contends for…suppose vibrations, perceptions, judgments, passions, tempers, actions, ever so naturally to follow each other: What is all this to the God of nature?…[N]ecessity has no power over those 'who have the Lord for their God.' Each of these can say, through happy experience, 'I can do all things through Christ strengthening me.'[23]

Wesley allows his a priori commitment to his understanding of the truth of Scripture to override both Wilson's account and Hartley's argument. This makes his approach problematic in terms of epistemology, but he does not seem to care.

Moving away from his interaction with others to his own "original" work, we can see that Wesley continues in this vein. He affirms the limited but useful role of understanding gained by physical experience and experiment, and he grounds his approach to science, not in a scientific worldview, but in his faith in God as Creator. This can be seen in his medical work, in his compendium of science, and in many passing references to scientists in his *Journal* and elsewhere.

Wesley's study of medicine dates at least as far back as his sailing for Georgia, "where I imagined," he writes, "I might be of some service to those who had no regular Physician among them."[24] Struck by the condition of the poor in London, he used his Society there to begin providing some medical care and medicines to them.[25] In support of that aim, and on the principle of "doing as much good as I can,"[26] Wesley compiled and published his own *Primitive Physic: Or an Easy and Natural Method of Curing Most Diseases.*[27] He publishes this in as cheap a format as possible to ensure that some form of medical advice was available to those who most needed it and yet could not afford professional physicians, who did not hold a very high place in Wesley's opinion.[28] The tract *The Desideratum; or Electricity made plain and useful*, which Wesley authors as "A Lover of Mankind, and of Common Sense" has a similar purpose.[29]

In both works, Wesley endorses a practice-based, non-speculative approach to medicine. In *Primitive Physic*, he decries doctors who practice on theory,[30] and in *The Desideratum* he notes, "Indeed, I am not greatly concerned for the philosophical part, whether it stand or fall. Of the facts we are absolutely assured...But who can be assured of this or that hypothesis, by which he endeavors to account for those facts?"[31] Such statements need not indicate that Wesley is opposed to the idea of scientific theory, but he insists that physical experience and physical utility be its judge.

Such a hard and fast rule has led many to see in Wesley a firm metaphysical dualism, in which physical things like bodies are subject to physical laws and scientific understanding but spiritual things are governed by other laws, known chiefly through revelation. If this were true, it would complicate any investigation of the role experience could play in the formation of theology. However, a deeper investigation of Wesley shows that he actually works to re-connect the physical and the spiritual in the face of a culture that was beginning to overemphasize the former and exclude the latter. Even if he is a metaphysical dualist, his practical approach makes his a strongly integrated dualism.

In the introduction to *Primitive Physic* Wesley explicitly connects spiritual reality with the physical and demonstrates their interrelationship in strict opposition to any materialist worldview. For example, Wesley cites sin and the Fall as the source of bodily ills,[32] he notes that the only trustworthy physician is the one who fears God,[33] and he claims that proper spiritual health is the key to maintaining proper physical health.[34] However, this does not mean that all physical ills are the result of spiritual maladies, and Wesley notes on several occasions the fact that Christians can praise God even while enduring the worst of physical ills.[35] So, while Wesley sees the physical and the spiritual working together and is interested in things pertaining to the former, he gives clear and unashamed priority to the latter.

The interaction of faith and science, and Wesley's affirmation of their complementary rather than antagonistic relationship, can also be seen in his most extensive scientific work, a compilation and abridgement of the work of several of "natural philosophers" in a five-volume piece he calls *A Survey of the Wisdom of God in Creation*, and only subtitles as *A Compendium of Natural Philosophy*.[36] The title alone reveals his concern for science as a window on God the Creator, and the end of the first paragraph leaves little doubt of that. "I wished to see this short, full, plain account of the visible creation directed to its right end: Not barely to entertain an idle, barren curiosity; but to display the invisible things of God, his power, wisdom, and goodness."[37]

This theological framework for reading science is consistent throughout Wesley's work. In his *Journal*, he commends those who explicitly bring God into their scientific understandings[38] and condemns those who leave God out.[39] He roundly condemns a preoccupation with scientific knowledge as no less than spiritual idolatry,[40] and he asserts that "[N]o system, either of morality or philosophy, can be complete, unless God be kept in view, from the very beginning to the end."[41] This affirmation of the interrelationship of the spiritual and physical realms even shows up in the odd delight Wesley took in pointing to things that he felt proved the inadequacy of a wholly scientific or materialist worldview. Throughout his *Journal*, we find references to (and Wesley's rather credulous disposition toward) such things as ghost stories, dreams, miracles and scientifically unexplainable phenomena.[42] In relating these stories, Wesley knows full well that he is challenging the scientific worldview, and he does so deliberately. In arguing against the Enlightenment worldview he asserts:

> They well know, (whether Christians know it, or not,) that the giving up witchcraft is, in effect, giving up the Bible; and they know, on the other hand, that if but one account of the intercourse of men with separate spirits be admitted, their whole castle in the air (Deism, Atheism, Materialism) falls to the ground.[43]

To conclude, we can see that Wesley's interest in science, particularly the experimental and practical kind, was genuine, but it was subservient to other purposes. As we saw above in his appropriation of Aristotle, Wesley saw experience (here represented by natural science) as necessary but insufficient for true knowledge. He believed a materialist approach would always fall short of complete truth because it was not properly pre-conditioned in a way that would allow for a proper interpretation of experience. It is the same critique he will offer to that most influential system of philosophy during Wesley's time: British Empiricism.

Notes

1. Cf. Bertrand Russell's critique that he was generally ignorant of the scientific advancements being made during his lifetime, (Bertrand Russell, *History of Western Philosophy and its Connection with Political and Social Circumstances from the Earliest Times to the Present Day* [London: George Allen and Unwin, 1946], 566) and the statement by W. T. Jones that Bacon himself did not fully understand what scientists of his day were doing (W. T. Jones, *A History of Western Philosophy* [New York: Harcourt, Brace and World, 1952], 596-97). On the idea that men like Bacon were merely

interpreting their time and were not themselves forging a new worldview, cf. William Babcock, "The Commerce between the Mind and Things. A Re-shaping of the World in the 17th Century," in *The Unbounded Community: Papers in Christian Ecumenism in Honor of Jaroslav Pelikan*, ed. William Caferro and Duncan G. Fisher, (New York: Garland, 1996), 163-186.

2. Francis Bacon, *Novum Organum* [§I.3], in *English Philosophers from Bacon to Mill*, ed. Edwin Burtt (New York: The Modern Library, 1939), 28.

3. Ibid. [§I.29], 31.

4. Ibid. [§I.63], 43.

5. Ibid. [§I.97], 68. Emphasis added.

6. Hobbes was apparently Bacon's favorite secretary and the only one whom Bacon felt truly understood him (Jones, *History*, 635).

7. Thomas Hobbes, *Leviathan* [§I.1], in Burtt, *English Philosophers*, 131.

8. On this point, cf. Frederick Copleston, *A History of Philosophy*, vol. 5, (London: Search Press, 1959), 7-8.

9. Hobbes, *Leviathan* [§I.12], 89.

10. On this trend and the importance of Hobbes for British atheism, cf. John Redwood, *Reason, Ridicule and Religion: The Age of Enlightenment in England 1660-1750* (Cambridge, MA: Harvard University Press, 1976), 34.

11. See the review of this discussion in J. W. Haas, "John Wesley's Views on Science and Christianity: An Examination of the Charge of Antiscience" *Church History* 63 (1994): 378-392. For an earlier overreaction to these criticisms, cf. Frank W. Collier, *John Wesley Among the Scientists* (Nashville: Abingdon, 1928).

12. See Wesley's comments on Bacon in *Journal* 5 November 1787 (*Jackson* 4:404) and *Thoughts On Genius* §4 (*Jackson* 8:478), written three days later.

13. *Of the Gradual Improvement of Natural Philosophy* §6, which introduces Wesley's *A Survey of the Wisdom of God in Creation* (*Jackson* 8:482).

14. *Journal* 11 May 1786 (*Jackson* 4:331).

15. See Wesley's comments on a kind of "Social Contract" theory of government in *Some Observations on Liberty* §31 (*Jackson* 11:104).

16. Sermon #44 "Original Sin" §III.4 (*Jackson* 6:64).

17. Sermon #70 "The Case of Reason Impartially Considered" §4 (*Jackson* 6:356-57).

18. Namely, *The History and Present State of Electricity, with Original Experiments*, published in 1767. Interestingly enough, Priestley cites approvingly Wesley's own work on electricity, *Desideratum: or Electricity made Plain and Useful* (1760), a book whose title itself is instructive.

19. *Journal* 4 January 1768 (*Jackson* 3:311).

20. Cf. *Journal* 28 June 1770 (*Jackson* 3:402), "Letter to the Lord Bishop of London" ¶14 [11 June 1747] (*Jackson* 8:490), and *Thoughts Upon Nervous Disorders* ¶6 (*Jackson* 11:518) as well as the introduction to his own *Primitive Physic* ¶16 (*Jackson* 14:314)

21. *Journal* 10 July 1782 (*Jackson* 4:232).

22. Cf. *Journal* 16 January 1789 (*Jackson* 4:444). Interestingly enough, Wesley is intrigued enough by this account to go back to it later that year (*Journal* 1 December 1789 [*Jackson* 4:476]) and give it an extended treatment in a tract entitled *Thoughts Upon a Late Publication* (*Jackson* 13:411), and though he does not change his opinion of it he still takes the time to publish an abridgement of it (minus, of course, the parts he found most objectionable) in his multi-volume *Christian Library* (see *Jackson* 14:294).

23. *A Thought on Necessity* §VI.1 (*Jackson* 10:478).

24. *A Plain Account of the People Called Methodists* §XII.2 (*Jackson* 8:264)

25. *Journal* 4 December 1746 (*Jackson* 2:39).

26. "Letter to Mr. T. H." [12 December 1760] (*Jackson* 13:391).

27. First published in 1747, this work went through twenty-three editions in Wesley's lifetime, the last in 1791, making it Wesley's single most popular work. In subsequent editions, Wesley frequently took pains to correct, add and remove various cures as further experience with them warranted, cf. the various postscripts appended to several of the editions (*Jackson* 14:316-318).

28. Cf. some of Wesley's comments on professional physicians in *Journal* 12 July 1739 (*Jackson* 1:210) and 5 April 1756 (*Jackson* 2:360); Sermon #50 "The Use of Money" §I.5 (*Jackson* 6:129); Sermon #84 "The Important Question" §III.7 (*Jackson* 6:501); and *Thoughts Upon Nervous Disorders* §1 (*Jackson* 11:515). Again his criterion for evaluating them is their utility.

29 *The Desideratum; or Electricity made plain and useful* §2-3 (*Jackson* 14:242). For more on Wesley's view of medicine and health cf. Maddox, *Responsible Grace*, 146-47; and the studies of Philip W. Ott ("John Wesley on Health. A Word for Sensible Regime," *Methodist History* 18 (1980):193-304; "John Wesley and the Non-Naturals," *Preventive Medicine* 9 (1980): 578-84; "John Wesley on Mind and Body. Toward and Understanding of Health as Wholeness," *Methodist History* 27 (1989): 61-72; and "John Wesley on Health as Wholeness," *Journal of Religion and Health* 30 (1991): 43-57.

30. "Preface" to *Primitive Physic* §6-12 (*Jackson* 14:309-312).

31. *The Desideratum* §2 (*Jackson* 14:242).

32. "Preface" to *Primitive Physic* §2 (*Jackson* 14:308)

33. Ibid., §15 (*Jackson* 14:313). Cf. also *Journal* 12 May 1759 (*Jackson* 2:479), where Wesley notes, commenting on a medical case, that "no man can be a thorough Physician without being an experienced Christian."

34. Ibid., §16.VI.5 (*Jackson* 14:316).

35. Among many examples, cf. *Journal* 11 September 1740 (*Jackson* 1:287), 23 March 1741 (*Jackson* 1:304), and 11 March 1762 (*Jackson* 3:81).

36. Wesley began working on this piece in the late 1750s (cf. *Journal* 11 December 1758 [*Jackson* 2:464]), which originally comprised three volumes but grew to five before the end of Wesley's life.

37. "Preface" to *A Survey of the Wisdom of God in Creation* ¶1 (*Jackson* 14:300). Cf. also Wesley's *Address to the Clergy* where he recommends natural philosophy as a means of better understanding Scripture (*An Address to the Clergy* §I.2 [*Jackson* 10:484]).

38. Cf. his comments on Dr. Hales in *Journal* 3 July 1753 (*Jackson* 2:295).

39. Cf. Wesley's comments on Dr. Robertson's and Dr. Hawkesworth's work in *Journal* 6 July 1781 (*Jackson* 4:210) and his *Remarks on the Count de Buffon's 'Natural History'* (*Jackson* 13:454-55).

40. Sermon #78 "Spiritual Idolatry" §I.14 (*Jackson* 6:440).

41. *Thoughts Upon Necessity* §IV.4 (*Jackson* 10:473).

42. Among many examples cf. *Journal* 25 December 1742 (*Jackson* 1:406); 24 July 1761 (*Jackson* 3:69); 4 July 1770 (*Jackson* 3:403-04); 8 October 1778 (*Jackson* 4:138); and 19 April 1784 (*Jackson* 4:271).

43. *Journal* 25 May 1768 (Jackson 3:324-25).

4

Wesley and British Empiricism

Just before Wesley's time, the empirical ideas of Bacon and Hobbes were given their fullest and most influential treatment by John Locke. During Wesley's lifetime, these ideas were further explored by David Hume. Together with George Berkeley,[1] they make up the philosophical movement called British Empiricism, which firmly established in England an empirical tradition with a strong epistemological drive that survives in Anglo-American philosophy to the present day. In our investigation, we will also include Peter Browne, an Irish bishop who is largely forgotten today but who published his own adaptation and critique of Locke's ideas while Wesley was at Oxford.

Wesley inclusion in this group has long been assumed, and most attempts to understand his epistemology and the role of experience in his thought begin with the presumption that he does, indeed, belong here. While there is no doubt that these men, at least Locke and Browne, had an influence on Wesley, his approach nevertheless should be distinguished from theirs. The reasons for this will become evident as we examine his interactions with these men, particularly in light of the features of his epistemology we have explored above: his devotion to logic with its metaphysical implications and his commitment to the inadequacy of purely material knowledge.

The British Empiricists

John Locke

Born in 1632, John Locke studied philosophy and medicine at Oxford and had a varied career as a doctor, political secretary and gentleman philosopher before his death in 1704. His most influential work was called *An Essay Concerning Human Understanding* (1690), which defined the doctrine of empiricism in its Enlightenment form and became the touchstone for almost all future discussions on the issue. Despite the fact, however, that in Wesley's day, Locke was "the intellectual ruler of the century,"[2] there is much debate as to how deeply his ideas had penetrated the popular culture of the time.[3] Certainly the book was popular, but it was often read only to be refuted or critiqued, usually by English clergy who opposed Locke's heterodoxy (Peter Browne being one good example of this). We should, therefore, be suspicious of any attempt to liken Wesley to Locke simply because the latter is supposed to have been the dominant voice in British philosophy during Wesley's collegiate years.

To begin with, Locke, like Bacon and Hobbes, is a strong empiricist, one who will allow no other source of ideas than experience. He spends the first book of his *Essay* challenging the rationalist notion of "innate ideas," in which reason has some unmediated access to truth. He then sets up at the beginning of the second book his own empirical stance: "Let us then suppose the mind to be, as we say, white paper, devoid of all characters, without any ideas; how comes it to be furnished?…To this I answer in one word, from EXPEREINCE: in that all our knowledge is founded, and from that it ultimately derives itself."[4]

It is this attack on rationalism and defense of empiricism for which Locke is chiefly known, and it is for agreeing with him in this that Wesley is usually placed in Locke's camp. The problems with this will become clear as we examine Wesley's interaction with Locke, but at this point it should be noted that people easily reduced Locke's project to the mere establishment of empiricism, his work *against* rationalism being far better known than the details of his own position *for* empiricism.[5] As Clark notes, many of the figures of the "long eighteenth century" in England were treated as representatives of set of opinions by later historiographers,[6] and so Locke becomes the representative empiricist, much as Bacon had already become by Locke's day the representative scientist. This leads to an easy but unfortunate association of all empiricists with Locke's name. There is, then, an implicit logical fallacy that seems to be at work among many readers of Wesley, which runs as follows: all Lockeans are empiricists; Wesley is an empiricist; therefore Wesley is a Lockean.[7] Wesley himself would have been at pains to note that this conclusion does not follow.

To return to Locke, we find that his understanding of experience is two-fold, involving our sensation of the external world and also our perception of the operations of our mind (what Locke calls "internal sense" or "reflection"). While this second category becomes controversial, it is enough for us to note at this point that, in Locke's view, the mind can know things *outside itself* only through sensation and experience (with the problematic exception of God). And aside from its own existence, the mind knows all else only by probability, not with certainty. "Probability," writes Locke, "is the appearance of agreement upon fallible proofs…The grounds of probability are two; conformity with our own experience, or the testimony of others' experience."[8] And the experience of others is only to be trusted on the basis of reasoned criteria from our own experience.

Thus, Locke shares with Wesley a strong sense of the limited nature of human understanding, but for Locke this is a problem that one must simply cope with. It cannot be solved. In fact, Locke wrote his *Essay* so that reason might "stop when it is at the utmost end of its tether, and to sit down in a quiet ignorance of those things which, upon examination, are found to be beyond the reach of our capacities."[9] This means that Locke, *unlike* Wesley, is explicitly against any metaphysical a priori which would supplement one's ability to experience the material world. In the fourth book of the *Essay*, Locke inveighs against any metaphysical scheme that would replace experience, and, like Bacon, his main object of attack is Aristotle's logic. It is there he famously quips:

> But God has not been so sparing to men to make them barely two-legged creatures, and left it to Aristotle to make them rational...He has given them a mind that can reason, without being instructed in methods of syllogizing: the understanding is not taught to reason by these rules; it has a native faculty to perceive the coherence or incoherence of its ideas, and can range them right, without any such perplexing repetitions.[10]

Our "native faculty" means we need no help from outside ourselves to reason well. If that reasoning is imperfect, so be it; it cannot be helped. We will naturally associate ideas together that belong together, and logic only obscures the issue.[11] The entirety of Book Four of the *Essay* reveals how anti-metaphysical Locke's approach is, and this becomes most clear when he turns to the subject of religion or faith, particularly revelation and the problem of enthusiasm.

Locke has much to say on the topic of faith and reason, as it was this very thing that got him started on the line of thinking that led to his writing the *Essay*.[12] Locke is much more avowedly religious than either Hobbes or Hume, and he has even been called a "theological philosopher,"[13] although he was apparently not an orthodox one. Still, against the general tenor of the rest of his epistemology, Locke allows one to have certain knowledge of God as a necessary corollary to one's own existence (*a la* Descartes).[14] There is, therefore, a place for faith and revelation in Locke's thought, if revelation is understood to be the testimony of God concerning things *above* human reason. The difficulty comes with the question of how one knows that a given revelation is from God, and here Locke's anti-metaphysical empiricism is at odds with Wesley's more metaphysically friendly version.

One of the very last chapters of Locke's *Essay* is his discussion of the problem of enthusiasm, or irrational religion, that "which, laying by reason, would set up revelation without it."[15] Locke had earlier noted that faith must be regulated by reason,[16] and in this chapter he is clear that reason and reason *alone* is capable of determining whether or not we should asset to a proposition as coming from God—although we would not, of course, be expected to make sense of it ourselves.

> God, when he makes the prophet, does not unmake the man. He leaves all his faculties in the natural state, to enable him to judge of his inspirations, whether they be of divine original or no. When he illuminates the mind with supernatural light, he does not extinguish that which is natural. If he would have us assent to the truth of any proposition, he either evidences that truth by the usual methods of natural reason, or else makes it known to be a truth which he would have us assent to, by his authority; and convinces us that it is from him, by some marks which reason cannot be mistaken in. *Reason must be our last judge and guide in*

everything. I do not mean that we must consult reason, and examine whether a proposition revealed from God can be made out by natural principles, and if it cannot, that then we may reject it: but consult it we must, and by it examine, whether it be a revelation from God or not.[17]

For Locke then, religion which is exclusively grounded on faith and not reason has no place. And the reason which grounds faith is itself grounded in our normal, everyday experience. Unlike Bacon and Hobbes, Locke does not limit real knowledge to physical reality. He affirms that there are truths above reason, revelations from God among them, but he feels he must guard against those who would abuse this possibility. So, while not denying the workings of a spiritual realm, Locke is at pains to show how such workings must be consonant with the workings of this non-spiritual, physical realm. Faith and reason go together, but because we live in this world, and not in the spiritual one, it must be reason—which is also based in this world—which grounds us. The role of faith is to supplement—not supplant—reason in connecting us to the world that transcends us by means of God's revelation to us.

Locke's position is problematic, as we shall see, but it remains a powerful and serious attempt to grapple with the question of knowledge and how we might integrate physical knowledge with spiritual knowledge. But the truce he forms between these two kinds of knowledge is not one that can stand. After his death, people like Peter Browne will affirm the priority of the spiritual, while people like David Hume will flatly deny that we can have anything like knowledge of it.

Peter Browne

While Wesley was still a young Fellow and Tutor at Oxford, Locke's ideas were picked up, critiqued, and given an even more explicitly religious cast by the then Bishop of Cork, Peter Browne, in *The Procedure, Extent and Limits of Human Understanding* (1728).[18] While Browne has been largely forgotten today and little case can be made for his having impacted the history of empirical philosophy to any great extent, Browne's significance to Wesley is undeniable. Browne is essentially a Lockean, but he makes some modifications to Locke that may have influenced the young Mr. Wesley.

Browne accepts Locke's refutation of innate ideas, but he seems more positive about the reliability of the knowledge that comes from the senses than Locke is. Here, Browne reverts to a much more commonsensical approach, as Browne, like Wesley, does not appear to be driven by the issue of proving the certainty of our knowledge. He simply affirms that our sensory knowledge of the world represents what is objectively real. Browne's reason is that knowledge of the external world comes to us without our consent and is not contingent upon us or our fallible reasoning processes. We receive representations of the world from our senses—"ideas," Browne calls them and compares them to wax impression—"without any immediate concurrence of the pure intellect."[19] So, for example, upon seeing a tree, we are compelled to believe a tree exists—no reasoning is necessary.[20]

This positive evaluation of the senses allows Browne to be more insistent than Locke that all ideas come only through our five physical senses, eliminating Locke's second category of ideas—those based on reflection or on the mind perceiving itself. Browne's objection to this doctrine seems to anticipate Hume's critique of allowing the self to be an object of perception by the mind, somehow allowing one to be at the same time perceiver and perceived.[21] However, despite his attempt to distance himself from Locke, Browne ends up with an idea rather close to Locke's idea of intuition, and so we have necessary and immediate knowledge of our states of self and necessary and mediate knowledge of the external world via our senses.[22] This immediate knowledge of ourselves, however, is not so much an act of perception as a by-product of our conscious minds.

> The necessary assent of the mind doth not only follow of course upon this consciousness, as it is in the case of external sensation, but falls in with it: they are so closely connected that the consciousness is itself the immediate act of assent or knowledge; at least they are so inseparable that they cannot be distinguished even in thought.[23]

A third and final modification of Locke in Browne relevant to our purposes is the role he gives to revelation. While Locke allows for the *possibility* of revelation and spends the last section of his *Essay* guarding against its abuse, Browne gears his entire essay toward an insistence on the *necessity* of revelation, pointing out, as we have seen Wesley do above, the inadequacy of human knowledge without it.[24] This orientation, directed against Browne's deistic opponents gives his work a religious, even apologetic cast, something of which Wesley would have approved.

David Hume

The next significant development in empiricism in Eighteenth Century England comes from the pen of David Hume. Born eight years after Wesley (1711) and preceding him in death by some fifteen (1776), Hume was entirely Wesley's contemporary. His principle work on epistemology is his *Enquiry Concerning Human Understanding*, which was published in 1751 as a revision of *A Treatise of Human Nature*, which had appeared in 1738-40. Hume's importance for modern philosophy is immense, but for Wesley he is merely a foil, demonstrating how far Wesley is from the project of epistemology in which Hume is engaged.

David Hume develops Locke's empiricism back toward the direction originally set by Bacon and Hobbes, concentrating on the physical world. Hume, however, is much more pessimistic about our knowledge, and in his work the epistemological drive to determine what exactly we can know is clear. A true skeptic, albeit a positive and happy one, Hume affirms that, while we cannot avoid believing that there is a world out there to be known, we have no way of knowing for certain whether or not this is a justified belief. If all knowledge comes from experience, then all we can know is experience, and thus it is only ever circular reasoning that can be used to demonstrate that our experience is indicative of anything higher than itself, that it faithfully represents objective reality.

Hume is best remembered for calling into question the reality of our idea of cause and effect, the validity of which is arguably the single most important presupposition of empiricism. He claims that we cannot know whether or not it is a function of reality, even if it is an inescapable habit of the mind. In doing this, Hume makes problematic the very idea of knowledge with any certainty, if knowledge is the effect of which experience is the cause. In a way, this is just Hume making explicit some of the implications inherent in Locke's presuppositions and extending Locke's cautions about the limitations of knowledge to their utmost degree.

This view of knowledge and experience has implications for the idea of religious experience or for any knowledge of the spiritual world. After all, if knowledge of this concrete world is problematic, knowledge of something like God is practically excluded. This is seen most clearly in Hume's *Essay on Miracles*, but it is also evident in his *Dialogues on Natural Religion*, which Hume knew would cause a religious reaction and so directed not to be published until after his death.

Hume's position is one of profound agnosticism and, as has already been mentioned, is the natural culmination of the epistemological drive in philosophy that Locke initiated. In answer to the question of "How do we know what we know," Hume answers, "We don't. Full stop." Given an purely empiricist approach to knowledge, Hume states that the question of knowledge has no answer. Understanding Hume in this way helps one to understand Wesley's reaction to him, and it sets off Wesley's own view in much better relief.

British Empiricism is deeply written into the intellectual milieu of Eighteenth Century England, and it should come as no surprise that Wesley, like any well-educated man of his day, would have encountered it. What is surprising when one looks at Wesley's reaction to this empirical tradition is not how much he was influenced by it but how clearly his deeper commitments come to the fore when he interacts with it. To explore what we mean by that, we will trace Wesley's reaction to the various figures in this movement.

Wesley the Empiricist

Wesley's Reaction to Locke

Wesley's interactions with Locke seem to begin at Oxford, where we know that Locke's work appeared on his self-appointed reading lists[25] and where we know that he discussed Locke with friends.[26] However, there is no direct evidence of Wesley's engagement with Locke from this time, at least not of the kind we find for his engagement with Peter Browne. In his diaries, he notes engagements with commentaries on Locke,[27] so he seems to have been interested in the issues Locke raised, but of citations or comments on Locke himself, there is almost nothing. Even where mediated influences might exist, such as that of Richard Fiddes, who discussed faith in Lockean terms as "the assent to a proposition on rational grounds," we find him distancing himself from this way of thinking.[28] Wesley's association of this idea with Fiddes rather than with the much more well-known figure of Locke may also reveal a lack of familiarity, and in any case his rejection of the idea entails a rejection of a major feature of Lockean epistemology—the foundational priority of reason.

Throughout his life, as Wesley engages the basic questions of knowledge and experience that Locke engages, he never does so with explicit reference to Locke. He includes Locke's *Essay* in the curriculum for the Kingswood school in the late 1740s and recommends its reading in a letter to Miss Lewin in 1764, but those recommendations may be as easily explained as a nod to the importance of the work as indicating a personal indebtedness to it. It is not until 1781, in the last decade of his life, that we find Wesley seriously engaging Locke's *Essay*, and that with some surprise as to how good that work was. This engagement, published with excerpts from Locke's work in the *Arminian Magazine*, was entitled *Remarks upon Mr. Locke's 'Essay on Human Understanding.'* In it, we can see the common empirical ground Wesley and Locke share, but we are also confronted with the clear distance between Wesley's naïve (Aristotelian) empiricism and Locke's anti-metaphysical version.

Wesley begins his *Remarks* with this comment:

> For some days I have employed myself on the road in reading Mr. Locke's "Essay on Human Understanding:" And I do not now wonder at its having gone through so many editions in so short a time. For what comparison is there between this deep, solid, weighty treatise, and the lively, glittering trifle of Baron Montesquieu? As much as between tinsel and gold; between glass-beads and diamonds. A deep fear of God, and reverence for his word, are discernible throughout the whole: And though there are some mistakes, yet these are abundantly compensated by many curious and useful reflections.[29]

Two things should be noted at the outset. First the comment reflects a lack of previous familiarity with Locke's work ("I do not now wonder..."). It is, of course, very likely that Wesley read the *Essay* at Oxford, but even so, it made no lasting impression on him, and Wesley treats this reading of Locke as if it is his first. Second, the ground of Wesley's approval of Locke is *not* epistemological but religious ("A deep fear of God..."). He had been reading at the same time Montesquieu's *Spirit of Laws*, which Wesley took to be an anti-religious work, and Locke comes off so much better in the comparison.[30] The sum is that the work is pronounced useful despite some mistakes, and it is in elucidating these mistakes that Wesley's a priori religious and metaphysical concerns consistently clash with Locke's reason-based, anti-metaphysical claims.

To begin with, Wesley will often critique Locke's philosophical anthropology by referencing explicitly faith-based ideas. Regarding Locke's identification of identity and consciousness, to take one example among several possibilities, Wesley has this to say: "That 'Socrates asleep and Socrates awake is not the same person,' (Book II., chap. i., sec. 11,) I can by no means allow." His reasons for rejecting this idea are explicitly grounded in his religious understanding. For Wesley, one's soul—not one's consciousness—determines one's identity. As evidence against Locke's idea, he points out the implications of it for a person's accountability before God, and he concludes that part of his critique as follows:

> Upon the whole, if you take the word "person" for a thinking intelligent being, it is evident, the same soul, conscious or unconscious, is the same person. But if you take it for the same soul, animating the same human body, (in which sense I have always taken it, and I believe every one else that has not been confounded by metaphysical subtlety,) then you and I and every man living is the same person from the cradle to the grave. And God will accordingly reward every man, or every person, (equivalent words,) according to his own works; and that whether he be conscious of them or no; this will make no manner of difference.[31]

Wesley's argument against Locke here is clearly a religious argument against a philosophical point. One could argue the appropriateness of such a move, but it does indicate where Wesley's sympathies lie. Locke has reasons for his position, but they seem to be worth nothing against Wesley's a priori commitment to revelation. This attitude shows through in other places as well, as we will see below, but that discussion immediately leads into a much more important critique of Locke by Wesley: Wesley's explicit avowal of Aristotelian logic against Locke's rejection of it.

Already in commenting on the first half of the *Essay*, Wesley notes that, "The operations of the mind are more accurately divided by Aristotle than by Mr. Locke. They are three, and no more: Simple apprehension, judgment, and discourse."[32] He also cites Aldrich's work, which have seen is a re-presentation of Aristotle's logic, as being clearer and more succinct than Locke's on the subject of "signs".[33] But it is in coming to his analysis of the second half of Locke's *Essay* that Wesley's real concerns come to the fore.

> In reading over the second volume [i.e. books three and four] of Mr. Locke's Essay, I was much disappointed: It is by no means equal to the first. The more I considered it, the more convinced I was, 1. That his grand design was, (vain design!) to drive Aristotle's Logic out of the world, which he hated cordially, but never understood: I suppose, because he had an unskilful master, and read bad books upon the subject. 2. That he had not a clear apprehension. Hence he had few clear ideas; (though he talks of them so much;) and hence so many confused, inadequate definitions. I wonder none of his opponents hit this blot. I have not time to point out half the mistakes in this volume. I can only make a few cursory strictures.[34]

These remarks are telling for several reasons. First of all, the very fact that Wesley will undertake to critique the philosophical paragon of the century reveals his deep confidence (perhaps even bordering on arrogance) in his own position and its superiority to Locke's. Second, Wesley speaks much more approvingly of the first part of the *Essay*, in which Locke attacks the concept of innate ideas, than he does of the second part, in which Locke begins to build his own empirical system. Thus, while he shares Locke's empiricist premise, he is not wholly appreciative of Locke's efforts to flesh that premise out. Finally, Wesley avows the metaphysical truth of Aristotle's logic by both citing Locke's explicit rejection of it as a problem and by using metaphysical-logical issues to counter Locke's claims. He asserts that Locke must not have understood logic, because if he had, he would have believed it and used it to gain a better apprehension, which is to say, a better pre-informed experience of the world. The reason why "none of his opponents hit this blot" is probably because few of them would have been as deeply Aristotelian as Wesley shows himself to be, especially in the comments that follow.

Wesley quotes Locke as saying, 'Logic has much contributed to the obscurity of language.' His rejoinder is clear:

> The abuse of logic has; but the true use of it is the noblest means under heaven to prevent or cure the obscurity of language. To divide simple terms according to the logical rules of division, and then to define each member of the division according to the three rules of definition, does all that human art can do, in order to our having a clear and distinct idea of every word we use. Had Mr. Locke done this, what abundance of obscurity and confusion would have been prevented!...Whatever Mr. Locke says against the terms 'essence' or 'species,' he can find no better words. But I impute this to his violent spleen against logic, which he never rightly understood.[35]

Finally, Wesley even cites Peter Browne *against* Locke on this point: "Here comes his main attack upon logic, by that marvellous invention of substituting juxtaposition of ideas in the place of syllogism. But Bishop Browne has so thoroughly confuted this, (in his Essay on "Human Understanding,") that to add anything more is quite superfluous."[36]

While this surface defense of logic is interesting, far more significant is Wesley's explicit endorsement of the metaphysical implications of Aristotle's logic over and against Locke's pure empiricism. Citing book 3, chapter 3 of the *Essay*, Wesley notes, "Here his hatred of logic breaks out: 'Defining by genus and difference may be the shortest way, yet I doubt whether it be the best.' Then what is the best? No man living can tell a better than this; only if we do not know the difference, we must assign the properties."[37]

The ideas of *genus* and *difference* were Aristotelian categories that enabled one to process information given to the mind from the senses. Here Wesley is specifically defending the a priori role of Aristotle's logical metaphysical taxonomy against Locke's (and Bacon's) mind-as-*tabula-rasa* view. Wesley maintains that differences or essences we have *in* the mind belong—not *to* the mind—but to the nature of the thing itself, which is why they can guide our perception of reality. This accords with what we noted earlier, that Wesley maintains that a proper metaphysic is necessary for proper apprehension. He makes this position even clearer in the following series of comments on Locke, and here we also see how Wesley ties this understanding to the Scripture itself, further showing the priority of religious (or biblical) thinking over philosophical thinking in his mind.

> A man need only read the first chapter of Genesis, to be convinced that God made every species of animals 'after its kind;' giving a peculiar essence to each, whether we know that real essence or no...[quoting Locke] 'Species and their essences have no real existence in things.' Moses says otherwise, and so does Mr. Locke, page 44: 'By real essence, I mean that real constitution of anything which is the foundation of all its properties. But this we do not know.' True; but it exists...[quoting Locke again] 'Each abstract idea makes a distinct species.' (Ibid.) What! Does my idea of them make a horse, a cow, and a dog, three distinct species? Would not these species be equally distinct, if I had no idea of them at all?...[again Locke]'It is a false supposition, that there are certain precise essences by which things are distinguished into species.' It is a most true supposition. The Scripture asserts it; and all experience agrees thereto.[38]

In these comments, we see that Wesley admits, with Locke, the limitations of human knowledge concerning things like essences, that they are not knowable via experience. However, Wesley will affirm the existence of these essences, and he calls upon experience to affirm that things are different in essence, not because we make them different or because we construe them differently but because they are, in reality, different. We don't experience essences, he seems to say, but our experience is not understandable without them.

Of course, this immediately raises the epistemological question: How does one know that these essences exist if in themselves they are not knowable through our experience of them or through innate ideas, as the rationalists would have affirmed? Wesley's answer seems decidedly medieval and definitely un-philosophical—because the Scripture so asserts it. This interplay between an a priori authority (here Scripture) and experience is something we will explore more deeply when delving into Wesley's own thought on experience.

One final comment from Wesley on Locke will suffice to show his distance from both British Empiricism and Scientific Materialism. Again the subject is logic, specifically the a priori rule of constructing a syllogism: that one cannot argue from the particular to the general. Citing Locke, Wesley begins, "'I take notice of one manifest mistake in the rules of syllogism, — that particular premises prove nothing.' Can anything show more clearly his total ignorance of logic?"[39] This points to the fundamental difference between Wesley's empiricism and the burgeoning scientific empiricism that Locke endorses and that will eventually take hold in Modernity. It also shows that Wesley is aware of this difference. Logic speaks of generalities and their relationship to particularities, and that is why a syllogism with two particular premises proves nothing general—they only speak to one specific case. However, from the standpoint of the scientific empiricism of Bacon and Locke, there are only specific cases, only particular premises—no general cases or premises exist. They must be created on the basis of specific cases. It is against Aristotle that the whole tradition rebels, and by maintaining a loyalty to Aristotle, Wesley espouses a different philosophical outlook.

So we can see that there are similarities between Wesley and Locke, but they are the same similarities as would exist between Locke and Aristotle. More clear are the parallels between Wesley and Aristotle *against* Locke. As we explore Wesley's interaction with the rest of this British empirical tradition (which we can now do in much less detail), we will see that the general lines of Wesley's reaction to Locke—the defense of a priori metaphysical convictions about logic and religion—continue to hold almost without exception.

Wesley's Reaction to Browne

As we noted above, and as has been off and on acknowledged,[40] the influence of Peter Browne on Wesley is more significant than the influence of Locke. Even here, however, this influence must be contextualized within Wesley's logical and religious training.

Browne publishes his *Procedure* in 1728, and Wesley reads it in 1730, several years after he had become a moderator in logic at Oxford. His initial reaction was not enthusiastic. He had apparently recommended the book without reading it fully, and later, in a letter to one Miss Pendarves, regretted that recommendation:

> I own I deserve a severer censure for my want of consideration in positively recommending to them a book of which I had read but a few pages, the beauties of which I find, upon closer examination, to be joined with so many imperfections, with so many fallacies and falsehoods and contradictions as more than balance them, and make it highly unworthy to take up any of their hours who know so well how to employ every moment.[41]

Despite these critical remarks, Wesley promises to abridge the text (thus at least showing he felt it that much worthy of his time) and send that to her. Miss Pendarves, in her reply, assumes this is Browne's book, and later acknowledges receipt of that abridgement. We can reasonably assume that this is the abridgement of Browne that eventually shows up as an appendix to Wesley's *Compendium of Natural Philosophy*.

It seems that Wesley's deeper engagement with Browne through the abridgement process softens his initial criticism. Whether his initial critique was overstated, perhaps in an attempt to impress a lady with his academic acumen, or whether he actually comes to change his mind is largely irrelevant. The fact remains that Wesley uses Browne, recommends its reading (once alongside Locke's *Essay*,[42] once without it[43]), and endorses Browne's general conclusion concerning the necessity of revelation in a letter to William Law.[44] He will even call Browne to his defense of logic against Locke in the *Remarks* cited above.

However, even in light of these endorsements, the idea that Browne stands as the primary philosophical influence on Wesley is not, in the end, tenable.[45] As we investigate Wesley's own epistemology in the next chapter, his differences from Browne will emerge more clearly, but a few remarks can still be made at this stage. First, it is true that Wesley is closer to Browne than he is to Locke, especially on the matter of the reliability of the senses and the necessity of revelation, but this is to be expected in light of what we already have seen of Wesley. Concerning the reliability of the senses, Browne is merely reaffirming a more classically Aristotelian position over and against Locke, a position Wesley seems already to have owned. Concerning the necessity of revelation, Browne reveals the same priority of the religious over the philosophical that we have already seen in Wesley. Both agree that sensory-experience-based ideas are insufficient for true knowledge, but Wesley already affirmed that in a letter to his mother five years before he read Browne.[46] Thus, it is not necessary to assume Browne's direct influence on Wesley in these matters, Browne being treated much more like a colleague than a mentor in Wesley's writings. In one crucial point, Wesley find himself in direct opposition to Browne, whose confining of sensation to the physical senses leaves no room for Wesley's own doctrine of the spiritual senses.

Wesley's Reaction to Hume

The final figure in British Empiricism provides an interesting foil for Wesley. Wesley has a class of philosophers whose ideas he treats with nothing but contempt. This list includes the French humanists Voltaire, Rousseau, and Montesquieu, but the chief among these contemptible thinkers is David Hume, whom Wesley calls "the most insolent despiser of truth and virtue that ever appeared in the world…an avowed enemy to God and man, and to all that is sacred and valuable upon earth."[47] Given what we have seen of Wesley thus far, his contempt for Hume is understandable, perhaps even predictable. Hume's avowed agnosticism and his carrying of Locke's project to rather un-Lockean (but nevertheless more consistent) ends would not make him the object of respect by someone like Wesley, whose commitments to a priori metaphysical and religious claims were challenged by Hume's position.

It is difficult to tell if Wesley had read Hume himself or simply knew him by reputation, as all of Wesley's remarks about Hume come rather late in his life and well after the publication of the *Enquiry*, time enough for Hume's reputation to be established. However, Wesley was careful to read a number of the critical replies that were made to Hume by men such as George Campbell,[48] James Beattie,[49] and Thomas Reid,[50] thus indicating that he had a continuing interest in the matter. The interest, however, does not seem to be that of a serious epistemologist. Whatever it is that these men say against Hume, Wesley seems to accept, and the comments have much more the character of someone simply rejoicing in the victory over an common enemy than of someone thinking seriously about the epistemological issues involved. In any case, it is clear from all of Wesley's comments that he thought of Hume first as an enemy of religion and only second as a philosopher—and one of those despised "minute philosophers"[51] at that.

Wesley's Own Empiricism

That Wesley was an empiricist is evident both from his own statements and the general way he treats the question of knowledge. However, as we have already noted, Wesley's empiricism is much closer to the metaphysical empiricism of Aristotle than it is to the scientific empiricism of Bacon and Locke. When the two types of empiricism are set against each other, as they are in Locke, Wesley staunchly defends Aristotle's version. The main issue between these two camps seems to be the role of a priori factors in the human acquisition of knowledge, not the issue of where human knowledge comes from. On this latter point, Locke, Bacon, Aristotle and Wesley would agree. The source of knowledge is experience, and there is no other. Where the disagreement comes is whether experience functions best when laid on a *tabula rasa* in the mind or when it is attuned and shaped by prior influences in the mind. Here we find Wesley closer to the Kantian and post-modern concerns about the way human experience is shaped by things that already exist in the mind than he is to the Scientific Materialists and British Empiricists, who believe that knowledge comes into the mind with no interference from it. Wesley's commitment to logic and religion as being *true* reflections of reality leads him to affirm that they are needed to shape our experience of reality—*contra* Bacon and Locke. This modifies his empiricism in interesting ways, as we shall see when we examine his own thought in some detail in the next chapter.

One final thing to note about Wesley's empiricism is that his epistemology is not something that drives him. Wesley is not concerned with being philosophically respectable, and his philosophical concerns are governed by his religious ones, as we saw in his condemnation of Hume. As we turn to our final set of philosophical interactions, we see that he has no difficulty recommending distinctly non-empirical, rationalist-oriented philosophical works right alongside empirical ones, and that with little apology or concern for contradiction. This could only be the case if he approached the whole epistemological question as someone who is not ultimately concerned with it.

Notes

1. Berkeley does not seem to be very important to Wesley, and so we will not treat him here, though he was popular with many other British clergy who found his brand of empiricism more congenial to faith than Locke's (see below). We know that Wesley read Berkeley at Oxford, as he critiques the logic of one of his points in a letter to his mother ("Letter to Susanna Wesley" [22 November 1725] [*Telford* 1:23-26]), and Wesley makes a passing comment about the "ingenious and benevolent Bishop of Cloyne" and his penchant for extolling the virtues of tar-water in his *Desideratum* (¶4 [*Jackson* 14:242]), but there seems to be little or no influence on Wesley's thought from any of Berkeley's distinctive ideas. Perhaps this is because Wesley's Aristotelian orientation already allowed him to have a faith-inclusive empiricism.

2. Stephen, *History of English Thought*, vol. 1, 35.

3. On this point, see the discussion in J. C. D. Clark, *English Society 1660-1832* (Cambridge: Cambridge University Press, 2000), 124-42.

4. John Locke, *Essay Concerning Human Understanding* [§II.1.2], 29th edition (London: Thomas Tegg, 1841), 51, http://books.google.com/books?id=cjYIAAAAQAAJ.

5. Cf. Stephen, *History of English Thought*, vol. 1, 35; and Russell, *History of Western Philosophy*, 637, 666-72.

6. Clark, *English Society*, 125.

7. As we noted above, this assumption often shows up in works on Wesley. To cite merely one example, Richard Brantley claims, "[Wesley's] 'An Earnest Appeal'...is so Lockean as to suggest that Wesley had the *Essay* in view" (*Locke, Wesley, and the Method of English Romanticism* [Gainesville, FL: University Presses of Florida, 1984], 48.), upon which he quotes a couple of paragraphs from that work (¶ 32 & 33). The paragraphs are certainly empiricist, but they are not Lockean but Aristotelian. One telling indicator of this that throughout those very paragraphs Brantley quotes, Wesley uses the word *apprehension* with its Aristotelian meaning of *perception* where Locke consistently uses the word to mean not perception but *understanding*.

8. Locke, *Essay* [§IV.15.1, 4], 483-84.

9. Ibid., [§4], 2.

10. Ibid., [§ IV.17.4.3], 496 .

11. Ibid., [§ III.10.6-7], 349 .

12. Paul Helm, "Locke on Faith and Knowledge," *Philosophical Quarterly* 23 (1973): 52.

13. Stephen, *History of English Thought*, vol. 1, 36.

14. "Though God has given us no innate ideas of Himself, though He has stamped no original characters on our minds wherein we may read His being...He hath not left Himself without a witness; since we have sense, perception, and reason, and cannot want a clear proof of Him as long as we carry ourselves about us," Locke, *Essay* [§IV.10.1], 458.

15. Ibid. [§IV.19.3], 516.

16. Ibid. [IV. 17.24], 508.

17. Ibid. [§IV.19.14], 520. Emphasis added.

18. Peter Browne, *The Procedure, Extent, and Limits of Human Understanding*, (1728; reprint, New York: Garland, 1976). One would be hard pressed to find any mention of Browne, let alone an explanation of his thought, in even the most extended of histories of philosophy. Copleston mentions his name in passing (Copleston, *History of Philosophy*, vol. 5, 141), but that is the extent of the recognition he is given in the wider philosophical world. Some modest explications of certain aspects of his thought can be found in J. Clifford Hindley, "The Philosophy of Enthusiasm: A Study in the Origins of 'Experimental Theology,'" *The London Quarterly and Holborn Review*, 182 (1957): 102-06. For a broader view, cf. Arthur R. Winnett, *Peter Browne. Provost, Bishop, Metaphysician* (London: S. P. C. K., 1974).

19. Browne, *Procedure*, 88.

20. That fact that Browne must argue for a *passive* understanding of experience may also be taken as evidence that the ordinary understanding of the word had more active connotations.

21. Browne, *Procedure*, 92-93. For further analysis of this point, cf. Hindley, "Philosophy of Enthusiasm," 104-05.

22. Ibid., 222.

23. Ibid., 224.

24. The last chapter of his essay, and the one that is the most explicitly apologetic, is entitled "The Necessity and Manner of Revelation," especially Browne, *Procedure*, 462.

25. Vivian H. H. Green, *The Young Mr. Wesley: A Study of John Wesley and Oxford* (London: Edward Arnold, 1961), 116n1.

26. Ibid., 218.

27. Ibid., 71, 191.

28. *Letter to Susanna Wesley* [22 November 1725] (*Telford* 1:25).

29. *Remarks upon Mr. Locke's 'Essay on Human Understanding,'* (*Jackson* 13:455).

30. Wesley faults Montesquieu on a number of accounts, but concludes his critique by saying, "What I least of all admire is, his laying hold on every opportunity to depreciate the inspired writers; Moses, in particular." His final summation against Montesquieu, interestingly enough, clearly reveals the two a priori concerns that Wesley felt were necessary to proper reasoning and experience. "Other talents he undoubtedly had; but two he wanted, — religion and logic. Therefore, he ought to be read warily by those who are not well grounded in both" (*Thoughts upon Baron Montesquieu's "Spirit of Laws"* ¶8,9 (*Jackson* 13:415-416).

31. *Remarks on Locke* (*Jackson* 13:459).

32. Ibid. (*Jackson* 13:456).

33. Ibid. (*Jackson* 13:460). He will say the same thing for Aldrich's discussion of degrees of assent (*Jackson* 13:463).

34. Ibid. (*Jackson* 13:460).

35. Ibid. (*Jackson* 13:462).

36. Ibid. (*Jackson* 13:463).

37. Ibid. (*Jackson* 13:461).

38. Ibid. (*Jackson* 13:461-62 *passim*)

39. Ibid. (*Jackson* 13:463-64). Cf. also Wesley's translation of Aldrich, *A Compendium of Logic* §I.III.III.9 (*Jackson* 14:168).

40. Cf. Brantley, *English Romanticism*; Frederick Dreyer, "Faith and Experience in the Thought of John Wesley," *American Historical Review*, 88 (1983): 12-30; Hindley, "Philosophy of Enthusiasm"; and George Allen Turner, *The More Excellent Way: The Scriptural Basis of the Wesleyan Message* (Winona Lake, IN: Light and Life, 1952).

41. "Letter to Mary Pendarves" [3 October 1730] (*Telford* 1:56-57).

42. "Letter to Miss Lewin" [n.d.] §14 (*Jackson* 12:262).

43. "Letter to Samuel Furley" [18 February 1756] (*Telford* 3:163).

44. *An Extract to a Letter to the Rev. Mr. Law* §II.7 (*Jackson* 9:506).

45. Hindley argues that Browne's book established the philosophical framework in which Wesley then develops his own doctrines of experience and which provided the key source of tension leading up to Wesley's so-called "Aldersgate experience." The argument is interesting and not without merit, but it depends on Hindley's ignoring the prior influence of the Aristotelian logical tradition on Wesley. Cf. Hindley, "Philosophy of Enthusiasm," 104-105.

46. *Letter to Susanna Wesley* [22 November 1725] (*Telford* 1:25).

47. *Journal* 5 May 1772 (*Jackson* 3:462). Cf. similar sentiments expressed in Sermon #114 "On the Unity of the Divine Being" §19 (*Jackson* 7:271); and Sermon #123 "The Deceitfulness of the Human Heart" §3 (*Jackson* 7:342), among others.

48. *Journal* 5 March 1769 (*Jackson* 3:354).

49. *Journal* 5 May 1772 (*Jackson* 3:462).

50. *Journal* 30 May 1774 (*Jackson* 4:16).

51. *Journal* 5 May 1772 (*Jackson* 3:462).

5

Wesley and the Rationalist Tradition

The last set of philosophical influences we will examine is of a decidedly different stripe than the three empirical traditions mentioned above. In the early seventeenth century, while the Aristotelians were busy at Oxford, there was a revival of Platonic philosophy at Cambridge. The group of Cambridge Platonists was an informal collection of thinkers, mostly associated with Emmanuel College, whose names include Benjamin Whichcote, Henry More, John Smith, and Ralph Cudworth. In addition to their own thoughts, these men also contributed to the filtering into England of the Continental Rationalist tradition, here represented by Nicolas Malebranche, and his English interpreter—and philosopher in his own right—John Norris.

The Cambridge Platonists

The Cambridge Platonists are something of an anomaly in British thought, a group of unashamed rationalists who sought to revitalize religion in England by reaffirming classical, Platonic positions. Disapproving of both the scholastic Aristotelian tradition and the new empiricism of Bacon and Hobbes,[1] the Cambridge Platonists sought to recover the ancient Christian tradition, and so the spiritual-metaphysical tradition of Plato and Plotinus in which that early tradition was articulated. One of their contemporary and sympathetic observers describes their concerns and goals this way:

> New Philosophy will bring in New Divinity. True philosophy can never hurt sound Divinity…The Christian religion was never bred up in the Peripatetic School, but spent her best and healthfullest years in the more Religious Academy, among the primitive Fathers; but the Schoolmen afterwards ravished her thence, and shut her up in the decayed ruins of the Lyceaum.…[L]et her old loving Nurse the Platonick Philosophy be admitted again into her family.[2]

It is important to see that the Cambridge Platonists were driven by very religious concerns, and that their philosophical stance is largely dependent upon their religious stance.[3] They are thus not rationalists in the sense of seeing the truth of religion as founded on reason. To them, "the Gospel is not a book, but a power,"[4] and moral living is not only more important than dogmatic understanding—it is absolutely essential to it.[5] It is only the moral or virtuous mind that has any hope of understanding spiritual reality, and thus Christian understanding is built on two pillars: the proper use of reason and the exercise of virtue.[6] As John Smith puts it in *A Discourse concerning the True Way or Method of attaining to Divine Knowledge*, "Some men have too *bad hearts* to have *good heads*. They cannot be good at theorie who have been so bad at the practice."[7] So, where Bacon and Locke might have divorced religion and reason in order to protect religion, the Cambridge Platonists hold the two forever together, making the exercise of reason dependent upon the proper exercise of religion.[8] We might call such men *Rational Devotionalists*, pre-eminently concerned with living the Christian life and using rationalist philosophy to further that aim.

In bringing Christianity out of "the decayed ruins of the Lyceaum," the Cambridge Platonists felt it necessary to emphasize the power of reason to immediately grasp spiritual truths, independent of the physical senses. So, whereas reason, via the senses, might actively *discover* truth about the material world, it is more appropriately suited to passively *receive* the truths of the spiritual world.[9] Reason can do this, they believe, because it belongs to the spiritual realm. Human reason is a partial likeness of that one Eternal Reason,[10] and by virtue thereof is the "candle of the Lord," as Benjamin Whichcote notes: "I have declared the quality and fitness of the principle [i.e., reason], as from God, in the hand of God: 'the candle of the Lord', *res illuminata illuminens*."[11] Elsewhere Whichcote notes "To go against reason is to go against God...[It] is the very voice of God."[12]

Again, fundamental to the concerns of the Cambridge Platonists was a religious and moral life, and so they saw the most important of these eternal truths as those fitting into that category. Ralph Cudworth writes a book entitled *Treatise concerning eternal and immutable Morality*, and Henry More outlines twenty-three immediately perceptible moral truths in his *Enchiridion ethicum*. In these and works by other members of this movement, there is a concern to anchor religion and morality in the "trans-sensory" world. This is clear in their initial appreciation of, and subsequent reaction against, the work of Rene Descartes.[13] Descartes' rationalism initially brought their favor and praise, but his dualism and his mechanical view of the material world would not admit to the very close connection the Cambridge Platonists wanted to make between the material and the spiritual, a connection they will anchor in the faculty of reason.

From the foregoing, one can see the antagonism between this view of reason and that of the empirical thinkers described above.[14] While the Cambridge Platonists would not deny the importance of sensory knowledge, they nevertheless could not accept an empiricist worldview as adequate for preserving the type of truth—eternal, moral truth—that they valued most. From their point of view, empiricism was fundamentally and unalterably materialist, and therefore of little use to them. Theirs was explicitly a philosophical movement aimed at shoring up the intellectual foundations of religion, which they saw people like Hobbes as eroding. In fact, it was one of their number,

Ralph Cudworth, who first called Hobbes the "principle enemy of true religion,"[15] an epithet strongly reminiscent of Wesley's treatment of Hume.

By confining knowledge to sensory knowledge, empiricism (at least in the eyes of these men) not only refused a place for truly spiritual truth, they distorted the very idea of knowledge by making it a matter of power. Scientific knowledge was knowledge for the sake of control. Spiritual knowledge, at least in the minds of the Cambridge Platonists, was knowledge for the sake of surrendering one's life to it. In order to protect that truth, the Cambridge Platonists gave the "spiritual" realm a priority over the physical and maintained the connection between reason and faith that Bacon and Hobbes were at pains to severe. This seems to be the real reason why they gave to Reason the role of an "organ of the supersensuous," operating above the realm of merely physical senses and having direct contact with the realm of eternal ideas and their eternal relationships (which, to them, is what Truth is).[16] If reason's real goal is to have immediate access to a "trans-sensory" knowledge beyond the natural world, such knowledge could not, by its very nature, be exploited by science.[17]

Having delineated the difference between the Cambridge Platonists and the Empiricists on the role of reason, one notices a curious feature of the language used by some of these Platonists to describe the way reason works. In having immediate access to eternal truth, it functions very much like a "spiritual sense." This is John Smith's view in the *Discourse* cited earlier: "Were I indeed to define *Divinity*, I should rather call it *a Divine Life*, than *a Divine Science*; it being something rather to be understood by a Spiritual sensation, than by any *Verbal description*, as all things of Sense and Life are best known by Sentient and Vital faculties."[18]

Later in that same treatise, he makes the analogy even more explicit: "When Reason once is raised by the mighty force of the Divine Spirit into a converse with God, it is turned into *Sense*."[19] This curious use of empirical language to describe an anti-empirical idea might help us understand Wesley's reaction to these men and appreciate his attempt (the success of which we will debate later) to weave together their concerns with an empirical orientation.

While a revival of spirituality in a Platonic mode was their chief aim, the Cambridge Platonists also served the role of filtering Continental Rationalist thought into Britain. As mentioned above, they initially received with favor the work of the great French rationalist Rene Descartes and introduced the teaching of his thought at Cambridge, although they later grew disenchanted with its skepticism and its complete divorce of mind and matter.[20] As Descartes seems to have little if any influence on Wesley, we may dispense with a treatment of him. More important for our study are the figures of Nicolas Malebranche and John Norris.

Nicolas Malebranche and John Norris

The son of a secretary to Louis XIII of France, Nicolas Malebranche (1638-1715) was a monk who turned to philosophy upon reading Descartes' *Treatise on Man* after failing in his studies of church history and Bible.[21] A follower of Descartes, Malebranche also developed quite a few of his own ideas, among the most important for our discussion being his idea of sensation (or experience) and perception. Malebranche was a rationalist (although he is also important for the history of science), and like the Cambridge Platonists he held that ideas were real, eternal, universal and immutable and that truth could best be described as the relationship between all these ideas.[22] However, Malebranche will not allow the mind or reason to perceive these ideas directly, as did men like Whichcote or Smith. According to Malebranche, the mind perceives these ideas, indeed perceives anything at all, only through the activity of God. He notes:

> When we perceive something sensible, two things are found in our perception: *sensation* and pure *idea*. The sensation is a modification of the soul, and it is God who causes it in us…As for the idea found in conjunction with the sensation, it is in God, and we see it because it pleases God to reveal it to us. God joins the sensation to the idea when the objects are present so that we may believe them to be present and that we may have all the feelings and passions that we should have in relation to them.[23]

Malebranche's idea is that we neither perceive reality directly through our senses (as in empiricism) nor do we have a special "organ of the supersensuous" that is capable of directly sensing ultimate reality. We see anything at all, we know what we know, because God acts upon the human soul. This theory of "seeing all things in God" makes God the direct causal agent of all knowledge (in reality, the direct causal agent of everything), and this knowledge comes to the human mind directly from God on the occasion of a perception. Our interactions with the world, then, are God's opportunities to interact with us.[24]

Like much of the empirical tradition, Malebranche seems to have a dim view of any innate human capacity for knowledge—through either sense or reason. The senses may be good for practical knowledge, but senses can be deceived[25] and a focus on sensory information only obscures the revelation of eternal Truth.[26] Unfortunately, the innate power of human reason fares no better. "The mind of man is incapable of framing an idea sufficiently great to encompass and comprehend the least extension in the world, since the mind is limited whereas the idea must be infinite."[27] Since the mind cannot grasp truth on its own, it needs the activity of God. This means that, in Malebranche's system, God is not just a possible entity or an object we might strive after in our pursuit of truth; God is the only way we can explain that we know anything at all.[28]

Even though Malebranche's brand of rationalism is different from that of the Cambridge Platonists, there are striking points of commonality, particularly the strong religious orientation of their philosophy. Malebranche's philosophy might seem odd to contemporary ears, but he earned respect and a small following in his own day for his attempts to unite religion and serious philosophical thinking. Once his work was translated into English in 1694, it provoked, perhaps predictably, a rebuttal from John Locke the next year. Later, Malebranche's ideas were propounded and defended by the Englishman John Norris (1657-1711) in *An Essay toward the Theory of the Ideal or Intelligible*

World (1701-04). Because of the similarity between Norris' Malebranchian rationalism and the perspective of men like Whichcote and More, Norris is sometimes referred to as the last of the Cambridge Platonists, despite the fact that he himself was an Oxford man.[29]

While people like the Cambridge Platonists and Malebranche, and the rationalism that they represent, were not as influential in society at large as the science and empiricism of Bacon and Locke, they are nonetheless important background for understanding Wesley. Their project of holding reason and faith together is one that Wesley would have appreciated, and Wesley himself developed an idea about "spiritual sensation," which, at least at first glance, contains strong affinities to the ideas of Malebranche. Understanding how and to what extent he appropriated this tradition is then very important for understanding Wesley's ideas on experience and the use he made of them in theology.

Wesley The Rational Devotionalist

Given what we have already established concerning Wesley's empirical orientation, his reaction to this rationalist school may be surprising. That reaction is only a positive one, but it is also a reaction that reveals his own lack of epistemic concern and his avowal of a priori metaphysical concerns in experience.

The names of the Cambridge Platonists themselves do not show up very often in the Wesleyan corpus, confined mainly to a recommendation of Henry More's works (along with Malebranche's) in Wesley's *Address to the Clergy*, in the place where he discusses the usefulness of metaphysics. That alone is an interesting recommendation, given what we stated above about Wesley's own philosophical outlook. A couple of times he will use their terminology of reason as the "candle of the Lord" in a positive way,[30] but he will just as often use the phrase to refer to God's coming into a person's life in more explicitly spiritual way.[31] However, far more interesting is the inclusion of several of the Cambridge Platonists in his *Christian Library*, his fifty-volume collection of abridged and edited works by various authors designed to make works of practical divinity accessible to his societies and preachers.

Seven of the fifty-volumes of the *Christian Library* are given over to the work of Cambridge Platonists—two volumes for John Smith, and one each for Ralph Cudworth, Nathanael Culverwel, Henry More, Simon Patrick, and John Worthingon—all appearing between 1752 and 1753. To John Smith's works, he appends a personal note, indicating that they are a "great treasure," but he acknowledges that they are difficult to read.[32]

As John English has noted, Wesley does not simply reprint the work of these men but abridges and edits their writings, both in terms of style and content, eliminating references to mysticism and Calvinism as well as references to their rationalist philosophical orientation.[33] But the very fact of their inclusion in the library at all—even in their philosophically purged form—indicates that Wesley thought very highly of the divinity, if not the philosophy, contained in their work. This is consistent with what we have seen of Wesley, laying as he does more stress on the religious than on the philosophical. Thus his appreciation of the Cambridge Platonists, with whom he disagreed philosophically, is as unsurprising as his deprecation of David Hume, who shared his empirical outlook.

Turning to Wesley's appreciation of Nicolas Malebranche and John Norris, we find an even more striking example of the priority of religion over philosophy and of Wesley's lack of epistemic concern.[34] Despite his being an empiricist, Wesley appreciatively read Malebranche and recommended that reading to others. In fact, whenever he recommends the reading of Locke's *Essay*, it is always in conjunction with (sometimes even after) the recommendation of Malebranche's *Search After Truth*.[35] Wesley also includes the *Search After Truth* as one of the exemplary works on metaphysics in his *Address to the Clergy*,[36] a work, interestingly enough, in which neither Locke nor Browne is mentioned.

John Norris, too, receives his share of positive evaluation in Wesley. Not only does Wesley extract Norris' *Reflections Upon the Conduct of Human Life* and *A Treatise on Christian Prudence*, but he comments in a letter to one Samuel Furley that the former is a "masterpiece of reason and religion...every paragraph of which must stand unshaken (with or without the Bible) till we are no longer mortal."[37] Several times in his correspondence, Wesley makes passing reference to some devotional ideas of Norris, for which he gives Norris credit.[38] This indicates not only a good familiarity with Norris' work but also a concern that other people are aware of the source of the ideas he notes.

This positive attention to the contemporary rationalist scene has led a few scholars to posit a view of Wesley's epistemology as more than just a thoroughgoing empiricism, either portraying him as a hidden rationalist or as one who tried to combine the epistemological views of both camps. We will look more closely at the substance of these contentions in examining Wesley's own thought. However, at this juncture it is appropriate to point out that, while Wesley looks with favor on both Malebranche and Norris, he does not explicitly interact with their philosophy. All we have of Malebranche are passing references—no explicit interaction at all. In abridging Norris' works, Wesley's condensations are so drastic (in the case of the *Reflections* he reduces a book of more than 200 pages to a tract of 36), that all he retains are a few essential elements of Norris' ideas on practical divinity and nothing whatsoever of the explicit philosophy that lies behind them.

These arguments from silence are, in themselves, naturally inconclusive. Any unacknowledged influence of any of these rationalists—Cambridge Platonists, Malebranche or Norris—will need to be examined when looking at Wesley's explicit thought, to which we will shortly turn. However, while the philosophical issues surrounding Wesley's interaction with these men might be in doubt, one clear explanation of his appreciation of them is immediately available. All of them were concerned to unite reason and religion, and for all them, their application of reason seemed to be dictated by their already-held religious assumptions. This was a project of which Wesley would have heartily approved. Their religion-first, philosophy-second attitude would have matched his own, even if their philosophical outlook did not. Their work as "Rational Devotionalists," as people who would use reasonable arguments to advance the ends of religion and personal faith, has many parallels with Wesley. It may, therefore, be possible to explain his appreciation of them entirely outside of any philosophical concerns. In fact, given what we have seen of his interaction with philosophy, it might even be more appropriate to do so.

Up to this point, we have consistently portrayed Wesley as one primarily interested in religion, albeit one perfectly willing to use reason and the tools of philosophy and epistemology to advance that cause. The priority of religion over philosophy is no more clear than in Wesley's appreciation of men like the Cambridge Platonists, Malebranche and Norris. And so it is at this point that we might appropriately offer a few brief remarks on the way religion and reason (including, therefore, any epistemological value given to experience) fit together in Wesley's thought.

Wesley wrote several sermons and tracts which focused on the relationship between reason and religion,[39] and he was often at pains to show that the two were eminently compatible. He says at one point, "It is a fundamental principle with us, that to renounce reason is to renounce religion; that religion and reason go hand in hand; and that all irrational religion is false religion."[40] However, it is Wesley's concerns for religion—not philosophy—which lie behind this stress. His sermons on reason and his *Appeals* are apologetic, meaning that they have religious—not philosophical—ends in view. To read these sermons and treatises (as has often been done) as works in philosophy seems to distort their nature. That Wesley was concerned about the proper application of reason is clear, but for him that proper application was always in the realm of the religious and never for its own sake. Where religious ends are advanced by appreciation and application of reason, he sounds very much like the child of his age, the "Age of Reason." However, when religious ends are served by recognizing the limitations and inadequacy of reason, then Wesley can affirm such, as is the case with the entire sermon on "The Imperfection of Knowledge." In either case the human capacity for reason and the desire for knowledge is seen as a religious faculty, designed "to raise our thoughts to higher and higher objects, more and more worthy our consideration, till we ascend to the Source of all knowledge and all excellence, the all-wise and all-gracious Creator."[41]

Conclusion to Part One

We have been examining Wesley's philosophical milieu and his explicit interactions with it in order to give us a proper orientation into Wesley's more implicit philosophical concerns. In light of this, we can draw a rough—but far from complete—sketch of Wesley's philosophical orientation, and thus something of his understanding of experience.

In looking at words like *experience* as people used them in Wesley's day, we see that they did not have the strong internal—meaning private or psychological—connotation that they often do today, and that experience was seen as an active concern, not just a passive one. In Eighteenth Century England, experience referred to that collective body of knowledge one got from living one's life and engaging the world. In this, it was closely related to the various cognates of *experiment*, which, in turn, were not always used in a technical or scientific sense. If Wesley's idea of experience follows these lines, then it would be a mistake to read his doctrine of experience as if it were internal or psychological, and therefore individualistic.

On the question of the relationship between experience and knowledge, we have seen that Wesley explicitly acts as an Aristotelian empiricist and not as a Lockean. This is important for two reasons. First, Wesley concerns himself with the proper application of reason to the data of experience but not with the epistemological problem of experience and question of certainty in knowledge. While there may be traces of those concerns in his early years, they do not endure into his mature work. The Wesley who interacts with his philosophical environment is a Wesley who does not seem driven by epistemology.[42] If that holds true, then importing an epistemological orientation into Wesley's thought might distort his meaning, raising questions that Wesley was not concerned with and ignoring others that may have been much more important. There has been an easy progression from the assumption of Wesley as a Lockean to the corresponding *epistemological* weight given his understanding of "spiritual senses" or the "witness of the spirit," and that might not be appropriate. To be sure, Wesley's epistemology was important to his theological method, and in the next chapter we will see just how important it was. But that epistemology may be obscured by the categories of a contemporary philosophy that divorces issues of faith from issues of reason. If Wesley is more at home in the philosophical world that precedes that divorce, then he should be read that way.

The second reason why Wesley's Aristotelian orientation is important is that this kind of empiricism allows him to admit to metaphysical pre-understandings that shape experience in direct contradiction to the more pure forms of empiricism current in his day. He assumes the a priori logical nature of the universe,[43] and his faith in logic, if we may call it "faith," was strong enough to allow him to use it even to critique Locke, the most well-known and well-respected empirical philosopher of the day. In addition to his faith in logic, Wesley also brings with him an a priori faith in Christian revelation. Religious concerns—especially the authority of Scripture—seem to allow him to critique scientific experiments, as well as fellow empiricists like Locke and Hume, all the while giving appreciation to religious rationalists like Malebranche and Norris. This complicates the picture of Wesley's epistemology, but further investigation will reveal whether he was simply incoherent in his epistemology or attempting to balance more than just philosophical concerns.

With this background and these warnings now in hand, we are ready to listen more attentively to Wesley's writing and thought on the nature of experience. So it is to the project of sketching out his more implicit religious epistemology we must now turn.

Notes

1. Copleston, *History of Philosophy*, vol. 5, 54. Cf. also Gerald R. Cragg, "Introduction," in *The Cambridge Platonists*, ed. Gerald R. Cragg, A Library of Protestant Thought (New York: Oxford University Press, 1968), 12-13; and John C. English, "The Cambridge Platonists in Wesley's 'Christian Library'," *Proceedings of the Wesley Historical Society* 36 (1968): 161-68.

2. S[imon] P[atrick]. *A Brief Account of the New Sect of Latitude Men*, The Augustan Reprint Society #100 (1662; reprint, Los Angeles: University of California, 1963), 22-24.

3. Robert Caponigri, *Philosophy from the Renaissance to the Romantic Age* (Chicago: University of Notre Dame Press, 1963), 291.

4. Ernst Cassirer, *The Platonic Renaissance in England*, trans. James P. Pettegrove (Austin: University of Texas Press, 1953), 33.

5. Cassirer, *Platonic Renaissance*, 41.

6. Cragg, *Cambridge Platonists*, 69.

7. John Smith, *A Discourse concerning the True Way or Method of attaining to Divine Knowledge*, in *The Cambridge Platonists*, ed. E. T. Campagnac (Oxford: Clarendon, 1901), 67. Emphasis in the original.

8. Cassirer, *Platonic Renaissance*, 52.

9. Ibid., 40.

10. Frederick. J. Powicke, *The Cambridge Platonists. A Study* (London: Dent, 1926), 27.

11. Benjamin Whichcote, *Third Letter*, in Cragg, *Cambridge Platonists*, 44. The Latin phrase may be translated "an illuminated illuminating thing" or "a thing which illuminates by being itself illuminated."

12. Benjamin Whichcote, *Moral and Religious Aphorisms*, quoted in Campagnac, xxxiii.

13. Cragg, *Cambridge Platonists*, 12.

14. For a detailed analysis of this antagonism, cf. Cassirer, *Platonic Renaissance*, 49-65.

15. Copleston, *History of Philosophy*, vol 5, 52; and Cragg, *Cambridge Platonists*, 12-13.

16. Cragg, *Cambridge Platonists*, 19-21.

17. Copleston, *History of Philosophy*, 56.

18. Smith, *Discourse*, 79.

19. Ibid., 93.

20. Cragg, *Cambridge Platonists*, 19-21.

21. For more on the thought of Malebranche, cf. R. W. Church, *A Study in the Philosophy of Malebranche* (London: George Allen and Unwin, 1931); Steven Nadler, *Malebranche and Ideas* (Oxford: Oxford University Press, 1992); and Beatrice K. Rome, *The Philosophy of Malebranche. A Study of his Integration of Faith, Reason, and Experimental Observation* (Chicago: Henry Regnery, 1963); as well as Caponigri, *Philosophy*, 259-66; and Copleston, *History of Philosophy*, vol. 4, 180-204. For more on John Norris specifically, cf. Bruno Morawetz, "The Epistemology of John Norris" (Ph.D. diss., Ontario University, 1963).

22. Rome, *Philosophy of Malebranche*, 117-19.

23. Nicolas Malebranche, *The Search After Truth*, trans. and ed. Thomas M. Lennon and Paul J. Olscamp (Cambridge: Cambridge University Press, 1997), 234.

24. Copleston, *History of Philosophy*, vol 4, 189-90.

25. "When we feel heat, when we see light, or ideas, or other objects, we do in fact see them, even in delirium. Nothing is truer than that all visionaries see what they see; their error lies only in their judgment that what they see really exists externally because they see it externally," (Malebranche, *Search*, 69-70).

26. Church, *Study*, 133.

27. Malebranche, *Search*, 28-29.

28. All this leads to an almost mystical view of knowledge (Cf. Joseph Vidgrain, *Le christianisme dans la philosophie de Malebranche* (Paris: Alcan, 1923), 349; and Yves de Montecheuil, *Malebranche et le quietisme* (Paris: Aubier, 1946), and the defense of Malebranche in Rome, *Philosophy of Malebranche*, 40n.154 and 158n.111), which might help to explain both Wesley's approval and critique of Malebranche.

29. For more on the general British reception of Malebranche, cf. Charles J. McCraken, *Malebranche and British Philosophy* (Oxford: Oxford University Press, 1983).

30. Sermon #70 "The Case of Reason Impartially Considered" §II.10 (*Jackson* 6: 359); and "Letter to a Member of the Society" [July 5 1768] (*Jackson* 12:284).

31. Sermon #46 "The Wilderness State" §III.1 (*Jackson* 6:84); and *An Earnest Appeal to Men of Reason and Religion* §54 (*Jackson* 8:21) [hereinafter cited as *Earnest Appeal*].

32. "Preface" to *The Works of Mr. John Smith* (*Jackson* 14:230).

33. English, "Cambridge Platonists," 161-68 *passim*.

34. There is some debate over the influence of Malebranche and Norris on the thought of Wesley, but that debate depends entirely on certain supposed congruencies between his work and theirs and not on Wesley's explicit interaction with their work. Those issues will become clearer as we further analyze Wesley's own thought in the next chapter.

35. Cf. "Letter to Miss Lewin" [n.d.] §14 (*Jackson* 12:262); "Letter to Miss Bishop" [August 18, 1784] (*Jackson* 13:39); and the curriculum for fourth year students at Kingswood in *A Short Account of the School at Kingswood* (*Jackson* 13:288).

36. *An Address to the Clergy* §II.5 (*Jackson* 10:492).

37. "Letter to Samuel Furly" [14 March 1756] (*Telford* 3:173).

38. Cf. *Letter to Mr. John Smith* [28 September 1745] §III.21 (*Jackson* 12:64); and "Letter to a Member of the Society" [14 April 1771] and [1 July 1772] (*Jackson* 12:289, 294).

39. Cf. especially Sermons #69 "The Imperfection of Human Knowledge" (*Jackson* 6:337-50); Sermon #70 "The Case of Reason Impartially Considered" (*Jackson* 6:350-60); *Earnest Appeal* (*Jackson* 8:3-42); and *A Farther Appeal*, all three parts (*Jackson* 8:46-247).

40. *A Letter to Rev. Rutherforth* [March 28, 1768] §III.4 (*Jackson* 14:354)

41. Sermons #69 "The Imperfection of Human Knowledge" (*Jackson* 6:337).

42. Much of what has been written on Wesley has assumed the contrary. Mitsuo Shimizu, whose dissertation remains an important work on the subject, even goes so far as to say, "It is possible to characterize his [Wesley's] theology as an epistemologically oriented theology...Wesley's position on matters of epistemology was ultimately decisive for many of his relationships" ("Epistemology in the Thought of John Wesley" [Ph.D. diss., Drew University, 1980]), 5; see also the work of Shimizu's theological mentor: Yoshio Noro, "Wesley's Theological Epistemology," *Iliff Review* 28 (1971): 59-76. Rex Matthews makes the resolution of the question of epistemological dualism (between material or physical-sense based knowledge and spiritual knowledge) a central concern of his investigation of Wesley's understanding of reason (Matthews, "Reason and Religion," 247-312). J. Clifford Hindley admits that Wesley was far more religious

than philosophical, but then immediately sets Wesley's religious concerns aside in order to work out the implications of his Brownean epistemology in a way that "proves" Wesley to be an enthusiast (Hindley, "Philosophy of Enthusiasm," 106). Finally, Robert Tuttle makes the resolution of the problem of epistemology—Aristotelian versus Platonic—the central defining feature of Wesley's early intellectual development (Tuttle, *John Wesley*, 69-77, 143-155, 215-229). In Part Two, we will investigate whether these concerns are features of Wesley's work or merely of our modern (and thus epistemologically charged) reception of it.

43. The importance of a priori authorities in Wesley should not be confused with a completely deductive orientation in Wesley, which would be inconsistent with Wesley's empiricism. Matthews is correct when he cites that a priori argumentation in Wesley is very rare (Matthews, "Reason and Religion," 110), but all of Wesley's logical argumentation is based on the implicit a priori claims that underlie Aristotle's logic.

Part Two

6

The Epistemic Role of Experience

In turning to the question of Wesley's religious epistemology, we intend to pick up the threads from his philosophical interactions and see if they are woven through the rest of his work. While Wesley wrote no explicit treatise on epistemology, his implicit epistemological orientation is evident throughout his writing. Our task in Part Two will be to bring out that implicit understanding and see what kind of coherence it has. Seeing how experience functions in knowledge in general could give us a clearer picture as to how it should function in terms of knowledge of God.

In picking up the loose threads from Part One, there are three particularly relevant issues that arise in examining Wesley's interaction with his philosophical environment. The second of these, Wesley's lack of epistemological concern, we have already dealt with as a background issue. That leaves us with the meaning and implication of the other two: experience as public concern and experience as active concern, which we will explore in this chapter. This will then lead us to the importance of Wesley's a priori metaphysical claims, which will be the subject of Chapters 7 and 8. Chapter 9 will then discuss the dynamic created by the interaction of Wesley's epistemological and metaphysical commitments, and we will conclude Part Two by exploring the implications of this interaction for Wesley's doctrine of the so-called *spiritual senses* in Chapter 10.

Wesley's Implicit Epistemology

In attempting to reconstruct Wesley's implicit epistemology, we must remember that he does not function primarily as a philosopher. If he is not driven by epistemology, as we have contended, then he will not always answer the questions raised by epistemology in ways that would satisfy a epistemologist. He will often make comments that overstate the case, comments that he must then explain or reinterpret. Focusing, then, on any one given statement, and taking that as if it represented the *real* John Wesley, may only distort his thought.[1] To investigate Wesley's general epistemology, we must look at the overall tenor of his whole work, establishing whether or not there is a general framework that can help us make sense of the varieties of individual references.

If his epistemology proves to be coherent, then it will only be from within this general context on questions of knowledge that we can properly address the knowledge of God.

In treating Wesley this way, we are taking a different approach than the one usually taken with his epistemology. As we noted in the beginning, many authors have made a more or less sharp distinction in Wesley between experience in general and *religious experience*, the former having use in discussing the world and the latter being the part most interesting for theology. They recognize that Wesley himself did not make these distinctions,[2] but their analyses nevertheless proceed on the basis of discerning a dualism between his concept of religious experience and a more general or philosophical understanding of it.[3] Some of this may be a reaction against the early twentieth century move by people like George Croft Cell and George Eayrs to make Wesley into a Christian philosopher, one whose religious concerns were dominated by his philosophical orientation. We have already seen that such a picture is inadequate, but failing to let Wesley be as philosophical as he was may be equally dangerous. If we bifurcate the idea of experience between the *religious* and the *ordinary*, we threaten to bifurcate life into ordinary and religious spheres as well, and that is something Wesley himself would never have done.

Since Wesley himself does not separate religious experience from other types of experience, it may be better for us to assume a single understanding of experience in his thought than a dualistic one. We may then see if the features one discerns of his general epistemological use of experience are also relevant to his use of experience in theology. Allowing Wesley his own integration of the question of faith and knowledge may be the best way to allow him both to speak for himself and to speak to the present day.

Given the nature of building a case for an implicit understanding in any thinker, we must be careful to trace these ideas as deeply and as broadly through Wesley's corpus as we can. Wesley is frequently misunderstood on these issues, and so the more we can trace these ideas through the length and breadth of his writings, the more we may be assured that they are his. Once we have examined these issues as descriptively as we can in Wesley's work, we will turn to the more creative and less descriptive work of synthesizing these concerns, fitting them into a coherent framework and showing that they can all be grounded in his Aristotelian approach to reality, which is solidly philosophical without being as driven by epistemology as the British Empirical approach tends to be. Although we must go beyond Wesley's own thought to create this synthesis, this move is still aimed at making that thought clearer. If such a reconstruction is faithful to the way that Wesley deals with experience, then it may be used to understand him better, even if it is not something that he explicitly articulated himself. Once we have an adequate understanding of the dynamics surrounding experience in Wesley, we will be ready to see how those dynamics work themselves out in Wesley's theological method in Part Three.

Experience as Public Appeal

As we noted in Part One, we tend to use the word *experience* today with psychological connotations that do not seem to be present in eighteenth century England. These psychological connotations bias our interpretation of experience toward the private and passive mental synthesis of sensory input into quantifiable events. Additionally, we are very sensitive to the differences between individual experiences, particularly in those areas where we suspect that people are more shaped by their experience than are shapers of it.

As we have also seen, however, we have reason to suspect that Wesley does not share these biases. He never refers to "an experience," never talks about "having an experience," nor does he refer to the now famous "Aldersgate experience"—or any other such discrete psychological event for that matter—as a definable, nameable experience. The word experience as Wesley uses it cannot be quantified except in the rare cases in which he refers to the experience of two or more people. It is never the succession of psychological events in one individual person. If experience is not a private or internal thing, then it can only be something both public or external, something that refers to a reality common to all.

This recognition helps allay one of the main fears that many people have when admitting experience to the theological dialogue. It has often been assumed by interpreters of Wesley that Wesley's use of experience admits to a certain degree of subjectivism. Here Scott Jones may be seen as representing the opinion of many students of Wesley when he notes, "A reliance upon experience as a source of knowledge opens the possibility that the experience of others may not always confirm what Scripture teaches."[4] Experience, or so this claim goes, varies from person to person and could even be at variance with Scriptural truth. While this may be a natural concern to a contemporary reader who understands experience in a psychological way, it was not a concern to Wesley. This is because his conception of experience is primarily public and external and is aimed precisely at a providing objective standards for references (even if they are not completely free from subjective variation, as we shall see).[5] Wesley was a philosophical realist, one who believes that there is an objective reality out there to be encountered, and his doctrine of experience revolves around what one learns through these encounters.[6] Since that reality is the same for everyone, experience as *encounter-with-reality* is common to all. Wesley reveals this solidly empirical stance in the way he appeals to experience as an authority.

When Wesley appeals to experience as an authority—especially when it is supposed to inform theology—he does so with a clear focus on the objective reality that experience *re-presents*, not on the subjective appropriation of that reality. In the first place, he will frequently modify the noun experience, broadening his appeal to "daily experience,"[7] "constant experience,"[8] or "long experience."[9] This reflects an understanding of experience as established by "frequent trial," time being needed to secure the objective nature of experience against the vagaries of any momentary subjective impression. He will also refer to such things as "universal experience," "the experience of all ages," and "the experience of every true believer,"[10] further reinforcing its objective nature. A couple of examples are sufficient to convey the general tone of Wesley's argumentation.

When Wesley decries the absence of the "Catholic Spirit" among Christians, he asks, "All men approve of this [i.e., the Catholic Spirit]; but do all men practise it? Daily experience shows the contrary. Where are even the Christians who 'love one another as He hath given us commandment?'"[11] Wesley throws open to the experience of his congregation or readers the question of whether or not Christians are really tolerant and forgiving of other Christians with whom they differ. In so doing, he tacitly assumes that they will answer his rhetorical question based on their experience in the same way he would answer it based on his. The experience to which he appeals is a public matter.

We find the same attitude at work in a discussion Wesley has with one Rev. Church concerning the problems that have arisen in consequence to his revival. Wesley writes, "That, whenever God revives his work upon earth, many tares will spring up with the wheat, both the word of God gives us ground to expect, and the experience of all ages."[12] In making a broad rhetorical appeal like this, Wesley assumes that anyone reading history will read it in the same way the he does, that the "experience of all ages" is public domain and confirms that the results of revival are always a "mixed bag."

Even without modifying the word, Wesley's use of experience in his sermonic and apologetic work always refers to an encounter with reality to which both he and his readers or hearers have the same access. For example, Wesley records in his *Journal* the following appeal, a piece of a sermon he preached on "Do this in remembrance of me":

> But experience shows the gross falsehood of that assertion, that the Lord's Supper is not a converting ordinance. Ye are the witnesses. For many now present know, the very beginning of your conversion to God (perhaps, in some, the first deep conviction) was wrought at the Lord's Supper. Now, one single instance of this kind overthrows the whole assertion.[13]

Here Wesley's appeal to experience is an appeal to the public memory of his congregation. He uses the fact that many of them did indeed receive faith in the taking of the sacrament as an experiential argument against those who would limit the Eucharist to people who already had faith. One could claim that this argument would be more effective for the people who actually underwent such a conversion, but those so converted would be least likely to need arguments about this matter. Wesley's appeal is to everyone, and his argument rests more on the public testimony to the events in question than on any inward or subjective impressions that individual members may have felt.[14]

Wesley will use the same kind of appeal in discussing the importance of fasting. He observes "How fullness of bread increased not only carelessness and levity of spirit, but also foolish and unholy desires, yea, unclean and vile affections. And this experience puts beyond all doubt. Even a genteel, regular sensuality is continually sensualizing the soul, and sinking it into a level with the beasts that perish."[15] It does not seem to matter to him whether each individual hearer had experienced this personally; his claim is that experience in general proves the assertion.

In these instances, as well as many others, Wesley appeals to experience as a public reality to which both he and his readers have the same access and the same apprehension. There are even times when he allows his arguments to turn on the fact that he can predict the experience of his readers because he assumes it is the same as his own. For example, Wesley raises the question of the compatibility of our freedom and God's glory in his *Predestination Calmly Considered*, assured that he and the reader share the same experience. "Has not even experience taught you this?…when you have yielded to 'work together with Him,' did you not find it very possible, notwithstanding, to give him all the glory?"[16] In discussing the reality of the "Witness of the Spirit," Wesley boldly asserts to his reader that "It is confirmed by your experience and mine. The Spirit itself bore witness to my spirit that I was a child of God, gave me an evidence hereof, and I immediately cried, 'Abba, Father!' And this I did, (and so did you,) before I reflected on, or was conscious of, any fruit of the Spirit."[17] In raising the issue of faith being a gift of God in the *Earnest Appeal*, Wesley asks, "May not your own experience teach you this? Can you give yourself this faith?"[18]

We may deem it presumptuous, even arrogant, for Wesley to assume he can "get inside his reader's head" like that. But the very fact he does reveals his confidence in the universal and public nature of the experience to which he appeals. Contrary to what many have assumed, Wesley does not seem to throw open these questions so that the reader may decide for himself or herself based on that reader's own, particular, individual experience. The rhetorical, sermonic and apologetic nature of these appeals make such an assumption difficult. In all of these cases, Wesley is making an argument with a clear purpose; he is not raising an open epistemological question. He appeals to experience because he knows in advance what experience will say. These rhetorical appeals are designed to lead the reader to agree with Wesley's presentation of things, and they reveal his faith in an idea of experience that transcends the individual. We should not, therefore, read him as if he were allowing his readers to base their understanding of religion or God's activity on the *ground* of their own individual experience. If that were so, such appeals would as much endanger as aid his argument.

The Public Nature of Private Experience

The priority of the external and public over the internal and private in Wesley's understanding of experience is evident even in his references to "inward experience" and "personal experience." Wesley understands "inward experience" not as describing a private possession but as the *spiritual* location of an encounter with something that still transcends the individual. In the sermon "On Living Without God," which is about the inwardness of Christianity, Wesley states,

From hence [the need for inward renewal] we may clearly perceive the wide
difference there is between Christianity and morality. Indeed nothing can be more
sure, than that true Christianity cannot exist without both the inward experience
and outward practice of justice, mercy, and truth; and this alone is genuine
morality.[19]

Aside from arguing against an artificial duality between inward and outward
life (and perhaps arguing against a duality between the spiritual and the physical
as well), Wesley's idea of experience here can only refer to something that
transcends his reader. The reader is exhorted that he or she needs and inward
and outward encounter with the same things. It would, therefore, make little
sense to treat "justice, mercy, and truth" as if they were subjective emotions or
states of religious consciousness. A better explanation would be to see the
"inward experience" of these things as taking these external realities to heart,
ensuring that one's encounter with them affects the core of one's being.

A similar affirmation is found in the first part of the *Farther Appeal*, where
Wesley notes, "And as we are figuratively said to see the light of faith; so, by a
like figure of speech, we are said to feel this peace and joy and love; that is, we
have an inward experience of them, which we cannot find any fitter word to
express."[20] Here, Wesley uses the phrase "inward experience" to explain what
he means when he claims that we *feel* peace, joy and love. One could (and many
have) simply assumed that Wesley is talking about something subjective here
and equate his understanding of experience to an idea of feeling-as-emotion.
However, that does not do justice to the context of the statement, particularly the
parallel with "the light of faith." Faith, for Wesley, is not a subjective emotion,[21]
and he uses the word *feeling* here in its empirical sense of touch, not in the sense
of emotion. This explains Wesley's awareness that he is stretching his words
and why he says that he can find no "fitter word to express" it. He is dealing
with an inward encounter with the objective realities of peace, joy and love, not
with our subjective creation of these emotions. The inwardness describes the
location of the encounter, but the realities encountered are external to the
believer.

Even where Wesley gives weight to individual and personal experience, he
does so because such personal experience establishes a general truth. In telling
the story of what happened at Aldersgate, Wesley is forced to admit a general
truth about the reality of conversion on the basis of the personal testimonies of
those Peter Böhler brought to meet him.[22] In his letter to Conyers Middleton, he
rejects the idea (typical of British Empiricism) that "personal experience" only
has epistemological force for the one who experiences it.[23] Instead, he affirms to
Middleton that he can indeed learn from the personal experiences of others
because he can see its outward effects, that accepting the testimony of others is a
"easier or surer way" to find knowledge of things beyond one's own experience,
and that this public testimony of "personal experience" gives one "a very strong
evidence of the truth of Christianity; as strong as can be in the nature of things,
till you experience it in your own soul."[24] Wesley does not deny that "personal
experience" has greater force for the one whose experience it is, but he lays the

weight of his appeal on the public facets of that experience, those which are accessible to everyone.

There is one final indication that Wesley's idea of experience is something public and not merely the private province of individuals, and we see it when Wesley will cite the idea of experience-as-public-criterion *against* experiences-as-private-feelings," even his own.

In the first volume of his *Journal*, Wesley reflects on his first sermon in Savannah, Georgia. He is preaching, ironically enough, on a passage where Jesus speaks of his own persecution (and those of his followers). Wesley's own experience and the experience of "all the sincere followers of Christ whom I have ever talked with, read or heard of" would affirm that those who follow Christ will experience persecution from those who do not. However, the present circumstances of that first sermon lead him to call that bit of wisdom into question. He writes,

> I do here bear witness against myself, that when I saw the number of people crowding into the church, the deep attention with which they received the word, and the seriousness that afterwards sat on all their faces; I could scarce refrain from giving the lie to experience and reason and Scripture all together. I could hardly believe that the greater, the far greater part of this attentive, serious people would here after trample under foot that word, and say all manner of evil falsely of him that spake it.[25]

By the time Wesley publishes that bit in the *Journal*, he knows that those people turned against him. What is interesting to note is that Wesley contrasts his own feelings and impressions with the teachings of experience; he does not label these feelings and impressions as *experience*. In addition, Wesley is clear that his feelings and impressions misled him and that experience-as-public-criterion proved more trustworthy than these subjective and psychological indicators.

One final example of this contrast between individual, psychological impressions and experience-as-public-criterion comes out in his sermon on "The Nature of Enthusiasm," where he explicitly sets the two against each another. In discussing how a true enthusiast may be cured of thinking that his visions or dreams really are messages from God, Wesley offers experience as the remedy. "When plain facts run counter to their predictions, experience performs what reason could not, and sinks them down into their senses."[26] Here experience refers—not to the dreams or psychological delusions of the enthusiast—but to the hard encounter with reality that thwarts such delusions. Experience is thus an authority precisely because it is not individual, because it transcends subjective and individual impressions.

In all these examples, as well as in numerous other places, we see the priority of the external and public in Wesley's understanding of experience. Experience is an authority because it is not subjective, not a matter of internal states or emotions. In this, Wesley functions as a good empiricist, one who appeals to experience when arguing questions of truth or knowledge. But the empirical positions of his own day—particularly that of Peter Browne—relied on the passive nature of our encounters with reality to guarantee their trustworthiness. As we shall see, Wesley is willing to admit that some experience cannot be trusted.

Experience as Active Concern

As we saw in Chapter 1, the word *experience* was defined using active words (*try, practice, trial*) in Wesley's eighteenth century England, despite the fact that experience-as-empirical-criterion needs to be passive to be reliable. By contrast (perhaps under the influence of that cultural empiricism), our contemporary understanding of experience is more passive than not. When we want *to experience* something, we generally mean we want it to happen to us, not that we want to do it. And if we are looking at active or contrived encounters with reality, we tend to refer to them as *experiments*. The issue of passivity is important to epistemology because the more pro-active experience is, the more fallible it is likely to be. If all our knowledge comes from experience, and experience is not reliable, then neither is knowledge. That was the general conclusion of both Locke, who would discuss knowledge only in terms of probability, and Hume, who was an outright skeptic. Peter Browne resists this trend, but he can only do so by making experience completely passive. Wesley, however, did not follow him in this, as we can see in the way he used experience as a verb and in the way he treated sensory input, the primary channel through which experience comes.

While it would be dangerous to build too much on merely grammatical points, it is nevertheless interesting to see that Wesley uses the word experience in ways that reinforce its active nature. To begin with, Wesley consistently uses the verb in the active voice, placing the grammatical focus on the one who experiences rather than on the thing experienced.[27]

Even more telling are the times when Wesley will invoke the verb *experience* as the culmination of a series of activities, implying deeper levels of active engagement and even diminishing passivity. For example, in describing his preaching in Hayes, Wesley notes, "All but the Gentry of the parish patiently hear the truth. Many approve of, and some experience it."[28] The progression from hearing to approving implies a greater degree of engagement, and if experience is the apex of this triad, then it must be more active than mere approval. The experience of truth—that is, the encounter with truth in the world—seems to be something one must work at. Wesley makes this idea explicit in his favorable comments on the Methodist Society in Whitehaven in his *Journal* when he notes, "The society is united in love, not conformed to the world, but labouring to experience the full image of God, wherein they were created."[29] The members of this society are doing more than just acquiring information from their encounters with reality; they are seeking to shape that encounter by something they understand. Whatever it means to "experience the full image of God," it is more than something that just happens to a believer.

The idea of experience as an active encounter also shows up when Wesley indicates that one can *lose* experience. Relating a preaching tour through Limerick, Wesley writes, "I preached on, 'Thou shalt love the Lord thy God with all thy heart.' Many here once experienced this; but few, if any, retain it now!"[30] Unless Wesley is talking about forgetting some information, which does not seem to be the case, he must be referring to an experience of—an encounter with—love that demands reciprocal activity. We see the same concern in Wesley's letter to John Trembath, where he writes, "Certainly some years ago you was [sic] alive to God. You experienced the life and power of religion. And does not God intend that the trials you meet with should bring you back to this?"[31] Here again, experience is something that is acquired through engagement with reality, not merely the passive reception of data from it.

Such examples could be multiplied, but these are sufficient to make the point. Despite the epistemological problems it raises, experience in Wesley is not merely passive. It is an active encounter with reality which requires something from the one whose experience it is. This idea of active engagement in Wesley even extends to the very basis of empirical experience—the reception of sense data.

Activity and Passivity in the Senses

Wesley does not often address the manner in which sense data comes into the mind through experience, but the few places where he does so are telling. They reveal a common-sense realization that even our sensation of the world is actively shaped and misshaped by the way we engage it. Again, a pair of examples are sufficient to make this evident.

In *Thoughts Upon Necessity*, Wesley reacts against the idea that all human actions are *necessary* and that there is no such thing as free will. In making his case against this position, he both affirms both the reliability and limitedness of our sensory experience. On the one hand, Wesley argues that our brain receives the impressions of our senses, it does not create them. So, contrary to his opponent's opinion, Wesley believes that qualities like color exist in reality and are not illusions within the human brain.[32] But just a few paragraphs later, he qualifies the degree to which our senses are passive. Quoting his opponent, he begins, "'Man is passive in receiving the impressions of things.' Not altogether. Even here much depends on his own choice. In many cases he may or may not receive the impression; in most he may vary it greatly."[33] Wesley affirms an active role for the mind in sensory perception because it is important to his defense of freewill,[34] but this seems to reflect his true opinion. He notes two possible ways in which sensory experience is active, and so possibly fallible. The receiver may not receive the information, and he or she may vary the impression once it is received. In either case, Wesley leaves open the possibility that proper sensory perception is partially dependent upon the active co-operation (or the active restraint) of the will.

Wesley makes the same basic point in his first sermon on the "Witness of the Spirit," comparing the physical and spiritual senses (an idea to which will return in Chapter 10). There he asks, "How do you distinguish light from darkness; or the light of a star, or a glimmering taper, from the light of the noon-day sun? Is there not an inherent, obvious, essential difference between the one and the other? And do you not immediately and directly perceive that difference, *provided your senses are rightly disposed?*"[35] Again, his realist stance shows through (in speaking of an "inherent, obvious, essential difference"), and again he indicates that there is more to proper perception than passive reception. Whatever he means by having one's senses "right disposed," Wesley indicates that proper orientation is a part of proper perception.

What is true for the physical senses (*apprehension* in Aristotle's terms) is also true for the understandings we build on them. The tract entitled "Free Thoughts Upon the Present State of Public Affairs in a Letter to a Friend" was written to respond to a friend's request for Wesley's opinion regarding some actions taken by the King and Parliament. Before Wesley offers his "free thoughts," he feels compelled to state explicitly upon what shaky foundation they lie. He notes,

> And it is no easy matter to form any judgment concerning things of so complicated a nature. It is the more difficult, because, in order to form our judgment, such a multitude of facts should be known, few of which can be known with tolerable exactness by any but those who are eye-witnesses of them. And how few of these will relate what they have seen precisely as it was, without adding, omitting, or altering any circumstance, either with or without design! …But supposing we have ever so much information, how little can one rely on it! on the information given by either party! For is not one as warm as the other? And who does not know how impossible it is for a man to see things right when he is angry? Does not passion blind the eyes of the understanding, as smoke does the bodily eyes? And how little of the truth can we learn from those who see nothing but through a cloud?[36]

Working as a true Aristotelian, Wesley insists that his judgment must be founded on information (apprehension), but that information may not be reliable because people often, even without intending it, do not relate an event "as it was." This is the perennial problem in empiricism with relying on the experiences of other people. Our access to the world is shaped and misshaped by our feelings about it, and "it is impossible for a man to see things right when he is angry." We do not, Wesley realizes, merely receive impressions from the world in passive way; we actively engage it.

The idea of active experience raises some thorny problems to an empiricist epistemology. If experience is active, and we can shape it or distort it, then experience alone is insufficient for sure knowledge. At this point, as we noted above, Locke will find the "end of reason's tether" and speak only in terms of probability, and Hume seems to give up the project of real knowledge altogether. Wesley, however, as a different approach. If we must have senses that are "rightly disposed," then there may be a priori conditions that are necessary to proper experiencing. These conditions are not alternative sources of knowledge opposed to experience. Instead, they function as a set of pre-conditions that allow one to obtain knowledge from experience. It is to examining the role of these a priori authorities in Wesley that we now turn.

Notes

1. The classical example of this is Hindley's taking Wesley's off-abused quote about "the most infallible of all proofs, inward feeling" (*Journal* 8 January 1738 [*Jackson* 1:72]) and further abusing it by grounding Wesley's entire epistemology upon it (cf. Hindley, "Philosophy of Enthusiasm").

2. Though some wish he would have, as can been seen in Thorsen's comment that Wesley's failure to make this distinction "leads to confusion in understanding his theology" (*Wesleyan Quadrilateral*, 203 n. 7).

3. So the work of Maddox, *Responsible Grace*, 44-45; Thorsen (despite his protestations to the contrary), *Wesleyan Quadrilateral*, 203; Matthews, "Reason and Religion," 289; and Shizimu, "Epistemology," 171. We will deal with their concerns in the material that follows.

4. Scott Jones, *Conception and Use*, 31.

5. Both Randy Maddox (*Responsible Grace*, 46) and Scott Jones (*Conception and Use*, 179) recognize the external or objective role of experience in Wesley, and Maddox intimates that this externality has a role in confirming religious doctrine. Both scholars, however, separate out this external factor from the supposed *internal* nature of religious experience, and thus attribute to Wesley an essentially dualistic epistemology. It remains to be seen if this distinction is warranted.

6. There are fascinating, but as yet not fully explored, parallels between Wesley's approach to the question of knowledge and the "critical realist" approach of the Neo-Thomist school of Catholic philosophy, as exemplified by Joseph Marechal and Bernard Lonergan.

7. Sermon #8 "The First Fruits of the Spirit" §II.5 (*Jackson* 5:91). This is a favorite appeal in Wesley and can also be found in many places. Cf. Sermon #24 "Sermon on the Mount—Discourse IV" §I.1 (*Jackson* 5:297); Sermon #29 "Sermon on the Mount—Discourse IX" §9 (*Jackson* 5:283); Sermon #44 "Original Sin" §II.2 (*Jackson* 6:58); *The Doctrine of Original Sin—Part II* §[II].20 (*Jackson* 9:295); and *An Extract of a letter to the Reverend Mr. Law* [6 January 1756] (*Jackson* 9:502), among many others.

8. In speaking of the reality of liberty, Wesley states that "To deny this would be to deny the constant experience of all human kind" (Sermon #109 "What is Man" §11 [*Jackson* 7:228]). Cf. also Sermon #13 "On Sin in Believers" §V.1 (*Jackson* 5:155); "Second Letter to Rev. Mr. Walker" [3 September 1756] (*Jackson* 13:199); *Reasons Against a Separation from the Church of England* §3.5 (*Jackson* 13:231); again, among others that could be cited.

9. *Journal* 6 August 1746 (*Jackson* 2:19). Cf. also Sermon #107 "On God's Vineyard" §II.6 (*Jackson* 7:208), and "Letter to Rev. Mr. Walker" §1 (*Jackson* 13:194).

10. Discussing the vanity of worldly hopes, Wesley notes, "So that universal experience, both our own, and that of all our friends and acquaintance, clearly proves, that as God made our hearts for himself, so they cannot rest till they rest in him" (Sermon #78 "Spiritual Idolatry" §II.2 [*Jackson* 6:442]). Cf. also *Journal* 3 November 1766 (*Jackson* 3:269). For the "experience of all ages," cf. Sermon #70 "The Case of Reason Impartially Considered" §1 (*Jackson* 6:350). In arguing against the author of a work called *Letters to the Author of 'Theron and Aspasio'*, Wesley notes, "Whereas our Lord

gives a general command, 'Seek, and ye shall find;' you say, 'Saving faith was never yet sought, or in the remotest manner wished for, by an unbeliever:' (Page 372:) A proposition as contrary to the whole tenor of Scripture, as to the experience of every true believer" (*A Sufficient Answer to 'Letters to the Author of "Theron and Aspasio"'* [*Jackson* 10:303]) Cf. also Sermon #34 "The Original, Nature, Property, and Use of Law" §IV.5 (*Jackson* 5:444). That these usages and modifications of the word experience were not unique to Wesley but part of ordinary usage may be deduced from the fact that these phrases also occur in quotes that Wesley makes from other authors: cf. *Journal* 19 April 1761 (*Jackson* 3:173); *The Doctrine of Original Sin—Part IV* §3 (*Jackson* 9:361); and *The Doctrine of Original Sin—Part VII* §[II].[II].2.[III].2 (*Jackson* 9:451).

11. Sermon #39 "The Catholic Spirit" §3 (*Jackson* 5:493).

12. *An Answer to the Rev. Mr. Church's Remarks on the Rev. Mr. John Wesley's Last Journal* §III.13 (*Jackson* 8:413).

13. *Journal* 27 June 1740 (*Jackson* 1:279).

14. Note, too, how Wesley the logician points out that it only takes a single counterexample to overthrow a general assertion: "No conversions happen at the Lord's Supper"; but "Mr. X was converted at the Lord's Supper"; therefore the first statement is false.

15. Sermon #27 "Sermon on the Mount—Discourse VII" §II.4 (*Jackson* 5:350).

16. *Predestination Calmly Considered* §46 (*Jackson* 10:230).

17. Sermon #11 "The Witness of the Spirit—Discourse II" §III.6 (*Jackson* 5:127).

18. *Earnest Appeal* §10 (*Jackson* 8:5).

19. Sermon #125 "On Living Without God" §14 (*Jackson* 7:353).

20. *Farther Appeal—Part One* §V.28 (*Jackson* 8:106).

21. Cf. Wesley comments on the what happened at Aldersgate (*Journal* 24 May 1738, especially §12 [*Jackson* 1:102]); as well as *Journal* 13 April 1759 (*Jackson* 2:474); Sermon #1 "Salvation by Faith" (*Jackson* 5:7-16); Sermon #5 "Justification by Faith" (*Jackson* 5:53-64); and the many times when he quotes Ephesians 2:8 about faith being the "gift of God."

22. *Journal* 24 May 1738 §12 (*Jackson* 1:102)

23. In his *Essay*, Locke relates the story of the Dutch ambassador telling the King of Siam about snow and the King's inability to believe the story because he had not experienced it for himself (*Essay*, 485). Hume retells that story, displacing the events to India, and notes that the Indian prince in question "reasoned justly" in disbelieving the account (*An Enquiry Concerning Human Understanding*, ed. Tom Beauchamp [Oxford: Oxford University Press, 2000], 86, http://books.google.com/books?id=R6d35Aei0KoC).

24. *A Letter to the Reverend Conyers Middleton* [4 January 1748-9] §III.10 (*Jackson* 10:78).

25. *Journal* 7 March 1736 (*Jackson* 1:28).

26. Sermon #37 "The Nature of Enthusiasm" §18 (*Jackson* 5:472).

27. In those few times when Wesley will revert to the passive voice to emphasize the object rather than the subject of experience, it is still clear that the experience is not passively received. For example, Wesley will speak of "inward religion" as "being experienced," but that does not imply that such religion is primarily passive (cf. Sermon #102 "Of Former Times" §11 [*Jackson* 7:162]; Sermon #114 "The Unity of the Divine Being" §18 [*Jackson* 7:270]; and *Letter to Bishop Lavington* [1 February 1749-50] §20 [*Jackson* 9:8]).

28. *Journal* 11 February 1753 (*Jackson* 2:280).

29. *Journal* 20 April 1784 (*Jackson* 4:271).

30. *Journal* 15 May 1787 (*Jackson* 4:375).

31. "Letter to Mr. John Trembath" [17 August 1760] (*Jackson* 12: 253).

32. *Thoughts Upon Necessity* §IV.3 (*Jackson* 10:471).

33. Ibid. (*Jackson* 10:472).

34. For now we can ignore Wesley's unconscious circular reasoning—that he assumes we have choice in order to prove that we have choice—as even this faulty argument reveals Wesley's opinion on the contingent nature of the senses.

35. Sermon #10 "Witness of the Spirit—Discourse I" §II.9 (*Jackson* 5:121), emphasis added.

36. "Free Thoughts Upon the Present State of Public Affairs in a Letter to a Friend" (*Jackson* 11:14-15).

7

The A Priori Role of Logic

As we intimated in our philosophical contextualization of Wesley, his Aristotelian empiricism is not as "anti-metaphysical" as that of the British Empirical tradition. For good or ill, Aristotle's brand of empiricism allows for certain pre-understandings or pre-conditions to be attached to the question of experience. Being the good Aristotelian that he was, the first a priori that we find in Wesley is that great "idol of the mind," logic. We will, therefore, first examine in this chapter the way in which logic pre-informs experience in Wesley. In doing so, we will show both *that* there is an a priori role for logic and the general shape of that role in both opening up and in limiting possible experience.

In Chapter 8, we will examine the other a priori lens that orients and filters experience in Wesley, namely his religious faith, or more precisely, his affirmation of Scripture-based religious understandings. While it may seem odd to place our discussion of the interaction between Scripture and experience here in our analysis of religious epistemology, rather than in our discussion of theological method, the move is nonetheless warranted. Wesley's affirmation of Scripture, like his affirmation of logic, pre-informs all experience (including such secular areas as history and science), not just supposedly religious experience. Recognizing this interplay between areas that contemporary thinking often keeps separate reinforces the need to view Wesley's approach to experience as a unified whole and not as divided between religious and non-religious arenas.

We have already seen that Wesley was influenced by Aristotle's logic, and that this logic entails a priori faith it its connection to reality. This logic is a system of processing information by means of apprehending (or perceiving), judging, and discoursing (by which one strings together judgments). Logic, in Wesley, is also equated to reasoning in general[1] or, as he often prefers to put it, *understanding*.[2] This means that when we investigate the a priori role played by logic, we will also need to be aware of the role of reasoning in general. Even where the formal structures of Aristotelian logic are absent, one might still detect a role for reason or understanding that pre-informs experience.

There are two significant ways that logic and reason may function prior to experience within an Aristotelian system, one positive and one negative. We will examine each in detail and in turn. In a positive way, logic may serve as a heuristic device. If one believes the world to be reasonable and knowable by the rules of logic, then any statement about truth will have a logical form. This means logic is sufficient to establish the truth of a conclusion even in the absence of experience, provided that one's premises are grounded in experience. So, if by experience we know that "All students at Cheltenham are girls," and by experience we know that "Pat is a student at Cheltenham," then we may act on the truth of the conclusion that "Pat is a girl" even in the absence of a direct experience of that truth.[3] In fact, we "know" that we will experience this fact in advance, and so logic can pre-inform experience by expectation.

Logic can, however, also perform a delimiting or negative role. Certain ranges of experience and their interpretation may be deemed illogical and impossible, or in more Wesleyan terms, *irrational* or *absurd*. If the world is indeed governed by logic, then the experience of certain things (such as square circles) is excluded a priori, and no amount of experience *can* establish them. To someone holding a logical view of the world, it would make no difference how strenuously one insisted that square circles were a part of one's experience or how many testimonies for them were amassed. The authority of experience in such a case is nullified at the outset; experience is not allowed to validate something that logic pronounces absurd. Note that for the true Aristotelian, there is no conflict of authorities here, as if it might be possible that reason and experience were contending for different truths. Rather, the congruency of them is simply assumed as part of the framework of reality. If there *seems* to be a conflict, it either lies in a misapplication of reason or in a misinterpretation of experience. In turning our attention to Wesley's use of logic as it relates to experience, we can see both the positive and the negative a priori roles that logic plays. Some of this information we have seen before, but it will be good to review it here with the foregoing analysis in view.

Wesley affirms the sheer fact of logic's a priori role in proper experiencing in several places, the clearest being his *Address to the Clergy*, at which we have already looked. In listing the "acquired endowments" necessary for good ministry, Wesley's remarks on logic come after he has discussed other arenas of knowledge like history and the original biblical languages. However, he calls specific attention to the importance of logic by saying that it is "even necessary next, and in order to, the knowledge of the Scripture itself."[4] He first notes that, in addition to being the "art of good sense," logic is also the "art of learning and teaching." That logic has rhetorical power was hardly a matter of controversy, but in order for logic to be a "learning art," it must be able to inform experience. He goes even further than this, noting the way in which metaphysics, as the second part of logic, allows one "to clear our apprehension...by ranging our ideas under general heads."[5] For Wesley, some pre-understanding was necessary for proper apprehension, which in this context can be more or less equated with proper experiencing.

These remarks accord with the foundational role Wesley gives to logic in numerous other places. Latter in that *Address*, Wesley refers to logic as the "gate" of the sciences.[6] Since he understood science as an experimental endeavor, logic as a gate allows one entry into these proper forms of experiencing. As we have already seen, almost all of Wesley's critiques of John Locke flow from his Aristotelian-logical presumptions. He blames a lack of clarity in the ideas of John Locke (and also of Alexander Gerard) on the fact that they neglected logic, and thus they could not apprehend reality well enough to think clearly about it.[7] Finally, as if to underscore its metaphysical importance, Wesley understands that logic is so difficult to learn that few undertake it except on "principle of conscience."[8] This phrase implies that one must have solid convictions about the world and its logical nature to force oneself to endure its study.

Logic as Positive A Priori

The heuristic use of logic to open up possibilities for experience, either certain or as worth exploring, can be seen in a number of places where Wesley employs, as he often does, logical forms of argument. Although these arguments are designed to advance religious causes, we will not take up their theological implications now but simply note the dynamic of the interplay between logic and experience.

In the late tract "Thoughts on Salvation by Faith," Wesley examines the idea of unconditional predestination, attempting to show that such a doctrine obviates the need for both faith and works, as these can only be understood as conditions on one's salvation. The conclusion of his argument runs like this: "It is plain, then, if we affirm, No man is saved by an absolute, unconditional decree, but only by a conditional one; we must expect, all who hold unconditional decrees will say, we teach salvation by works."[9] Wesley is warning his Arminian followers that, *by logical necessity*, they will be accused of preaching a works-based salvation by those who hold to unconditional election. The tract is occasioned by his own experience, but he does not know how to interpret the experience until he figures out this logical connection.[10] Then, in offering his conclusion to his readers, he tells them that they may expect to experience this persecution because it is the logical conclusion of the clash between the two doctrines—not because Wesley himself had experienced these things before.

In the same way, Wesley logically analyzes some statements by Jesus to conclude that contempt by the world in general is a *necessary* consequence of being a Christian. He writes to his father in a letter that he places in his published *Journal*:

> Till he is thus despised, no man is in a state of salvation. And this is a plain consequence of the former; for if all that are 'not of the world,' are therefore despised by those that are, then, till a man is despised, he is 'of the world;' that is, out of a state of salvation. Nor is it possible for all the trimmers between God and the world to elude the consequence; unless they can prove that a man may be 'of the world,' and yet be in a state of salvation...insomuch that though a man may be despised without being saved, yet he cannot be saved without being despised.[11]

Whether or not one agrees with this theological position as stated in such stark terms, the dynamic interplay between logical analysis (involving the equivalency rule of contraposition[12]) and experience (in this case, of contempt by the world) is noteworthy. We may be certain that we will experience contempt as a logical consequence of being a Christian, and the lack of such an experience is proof—not against the logic of the argument—but against one's own salvation! Now, this letter and the section of the *Journal* in which it is related are relatively early, and we must leave room for Wesley to have modified his theological position. Nevertheless, the a priori way in which logic dictates the possible interpretations of an experience shows the power it had in his thinking.

Logic as Negative A Priori

Just as logic leads one to expect with certainty some outcomes, so, too, it may a priori eliminate others with equal certainty. In investigating this dynamic, we find Wesley not only delineating out possible experiences as absurd but also clearing away what we might understand as false delineations, in which improper logic had eliminated an experience that he was interested in promoting. In both of these cases, Wesley's faith in the power of logic priori to—sometimes even over and against—experience is noteworthy.

In his sermon on "Wandering Thoughts," Wesley lays out the various possible sources of such thoughts and then shows how only those that stem from sin are likely to be eliminated in the life of the believer. One cannot expect to be delivered from wandering thoughts occasioned by the Devil or by other people, because both will always be around. One must also contend with wandering thoughts occasioned by our embodied nature.

> To pray for deliverance from those [wandering thoughts] which are occasioned by the body is, in effect, to pray that we may leave the body: Otherwise it is praying for impossibilities and absurdities; praying that God would reconcile contradictions, by continuing our union with a corruptible body without the natural, necessary consequences of that union. It is as if we should pray to be angels and men, mortal and immortal, at the same time.[13]

The possibility of experiencing such a deliverance or even of praying for it is eliminated by Wesley as impossible and absurd (i.e., contrary to logic) a priori. Once again, no Scripture is cited for this conclusion, and it is offered on purely logical grounds.[14]

Replying to some of his critics in the third part of his *Farther Appeal*, Wesley advances the same kind of argument to show that people should not expect miracles as proof that the revivals occasioned by his preaching were indeed from God. Such extraordinary experience is quite beside the point, according to Wesley. Summarizing his arguments at the end of one section and the beginning of another, he says:

Miracles, therefore, are quite needless in such a case. Nor are they so conclusive a proof as you imagine. If a man could and did work them in defence of any doctrine, yet this would not supersede other proof; for there may be *terata pseudous*, 'lying wonders,' miracles wrought in support of falsehood. Still, therefore, his doctrine would remain to be proved from the proper topics of Scripture and reason: And these even without miracles are sufficient; but miracles without these are not...I presume, by this time you may perceive the gross absurdity of demanding miracles in the present case; seeing one of the propositions in question, (over and above our general doctrines,) viz., 'That sinners are reformed,' can only be proved by testimony; and the other, 'This cannot be done but by the power of God,' needs no proof, being self-evident.[15]

One interesting feature of this quote is that it shows the greater value Wesley places on ordinary experience (testimony) over the extraordinary (miracles). But aside from that, we also see Wesley placing around experience a boundary by means of logical analysis, dictating what such experience may (or in this case may not) prove. Proof of doctrine cannot be verified by certain types of experience, namely miracles, but by "Scripture and reason."[16] To believe otherwise is a category mistake and is classified as an absurdity, something contrary to logic.

In addition to eliminating the possibility of some experience, Wesley will also work to restore parts of experience that had been improperly eliminated by bad thinking. This, too, reveals his faith in the a priori role of logic and reason to experience, and a few instances of this kind are worth noting.

In reflecting upon some of the extraordinary epiphenomena that were sometimes occasioned by his preaching (such as visions or convulsions or the like), Wesley takes great care in using logic to distinguish the proper and improper bounds on experience. Early on in the revival, he notes, one might have been tempted to see those extraordinary phenomena as necessary to revival, but at the time of his writing he feels the greater danger would be to disparage all such phenomena as either feigned or demonic. Wesley feels neither extreme to be appropriate. After affirming the possibility that visions or trances *might* be from God, Wesley reflects on the implications that they are not *always* so.

Let us even suppose that in some few cases there was a mixture of dissimulation; that persons pretended to see or feel what they did not...Yet even this should not make us either deny or undervalue the real work of the Spirit. The shadow is no disparagement of the substance, nor the counterfeit of the real diamond. We may further suppose, that Satan will make these visions an occasion of pride: But what can be inferred from hence? Nothing, but that we should guard against it; that we should diligently exhort all to be little in their own eyes, knowing that nothing avails with God but humble love. But still, to slight or censure visions in general, would be both irrational and unchristian.[17]

Using the language of logic (*suppose, infer*), Wesley points out that an a priori elimination of the possibility of visions is irrational, which is to say that it is not a warranted conclusion based on the evidence of experience. No general conclusions can be drawn from particular affirmations. To say that some extraordinary manifestations are from God and that some extraordinary manifestations are not allows for no further affirmations or denials. Thus, Wesley takes care that no artificial boundary be laid against experience on the basis of faulty logic.

In his sermon "On the Repentance of Believers," Wesley draws out the logical implications of the assumption that one receives all the sanctification one will ever receive at justification. Again, Wesley does not cite Scripture for his conclusion (although he does so in establishing his premises). He merely asserts, "For it is manifest, 'they that are whole need not a Physician, but they that are sick.' If, therefore, we think we are quite made whole already, there is no room to seek any farther healing. On this supposition it is absurd to expect a farther deliverance from sin, whether gradual or instantaneous."[18] He goes on to argue against this idea, but it is clear that he believes a misunderstanding about the nature of justification may a priori limit experience in this area. A similar example can be found in Wesley's "A Call to Backsliders," where he argues against using a metaphor as a premise because it results in improper expectations. These backsliders seem to have reached the conclusion that they cannot expect two pardons from their Heavenly King on the basis of the idea that God is like earthly kings, from whom one should not expect multiple pardons.[19] In both of these cases, Wesley feels that he must combat improper conclusions so that the proper expectations might be restored. When we examine in more detail Wesley's theological method, this practice of properly pre-informing experience will have enormous significance.

Experience Beyond Logic

While we can see how Wesley's understanding of experience can be pre-informed by his understanding of, and faith in, the logical nature of reality, we must guard against the temptation to make Wesley a "closet rationalist," one who occasionally allows rationalist metaphysical premises to override his empirical ones. In first place, despite the a priori role that Wesley gives to logic in enabling such things as proper apprehension or proper construal of experience, he nevertheless strongly affirms that logic is an "acquired endowment" or art and is *not* innate. Aside from his explicit avowal of that Aristotelian dictum that "nothing is in the intellect which is not first in the senses," Wesley decries how rarely good logic is found in the world[20] and notes how much work it takes to properly acquire it.[21]

As further evidence that experience is not wholly constrained by reason and logic, we can also look at those times when Wesley allows experience to function outside of them. The quote from Wesley, examined above, concerning the role of experience and reason in combating enthusiasm points to this. If it is true what he says, concerning a prophetic enthusiast, "When plain facts run counter to their predictions, experience performs what reason could not, and sinks them down into their sense,"[22] then we cannot say experience is always constrained by reason.

Wesley will also note that some believers "are not able to reason either strongly or clearly...They know not how to prove what they profess to believe; or to explain even what they say they experience."[23] This seems to allow for true experience even when reason is not competent to explain it or inform it. That bad reasoning cannot wholly inhibit experience is evident in the comments Wesley records in his *Journal* upon reading a history of the Trappist order. "I am amazed," Wesley writes, "at the allowance which God makes for invincible ignorance. Notwithstanding the mixture of superstition which appears in every one of these, yet what a strong vein of piety runs through all! What deep experience of the inward work of God; of righteousness, peace, and joy in the Holy Ghost!"[24]

Of course, this position is burdened with an ambiguous epistemology, and it raises some serious questions concerning the role Wesley gives to experience and how that relates to logic and reason, not the least of which is the question of where knowledge begins. However, as the analysis of that dynamic will parallel the analysis of the role played by the other a priori authority in Wesley— Scripture—we will hold off examining it until we have seen the ways that Scripture pre-informs, expands and constrains experience as well.

Notes

1. Cf. *Journal* 15 June 1741 (*Jackson* 1:315). This is the main thesis of Matthews, "Reason and Religion."

2. Sermon #60 "On General Deliverance" §I.5 (*Jackson* 6:244) and Sermon #70 "The Case of Reason Impartially Considered" §I.2 (*Jackson* 6:353).

3. Of course, a true Lockean or Baconian would challenge that we can ground in experience any such absolute general statements, and that is part of their critique of logic. But for one who accepts the Aristotelian framework, which is not driven by these epistemic concerns, this does not seem to matter.

4. *An Address to the Clergy* §I.2 (*Jackson* 10:482).

5. Ibid. Latter in the tract he re-echoes much the same words (*Jackson* 10:492). The remarks also echo the justification for the study of logic found at the beginning of *A Compendium of Logic* §I.I.II (*Jackson* 14:161).

6. *An Address to the Clergy* §II.1.(5) (*Jackson* 10:491).

7. Cf. *Remarks upon Mr. Locke's 'Essay on Human Understanding'* (*Jackson* 13:460-461) and his remarks on Dr. Gerhard's "Essay on Taste" in his *Journal* 1 November 1787 (*Jackson* 4:403).

8. *Journal* 13 March 1747 (*Jackson* 2:49).

9. "Thoughts on Salvation by Faith" §8 (*Jackson* 11:494).

10. "I was in this perplexity," Wesley notes, "when a thought shot across my mind, which solved the matter at once" (Ibid.).

11. *Journal* 28 March 1739 §20 (*Jackson* 1:184).

12. That is, if not "of the world," then despised = if not despised, then "of the world"

13. Sermon #41 "Wandering Thoughts" §IV.7 (*Jackson* 6:31).

14. That is, by the law of non-contradiction, which states that a thing cannot be both

"A" and "not A" in the same way at the same time.

15. *Farther Appeal—Part Three* §III.29-30 (*Jackson* 8:235).

16. Earlier in the section, Wesley added "and, if need be, by antiquity," (§III.2, [*Jackson* 8:233]). The idea of the inefficacy of miraculous proofs is echoed by Wesley in several other places; cf., among others, Sermon #112 "The Rich Man and Lazarus" §III.2-5 (*Jackson* 7:253-55); *The Principles of a Methodist Farther Explained* §V.8 (*Jackson* 8:467), and "A Letter to the Reverend Mr. Fleury" [18 May 1771] §12 (*Jackson* 9:186).

17. *Journal* 25 November 1759 (*Jackson* 2:519-20).

18. Sermon #14 "The Repentance of Believers" §III.1 (*Jackson* 5:168).

19. Sermon #86 "A Call to Backsliders" §I.1, II.1 (*Jackson* 6:516, 519).

20. Cf. Sermon #134 "True Christianity Defended" §II.7 (*Jackson* 4:459); *Farther Appeal—Part Three* §III.8 (*Jackson* 8:219); and *A Plain Account of Kingswood School* §18 (*Jackson* 13:298).

21. Cf. "Letter to Ms. Lewin" [n.d.]§9 (*Jackson* 12:261); "Letter to a Member of the Society" [1 July 1772] (*Jackson* 12:294); and "Letter to Mr. Joseph Benson" [7 November 1768] (*Jackson* 12:409).

22. Sermon #37 "The Nature of Enthusiasm" §18 (*Jackson* 5:472).

23. Sermon #31 "Upon Our Lord's Sermon on the Mount—Discourse XI" §II.9 (*Jackson* 5:411).

24. *Journal* 21 December 1747 (*Jackson* 2:77). Cf. a similar comment concerning Cardinal Bellarmine in Sermon #20 "The Lord Our Righteousness" §II.4 (*Jackson* 5:238).

8

The A Priori Role of Scripture

Few who read Wesley can doubt that Scripture was central to his life, and that he was proud of that fact. Early on in his life, he resolved to be a *homo unius libri*,[1] "a man of one book," and that book was the Bible. Many scholars have taken great pains to show the centrality of the Bible in his thought,[2] and even Wesley's English breathes with the phraseology of the Authorized Version.[3] Our concern here, however, is not with Wesley's ideas about the Bible *per se* but with the way in which his understanding of Scripture functions as an a priori to experience, opening up arenas for experience that might otherwise go unnoticed and closing off other arenas as impossible. This function for Scripture is not confined to theology, extending to the entirety of experience, both secular and sacred, and it seems to be a natural expression of Wesley's tendency to contextualize his philosophy within his religion.[4]

Scripture, at least the way Wesley understands it, stands in an unquestionably primary position of authority, and his faith in its ultimate veracity seems to be a non-falsifiable position, one not subject to doubt or challenge from experience. He offers no original arguments for Scripture's truth or priority,[5] but that is to be expected if this is a foundational belief for him. Had he offered extensive arguments, he might have implied that Scripture was true *because* of the arguments and so make the authority of Scripture dependent upon some other authority, namely reason. Instead, Wesley assumes the unimpeachable truth of Scripture, referring to it as "unquestionable true,"[6] as "an infallible test,"[7] and affirming that it must be completely free of mistake, since it has come from the God of Truth.[8] No doubts are raised on that score whatsoever.[9]

Wesley's strong faith in Scripture will also lead him to deride those who do not accept its authority (in the same way he assails those who denigrate logic), asserting that they are incapable of proper understanding or belief. In a tract evaluating a comparison of the Hindu religion with Christianity, he concludes by saying, "I cannot but repeat the observation, wherein experience confirms me more and more; namely, They that do not believe the Bible will believe anything. They may believe Voltaire, or the Shastah. They may believe that a man is able to put himself into a quart bottle!"[10] In other words, without the a priori role of Scripture creating certain boundaries, one's judgments will not be completely sound. A similar belief seems to lay at the root of Wesley's contention, noted in the previous chapter, that "No man can be a thorough Physician without being an experienced Christian."[11] His final comment on Rousseau's treatise on education reveals much the same thing: "Any one may observe concerning the whole, the advices which are good are trite and common, only disguised under new expressions. And those which are new, which are really his own, are lighter than vanity itself. Such discoveries I always expect from those who are too wise to believe their Bibles."[12]

Scripture as Positive A Priori

As he does with logic, Wesley used Scripture as an a priori in order to open up possibilities for experience and its interpretation, both religious and otherwise. One indication of this is the way Wesley approaches that quintessential sphere of *non-religious* experience, namely science or "natural philosophy," including medicine. In his *Address to the Clergy*, admittedly biased toward a religious perspective, Wesley affirms that "natural philosophy" has value because it can help one understand the Scriptures. The possibilities of science are validated because they can be used for scriptural ends, namely to see "how the invisible things of God are seen from the creation of the world; how 'the heavens declare the glory of God, and the firmament showeth his handiwork;' till they cry out, 'O Lord, how manifold are thy works! In wisdom hast thou made them all.'"[13] It is this scriptural perspective that pre-informs how one is to interpret scientific experience. Science may aide one in understanding and interpreting Scripture, but it cannot challenge its authority.

Wesley says much the same thing in the very first paragraph of the "Preface" to his *Survey of the Wisdom of God in Creation*. In laying out why he took on this work himself, his culminating reason is this: "I wished to see this short, full, plain account of the visible creation directed to its right end: Not barely to entertain an idle, barren curiosity; but to display the invisible things of God, his power, wisdom, and goodness."[14] From Wesley's perspective, this proper, scriptural, a priori contextualization of scientific experiments and experience protects them from becoming objects of what Wesley calls "Spiritual Idolatry."[15]

Perhaps the most interesting place in which we can see the a priori role of Scripture outside of religion is in Wesley's interactions with the scientific thought of John Hutchinson. Hutchinson was a scientific opponent of Sir Isaac Newton's idea of gravitation, which he challenged with ideas taken from a symbolic reading of the un-pointed Hebrew of the Old Testament. His approach intrigued Wesley, as he interacts with the thought of Hutchinson and his disciples several times[16] and even recommends the reading of his works.[17] All those interactions together reveal both Wesley's appreciation of Hutchinson's attempt to "do science" on the basis of Scripture, but also a deep skepticism about Hutchinson's success. In the end, he cannot buy Hutchinson's system, *not* on the basis of inadequate experimental verification,[18] but because the arguments are unconvincing (a logical concern) and because he finds fault with his scriptural interpretation. The ideas, Wesley notes, "have no foundation in Scripture or sound reason."[19]

In turning away from secular examples to more sacred ones, we can see several areas in which Scripture opens up possibilities for experience. Since we will be returning to this point in more detail in the next chapter, all we need to do at this point is briefly foreshadow a few relevant issues to show how Wesley's religious thought is consonant with his non-religious thought on the matter of Scripture and experience.

Two of Wesley's most distinctive doctrines—the doctrine of entire sanctification and the doctrine of the witness of the spirit—are precisely those in which Wesley urged believers to expect something in their experience on the basis of Scripture. In both cases, he often contends for an interpretation of Scripture that opens up possibilities for the believer to experience something that he or she otherwise would not. In these cases (as in others), Scripture provides a platform on which experience can be built and the means by which experience is to be interpreted.

In his *Plain Account of Christian Perfection*, Wesley explicitly grounds the expectation of the deliverance from sin on Scripture. After enumerating the points of agreement between his followers and his opponents on the subject of sanctification, he boils down their disagreement to one question: "Should we expect to be saved from all sin before the article of death?"[20] Wesley then proceeds to ground this expectation on a long list of direct scriptural promises and indirect ones in the form of prayers and commands. His sermon on the same subject concludes with much the same emphasis, in which readers or hearers are encouraged to seek in their experience what is promised in Scripture:

> 'Having therefore these promises, dearly beloved,' both in the Law and in the Prophets, and having the prophetic word confirmed unto us in the Gospel, by our blessed Lord and his Apostles; 'let us cleanse ourselves from all filthiness of flesh and spirit, perfecting holiness in the fear of God.'... 'let us press toward the mark, for the prize of the high calling of God in Christ Jesus;' crying unto him day and night, till we also are 'delivered from the bondage of corruption, into the glorious liberty of the sons of God!'[21]

Much the same dynamic is a work in Wesley's doctrine of the "witness of the spirit." After citing the key text for this doctrine,[22] he opens his second sermon on the "Witness of the Spirit" like this:

> None who believe the Scriptures to be the word of God, can doubt the importance of such a truth as this; — a truth revealed therein, not once only, not obscurely, not incidentally; but frequently, and that in express terms; but solemnly and of set purpose, as denoting one of the peculiar privileges of the children of God.[23]

One of Wesley's chief aims in writing this sermon seems to be establishing the biblical basis for something that ought to be a part of a Christian's experience. The method he uses to establish this provides an interesting example of how experience and Scripture interact. He begins by showing that Romans 8:16 and Galatians 4:6 cannot be understood in any way other than by allowing an "immediate and direct" testimony of God's Spirit in and with ours. Then, after establishing this scriptural basis, he moves to adduce experiential evidence to confirm it and defend his method against possible objections.

> It is objected, First, 'Experience is not sufficient to prove a doctrine which is not founded on Scripture.' This is undoubtedly true; and it is an important truth; but it does not affect the present question; for it has been shown, that this doctrine is founded on Scripture: Therefore experience is properly alleged to confirm it.[24]

Once the scriptural basis of the doctrine has been established, the role of experience is to confirm it, to actualize the potential implied by this scriptural understanding. Finally, in the conclusion of the sermon, Wesley exhorts his readers or hearers to seek this witness as confirmed by both Scripture and experience.

Scripture also provides the means by which one may properly interpret one's own experience of this witness. In analyzing how we may distinguish between a true "witness of the spirit" and false delusions, Wesley provides scriptural benchmarks. "For the Scriptures lay down those clear, obvious marks, as preceding, accompanying, and following that gift, which a little reflection would convince him, beyond all doubt, were never found in his soul."[25] Thus, even a person's own experience is not enough to settle the matter outside of the proper and a priori context of Scriptural testimony.

Wesley's attitude on this point is consistent and extends beyond these doctrines into his investigation of all so-called "religious experience." When examining the experience of those of his societies and bands or of those he has read about, he frequently makes comments like this, concerning the select society in Worcester: "I have seen very few, either in Bristol or London, who are more clear in their experience. The account all whom I had time to examine gave, was scriptural and rational."[26] Giving a positive evaluation of Mrs. Rowe's "Devout Exercises of the Heart," he notes, "Her experience is plain, sound, and scriptural, no way whimsical or mystical."[27]

In contrast, Wesley notes about Baron Swedenborg and his visions, "He is one of the most ingenious, lively, entertaining madmen that ever set pen to paper. But his waking dreams are so wild, so far remote both from Scripture and common sense, that one might as easily swallow the stories of 'Tom Thumb,' or 'Jack the Giant-Killer.'"[28] In examining and abridging the life of Madam Guyon, Wesley's chief concern was to remove her "unscriptural" interpretations of experience while still preserving what was valuable in it.[29] Throughout his work, Wesley gives Scripture priority over experience in determining what it should be and judging it when it falls short.

Thus, in both secular and sacred contexts, Wesley uses Scripture as an a priori to experience, pre-informing it by setting up proper expectations, alerting one to possibilities that might otherwise be missed, and guarding against improper interpretations. This is not to say that Scripture simply dictates experience; the question is not so simple as that, as we shall see in examining the dynamic interplay between experience and its a priori authorities below. But there is nonetheless a role for Scripture to play before experience is given its full say.

Scripture as Negative A Priori

Turning toward the negative heuristic role of Scripture in experience, we again see parallels between the way logic eliminated possibilities for experience and its interpretation and the way that Scripture operates. Certain experiences and their interpretation are a priori invalidated. We can see this in Wesley's approach to science (including history as a social science), in his approach to religious experience, and—again in parallel with his understanding of logic—the way he deconstructs improper interpretations that close off possibilities of true experience.

Scripture and Science

Wesley's critique of Locke demonstrates his use of Scripture to critique matters of science. One can see this in his discussions of personal identity and the soul[30] and his assertion that the idea of species is a feature of reality and not merely our human organization of it.[31] Locke's views on these matters are dismissed because they constitute an interpretation of experience that Wesley finds at odds with Scripture. He reveals the same attitude in his approach to the Lisbon earthquake of 1755, which almost destroyed the town and which confirmed the doubts that many had, most notably Voltaire, about a supposedly good God overseeing the world. Wesley reflects on the event in order to address those doubts, challenging the idea that the earthquake was a merely natural event:

> If by affirming, 'All this [the earthquake] is purely natural,' you mean, it is not providential, or that God has nothing to do with it, this is not true, that is, supposing the Bible to be true. For supposing this, you may descant ever so long on the natural causes of murrain, winds, thunder, lightning, and yet you are altogether wide of the mark, you prove nothing at all, unless you can prove that God never works in or by natural causes. But this you cannot prove; nay, none can doubt of his so working, who allows the Scripture to be of God…what is nature itself, but the art of God, or God's method of acting in the material world? True philosophy therefore ascribes all to God.[32]

Despite the theological difficulties the event raised, Wesley had a priori eliminated, on the basis of Scripture, one possible interpretation of the event— that God had nothing to do with it. His response was to defend God's purposes in such a terrifying event (and even use it as an evangelistic tool). Unlike Voltaire, Wesley could not allow experience to challenge the idea of a good and sovereign God.

In fact, Wesley will allow science no role whatsoever in determining anything related to the spiritual realm; all of science's conclusions on that matter are suspect, as Wesley makes clear in the closing words of the "Preface" to his *Survey of the Wisdom of God in Creation*:

> What remains of natural philosophy is, the doctrine concerning God and spirits. But in the tracing of this we can neither depend upon reason nor experiment. Whatsoever men know or can know concerning them, must be drawn from the oracles of God. Here, therefore, we are to look for no new improvements; but to stand in the good old paths; to content ourselves with what God has been pleased to reveal; with 'the faith once delivered to the saints.'[33]

The experiential authority of science is a priori constrained by a belief in the veracity of Scripture. Where science confirms Scripture, so much the better for faith. Where it might be seen to challenge it, such inconsistency indicates a failure in human understanding. It is not that Wesley dismisses science, but he is very suspicious about our command of it. This attitude, too, he articulates as a product of learning-by-experience. In a reply to critics of his *Survey*, published in the *London Magazine*, Wesley lays out a minute and experimentally-based discussion of the solar parallax and the inhabitability of the moon, but then concludes with these words:

> Be not so positive; especially with regard to things which are neither easy nor necessary to be determined. I ground this advice on my own experience. When I was young, I was sure of everything: In a few years, having been mistaken a thousand times, I was not half so sure of most things as I was before: At present I am hardly sure of anything but what God has revealed to man.[34]

In setting science—or indeed any exercise of human knowledge, which is all based on experience or experiment—against Scripture, Wesley's experience led him to trust the latter much more than the former. Because experience is active, it is fallible. To guard against that fallibility, Wesley will place a priori limits around the authority of experience based on his faith in Scripture.

Wesley's concern for the fallibility of human interpretation of our experience—and so his recognition of the need for a priori biblical parameters—also shows up in his approach to history, both ancient and contemporary. Wesley will only allow testimonial evidence (that is, evidence from the experience of other people) if it coheres with the biblical testimony.[35] As one example of this, Wesley's biblical understanding of original sin will not allow him to accept Henry Wilson's testimony of the virtuous but atheistic natives of Palau,[36] but he easily accepts another account of the native North-Americans, which falls in line with that understanding.[37] The validity of the interpretations of experience in each case is a priori constrained by Wesley's interpretation of the Bible. Commenting on Wilson's account (which, to be fair, he finds valuable enough to republish in an abridged form), Wesley is explicit in affirming what experience may or may not prove:

> The more I read and considered, the more convinced I was, that, if this account be true, the Bible is not true; for the Bible affirms, not in one place only, but through the whole tenor of it, that all mankind are 'by nature dead in trespasses

and sins.'...I cannot, therefore, but earnestly advise all those who still believe the Scriptures to be of God, to beware of this, and all other books of this kind, which either affirm or insinuate that there are any Heathens in the world who, like the supposed nations of the Pelew Islands, are unblamable by nature; since, if there be any such, all revelation is needless, and the Christian revelation utterly false.[38]

Rhetoric aside, Wesley sets out Wilson's account of his experience and Scripture as two opposing testimonies; one either believes Capt. Wilson or the Bible. Wesley's mind on this score is quite clear. The account cannot be true because Scripture has an a priori authority. "If it is true, then Scripture is not," is the substance of his argument (in good logical form). One should note that any doubt about the veracity of Scripture raised by this statement is purely rhetorical in nature, designed to help clarify the thinking of his audience and not evincing any true doubt on Wesley's part. His conclusion, which has been determined in advance and is not really open to question is that, since Scripture is true, then the account is false—perhaps not deliberately so, but false nonetheless.

This same orientation, at least in part, leads Wesley to doubt many of the historical accounts he reads[39] and to affirm (unaided by any outside source) the truth of others.[40] One finds the same perspective in his apology for composing his own *A Concise History of England*.[41] In some of these cases, Wesley feels that there is some scientific counter-evidence to the historical ideas presented therein, but his main line of evaluation—sufficient for him even in the absence of scientific evidence—is the weight of biblical testimony. That is what sets the boundaries around what testimonies may or may not be believed.

Scripture and Religious Experience

In turning to the arena of spiritual truth, one sees very much the same dynamic at work. Certain religious experiences or interpretations of experience are disallowed because they do not conform to what Wesley understands to be the truth as laid out in Scripture. One of the most striking instances of this kind occurs in a public letter that he wrote to William Law, to counter the latter's idea of *stillness*. The whole passage is worth quoting in some detail.

But how shall I know whether I have faith or not? [quoting Law]'I will give you an infallible touchstone. Retire from all conversation only for a month. Neither write, nor read, nor debate anything with yourself. Stop all the former workings of your heart and mind, and stand all this month in prayer to God. If your heart cannot give itself up in this manner to prayer, be fully assured you are an infidel.' (Spirit of Prayer, Part II., p. 163.) ... But I would gladly know by what authority you give us this touchstone; and how you prove it to be infallible. I read nothing like it in the oracles of God. I cannot find one word there of 'refraining from all conversation, from writing, and reading, for a month.' (I fear you make no exception in favour of public worship or reading the word of God.) Where does the Bible speak of this?... It would be no wonder, should any man make this unscriptural (if not anti-scriptural) experiment, if Satan were permitted to work in him 'a strong delusion,' so that he should 'believe a lie.'...Nearly related to this touchstone is the direction which you give elsewhere: 'Stop all self-activity; be retired, silent, passive, and humbly attentive to the inward light.' (Part I., pp. 77, 82.) But beware 'the light which is in thee be not darkness;' as it surely is, if it agree not with 'the law and the testimony.' 'Open thy heart to all its impressions,' if they agree with that truly infallible touchstone [i.e., Scripture]. Otherwise regard no impression of any kind, at the peril of thy soul, — 'wholly stopping the workings of thy own reason and judgment.' I find no such advice in the word of God. And I fear they who stop the workings of their reason, lie the more open to the workings of their imagination.[42]

Wesley struggled much with this doctrine of passivity, stillness, or "quietism" as he sometimes called it, and he found it to be a dangerous thing because it opened up its practitioners to *unbiblical experience*. In replying to Law as he does, Wesley intends to forestall this type of experience, and he does so almost entirely on his understanding of the Bible. He calls doing what Law suggests an "unscriptural (if not anti-scriptural) experiment." This would be an odd phrase did Wesley not have in mind a delimiting function for Scripture prior to experience. He is not denying that one might learn something from such an experiment, but he fears that whatever people might learn would be merely delusional, merely "the workings of their imagination." Any impressions, what we today might term *religious experiences*, are not only to be judged by Scripture (here referred to as "the law and the testimony") but only to be *sought* as they are in accordance with Scripture. That, and that alone, is the "truly infallible touchstone." Any experience promoted outside of the bounds allowed by Scripture may be judged dangerous ahead of time.

The same may be said of Wesley's approach to other mystical sounding doctrines. In a letter to one Dr. Robertson concerning Dr. Andrew Ramsay's *Philosophical Principles of Natural and Revealed Religion explained and unfolded in a General Order*, Wesley notes:

> The doctrine of pure love, as it is stated in the fourth book and elsewhere, (the loving God chiefly if not solely for his inherent perfections,) I once firmly espoused. But I was at length unwillingly convinced that I must give it up or give up the Bible. And for near twenty years I have thought, as I do now, that it is at least unscriptural, if not antiscriptural: For the Scripture gives not the least intimation, that I can find, of any higher, or indeed any other, love of God, than that mentioned by St. John: 'We love him, because he first loved us.' And I desire no higher love of God, till my spirit returns to Him.[43]

The idea of disinterested love for God might sound good, and Wesley admits that he believe in it in the past, but such an experience cannot find place in his thought when he believes it to be counter to his interpretation of Scripture.

Another such case, and one quite pertinent to this investigation, concerns Wesley's dealing with the problem or question of enthusiasm. His two chief weapons in combating extraordinary revelations from God—and protecting himself from charges of the same—were reason and Scripture, and it is on the latter that he grounds both his attack and his defense, as can be seen in his sermon on "The Nature of Enthusiasm."[44]

After taking pains to give a proper definition of *enthusiasm* as a species of religious madness (such concern for definition showing his strong Aristotelian bent), Wesley undertakes to outline the various kinds of enthusiasm and how they may be distinguished. The first enthusiasts are those who "imagine they have the grace which they have not," and they are labeled as enthusiasts because their lives do not conform to the scriptural pattern.[45] Enthusiasts may plead whatever experiences they like, but if they do not live as the Bible says they should, their interpretation of their own experience is invalid from the start. In dealing with the second sort of enthusiasm, the pretending to gifts of God, Wesley notes that some of these believe their "particular directions" or impression to have come from God. "But how many," decries Wesley, "impute things to him, or expect things from him, without any rational or scriptural ground!"[46] If Scripture and reason do not authorize such expectations, then they are not to be affirmed. He will later note, "But how is a sober Christian to make this inquiry? to know what is the will of God? Not by waiting for supernatural dreams; not by expecting God to reveal it in visions; not by looking for any particular impressions or sudden impulses on his mind: No; but by consulting the oracles of God."[47] Again, explanations or interpretations of experience, even subjective religious experience, are a priori hedged in by what can and cannot be supported by Scripture. A person's own understanding counts for nothing if cannot be based in Scripture.

Wesley applies these scriptural constraints to experience even to such a religious experience as worship. In his *Popery Calmly Considered*, he disallows the then Roman Catholic practice of only allowing the Mass to be said in Latin.

> This irrational and unscriptural practice destroys the great end of public worship. The end of this is, the honour of God in the edification of the Church. The means to this end is, to have the service so performed as may inform the mind and increase devotion. But this cannot be done by that service which is performed in an unknown tongue…It is manifest, then, that the having any part of divine worship in an unknown tongue is as flatly contrary to the word of God as it is to reason.[48]

Perhaps uncharitably, Wesley does not ask how such worship is experienced by those who participate in it, nor does he consider the reasons why the Roman Catholic church felt it necessary to enforce that practice. In this case, he judges solely on reason and Scripture, mainly on the latter.

Scripture and its Improper Interpretation

A final indication of the way in which Wesley understood the power of Scripture to pre-inform experience can be found in the way he dealt with false interpretations of Scripture, and he takes as much care in doing this as he did in eliminating improper logical constructions as noted above. As proper understanding of Scripture opens up positive possibilities and removes negative ones, so improper understanding of Scripture opens up negative possibilities and removes positive ones.

We begin with Wesley's treatment of "The Wilderness State," or what the Christian mystical tradition often refers to as the "dark night of the soul." That Wesley is no fan of this doctrine is clear, but what concerns us is the way he sees the interplay between Scripture and experience. In between dealing with spiritual darkness which is caused by sin and that engendered by temptation, Wesley has this to say:

> Another general cause of this darkness is ignorance...If men know not the Scriptures, if they imagine there are passages either in the Old or New Testament which assert, that all believers, without exception, *must* sometimes be in darkness; this ignorance will naturally bring upon them the darkness which they expect. And how common a case has this been among us! How few are there that do not expect it! And no wonder, seeing they are taught to expect it; seeing their guides lead them into this way. Not only the Mystic writers of the Romish Church, but many of the most spiritual and experimental in our own, (very few of the last century excepted,) lay it down with all assurance, as a plain, unquestionable scripture doctrine, and cite many texts to prove it.[49]

Here it is clear that a misconception of Scripture will lead to a misleading experience, the latter derivative of the former. In fact, Wesley even goes so far as to say that the improper expectation of experience brought on by the improper interpretation of Scripture would actually create such an experience. In other words, if you believe that mystical darkness is promised by Scripture, you will experience such a darkness. So even though his idea of experience is fundamentally concerned with an encounter with reality, he understood that this encounter was not a simple one. His understanding of the depth of the pre-informative power of expectation over experience shows that he did not conceive of experience in the same way as many of his philosophical and scientific contemporaries. Nor he is content to simply let experience prove William Law and those who follow him to be wrong. To challenge improper experience he must challenge its improper (i.e., unscriptural) basis.

Similar concerns govern Wesley's response to the prophetic enthusiasm of one George Bell. Bell had prophesied that the end of the world would occur on February 28, 1763,[50] and he caused no little disruption thereby in a number of places. Wesley's response is just what one might expect. He notes in his *Journal* for 21 February:

> Observing the terror occasioned by that wonderful prophecy to spread far and wide, I endeavoured to draw some good therefrom, by strongly exhorting the congregation at Wapping, to 'seek the Lord while he might be found.' But at the same time I thought it incumbent upon me to declare (as indeed I had done from the hour I heard it) that 'it must be false, if the Bible be true.'[51]

Wesley was happy to use the uneasiness created by the prophecy to some good, but he rejected the prophecy and the expectations to which that it gave rise as based on a false understanding of Scripture.[52]

In addition to forestalling improper experience created by faulty interpretations of Scripture, Wesley will also attempt to eliminate false interpretations of Scripture when they threaten proper interpretations of experience. A good example of this can be found in his sermon on enthusiasm, noted above. After dealing with three various kinds of enthusiasm (again, on scriptural grounds), Wesley then uses Scripture to guard against eliminating too much.

> It may be expected that I should mention what some have accounted a Fourth sort of enthusiasm; namely, the imagining those things to be owing to the providence of God which are not owing thereto. But I doubt: I know not what things they are which are not owing to the providence of God...So our Lord understood it, or he could never have said, 'Even the hairs of your head are all numbered;' and, 'Not a sparrow falleth to the ground, without' the will of 'your Father' which is in heaven. But if it be so, if God preside...'over the whole universe as over every single person, and over every single person as over the whole universe;' what is it (except only our own sins) which we are not to ascribe to the providence of God? So that I cannot apprehend there is any room here for the charge of enthusiasm.[53]

Using Scripture, Wesley preserves a space for interpreting the events of life in the context of God's provision. To cut off that possibility of interpretation would be to violate what he sees as a clear implication of biblical teaching, even if some would maintain that this is enthusiasm.

Another favorite theme of Wesley for restoring biblical interpretations of experience over and against a supposedly more scientific framework for experience is witchcraft. In his *Journal*, Wesley notes,

> It is true, likewise, that the English in general, and indeed most of the men of learning in Europe, have given up all accounts of witches and apparitions, as mere old wives' fables. I am sorry for it; and I willingly take this opportunity of entering my solemn protest against this violent compliment which so many that believe the Bible pay to those who do not believe it. I owe them no such service...They well know, (whether Christians know it, or not,) that the giving up witchcraft is, in effect, giving up the Bible; and they know, on the other hand, that if but one account of the intercourse of men with separate spirits be admitted, their whole castle in the air (Deism, Atheism, Materialism) falls to the ground...One of the capital objections to all these accounts, which I have known urged over and over, is this, "Did you ever see an apparition yourself?" No: Nor did I ever see a murder; yet I believe there is such a thing; yea, and that in one place or another murder is committed every day. Therefore I cannot, as a reasonable man, deny the fact; although I never saw it, and perhaps never may. The testimony of unexceptionable witnesses fully convinces me both of the one and the other.[54]

Wesley seems to be fully aware that what is at stake is a contest of worldviews. On one side is the worldview of the Bible, which accepts the existence of witchcraft,[55] or more properly, which affirms a spiritual world which interacts with this physical one. On the other is the edifice of Enlightenment understanding ("Deism, Atheism, Materialism"), which will not accept this. Wesley refuses to allow the smallest chink in the armor of his biblical understanding. He seems to realize that the transition between one worldview and the other will be made by small and incremental steps, and he will not grant even this single one. Wesley never uses the idea of witchcraft in theological discussions or as proof for any particular doctrinal point. The only reason he seems to defend it is that not to defend it—in his mind at least—compromises the possibility of the Bible's prescribing of experience. Only after dealing with the global and prescriptive issue of worldviews does he deal with the objection concerning personal experience. His evaluation of the validity of personal testimonies concerning witchcraft stems from his faith in the biblical worldview. Since these experiences (unlike the enthusiastic ones noted above) do not contradict Scripture, they may be—indeed must be—accepted alongside testimonies regarding non-spiritual matters like the reality of murder.

From the foregoing, we see that Scripture serves a role parallel to that of logic in placing or removing constraints around what may or may not be experienced and how one may or may interpret such experiences. However, as it is with logic, the knowledge of Scripture does not reside in one's mind as a set of innate ideas. The knowledge and understanding of Scripture must be acquired, which is to say that it must come from experience. The proper acquisition of the knowledge of Scripture is the result of long and hard study, and Wesley, in his sermon on enthusiasm quoted above, specifically decries those who think themselves to be illuminated by the Spirit to understand Scripture apart from such study.[56] Wesley understood the study of Scripture to be an academic enterprise of acquiring knowledge from without, as opposed to a Socratic or Deistic idea, in which Scripture just reminds one of what one already knows within or says much the same thing as does natural religion.[57] This is evinced, for example, in his strong affirmation of the importance of the original languages of Scripture, which no ordained minister is excused from not knowing.[58]

At the same time, just as we saw to be the case for logic and reason, Wesley will allow for some role for experience in approaching Scripture. This is a question to which we will return in the next chapter, but at this point, we can note two important examples. In discussing the question of assurance of salvation, Wesley relates the following incident in his *Journal*:

> When I met Peter Böhler again, he consented to put the dispute upon the issue which I desired, namely, Scripture and experience. I first consulted the Scripture. But when I set aside the glosses of men, and simply considered the words of God, comparing them together, endeavouring to illustrate the obscure by the plainer passages; I found they all made against me, and was forced to retreat to my last hold, 'that experience would never agree with the *literal interpretation* of those scriptures. Nor could I therefore allow it to be true, till I found some living witnesses of it.'...accordingly, the next day he came again with three others, all of whom testified, of their own personal experience, that a true living faith in Christ is inseparable from a sense of pardon for all past, and freedom from all present, sins.[59]

Note that what is at stake here is not the *truth* of Scripture but rather one's *understanding* of that truth. Wesley was not prepared to doubt Scripture, but he could doubt a particular interpretation of it if that interpretation were not *upheld* by experience. Experience has some possibility of correcting one's pre-understanding and is not inevitably conformed to it.

Wesley makes much the same point regarding the possibility of entire sanctification. In his *Plain Account of Christian Perfection*, he compares the weight given to personal testimonies to the experience of sanctification with the interpretation of the scriptural evidence for the doctrine.

> Q[uestion]. But what does it signify, whether any have attained it or no [i.e., testify to entire sanctification], seeing so many scriptures witness for it? A[nswer]. If I were convinced that none in England had attained what has been so clearly and strongly preached by such a number of Preachers, in so many places, and for so long a time, I should be clearly convinced that we had all mistaken the meaning of those scriptures; and therefore, for the time to come, I too must teach that 'sin will remain till death.'[60]

Although the passage has a rhetorical element in it, Wesley sounds prepared to give up his understanding of Scripture if he had no confirmation in experience. That gives experience significant weight in the *interpretation* of Scripture, and so the relationship between Scripture and experience, like that between logic or reason and experience, is not wholly one-sided.

The Relationship of Reason and Scripture

From what we have see in the foregoing two chapters, Wesley's approach to experience cannot be divorced from his high appreciation of both reason-as-logic and Scripture. In both so-called secular arenas of experience and sacred ones, each of these serves to pre-inform experience, opening up some possibilities and closing off others, and yet each is also acquired from experience. Interestingly enough, these two a priori authorities have an intimate connection between them in Wesley's thought, as well as a parallel and intimate connection between them and experience.

It comes as no surprise to anyone familiar with Wesley's works to find a similar function for Scripture and reason when it comes to approaching experience. In fact, many students of Wesley have recognized that reason and Scripture form a kind of unity in Wesley's thought. Donald Thorsen comments, "Either because of his own regard for the importance of reason or because he knew his theology needed to be well conceived from the standpoint of reason, Wesley regarded reason as inextricably bound up with the truths of Scripture and thus deserving of special recognition."[61] In the same vein, Randy Maddox notes, "Following Scripture, reason was the criterion that Wesley invoked most often in defending a belief or practice as authentically Christian. In fact, it was more typical for him to refer to Scripture and reason conjoined than to Scripture alone."[62] Similar sentiments are echoed by many others.[63]

These two canons of authority are frequently conjoined in Wesley's works, and one of his key phrases in evaluating things like ideas or testimonies is that they are or are not "scriptural and rational" or in accord with "Scripture and sound reason." The coupling of reason and Scripture as joint authorities in both positive and negative evaluations occurs literally hundreds of times throughout the Wesleyan corpus.[64]

Wesley's most important sermon on reason, "The Case of Reason Impartially Considered," is an extended reflection on the inextricability of reason and Scripture. In the first part of the sermon, Wesley says,

> The foundation of true religion stands upon the oracles of God. It is built upon the Prophets and Apostles, Jesus Christ himself being the chief corner-stone. Now, of what excellent use is reason, if we would either understand ourselves, or explain to others, those living oracles! And how is it possible without it to understand the essential truths contained therein?... Is it not reason (assisted by the Holy Ghost) which enables us to understand what the Holy Scriptures declare concerning the being and attributes of God?[65]

Wesley is clear that one cannot understand Scripture without the use of reason, a thought echoed in the quote from his sermon on enthusiasm cited above. He then spends the rest of the sermon outlining how useless reason is in producing the three theological virtues—faith, hope, and love—which human beings require to be happy, and so reason is as useless without Scripture as Scripture is without reason.

As criteria of evaluation, Scripture and reason are most often used in tandem, there are places in which they appear to be separated, though with no lessening of authority for either one. In terms of their authority, Wesley seems, at least a couple of times, to set them on more or less equal footing. He notes to Bishop Lavington in replying to the latter's charge of enthusiasm, "I am not above either reason or Scripture. To either of these I am ready to submit."[66] In a letter to one Freeborn Garrettson, he says, "If I have plain Scripture or plain reason for doing a thing [it is] well. These are my rules, and my only rules...I wish to be in every point, great and small, a scriptural, rational Christian"[67] This separation, however, does not seem to imply complete independence. Rather, throughout Wesley's corpus the two function is a completely complementary way. There is the tacit assumption that true reason and true interpretation of Scripture cannot conflict.

Seeing this interplay between Scripture, reason and experience in Wesley raises a critical question regarding his understanding of experience. Given that the three are so inextricably linked in Wesley's thought, it difficult to discern a clear and *philosophically* consistent epistemology there, and it confirms what our philosophical investigation in Part One led us to suspect. Wesley cannot be classified with the British Empirical tradition because his view of experience is clouded by the very things that tradition sought to free itself from—a priori authorities. Wesley makes no apology for his acceptance of the authority of logic and Scripture, but he nevertheless classifies himself as an empiricist. One could, of course, assume that Wesley was just philosophically uninformed and unaware of the contradictory nature of his *implicit* epistemology, but there is another option. Perhaps we can elucidate Wesley's epistemological intuitions about the best of both rational (a priori) and empiricist (a posteriori) approaches to knowledge and the dynamic between them in a way that reveals an inner coherence. It is to that task that we will now turn.

Notes

1. *Journal* 14 May 1765 (*Jackson* 3:213). Cf. also the *Preface to Sermons on Several Occasions* §5 (*Jackson* 5:3) and *A Plain Account of Christian Perfection* §10 (*Jackson* 11:373).

2. Cf. Scott Jones, *Conception and Use*; as well as Maddox, *Responsible Grace*, 36-39; Thorsen, *Wesleyan Quadrilateral*, 127-30; and Williams, *Wesley's Theology*, 23-27.

3. Cf. George Lawton, *John Wesley's English. A Study of His Literary Style* (London: Allen and Unwin, 1962), 164-90.

4. This also places Wesley firmly before the Enlightenment transition in biblical hermeneutics that Hans Frei decries in his *The Eclipse of Biblical Narrative: A Study in Eighteenth and Nineteenth Century Hermeneutics* (London: Yale University Press, 1974). Wesley sees the world through the lens of Scripture; he does not view Scripture through the lens of the world or of reason. On this point, cf. Scott Jones, *Conception and Use*, 27-31.

5. He will offer up an argument that Scripture must have God as its origin, which naturally has implications for its veracity, but the argument is a demonstration of something Wesley already believes, not his reason for believing it. Cf. *A Clear and Concise Demonstration of the Divine Inspiration of the Holy Scriptures* (*Jackson* 11:484), as well as Scott Jones's discussion of it (*Conception and Use*, 22).

6. Sermon #136 "On Corrupting the Word of God" (*Jackson* 7:472).

7. *The Principles of a Methodist Farther Explained* §V.6,8 (*Jackson* 8:466,468) and "A Letter to the Right Reverend The Lord Bishop of Gloucester" [26 November 1762] (*Jackson* 9:161,163).

8. *Journal* 24 July 1776 (*Jackson* 4:82).

9. Scott Jones's contention that Wesley's use of rhetorical statements (such as "If the Scriptures are true...") makes him a transitional figure to the modern, critical understanding of Scripture and so opens up the possibility that reason can *judge* Scripture, does not seem consonant with Wesley's own self understanding. That he used such statements is more naturally explained as an concession to his educated audiences, showing his understanding of *their* beliefs. Wesley knew that many educated folk of his day doubted the Bible, and he could not, as a matter of sermonic effectiveness, assume that everyone had his faith in it. However, this in no way indicates a personal lack of faith in the Scripture on Wesley's part. As we shall see when we return to this question in Part Three, Wesley himself is thoroughly pre-Enlightenment on this question, however much some parts of his audience may not have been. Cf. Scott Jones, *Conception and Use*, 26-31.

10. *Remarks on Mr. H.'s Account of the Gentoo Religion in Hindostan* §16 (*Jackson* 13:407-08).

11. *Journal* 12 May 1759 (*Jackson* 2:479).

12. *Journal* 3 February 1770 (*Jackson* 3:387).

13. *An Address to the Clergy* §I.2 (*Jackson* 10:483-84).

14. "Preface" to *A Survey of the Wisdom of God in the Creation: Or, A Compendium of Natural Philosophy* §1 (*Jackson* 14:300).

15. Cf. Sermon #78 "Spiritual Idolatry" esp. §I.14 (*Jackson* 6:440).

16. *Journal* 17 January 1756 (*Jackson* 2:353), 26 October 1756 (*Jackson* 2:388), 22 November 1756 (*Jackson* 2:389), 27 April 1758 (*Jackson* 2:441), 31 July 1758 (*Jackson* 2:454), 9 October 1765 (*Jackson* 3:238), 13 February 1770 (*Jackson* 3:387), and 20 November 1773 (*Jackson* 4:5); as well as Sermon #69 "The Imperfection of Human Knowledge" §I.5 (*Jackson* 6:339); and "Letter to the Rev. Dean D." [n.d.] (*Jackson* 12:464).

17. "Letter to Miss Lewin" [n.d.] §11 (*Jackson* 12:261). He also placed the abridgement to Hutchinson's works in the curriculum for the school at Kingswood (cf. *A Short Account of the School at Kingswood* [*Jackson* 13:288]).

18. Wesley does not seem to be aware of the actual state of these scientific questions, as one can see from the ambiguous evaluations in Sermon #77 "Spiritual Idolatry" §I.6 (*Jackson* 6:427); *Journal* 9 October 1765 (*Jackson* 3:238); and *Remarks on the Limits of Human Knowledge* (*Jackson* 13:490).

19. *Journal* 31 July 1758 (*Jackson* 2:454). It is instructive to compare this "pre-Enlightenment debate" with contemporary discussions about "Intelligent Design." Today, the ground of debate is unquestionably science, with most assuming that Scripture must be read from within the framework that science provides.

20. *A Plain Account of Christian Perfection* §17 (*Jackson* 11:388-89).

21. Sermon #40 "Christian Perfection" §II.30 (*Jackson* 6:19).

22. "The Spirit itself beareth witness with our spirit, that we are the children of God" (Rom 8:16, KJV).

23. Sermon #11 "The Witness of the Spirit—Discourse II" §1 (*Jackson* 6:123).

24. Ibid. §IV.1 (*Jackson* 6:129).

25. Sermon #10 "The Witness of the Spirit—Discourse I" §II.4 (*Jackson* 6:118).

26. *Journal* 15 March 1770 (*Jackson* 3:388).

27. *Journal* 2 July 1769 (*Jackson* 3:370).

28. *Journal* 28 February 1770 (*Jackson* 3:387).

29. Cf. "Preface" to *An Extract of the Life of Madam Guion* (*Jackson* 14:275-78).

30. *Remarks on Locke* (*Jackson* 13:458-60).

31. Ibid. (*Jackson* 13:461-62).

32. "Serious Thoughts Occasioned by the Late Earthquake at Lisbon" (*Jackson* 11:6-7).

33. *Of the Gradual Improvement of Natural Philosophy* §24 (*Jackson* 13:487).

34. "A Letter to the Editor of the 'London Magazine'" [1765] (*Jackson* 13:399). Similar thoughts are expressed throughout Wesley's work, including *Remarks on the Limits of Human Knowledge* (*Jackson* 13:488-99) and two whole sermons devoted to the topic: Sermon #69 "The Imperfection of Human Knowledge" (*Jackson* 6:337-50) and Sermon #70 "The Case of Reason Impartially Considered" (*Jackson* 6:350-360).

35. Scott Jones' contention that Wesley is uncritical in his acceptance of testimony (*Conception and Use*, 179) needs further nuance. True, Wesley's does not fall in with modern historiography, and Jones is correct that Wesley is "pre-critical" in this way, believing unless he has a reason to doubt rather than doubting unless there is a compelling reason to believe. Nevertheless, Wesley is very critical in his acceptance of testimonies which do not cohere with his understanding of Scripture, as we shall see.

36. Then known as "Pelew," cf. *Journal* 16 January 1789 (*Jackson* 4:444) and 29 November 1789 (*Jackson* 4:476). Perhaps the same may be said for his pert and unapologetic dismissal of Lady Mary Wortley Montague's favourable appraisal of Muslims (cf. Sermon #63 "The General Spread of the Gospel" §4 [*Jackson* 6:278]).

37. *Journal* 13 October 1790 (*Jackson* 4:497).

38. *Thoughts upon a Late Publication* §1, 6 (*Jackson* 13:411, 413)

39. Cf. *Journal* 25 April 1748 (*Jackson* 2:94), 24 May 1774 (*Jackson* 4:15-16), 27 April 1778 (*Jackson* 4:120), 24 November 1779 (*Jackson* 4:171-72), and 6 July 1781

(*Jackson* 4:210).

40. *Journal* 15 February 1773 (*Jackson* 3:487).

41. "Preface" to *A Concise History of England, from the Earliest Times, to the Death of George II*, esp. §5, 9 (*Jackson* 14:274-75).

42. *An Extract of a Letter to the Reverend Mr. Law* [6 January 1756] (*Jackson* 9:502-03).

43. "Letter to Dr. Robinson" [24 September 1753] (*Jackson* 12:212).

44. Sermon #37 "The Nature of Enthusiasm" (*Jackson* 5:467-78).

45. Ibid. §13-17 (*Jackson* 5:470-71).

46. Ibid. §20 (*Jackson* 5:473).

47. Ibid. §22 (*Jackson* 5:473-74).

48. *Popery Calmly Considered* §III.1 (*Jackson* 10:146).

49. Sermon #46 "The Wilderness State" §II.II.1 (*Jackson* 6:83-84).

50. Cf. *Journal* 7 January 1763 (*Jackson* 3:125).

51. *Journal* 21 February 1763 (*Jackson* 3:129).

52. Wesley knew that this false interpretation would shape other people's experience, and he notes on the fateful day itself, "I largely showed the utter absurdity of the supposition, that the world was to end that night. But notwithstanding all I could say, many were afraid to go to bed, and some wandered about in the fields, being persuaded, that, if the world did not end, at least London would be swallowed up by an earthquake. I went to bed at my usual time, and was fast asleep about ten o'clock." (*Journal* 28 February 1763 [*Jackson* 3:130]). It is worthy to note how Wesley attempts to show that he would not shape his own experience by something so contrary to both Scripture and reason.

53. Sermon #37 "The Nature of Enthusiasm" §28 (Jackson 5:476).

54. *Journal* 25 May 1768 (*Jackson* 3:324-35).

55. Cf. *Journal* 4 July 1770 (*Jackson* 3:404) and 23 May 1776 (*Jackson* 4:76); *A Letter to the Reverend Dr. Conyers Middleton* [4 January 1748-9] §III.19, V.12 (*Jackson* 10:36, 65-66); and the "Preface to a true Relation of the Chief Things which an Evil Spirit did and said at Mascon, in Burgundy" (*Jackson* 14:290).

56. Cf. Sermon #37 "The Nature of Enthusiasm" §27 (*Jackson* 5:475).

57. Cf. Wesley's comments on the works on natural religion of John Hutchinson (Sermon #106 "On Faith" §II.2 [*Jackson* 7:201]).

58. Cf. *An Address to the Clergy* §I.2, II.1.(2) (*Jackson* 10:483, 491). Add to this the fact that Wesley himself produces both a simple Greek and a simply Hebrew grammar for use in the Kingswood School and among his own preachers.

59. *Journal* 24 May 1738 §12 (*Jackson* 1:102).

60. *A Plain Account of Christian Perfection* §19 (*Jackson* 11:406).

61. Thorsen, *Wesleyan Quadrilateral*, 127.

62. Maddox, *Responsible Grace*, 40.

63. Dunning, *Grace, Faith, and Holiness*, 16-17; Scott Jones, *Conception and Use*, 74-80; Theodore Runyon, *The New Creation* (Nashville: Abingdon, 1998), 15; and Colin Williams, *Wesley's Theology*, 32-36.

64. To cite all the appropriate references for this would be to reproduce a sizeable chunk of Wesley's corpus. However, what can be noted is that the phrase is used both early and late in all the major categories of Wesley's writing, such as the *Journal* (3 September 1741 [*Jackson* 1:333] and 12 April 1784 [*Jackson* 4:270]); sermons (#5 "Justification by Faith" §II.4 [1742] [*Jackson* 5:57] and #126 "On the Danger of Increasing Riches"§17 [1790] [*Jackson* 7:362]); letters (*To Mr. John Smith* [28 September 1745] §14 [*Jackson* 12:61] and "Letter to Freeborn Garrettson" [24 January 1789] [*Jackson* 13:73]); and essays (*Earnest Appeal* §27 [1744] [*Jackson* 8:11] and *Thoughts upon Jacob Behmen* [i.e., Boehme] [1780] [*Jackson* 9:509]).

65. Sermon #70 "The Case of Reason Impartially Considered" §I.6 (*Jackson* 6:354).

66. *Letter to Bishop Lavington* [1 February 1749-50] §22 (*Jackson* 9:9).

67. "Letter to Freeborn Garrettson" [24 January 1789] (*Jackson* 13:73). Cf. also Wesley's favourable relating of a story of some who opposed Methodism. "When some gentlemen inquired of one of the Bishops in England, 'My Lord, what must we do to stop these new Preachers?' He answered, 'If they preach contrary to Scripture, confute them by Scripture; if contrary to reason, confute them by reason. But beware you use no other weapons than these, either in opposing error, or defending the truth.' Would to God this rule had been followed at Cork!" (*A Letter to the Rev. Mr. Baily, of Cork* [8 June 1750] §[III].12 [*Jackson* 9:87]).

9

The Dynamics of Experience

Up to this point, we have seen how both reason and Scripture affect experience in Wesley's thought and something of how they related to each other. While each of these binary relationships is clear (Scripture-experience, reason-experience, Scripture-reason) and the three are sometimes listed together as joint authorities,[1] Wesley nowhere undertakes an analysis of their interrelationship. However, if we are to process Wesley's general understanding of experience into our investigation of his theological method, we must address this issue using the threads that he has left to us. Fortunately, weaving those threads together is not a difficult task, as the manner in which Scripture, reason and experience relate in Wesley seems to be a clear consequence of his incorporating a faith in Scripture into his Aristotelian empirical framework. This framework ties together all the relevant features of experience that we have dealt with thus far—its fundamentally public nature, its active and passive concerns, and its interaction with a priori authorities. While the inclusion of Scripture at this point already points us toward theological method—and we have seen that Wesley's worldview is an avowedly religious one—we first need to clarify the explicitly epistemological concerns of the relationship between experience and authority. We will reserve the more theological issues raised by the use of Scripture for the discussion of Wesley's theological method in Part Three.

Reason and Experience:
An Aristotelian Interdependence

Recall that to a true Aristotelian, reason is a processing faculty of the mind, describing how the mind apprehends, discourses about, and judges data, and we have seen how well Wesley owns this approach. As a processing faculty, however, reason can in no way function as a true *source* of knowledge. In philosophical terms, that source can only be experience, which for Aristotle meant physical, sensory experience. Without experience, reason has no data with which to work. Wesley himself affirms this consequence when he quotes the Aristotelian dictum that "Nothing is in the intellect which is not first in the senses." He even adds that, without sensory experience of the "invisible world," our understanding, "having here nothing to work upon, can afford us no help at all."[2]

As we noted above, however, the rules by which reason processes experience, represented by logic, are not themselves products of experience. Aristotle believed the rules of logic to be self-evident to the mind, and so his original epistemology is not a pure empiricism free from rationalist taint (as Bacon and Locke were at pains to point out). Aristotle does, however, shift the kind of foundational role reason plays in knowledge away from being a *source of true ideas* to being a *reliable process* by which knowledge is derived from the external source of experience.

Thus, in addition to a *faith*, if we might call it that, in the veracity (or verifiability) of an external world, an Aristotelian empiricist adds a *faith* in the human logical mind. The rules of logic are seen as necessary structures of human thinking, and a good Aristotelian begins with the assumption that these structures are in harmony with reality (which, again, pure empiricists like Hume will call into question). This faith in the correspondence between the workings of the mind and the workings of reality also contributes to the public character of any discourse on experience. All minds work—when working properly— according to the same rules. Additionally, these minds can only work with the material from experience, which reflects a reality that is presumably the same for everyone. One sees Wesley's explicit ownership of these faith assumptions in his frequent assertions that his ideas or interpretations are agreeable to "unprejudiced reason," the generic "man of reason," or to "any reasonable man."[3]

Now, just as reason cannot do anything without the material from experience, so also is there no way to deal with the material of experience except through the exercise of reason. As far as Wesley is concerned, reason is an essential part of life. To Luther's derision of reason in his commentary on Galatians, Wesley responds, "What is reason (the faculty so called) but the power of apprehending, judging, and discoursing? Which power is no more to be condemned in the gross, than seeing, hearing, or feeling." Being the good Aristotelian, Wesley would understand "seeing, hearing and feeling" as avenues experience, and he deliberately sets out reason (the processor) as no more to be condemned than experience (the material processed). To those, like Luther, who would despise or under-value reason, Wesley has this to say in the conclusion to his sermon on the subject:

> Never more declaim in that wild, loose, ranting manner, against this precious gift of God...You see how many admirable ends it answers, were it only in the things of this life: Of what unspeakable use is even a moderate share of reason in all our worldly employments, from the lowest and meanest offices of life, through all the intermediate branches of business; till we ascend to those that are of the highest importance and the greatest difficulty![4]

Interestingly, Wesley will not use same unqualified language in discussing the dependence of experience on reason that he does in outlining the dependence of reason on experience, and this is significant. Still, it is clear that in his mind the two are intimately connected—even a "moderate share of reason" is of "unspeakable use."

So there is a mutual interdependence between reason and experience, but that dependence is, in some sense, lop-sided. Experience is larger than reason, and despite the fact that one cannot reason without the data from experience, one can experience something that one cannot process or talk about.[5] So the relationship between reason and experience is anchored in experience, and that is what keeps Aristotle's system empirical. In describing experience as an encounter with reality, the Aristotelian comes to the encounter with an a priori faith in that reality, a belief in the priority of the reality encountered over the understanding of the one who encounters it. This is the main reason why experience must, in the final analysis, be public, because the reality encountered is not dependent upon the one who encounters it. Private or subjective experience does not exist because private reality does not exist. This foundational assumption is critically important to an Aristotelian worldview, and no Aristotelian understanding of experience can be understood without it.

Having said that, however, we must note that this is primarily an *ontological* observation about the way reason and experience interrelate, a description of temporal priority, as it were. *Epistemologically*, the two cannot be separated so easily. When it comes to the question of knowledge, experience is as dependent upon reason as reason is on experience. If there are things in experience that reason is not sufficient to process, then there is no *other* way for them to be organized, explained, transmitted or otherwise dealt with. There is no other faculty of the mind which can handle them.

Reason can do nothing without material from experience, and experience goes nowhere without the processing power of reason. They are conjoined much like a pipe and the water that flows through it. The water (experience) cannot reach its destination without the pipe (reason), and the pipe is equally useless without the water. But what is that destination, to continue the analogy? Why must reason process the sensory data of experience and to what end is that processing directed? The quote from Wesley's sermon on reason, cited above, gives us the answer—at least as far as Wesley is concerned. One needs reason to process experience so that one can operate back in the realm of experience.

Wesley's Pragmatic Empiricism

With this loop from experience to reason back to experience, the practical bent of Wesley's empiricism comes to the fore. Knowledge, which may be thought of as experience-processed-by-reason (or more simply an *idea*), needs to be useful in order to have value. In other words, it must be able to affect experience. The question of knowledge does not flow in one direction from experience to reason—as is often assumed to be the case with any epistemological investigation of knowledge. Knowledge must also flow from reason to experience.

We have already seen Wesley's practical philosophical bent in examining his reaction to the Scientific Materialism of Bacon and Hobbes, but it is evident in almost every context where he deals with the question of knowledge. Wesley will frequently compare what he calls "speculative knowledge" and its concerns—those that simply remain in the mind—with other knowledge that he calls "practical" or "experimental," which one can apply to life. While he will not always demean the former, he gives clear priority to the latter, as can be seen in a few brief examples.

One clear expression of this priority is found in Wesley's evaluation, recorded in his *Journal,* of a set of listeners in Manchester. Wesley notes, "The speculative knowledge of the truth has ascended here from the least to the greatest. But how far short is this of experimental knowledge! Yet it is a step toward it not to be despised."[6] "Speculative knowledge" here is an understanding of the truth aided by reason, but this is insufficient unless it is applied back to experience in an effectual way, at which point it becomes "experimental knowledge." The former only seems to have value as a step toward the latter, but it is a step that Wesley affirms.

This same truth is evinced in an exhortation Wesley gives in a letter to an unnamed member of his Society: "press on to the mark, to the prize of the high calling of God in Christ Jesus; till you experimentally know all that love of God which passeth all (speculative) knowledge."[7] Again, engaged knowledge is of a higher value than knowledge that merely remains in the mind. This idea of experience-based-on-knowledge (and not just knowledge-based-on-experience) comes through in another letter Wesley writes, this time to Miss Frances Godfrey. Here he notes, "Certainly you have great reason to praise Him who has brought you to the knowledge of his truth; and not only given you to know, but to experience, the truth as it is in Jesus."[8] Here again, experience is something that follows knowledge, and by the way Wesley structures his comment, we can see that it is in some way superior to it.

While these comments show Wesley as valuing proper knowledge as a step toward proper experience, there are other times when he shows how leery he is of speculative knowledge that does not make a practical difference. After discussing one lady's purported private revelations concerning humans as fallen angels, Wesley notes in his *Journal,* "In the evening I earnestly besought them all to keep clear of vain speculations, and seek only for the plain, practical 'truth, which is after godliness.'"[9] Wesley certainly doesn't believe in this lady's revelations, but his critique is more against the uselessness of any idea that cannot be made practical than it is against whatever data the lady was offering. Wesley shows the same attitude when he gives this admonition about his preachers in Pembrokeshire when other preachers were disrupting the people with doctrinal disputes: "Let them never preach controversy, but plain, practical, and experimental religion."[10]

It is Wesley's strong practical concern that makes many epistemological approaches to the question of knowledge and experience in his thought inadequate. Experience is not just a source for knowledge, and Wesley is not that concerned with guaranteeing the veracity of the source—he takes that on faith. He is more concerned with applying knowledge to experience, and he has no more use for speculative theological ideas that make no difference in life than he does for the useless medical theories he condemns in *Primitive Physic*. Experience is important and useful not only because it is the source of knowledge but also because it serves as a testing ground, a crucible, in which knowledge can be tried. And since experience is really an encounter with reality, this testing ground can be understood as the "crucible of life."

A Hermeneutical Circle in Epistemology

Given what we have seen of the interplay in Wesley's thought between reason and experience, we can describe the dynamic between them as a kind of *hermeneutical circle*. The function of each when it comes to knowledge is strongly tied to the function of the other. Reason functions on the data from experience, but it must then re-apply that data to experience for the circle to be complete. In Wesley's vision of Aristotelian empiricism then, reason and experience are not just occasionally complementary, in the sense that they *can* function together; they are necessarily complementary, in the sense that they *cannot* function apart.

It is Wesley's implicit recognition of this interaction that allows him to balance both the active and the passive nature of experience. In its hermeneutical relationship with reason, experience both passively receives data that it transmits to reason and also actively acquires data as reason directs those senses that form the basis of experience. Experience is both the source of knowledge and the arena in which knowledge is applied. It is both our access to the world in which we encounter truth and our laboratory in which we put that truth to the test and put it to work. Even if this circle gives theoretical priority to experience, in practice one cannot approach experience in an unbiased manner. Indeed, Wesley would not have felt such an approach even desirable, given the positive a priori role he gives to reason in shaping experience.

This hermeneutical relationship between experience and reason changes the way Wesley deals with the question of the certainty of our knowledge, though, as we have seen, he is not too bothered by solving that problem. Like Aristotle's other heirs, Wesley will approach reality with two implicit assumptions, two *faiths*, as it were: a faith in a reality that can be encountered and a faith in the ability of reason to process that encounter properly. Unlike Descartes, who doubts his experience on the basis of his reason, or Locke, who seems to doubt logic on the basis of his experience, Wesley will just assume that both are reliable and that they function together.

The acceptance of these assumptions, however, does not make Wesley's approach to knowledge a kind of believe-it-or-not fideism because the dynamic interplay between experience and reason does allow *philosophical* falsification of particular constructions of knowledge. The fact that reason and experience must function together allows for any *dysfunction* to call into question the validity of any given idea. Since reason is concerned with giving direction to experience as well as receiving data from it, experience always serves to test the conclusions drawn by reason. While dissonance between reasoned conclusions and experience would not falsify the validity of either reason or experience, it could falsify any item of knowledge based on that process. So, for example, if one believed—based on experience—that all swans were white, and one were to encounter a black swan, one need not doubt either one's reason or one's previous experience. One simply adjusts one's judgments accordingly, either about this particular creature (maybe it's not a swan) or about swans in general (maybe they are not all white).

Wesley's implicit faith in reality and in reason, then, ground his method much more than they do any of his conclusions, and this will become very important for our reflections on his theological method. *Certainty*—or perhaps better *reliability*—is found not in the source of knowledge but arises out of its application. In other words, reliability comes in the hermeneutical move from reason to experience, in the testing and applying of knowledge in the crucible of life, much more than in the move from experience to reason, as if to say that all sense data by definition is epistemologically reliable (à la Peter Browne).

If one believes in the efficacy of this interaction, then one can begin one's quest for knowledge with even a very weak faith in either experience or in reason. What is required is not that one have full confidence in the nature of ultimate reality or in the ability of the mind to process it perfectly. It is enough that one suspects that there might be a reality out there and that human reason may correspond, however roughly, to that reality. Upon constant application of the data of experience to reason, the conclusions of reason to experience, and the new data from experience thus acquired back to reason—upon the successful workings of the process, in other words—one's faith in experience and in reason is confirmed or deepened. Thus the system can be affirmed even if one's conclusions or data are deemed to be false because the system functions reliably to achieve that falsification.[11]

Thus far, we have described the basic philosophical workings of Wesley's brand of Aristotelian empiricism. They allow for experience to have an active role, they enforce its public character, and they tie its workings to the workings of reason-as-logic. Where Wesley expands on this basic pattern is in his addition of a Christian faith in Scripture to his Aristotelian faith in both reality itself and the correspondence of reason to that reality.

Scripture and the Hermeneutical Circle

If the basic structure of Aristotelian thinking describes Wesley's own approach to knowledge, and we have ample reason to suppose that it does, then the next step in our investigation is to determine how something like Scripture—an authority foreign to Aristotle's understanding of the world—could be integrated into that hermeneutical circle. One would suspect that the addition of any new element could only be justified if either reason needed help in processing data or experience needed help in transmitting data to reason for processing. Since Wesley's faith in reason appears unshakeable, the inclusion of Scripture must come from his conviction of the inadequacy of experience. Wesley believes experience—at least sensory experience—to be inadequate because he also has an unshakeable faith in a world beyond the one that sensory experience can deliver to reason. Some other source of data about that world would be necessary in order for reason to receive and process data about that facet of reality and then (re)direct experience accordingly. So, *from a philosophical point of view*, one could fit Scripture into the Aristotelian framework by making it that description of *trans-sensory* reality.[12]

The addition of any new authority to the hermeneutical circle that reflects Wesley's approach to knowledge would not violate the dynamic of that circle so long as this new authority conforms to the pattern of those elements—reason and experience—that are already in place. Along with his faith in reason and in reality, we can easily add an unshakeable faith in Scripture, and it would become a new axiom of the system (accepted without need of proof) that Scripture does not conflict with reason or experience any more than they might conflict with each other. Scripture also shares the public nature of both reason (as logic) and experience, so one is not admitting an element of a different type, as if one were introducing a subjective dynamic into a system concerned with objective entities. Finally, the dynamic between experience and reason is extended, not disrupted, by the addition of Scripture as a new authority, extended so that data from the trans-sensory world can be interpreted into the world of our experience and used to shape it and data from the sensory world can be used to aid the interpretation of Scripture (as we have already seen Wesley affirm).

We should note at this point that the inclusion of a faith in Scripture as an adjunct to experience need not make Scripture an *epistemic* criterion, in the sense of that it guarantees the certain foundation of one's knowledge. Just as our experience can be doubted, and exercises of reason can be flawed, so, too, interpretations of Scripture can be found inadequate. Wesley's Aristotelian approach is not pre-occupied with grounding knowledge with certainty as much as it is with processing and applying it well. If Scripture can function in that framework, it will only do so on the same terms as reason and experience, based on the same type of faith which admits it to the circle and open to a dynamic interplay with the other two elements. Wesley believes in the reliability of Scripture, but that is different from saying that he believes in Scripture as an independent foundation of knowledge (a point we will explore more fully in the Part Three).

Given the inclusion of Scripture in this dynamic, we can appreciate how a focus on the functioning of a process rather than on the security of a source allows one to begin to engage Scripture with only a relatively weak faith in it (just as one could have a weak faith in our experience of reality or in reason). All that is required to set the process in motion is a commitment to test the reliability of Scripture as an adjunct to experience back in the arena of experience. One need not be a thoroughly convinced biblicist in order to avail oneself of this hermeneutical dynamic. The suspicion that Scripture might be true now and then would be enough to justify one's engagement with it.

It is for this reason—that faiths of this type can start small and be allowed time to deepen and grow—that Wesley kept the membership requirements for participation in his movement so low. "I have never read or heard of," Wesley avers in his *Journal*, "either in ancient or modern history, any other church which builds on so broad a foundation as the Methodists do; which requires of its members no conformity either in opinions or modes of worship, but barely this one thing, to fear God, and work righteousness."[13] The "fearing God" would, in Wesley's thinking, lead one to an appreciation of Scripture; the "working righteousness" is the commitment to actively engage reality and not just learn from it. Even such minimal faith as this is enough to set his dynamic of knowledge in motion.

To allow this philosophical dynamic of knowledge to function in the realm of faith—to add Scripture to the Aristotelian framework of reason and experience—is not, according to Wesley, merely a good idea or an option that some religious folks ought to consider. He considers such an extension to be demanded by the nature of our human limitations. Both times Wesley quotes his Latin empiricist dictum, he does so in sermons, the point of which is precisely to show the obvious limitation of purely sensory experience.

In the sermon "On the Discoveries of Faith," Wesley uses the quote to affirm an empirical stance concerning knowledge over and against a rationalist one, but he then immediately moves to the inadequacy of empiricism if one is to know anything beyond the world of the senses.[14] The first move is necessary because if reason has direct contact with reality or if there are innate ideas about anything stamped on the mind, then there would be no need of anything like faith (or experience or even Scripture) to ascertain spiritual reality—just a serious application of reason. The second move is just as necessary for Wesley unless one wants to restrict the domain of knowledge to things material, which Wesley will not do and assumes his readers would not want to do either.

In the sermon "The Difference Between Walking by Sight, and Walking by Faith," Wesley is even more deliberate in calling attention to the need for something more than a purely material empiricism. After discussing those parts of the material world which are beyond our experience, he aims at the immaterial world.

> But beside these innumerable objects which we cannot see by reason of their distance, have we not sufficient ground to believe that there are innumerable others of too delicate a nature to be discerned by any of our senses? Do not all men of unprejudiced reason allow the same thing,…that there is an invisible world, naturally such, as well as a visible one?[15]

We can, of course, debate whether Wesley's application of reason, which gives us *grounds* to believe in an invisible or spiritual world, is a good application or whether or not his evaluation of the results of *unprejudiced reason* is always true. But at least Wesley understood himself to be working out legitimate, perhaps even philosophical, implications of the nature of classical empiricism and its (to him) inherent insufficiency. From what he indicates, it seems that reason, on the basis of experience, can admit to the fact (or at least the strong possibility) of a world beyond the world of sensory experience, that reason can recognize its inherent limitation, the "end of its tether," as Locke put it. Reason cannot, however, provide anything more than that initial observation, and that is the point of both of these sermons. Something else is needed.

This brings us to the philosophical role of religious faith (something more than a mere grounding assumption) in Wesley's epistemology and to his much touted doctrine of the spiritual senses. That a religious concept like faith could have a philosophical role may seem strange, but it is how Wesley secures a role for Scripture in the Aristotelian dynamic between reason and experience. This is not to say that the concept is a philosophical and not a religious one in Wesley; it most certainly is religious, and as we shall see in the next chapter, its role goes beyond the question of epistemology. But its inclusion here serves as one more indication that Wesley is not all that concerned with maintaining a strict separation between philosophy and religion, and he has no qualms about subsuming the former in ultimate service to the latter.

Both of the key sermons noted above are designed to expound upon that part of reality to which we have access by faith, since we do not have access to it by sensory experience. Faith in Wesley, as has been recognized,[16] takes on the character of experience, and it is closely aligned with his understanding of the so-called spiritual senses, which may supply the defect inherent in physical senses. And so it is to a deeper investigation of this concept that we must now turn.

Notes

1. Cf. *Journal* 7 March 1736 (*Jackson* 1:28), 17 December 1772 (*Jackson* 3:485), and 12 July 1773 (*Jackson* 3:503); Sermons #14 "The Repentance of Believers" §I.2 (*Jackson* 5:157), #27 "Upon our Lord's Sermon on the Mount—Discourse VII" §II.6 (*Jackson* 5:351), #37 "The Nature of Enthusiasm" §38 (*Jackson* 5:478), and #86 "A Call to Backsliders" (*Jackson* 6:514-527), in which the triad forms the very structure of his sermon. The three are also used together in defence of some of the practices of Methodism in *A Plain Account of the People Called Methodists* §II.10, VI.7 (*Jackson* 8:255, 259), and they form the subtitle of *The Doctrine of Original Sin According to Scripture, Reason and Experience* (*Jackson* 9:192-464).

2. Sermon #113 "The Difference Between Walking by Sight, and Walking by Faith" §7 (*Jackson* 7:258). Cf. also Sermon #110 "On the Discoveries of Faith" §1 (*Jackson* 7:231).

3. Cf. among numerous possible examples, *Farther Appeal—Part Three* §IV.14 (*Jackson* 8:245); *Journal* 4 January 1753 (*Jackson* 2:278) and 22 April 1779 (*Jackson* 4:149); Sermon #28 "Upon Our Lord's Sermon on the Mount—Discourse VIII" §20 (*Jackson* 5:372), Sermon #60 "The General Deliverance" §III.11 (*Jackson* 6:252), and Sermon #84 "The Important Question" §III.4 (*Jackson* 6:499). The most striking instance of this is found in Sermon #113 "The Difference Between Walking by Faith, and Walking by Sight" §5 (*Jackson* 7:257), where Wesley unashamedly (though obviously rhetorically) cuts his cloth to fit his measure and will not allow "Materialists" and

"Atheists"—who do not believe as Wesley does in the invisible world—to be considered "men of reason."

4. Sermon #70 "The Case of Reason Impartially Considered" §II.10 (*Jackson* 6:359-60)

5. Cf. Wesley's comment, noted in Chapter Seven, on the world's perception of some true Christians, who enter by "the narrow gate" as "not able to reason either strongly or clearly: They cannot propose an argument to any advantage. They know not how to prove what they profess to believe; or to explain even what they say they experience." (Sermon #31 "Upon our Lord's Sermon on the Mount—Discourse XI" §II.9 (*Jackson* 5:411).

6. *Journal* 5 April 1772 (*Jackson* 3:457).

7. "Letter to a Member of the Society" [9 June 1775] (*Jackson* 12:300).

8. "Letter to Miss Frances Godfrey" [5 August 1788] (*Jackson* 13:42).

9. *Journal* 3 September 1740 (*Jackson* 1:286).

10. *Journal* 1 September 1767 (*Jackson* 3:296).

11. A notable instance of this interplay in Wesley shows up in his basic understanding that conviction of sin comes through preaching the law and that an awareness of grace comes through preaching the gospel. Wesley's original idea is grounded in his reasoned understanding of the function of law and gospel. However, when he encounters in his experience an instance or two of people being convicted of sin by the preaching of the gospel rather than law—that is, when reality challenges his construction of it—he does not dismiss this new experience because it does not fit his pre-existing framework. Instead, he adjusts his framework to account for these new facts. Cf. *Journal* 25 September 1748 (*Jackson* 2:117).

12. This accords with Rivers' observation that, in the end, there are only two sources for knowledge in Wesley, viz. Scripture and experience, though she does not integrate them as we are doing here. (Isabel Rivers, *Reason, Grace and Sentiment. A Study of the Language of Religion and Ethics in England 1660-1780*, vol. 1, *From Whichcote to Wesley* [Cambridge: Cambridge University Press, 1991], 208, 219-20).

13. *Journal* 26 August 1789 (*Jackson* 4:469) and Sermon #115 *The Ministerial Office* §21 (*Jackson* 7:281), written just a few months earlier.

14. Sermon #110 "On the Discoveries of Faith" §1-3 (*Jackson* 7:231-32).

15. Sermon #113 "The Difference Between Walking by Faith, and Walking by Sight" §5 (*Jackson* 7:257).

16. Cf. Matthews, "Reason and Religion," 232-240.

10

The Spiritual Senses

Wesley's doctrine of the "spiritual senses" has often been made to carry tremendous philosophical weight. It has lead some of his readers to posit a crypto-rationalist strand in his thought (by analogy with the Cambridge Platonists, who saw reason as a kind of spiritual sense) and led others to affirm him as an outright enthusiast, one who believes himself immediately inspired by God without the need of any worldly or material intermediary. As we will see, the concept, while important, is not nearly so disruptive of Wesley's approach to knowledge as it might initially appear. Properly understood, and properly contextualized within the larger hermeneutical circle of his epistemology, Wesley's idea of spiritual senses has far more to do with his appreciation of Scripture than it does with any direct epistemological access to the world Scripture describes.

Perhaps the clearest expression of Wesley's belief in spiritual senses can be found in the first part of his *Earnest Appeal to Men of Reason and Religion*. There, after a brief introduction, Wesley lays out his idea, and that in some detail. Since it is a key passage for understanding this idea, we will lay it out in its entirety.

Now faith (supposing the Scripture to be of God) is *pragmaton elegchos ou blepomenon*, 'the demonstrative evidence of things unseen,' the supernatural evidence of things invisible, not perceivable by eyes of flesh, or by any of our natural senses or faculties. Faith is that divine evidence whereby the spiritual man discerneth God, and the things of God. It is with regard to the spiritual world, what sense is with regard to the natural. It is the spiritual sensation of every soul that is born of God...Faith, according to the scriptural account, is the eye of the new-born soul. Hereby every true believer in God 'seeth him who is invisible.' Hereby (in a more particular manner, since life and immortality have been brought to light by the gospel) he 'seeth the light of the glory of God in the face of Jesus Christ;' and 'beholdeth what manner of love it is which the Father hath bestowed upon us, that we,' who are born of the Spirit, 'should be called the sons of God.' It is the ear of the soul, whereby a sinner 'hears the voice of the Son of God, and lives;' even that voice which alone wakes the dead, 'Son, thy sins are forgiven thee.' It is (if I may be allowed the expression) the palate of the soul; for hereby a believer 'tastes the good word, and the powers of the world to come;' and 'hereby he both tastes and sees that God is gracious,' yea, 'and merciful to him a sinner.' It is the feeling of the soul, whereby a believer perceives, through the 'power of the Highest overshadowing him,' both the existence and the presence of Him in whom 'he lives, moves, and has his being;' and indeed the whole invisible world, the entire system of things eternal. And hereby, in particular, he feels 'the love of God shed abroad in his heart.'[1]

In that quote, in an almost systematic way, Wesley lays out this idea of faith as a spiritual sense, comparing it to the work of all the physical senses except smell. He organizes his presentation of what it means to be "born of God" in his sermon "The Great Privilege of Those Born of God" in much the same way, noting the newfound powers of spiritual sight and spiritual hearing given at this new birth.[2] In several other places, Wesley will refer to these "spiritual senses" as "inlets of spiritual knowledge,"[3] and he compares the situation of the "natural man," whose spiritual senses are not awakened, to the state of a supposed toad who had been trapped inside an oak tree for fifty years and so had no sensory experience—and thus no knowledge—of the world beyond.[4]

Spiritual Senses and Epistemology

Given Wesley's consistent and avowed empirical position and the clear and deliberate parallels drawn between spiritual and natural senses, it has become standard practice when speaking of Wesley's doctrine of the spiritual senses to assume that it is an epistemological extension of Wesley's empiricism. Such an extension would allow him to maintain his basic philosophical orientation but not be restricted to the material realm when it come to acquiring epistemologically certain knowledge. This is what George Croft Cell affirms in calling Wesley a "transcendental empiricist,"[5] and the position has been taken up and argued, with varying degrees of nuance by many others. Laurence Wood affirms that "The key to Wesley's epistemology is faith. Here is where all the great metaphysical problems are resolved."[6] In discussing the epistemological importance of "spiritual sense," Mitsuo Shimizu makes the following claim: "The proper kind of religious knowledge Wesley seeks after is not indirect and mediate knowledge inferred from rational discourse, but direct and immediate knowledge derived from sensational evidence; he looks for religious knowledge as sure and certain as that perceived by the physical senses."[7] Matthews essentially agrees with this assessment, although he nuances his claim much more finely than does Shimizu.[8] Rivers will argue that it is precisely this broadening of senses to include the spiritual that separates Wesley's understanding from that of Locke.[9] Even those who will argue for a greater influence of the rationalist/intuitionalist camp in Wesley's thought will end up affirm much the same type of epistemological role, even if they use the terminology of intuition to explain it.[10]

Although this account of Wesley's doctrine of faith and the spiritual senses sounds epistemologically plausible and appears to allow Wesley the best of both worlds (that is, an empirical stance that can still affirm supernatural reality), the fact is that this *epistemologically oriented* perspective on spiritual senses does not cohere with Wesley's own self-understanding. It ignores the very basis for the doctrine in Wesley, Wesley's own aversion to enthusiasm and his approach to Quakerism, and the fact that Wesley himself casts serious doubts on the certainty of knowledge gained from any purely "spiritual impressions."

First of all, as virtually all of the forenamed scholars have noted, Wesley grounds his understanding of faith as a spiritual sense in Scripture. The key verse here is Hebrews 11:1, which in Wesley's Authorized Version reads, "Now faith is the substance of things hoped for, the evidence of things not seen." The language of "evidence of things not seen" or "unseen" is Wesley's preferred language for discussing the reality of faith, and it appears no less than 50 times in his work and in almost every different kind of writing. He defends this understanding of faith by grounding it in Scripture. "The term 'faith' I likewise use in the scriptural sense, meaning thereby 'the evidence of things not seen.' And, that it is scriptural, appears to me a sufficient defence of any way of speaking whatever."[11]

If Wesley's consistent reference to Hebrews does ground his doctrine, and is not simply an oft-employed proof-text, then his understanding of religious faith must be seen as a direct extension of his faith in Scripture. This means that Wesley's discussion of the doctrine of faith as a "spiritual sense," an "evidence" for an invisible world, is not fundamentally grounded in an epistemological need to provide an avenue for reliable or certain religious data to enter the mind to be processed by reason. For Wesley, reliable and certain religious data comes to reason through Scripture. To jump, as many commentators on Wesley are tempted to do, from this statement of faith into the framework of empirical philosophy ignores the scriptural basis of the statement itself. Working out the philosophical implications of the spiritual senses as a new type of sensory data is, then, a category mistake, putting, as it were, "the cart before the horse." It is not Wesley's understanding of faith as a spiritual sense that gives him an avenue of reliable and certain religious knowledge; it is Wesley's faith in Scripture as an avenue of reliable and certain religious knowledge that leads him to understand faith as a spiritual sense.

So, while one may not feel the same way about one's understanding of the spiritual world in the absence of the kind of faith-as-spiritual-sense that Scripture describes, this lack of feeling does not affect the *epistemological* reliability of that understanding. One discovers the reliability of one's understanding and begins to feel certain about it through that second-order move of reapplying reasoned data to experience and finding it fruitful. One does not find certainty merely in the first-order move of faith in the source of that data. And because the only source for data about the invisible world—as far as Wesley is concerned—is Scripture, one cannot understand Wesley's doctrine of faith as spiritual sense apart of his appreciation of Scripture, a point to which we will return shortly.

A second problem with interpreting Wesley's doctrine of the spiritual senses as if it were an epistemological move is that such an approach ignores Wesley's own aversion to enthusiasm and his anxiousness to defend himself against that charge. To interpret his doctrine of spiritual senses as an immediate and epistemically independent *source* of spiritual knowledge opens him to the charge of enthusiasm by his own definition.[12] Enthusiasm, to Wesley,

> May well be accounted a species of madness... a madman draws right conclusions, but from wrong premises. And so does an enthusiast. Suppose his premises true, and his conclusions would necessarily follow. But here lies his mistake: His premises are false...Enthusiasm in general may then be described in some such manner as this: A religious madness arising from some falsely imagined influence or inspiration of God; at least, from imputing something to God which ought not to be imputed to him, or expecting something from God which ought not to be expected from him.[13]

The problem of enthusiasm, at least as Wesley defines it, is precisely the problem of inadequate foundation, of building conclusions on falsely imagined premises rather than real ones.

The chief danger in doing this is that there is no way to dispute with an enthusiast who claims such subjective knowledge. Later in the same sermon, Wesley will comment on how difficult it is to convince such a "religious madman" of his error precisely because he believes himself to have a source of knowledge that can be described as independent and certain (even if Wesley does not use those words):

> Together with pride there will naturally arise [in the enthusiast] an unadvisable and unconvincible spirit. So that into whatever error or fault the enthusiast falls, there is small hope of his recovery. For reason will have little weight with him (as has been frequently and justly observed) who imagines he is led by an higher guide, — by the immediate wisdom of God. And as he grows in pride, so he must grow in unadvisableness and in stubbornness also. He must be less and less capable of being convinced, less susceptible of persuasion; more and more attached to his own judgment and his own will, till he is altogether fixed and immovable.[14]

Wesley will close the sermon with repeated affirmations that the only safe and secure course is to act on "the plain scripture rule, with the help of experience and reason, and the ordinary assistance of the Spirit of God."[15]

If Wesley's doctrine of spiritual senses and faith as "divine evidence" provide one immediate access to the truths of the spiritual realm in a way that parallels the access that one's physical senses provide to the material realm, then it is difficult to see how Wesley is not an enthusiast. One could defend him by saying that he is not imagining what he perceives, that it is not enthusiasm because it is really there, but that is a rather weak epistemological defense, and one that any enthusiast could offer without having to worry about being countermanded.

Related to this point is Wesley's attitude toward Quakers and their idea of "inner light," again making it difficult to cast his doctrine of faith as an epistemological one without making Wesley self-contradictory on the question. While he has nothing but love for individual Quakers and a great admiration for their simplicity, whenever he addresses their doctrine, he always does by consistently opposing any "direct and immediate" moving of the Spirit in the soul of a believer *independent* of the mediating rule of Scripture and reason.

The clearest statement of this can be found in Wesley's "Letter to a Person Lately Joined With the People Called Quakers," in which he lays out what he sees as the chief differences between Quakerism and Christianity. The very first difference he mentions is the role of *revelations* versus Scripture. To Robert Barclay's statement, "These revelations are not to be subjected to the extermination of the Scriptures as to a touchstone," Wesley firmly replies, "Here there is a difference. The Scriptures are the touchstone whereby Christians examine all, real or supposed, revelations. In all cases they appeal 'to the law and to the testimony' and try every spirit thereby."[16] Any direct and immediate spiritual knowledge is a priori constrained by the authority of Scripture and is only allowed to the degree that it corresponds to it.

Just a short while later, in attempting to define the role of the Holy Spirit and the role of Scripture, Wesley again emphasizes the place of Scripture, but that without demeaning the role of the Holy Spirit. Barclay notes, "Yet the Scriptures are not the principal ground of all truth and knowledge, nor the adequate, primary rule of faith and manners. Nevertheless, they are a secondary rule, subordinate to the Spirit. By Him the saints are led into all truth. Therefore the Spirit is the first and principal leader." To this, Wesley replies,

> If by these words 'The Scriptures are not the principal ground of truth and knowledge, nor the adequate, primary rule of faith and manners,' be only meant, that 'the Spirit is our first and principal leader;' here is no difference between Quakerism and Christianity. But there is great impropriety of expression. For though the Spirit is our principal leader, yet He is not our rule at all; the Scriptures are the rule whereby he leads us into all truth. Therefore, only talk good English; call the Spirit our *guide*, which signifies an intelligent being, and the Scriptures our *rule*, which signifies something used by an intelligent being, and all is plain and clear.[17]

Wesley does not doubt that the Holy Spirit is the ultimate source of truth, but he will allow no divorce between that ultimate truth and the role of Scripture. Although the perceptible operation of the Holy Spirit is not the same as the possession by a person of "spiritual senses," the same criteria for immediacy and reliability apply.

A third and related problem with understanding spiritual senses as an epistemological doctrine is that it would then contradict things that Wesley says in other places about the dubious business of using "spiritual impressions" or "inward feelings" as a guide or source of knowledge. The issue here, again, is not whether or not such impressions and feelings exist—Wesley will fight strongly for the existence of such feelings. The issue is whether or not these are valid epistemological criteria. And Wesley's answer to that is a resounding "No!"

In a letter written near the end of his life, Wesley notes,

> A great man observes that there is a three-fold leading of the Spirit. Some He leads by giving them, on every occasion, apposite texts of Scripture; some by

suggesting reason for every step they take, — the way by which He chiefly leads me; and some by impressions: But he judges the last to be the least desirable way; as it is often impossible to distinguish dark impressions from divine, or even diabolical.[18]

In another, slightly earlier letter, discussing the same categorization by Count Zinzendorf, Wesley adds, "I am very rarely led by impressions, but generally by reason and by Scripture. I see abundantly more than I feel. I want to feel more love and zeal for God."[19] Similarly, in a pastoral letter written in the middle of his career, Wesley says, "We know there are divine dreams and impressions. But how easily may you be deceived herein! How easily, where something is from God, may we mix something which is from nature! especially if we have a lively imagination, and are not aware of any danger."[20] Wesley is not denying the existence of such impressions, but he is denying them a role in obtaining certain knowledge. There may, of course, be a distinction between "spiritual impressions" and "spiritual sense," but it is hard to see how such a distinction can be strictly maintained.

In other places, Wesley will warn people of the dangers of relying on "inward feelings," an expression that employs the language of sense. In an early part of his *Journal* he notes to his society,

> I told them, they were not to judge of the spirit whereby any one spoke, either by appearances, or by common report, or by their own inward feelings: No, nor by any dreams, visions, or revelations, supposed to be made to their souls; any more than by their tears, or any involuntary effects wrought upon their bodies. I warned them, all these were, in themselves, of a doubtful, disputable, nature; they might be from God, and they might not; and were therefore not simply to be relied on, (any more than simply to be condemned,) but to be tried by a farther rule, to be brought to the only certain test, the Law and the Testimony.[21]

Over and over again, we see in Wesley a fundamental concern for the priority of Scripture as the only reliable access to *trans-sensory* reality. His doctrine of faith is built on it, and nowhere is any other access to the spiritual realm granted that would supersede it or relegate it to a secondary role. If that is the case, then Wesley's doctrine of faith as spiritual sense cannot be considered an epistemological idea. If it is to have any meaning, it must be contextualized in terms of the hermeneutical dialogue between reason and experience, the latter absolutely governed by the authority of Scripture when it comes to spiritual matters. When we do this, we find a much clearer and more consistent role for the "spiritual senses" than is given by placing them in an epistemological framework.

The real role of faith and the spiritual senses in Wesley is to allow the believe to apprehend the truth of Scripture and to re-apply that truth back into life. The role of faith as the "evidence of things not seen" and the role of spiritual senses as the "seeing eye" or the "hearing ear" is not to be a source of knowledge and grant immediate access to the realm of trans-sensory experience. Instead its role is to grant the believer apprehension of Scripture as the authoritative description of that trans-sensory reality. Religious faith is thus necessary to admit Scripture into the hermeneutical circle of reason and experience and allow reason to accept the data of Scripture as describing that which transcends our physical experience. As we have seen, however, the process is not complete by merely allowing the intellect to grasp the truth of Scripture. Faith is, in Wesley, this assent to spiritual truth, but it is not *just* this assent. Knowledge requires more than the move from experience to reason. Faith is thus also necessary to re-apply one's knowledge back into experience, to allow one to *have* the types of encounters with that trans-sensory reality that are merely *described* in Scripture. And so faith does have a function in contributing to the certainty of knowledge—not because it guarantees the believer an epistemologically unimpeachable perception of spiritual data but because it opens up the possibility of the (re)application of that truth to the realm of experience, which is the only way any certainty can be obtained. All of this is evident when we turn once again to Wesley's own words on the matter.

First of all, the intricate link between faith as spiritual sense and Scripture is evident to even the most casual reader of Wesley. A cursory glance at that quote from the *Earnest Appeal* that we used to introduce Wesley's concept of spiritual senses reveals that the whole section breathes with the language of Scripture, seen in all the quotes within the larger quote. That this is not an isolated incident but quite typical of Wesley can be seen in the following quote from the sermon "The Difference Between Walking by Sight, and Walking by Faith," in which we will add the Scriptures referred to in square brackets.

> How different is the case, how vast the pre-eminence, of them that 'walk by faith!'[2 Cor 5:7] God, having 'opened the eyes of their understanding,' [Eph 1:18] pours divine light into their soul; whereby they are enabled to 'see Him that is invisible,' [Heb 11:27] to see God and the things of God. What their 'eye had not seen, nor their ear heard, neither had it entered into their heart to conceive,' [1 Cor 2:9 quoting Is 64:4] God from time to time reveals to them by the 'unction of the Holy One, which teacheth them of all things.' [conflating 1 Jn 2:20 & 27] Having 'entered into the holiest by the blood of Jesus,' [Heb 10:19] by that 'new and living way,' [Heb 10:20] and being joined unto 'the general assembly and church of the first born, and unto God the Judge of all, and Jesus the Mediator of the New Covenant,' [Heb 12:23-24]— each of these can say, 'I live not, but Christ liveth in me;' [Gal 2:20] I now live that life which 'is hid with Christ in God;' [Col 3:3] 'and when Christ, who is my life, shall appear, then I shall likewise appear with him in glory.' [Col 3:4][22]

Many more such examples could be produced, all with the same general effect. The truths to which faith gives one access are precisely those truths revealed in Scripture and known independently *from no other source*, and Wesley will consistently use the scriptural language to portray them. In all the passages where Wesley employs the idea of spiritual senses and faith as divine evidence, much the same pattern is used. These descriptions are not systematic attempts to synthesize the various passages of Scripture cited; they merely reflect his conviction that only the language of Scripture is adequate for describing spiritual reality and that when one speaks of such, one should "speak as the Oracles of God."[23] Thus, despite the fact that Scripture is not always explicitly referred to, its words are woven into the warp and woof of all that Wesley says may be discovered "in faith."

There are, however, many times when Wesley will explicitly link the role of faith and the spiritual senses with the role of Scripture. One clear instance of this is in that key sermon "On the Discoveries of Faith," to which we have already referred several times in this discussion. Immediately upon pointing out the insufficiency of merely physical senses, Wesley states,

> But the wise and gracious Governor of the worlds, both visible and invisible, has prepared a remedy for this defect. He hath appointed faith to supply the defect of sense; to take us up where sense sets us down, and help us over the great gulf. Its office begins where that of sense ends. Sense is an evidence of things that are seen; of the visible, the material world, and the several parts of it. Faith, on the other hand, is the "evidence of things not seen;" of the invisible world; of all those invisible things *which are revealed in the oracles of God.* But indeed they reveal nothing, they are a mere dead letter, if they are 'not mixed with faith in those that hear them.'[24]

Here Wesley's introduction of the concept of spiritual senses leads immediately to the apprehension of that which God has revealed in Scripture, here called the "oracles of God." It is also clear that the Scriptures themselves are meaningless, "mere dead letter," without the operation of faith.

The same intimate connection can be seen in many other places. In his *Journal* Wesley reflects on the difference between himself and his opponent Dr. Erskine concerning the nature of saving faith. He notes,

> How marvellously small is the difference between us!... I do not quarrel with the definition [of Dr. Erskine] of faith in general, — 'a supernatural assent to the word of God;' though I think 'a supernatural conviction of the truths contained in the word of God' is clearer. I allow, too, that the Holy Spirit enables us to perceive a peculiar light and glory in the word of God, and particularly in the Gospel method of salvation: But I doubt whether saving faith be, properly, an assent to this light and glory. Is it not rather, an assent (if we retain the word) to the truths which God has revealed; or, more particularly, a divine conviction that 'God was in Christ, reconciling the world unto himself?'[25]

In replying to what he sees as inappropriate doctrines in the Roman Catholic Church (such as transubstantiation and purgatory), Wesley notes, "For as all faith is founded upon divine authority, so there is now no divine authority but the Scriptures; and, therefore, no one can make that to be of divine authority which is not contained in them."[26] In confuting Rev. William Law's conception of faith as the desire to move toward God, Wesley counters by stating that faith is "a supernatural, a divine evidence and conviction of the things which God hath revealed in his word; of this in particular, that the Son of God hath loved me and given himself for me."[27] There is, in all these quotes, no possibility of extricating the role of faith as a spiritual sense with the role of faith in enabling reason to apprehend (and apply) the truth of Scripture.

Even in Wesley's own life, a faith in Scripture was temporally prior to his finding what he considered to be full-orbed Christian faith, and the latter he only acquired through a steadfast application of the former. In all of Wesley's accounts of his own faith journey, he emphasizes that it was a faith in the reliability of Scripture that enable him to *experience* faith as the "divine evidence of things not seen." In one such account he notes,

> In 1730 I began to be *homo unius libri*; to study (comparatively) no book but the Bible. I then saw, in a stronger light than ever before, that only one thing is needful, even faith that worketh by the love of God and man, all inward and outward holiness; and I groaned to love God with all my heart, and to serve Him with all my strength.[28]

Without an a priori faith in the reliability of Scripture, Wesley would have never found "that one thing needful." And he assumes that this is not merely a peculiarity of his own experience but something to be found in the nature of the thing. He comments in his important sermon "The Scripture Way of Salvation," "'But what is that faith whereby we are sanctified; — saved from sin, and perfected in love?' It is a divine evidence and conviction, First, that God hath promised it in the Holy Scripture. Till we are thoroughly satisfied of this, there is no moving one step further."[29]

All this is not to say that the spiritual senses in Wesley only allow one to "experience Scripture." Scripture is completely instrumental in Wesley's thought, never an end in itself but always a means,[30] what we have referred to as a description of trans-sensory reality. Ultimately, it is that reality itself that is important and that one must experience (in the second-order sense of moving from reason back to experience). But there is no possible access to this reality which is ever, at any time, completely independent from the a priori affirmation or restraint of Scripture. It is Scripture which provides the avenue of knowledge, and not a supposed direct contact with that reality via one's spiritual senses. Wesley makes this clear in a comment to Dr. Rutherforth concerning the subject of "inward feelings." When asked what he believes on that head he says,

> I answer, (1.) The fruit of his ordinary influences are love, joy, peace, long-suffering, gentleness, meekness. (2.) Whoever has these, inwardly feels them; and if he understands his Bible, he discerns from whence they come. Observe, what he inwardly feels is these fruits themselves: Whence they come, he learns from the Bible.[31]

One's spiritual senses allow one to truly feel the love, joy and peace that are the product of the Holy Spirit's work. Like all feelings in a sense, they are the by-product of a certain type of encounter with reality, but one only *knows* anything about them from the Bible. Wesley explicitly denies any independent epistemic role for these feelings, and it is difficult to see how he could then turn around and grant such a role to any other "spiritual sense" besides these feelings.

Conclusion to Part Two

Wesley's idea (and ideal) of faith, then, is that capacity granted by God to engage ultimate or trans-sensory reality in a way analogous to the way we engage physical reality with our physical senses, but that engagement is always ruled or governed by the role of Scripture. The spiritual senses provide the capacity, but not the content. It is Scripture—and not the spiritual senses—that sets forth the authoritative description of that reality and provides both data about it and the parameters around one's experience once that data is applied. Since both sensory and trans-sensory reality are part of experience, reason has much the same job in both cases, the job of processing the appropriate data from experience and redirecting the results of that processing back to experience, and so on in an ever-cycling hermeneutical circle. That functioning is the same whether material or spiritual truth is at stake.

When it comes to physical reality, the first-order move is for reason to acquire data from the physical senses through one's encounter with reality. In this empirical process, reality is given theoretical priority and is assumed to be objective and available to anyone who has the appropriate senses with which to access it. This, however, is not enough to establish true knowledge. Reason must process these sense-data, upon which there is a second-order move in which that processed data—i.e., knowledge—is re-applied to life. This is where experience acquires its active component and where reason and logic get their a priori role in shaping experiencing, in opening up experience to the possibility of new encounters and closing off the possibility of others. Knowledge, then, is verified if it is effective in shaping experience and falsified if it is not. One's feeling of certainty about any idea arises from its practical efficiency. Truth is discovered in discovering what works, provided, of course, that one's faiths in reality and in the ability of reason to process it are well-placed.[32]

The uniqueness of Wesley's understanding of knowledge is that he allows the very same dynamic to function beyond the realm of the material by adding a faith in Scripture to the abovementioned faiths in reality and in reason. This is why Wesley believes that he can be both firmly rational and firmly scriptural, and why he consistently uses those two concepts to define himself and his vision of Christianity. The two can be understood as a kind of shorthand description of his understanding of knowledge. Wesley needs faith, in his own words, "to perfect my reason, that by the Spirit of God not putting out the eyes of my understanding, but enlightening them more and more, I may 'be ready to give' a clear scriptural 'answer to every man that asketh' me 'a reason of the hope that is in' me."[33] Wesley's spiritual knowledge arises from the same dynamic as does his ordinary knowledge.

Faith, as a spiritual sense, allows reason to acquire the data about that reality from Scripture. This is the first-order move that allows truths about spiritual reality to enter the mind and the mind to *assent* to those truths. Scripture is, in this sense, just as public and objective as the material world, describing a trans-sensory reality that is the same for all. But the interpretation of Scripture by reason through faith is not enough to produce true knowledge. As we shall investigate more deeply in Part Three, Wesley wanted more out of knowledge than *acknowledgement*. Just as ordinary knowledge is incomplete (or even meaningless) unless it can be re-applied to reality, so, too, the spiritual truths that reason has determined based on the data of Scripture must be re-applied to experience to have true value.

This is the role of faith as *trust*. Active experience, in this case, is shaped by the reasoned interpretation of Scripture rather than by the reasoned conclusions from physical sense data alone. It is in this second-order move that Scripture (more properly now the reasoned interpretations of Scripture) acquire their a priori authority over experience. Knowledge based on Scripture opens up possibilities for new encounters and closes off others. Here, too, one discovers reliable interpretations of Scripture in those that work, those that function in experience to shape a life after the pattern described by Scripture.[34] This idea becomes a foundational part of Wesley's theological method, which we will continue to explore in greater detail.

Thus far, we have been attempting to describe the dynamic of Wesley's understanding of knowledge and the role that experience plays as both the source for that knowledge and the arena in which that knowledge is brought to bear—tested, as it were, in the crucible of life. As both the source and the goal of knowledge, experience has a central place in Wesley's thought, but that place is inextricably linked with the roles of reason and Scripture. The functioning of these three together, in what we have described as a hermeneutical circle, forms the basic lines of his approach to the question of knowledge. Given the above construction, we can see that his epistemology addresses the question of certainty or reliability not in speculation about the source of knowledge or the means by which it is accessed but in the practical realm of its application. Through grounding faiths in the priority of reality, in the power of reason to process it, and in the ability of Scripture to provide reliable access to trans-sensory reality, Wesley lays out a religiously oriented view of knowledge that, at the same time, has some philosophical respectability.

This hermeneutical dynamic also allows us to understand both Wesley's view of knowledge and his view of experience in a more or less holistic way. The fact that the dynamic of knowledge remains the same whether one is speaking of sensory or trans-sensory reality mitigates against imposing an artificial dualism onto Wesley's thought, as does his concern that both material and spiritual knowledge be made practical in the same arena of life. Although one might still affirm some kind of epistemological dualism in Wesley—that some knowledge pertains primarily to spiritual and some primarily to material reality—that distinction must been seen as theoretical. In practice, the arena of experience is the same for the application of either physical or scriptural ideas, and thus even the fundamental distinction often drawn between the secular and the sacred becomes tenuous in Wesley. While this will become more important as we explore his theology in the next chapter, the general concern is evident even here, in the more or less doctrinally neutral realm of epistemology.

The dynamic that we have outlined is properly understood to be empirical, and that in a much more Aristotelian than Lockean way. This means that it has strong role for reason which not only feeds off of experience but must necessarily feed into it as well. This combination of empirical and rationalist elements is no great creative synthesis by Wesley but merely a result of his faithful adherence to an Aristotelian worldview. Wesley's creative contribution, if there is one, is that he found a way (in practice at least, even if he does not himself lay out the theory) to fit another authority (namely Scripture) into this philosophical framework without compromising either the religious authority of that Scripture or the philosophical functioning of that framework.

We have described a philosophical structure that Wesley nowhere explicitly lays out but is nonetheless implicit in a broad range of Wesley's thought and seems to be faithful both to his expressed ideas and his implicit concerns. Articulating his implicit understanding in this philosophically explicit way allows us to tie together many important Wesleyan threads concerning Scripture, reason and experience and guard against some historical misunderstandings. Using this framework as a background we are now better equipped to understand the dynamics of Wesley's own theological method and connect that method to contemporary concerns and issues. Having spent two lengthy parts dealing with these more or less philosophical concerns, it is time that we used this background to help us understand the theological concerns that are, after all, the true goal of our research.

Notes

1. *Earnest Appeal* §6-7 (*Jackson* 9:4-5).

2. Sermon #19 "The Great Privilege of Those Born of God" §I.9-10 (*Jackson* 5:226-27).

3. Sermon #9 "The Spirit of Bondage and of Adoption" §I.1 (*Jackson* 5:99) and Sermon #30 "Upon Our Lord's Sermon on the Mount—Discourse X" §17 (*Jackson* 5:400).

4. Sermon #125 "On Living Without God" (*Jackson* 7:349-54).

5. Cell, *Rediscovery*, 93.

6. Laurence Wood, "Wesley's Epistemology," *Wesleyan Theological Journal* 10 (1975): 53.

7. Shimuzu, "Epistemology," 184.

8. Matthews, "Reason and Religion," 296. Cf. also the work of Dreyer, "Faith and Experience," 12-30; Richard Heitzenrater, *Mirror and Memory: Reflections on Early Methodism* (Nashville: Kingswood, 1989), 88; and Theodore Runyon, "The Importance of Experience for Faith" in *Aldersgate Reconsidered*, ed. Randy Maddox (Nashville: Abingdon Press, 1990), 94. Thorsen assumes this epistemological framework without question, but he adds the helpful note that Wesley needs to be approached primarily religiously, and not philosophically, and that Wesley's doctrine of spiritual senses is religiously helpful however philosophically ambiguous it may be (Thorsen, *Wesleyan Quadrilateral*, 182-187). Maddox takes essentially the same position, and his concerns are fundamentally theological not epistemological. By the time he finishes nuancing the concept theologically, he will end up affirming in practice something very close to what we will affirm. However, in so doing, he admits the he reveals more epistemological ambiguities than he solves (Maddox, *Responsible Grace*, 27-28, 32). Hopefully, our

presentation of the spiritual senses in Wesley will allow us to affirm what Maddox does but on a more secure epistemological foundation.

9. Rivers, *Reason, Grace and Sentiment*, 235-36.

10. The most clear expression of this is Albert C. Outler's idea of Wesley's "transempirical intuition" (Albert C. Outler , ed., *The Bicentennial Edition of the Works of John Wesley*, vol. 1, *Sermons III*, Nashville, 1986, 361n.1). Cf. Outler, *John Wesley*, 28. This connection is also made in John English, "John Wesley's Indebtedness to John Norris," *Church History* 60 (1991): 55-69.

11. *Letter to Mr. John Smith* [28 September 1745] §(II)7 (*Jackson* 12:58).

12. Indeed, J. Clifford Hindley is perhaps alone in working out true implications of the doctrine of spiritual senses as a epistemological doctrine, not shying away from charging Wesley with enthusiasm as other commentators, ones more anxious to protect Wesley's reputation, are wont to do. Cf. Hindley, *Philosophy of Enthusiasm*.

13. Sermon #37 "The Nature of Enthusiasm" §11,12 (*Jackson* 5:469-70).

14. Ibid. §31 (*Jackson* 5:476).

15. Ibid. §38 (*Jackson* 5:478).

16. "A Letter to a Person Lately Joined with the People Called Quakers" [10 February 1748-9] (*Jackson* 10:178).

17. Ibid. Emphasis in original.

18. "Letter to Freeborn Garrettson" [15 July 1789] (*Jackson* 13:74). Note Wesley's self-identification as a man led chiefly by divinely guided reason.

19. "Letter to Mrs. Mortimer" [24 February 1786] (*Jackson* 13:66).

20. "Letter to Mrs. R—" [28 June 1766] §3 (*Jackson* 12:266).

21. *Journal* 22 June 1739 (*Jackson* 1:206).

22. Sermon #113 "The Difference Between Walking by Sight, and Walking by Faith" §13 (*Jackson* 7:260).

23. This quote from 1 Pet 4:11 is one of Wesley's explicit principles in speaking about spiritual reality, and he refers to it numerous times throughout his work. Cf. among others, *Journal* 18 July 1765 (*Jackson* 3:230) and 2 August 1789 (*Jackson* 4:467); Sermon #36 "The Law Established Through Faith—Discourse 2" §I.1 (*Jackson* 5:459); Sermon #49 "The Cure of Evil Speaking" §I.2 (*Jackson* 6:117); "Preface to the Second Series of Sermons" §6 (*Jackson* 6:188); and Sermon #117 "On Knowing Christ After the Flesh" §9 (*Jackson* 7:294).

24. Sermon #110 "On the Discoveries of Faith" §4 (*Jackson* 7:232). Emphasis added.

25. *Journal* 1 September 1769 (*Jackson* 3:377).

26. *A Roman Catechism, Faithfully Drawn Out of the Allowed Writings of the Church of Rome, with a Reply Thereto* §I.Q6 (*Jackson* 10:91).

27. *An Extract of a Letter to the Reverend Mr. Law* [6 January 1756] §II.4 (*Jackson* 9:496)

28. *Journal* 14 May 1765. (*Jackson* 3:213). Cf. also Wesley's chronicle of the events leading up to and immediately following his so-called "Aldersgate Experience" (*Journal* 24 May 1738 [*Jackson* 1:91-104]), in which Wesley tells his own spiritual story very much in terms of his own deeper understanding and finally experiencing of the truth of Scripture.

29. Sermon #43 "The Scripture Way of Salvation" §III.14 (*Jackson* 6:52).

30. So Wesley will make comments like the following, from the Preface to his first volume of sermons: "I want to know one thing, — the way to heaven; how to land safe on that happy shore. God himself has condescended to teach the way: For this very end he came from heaven. He hath written it down in a book. O give me that book! At any price, give me the book of God! I have it: Here is knowledge enough for me. Let me be *homo unius libri*" ("Preface" to *Sermons on Several Occasions* §5 [*Jackson* 5:3]). Cf. also his comment on 2 Tim 3:16, where he explains the phrase "all Scripture is

profitable" as "a means to this end, 'that the man of God may be perfect, thoroughly furnished to all good works'" [*Journal* 26 June 1740 (*Jackson* 1:279)].

31. *A Letter to the Rev. Dr. Rutherforth* [28 March 1768] §III.1 (*Jackson* 14:354).

32. This implicit epistemology seems very similar to the way Imre Lakatos describes the functioning of theory and experiment in science. New ideas take over from old as they function better in the process of acquiring and applying knowledge. This ever-circling dynamic gives one all the scientific certainty about any scientific theory that one can ever get, and the process has a phenomenal degree of integrity even though various theories and constructions of knowledge come and go. Cf. Imre Lakatos, "Falsification and the Methodology of Scientific Research Programmes," in Imre Lakatos and A. Musgrave, eds., *Criticism and the Growth of Knowledge: Proceedings of the International Colloquium in the Philosophy of Sciences, London 1965*, vol. 4 (Cambridge: Cambridge University Press, 1976), 91-196.

33. *Journal* 28 November 1750 (*Jackson* 2:216).

34. Thus Colin Williams is protecting Wesley a little too much from himself when he says, "In Wesley experience is not the test of truth, but truth the test of experience" (Williams, *Wesley's Theology*, 34). In fact, both of those statements are true, and it is in elucidating Wesley's dynamic understanding of knowledge that we are able to see how that is possible.

Part Three

11

From Experience to Scripture: Experience as Interpretive Tool

Having contextualized Wesley in his philosophical milieu and worked out the implications of his implicit understanding of the nature of knowledge and the dynamics between reason, experience and Scripture, we have sufficient general background to move on to more specific concerns. The one that interests us most is the way in which Wesley's general understanding of knowledge influenced the construction of that particular branch of knowledge we will label *theological:* knowledge of God, of the spiritual realm, and, in Wesley's mind at least, of its impact on the world of physical experience. The dynamic construct we developed in Part Two—the hermeneutical circle between reason and experience-authoritatively-informed-by-Scripture—will be of real use only if it can help us to better understand and appreciate the way in which Wesley used experience in the formation and application of his theology. Bringing out those implications is the purpose of Part Three.

Part Three will be organized into four chapters. The first two are devoted to analyzing the dynamics of Wesley's theological method itself, using our hermeneutical circle as a heuristic device to show how the relationship between Scripture and experience (aided by reason) becomes the central feature of the way Wesley formulates theology. This chapter will address what we will call the first-order move, the move in the hermeneutical circle that deals with the acquisition of data from Scripture with the help of experience. Chapter 12 will then cover the second order move, the move in the hermeneutical circle that re-applies reasoned constructions (i.e., interpretations of Scripture) back to experience. Both of these chapters will focus on the analysis of key texts, with notes that show how the dynamics contained in those specific passages can also be found in many other places in Wesley's writings.

Once we have seen how Scripture and experience function together in Wesley's theology, Chapter 13 will address the concerns about religious experience that have become important since Wesley's day. Here we will investigate both individual and communal facets of religious experience in order to lay the groundwork for a dialogue between Wesley's ideas and those engaged in modern debates on the subject.

In light of these methodological and content concerns for the use of experience, the final chapter in Part Three will discuss more broadly Wesley's entire theological method. Here we will deal in greater depth with the way Wesley relates his scripturally-informed Aristotelian epistemology to the other facets of Wesley's theological method, re-examining the well-known Wesleyan Quadrilateral, the now standard way of referring to the interplay of reason, experience, tradition and Scripture in Wesley's theological method.

The Beginning of a Circle

In exploring the close link between experience and Scripture in Part Two, we focused on how Wesley accommodated his implicitly Aristotelian understanding of knowledge to his religious faith in the Scriptures. In order for us to understand the full extent to which Wesley relied on experience in the construction of *theological* knowledge, we will need to explore a bit further the connection between experience and Scripture, both the way experience serves the interpretation of Scripture and the way in which Wesley hoped proper interpretation of the Scripture would shape experience.

The hermeneutical circle we used to describe Wesley's approach to knowledge can be seen as consisting of two movements, separable in theory however inseparable in practice they might be. We will use these movements to organize our exploration of the interplay of experience and Scripture for theology. The first-order move is that of acquiring the requisite data upon which to construct theological knowledge. As one may quickly see once a discussion of these issues is begun, the interrelationship between experience and Scripture in Wesley looks complicated without an awareness of the ever-cycling dynamic that we explored above.

First of all, if Scripture functions as the authoritative description of trans-sensory reality, a reality to which the ordinary avenues of experience have no clear access, then when our hermeneutical circle begins to acquire data about that reality, Scripture takes the place of experience as the *theoretical* starting point. The starting point is only theoretical, however, because no one approaches the Scripture from an unbiased or *un-experienced* perspective. The hermeneutical circle is always at work, and one cannot stop it merely because it becomes inconvenient. So even though Scripture may serve as the bedrock, the foundation, upon which all theology is built, it may take some experiential digging to get down to this foundation. We will return to this point shortly.

Because of the very nature of trans-sensory reality, theology *as knowledge* does not rest upon one's own experience. As far as Wesley is concerned, this type of knowledge cannot begin in our encounter with physical reality but must begin in revelation, in those testimonies to the encounter of that trans-sensory reality with our physical reality, to which—again according to Wesley—one only has reliable or definitive access through the Scripture. This odd substitution of Scripture for experience in Wesley's otherwise Aristotelian understanding of knowledge is the natural result of the inability of ordinary or sensory experience to convey accurate data about the spiritual realm to reason and the lack of any innate knowledge about God stamped on the human mind.[1]

The inclusion of Scripture into his hermeneutical circle of knowledge is in some sense mandated by the nature of the other components of that circle and

Wesley's unshakeable belief in a world beyond our physical one. This move, however, raises some interesting questions. First of all, what does this mean for the possibility of "natural theology" in Wesley? Second, if Scripture grounds theological knowledge, what is the role of experience in *approaching* Scripture? Since Scripture can only come to us as it is part of our experience, we cannot simply eliminate any experience prior Scripture or pretend that Scripture can be read in an absolutist way, divorced from the experiences of the people who both read it and wrote it. As we examine the answer to these questions in Wesley, we will begin to see how his implicit epistemology reveals itself at every turn.

Natural Theology in Wesley

If Scripture is the ultimate ground for true religious knowledge, then, for Wesley, there is no real possibility of anything like a *natural theology*, a theology that would take as its starting point something present in physical experience and could be processed by unaided reason into true knowledge of the spiritual realm. While Wesley will occasionally make rhetorical comments that suggest one can learn some things about God outside of what is revealed in Scripture, these remarks need to be understood in light of his more pervasive and typical idea that physical experience in itself cannot give one real (i.e., useable) understanding of God. Where Wesley admits to such extra-scriptural knowledge of God, he always does so to point out the insufficiency of such knowledge.

For example, Wesley will allow reason to conclude, based on physical experience, *that* there is a Creator, based on the mere fact of creation. But he immediately affirms that such information cannot be applied to our life and so is, in Wesley's way of viewing knowledge, useless. In his *Farther Appeal*, he notes:

> I grant, the existence of the creatures demonstratively shows the existence of their Creator. The whole creation speaks that there is a God. But that is not the point in question. I know there is a God. Thus far is clear. But who will show me what that God is? The more I reflect the more convinced I am, that it is not possible for any or all the creatures to take off the veil which is on my heart, that I might discern this unknown God; to draw the curtain back which now hangs between, that I may see Him which is invisible...I want to know this great God who filleth heaven and earth...and yet I am no more acquainted with him, than with one of the inhabitants of Jupiter or Saturn. O my friend, how will you get one step farther, unless God reveal himself to your soul?[2]

Knowing *that* there is a God is insufficient for the human soul unless one can know *who* that God is, and here Wesley is explicit that only God's self-revelation, and no natural theology, can fill that void.[3]

Some have argued that Wesley would have allowed for a knowledge of God's attributes known only through reason based on a remark he makes in one of his sermons on the Sermon on the Mount, but the arguments are based on a dubious reading of that sermon. Wesley states, "The name of God is God himself; the nature of God, so far as it can be discovered to man. It means, therefore, together with his existence, all his attributes or perfections," upon which he then lists those perfections, including God's eternity, fullness of being, omnipresence, wisdom and his "His Trinity in Unity, and Unity in Trinity, discovered to us in the very first line of his written word." [4] The argument[5] that Wesley would allow such things as God's attributes to be known via natural theology rests on a misreading of Wesley's use of the word *discover* as if it meant "learn by oneself." Wesley's actual intent in that sermon is to say that these are the things which are knowable about God *at all* by human beings, all else about God being far beyond our meager comprehension. He assumes, however, that they are knowable from Scripture, not from experience. His language suggests that these things are dis-covered *to* man (i.e., un-covered or revealed to him), not discovered *by* him, (i.e., learned independently). One can see that this is the case from the fact that Wesley includes God's Trinity on his list of attributes and uses the word for his (admittedly dubious) reading of the first words of Genesis. And Trinity is one doctrine that most agree must come from revelation if it is to come to humankind at all.

One final remark of Wesley that is sometimes cited as the proof for a place for natural theology in his thought is found in a letter he wrote to Dr. John Robertson, in response to the latter's annotations of Dr. Andrew Ramsay's *Philosophical Principles of Natural and Revealed Religion explained and unfolded in a General Order*. There he argues against Ramsay in saying, concerning the idea of God, "that the meanest plant is a far stronger proof hereof, than all Dr. [Samuel] Clarke's or the Chevalier's [i.e. Ramsay's] demonstrations." Maddox says, concerning this statement, "In this retort, Wesley joined the growing ranks of his contemporaries who favored 'scientific' evidence about God, arguing that the evident order in creation required a Designer (i.e., a teleological argument for God)."[6]

While this might be an appealing thought to some and could be used to demonstrate some commonality between Wesley and a whole host of modern, philosophical approaches to theology, to understand this remark as an endorsement of natural theology in Wesley is to stretch the comment beyond what Wesley intended. To see that, we need only put the quote in its larger context:

> The two first books [of Ramsay's work], although doubtless they are a fine chain of reasoning, yet gave me the less satisfaction, because I am clearly of Mr. H—'s judgment, that all this is beginning at the wrong end; that we can have no idea of God, nor any sufficient proof of his very being, but from the creatures; and that the meanest plant is a far stronger proof hereof, than all Dr. Clarke's or the Chevalier's demonstrations. Among the latter, I was surprised to find a demonstration of the manner how God is present to all beings; (page 57;) how he begat the Son from all eternity; (page 77;) and how the Holy Ghost proceeds from the Father and the Son. (Page 80.)...How much better to keep to his own conclusion, (page 95,) 'Reason proves that this mystery is possible!' Revelation assures us that it is true; Heaven alone can show us how it is.[7]

The entire quote reveals two important things about Wesley's approach to any supposed natural theology. First of all, Wesley comment on the "meanest plant" is in the context of a question of methodology. What Wesley is saying is that a rationalist approach, which deduces truths from general propositions, is inadequate to addressing the question of God, and in opposition to this he clearly affirm the opposite (i.e. empirical) stance—that one can only argue inductively, from the particular to the general, from the creature to the Creator. That is why the "meanest plant" is a *stronger* proof than the rational arguments of Ramsay and Clarke. This accords with what we saw Wesley conceding earlier, how the fact of a creation may lead us to the conclusion that there is a Creator.

This, however, does not mean that, in itself, such a plant is anything like a strong or useful proof of what we really need to know about God, as is evident from Wesley's subsequent remarks. The work of reason, even when re-oriented to focus on the material of experience rather than rationalist postulates, cannot provide anything like *proof* but only open up *possibility*. Thus Wesley affirms Ramsay's conclusion that "Reason proves that this mystery is possible," but he immediately adds that it is only through revelation that one has proof, that one may affirm that it is true, and even then no one can know the manner in which it is true, as that is something beyond the realms of merely human knowledge. That puts Wesley right back to the position we cited earlier, that whatever one can learn from creation, it is too little to be useful.

So, then, there seems to be no place in Wesley for natural theology, theology built fundamentally on the material of experience.[8] Natural experience is unable to serve as a *source* for knowledge of God, a place from which theologically sound data about the invisible world may be acquired. For Wesley, this methodological stance is dictated by a theological conclusion, namely his understanding of original sin. Wesley believed human beings to be both incapable of knowing—and even unwilling to know—anything about God until God begins to open up their spiritual senses, which, as we noted earlier, means teaching them to attend to the truth of Scripture. However, as the above quote indicates, this does not mean that there is no place for reflection on experience at the beginning of theology. Wesley affirms that experience can play a role, but that role is not to give us knowledge. Rather reasoned reflection on experience provides a space of possibility, opens up a place in our experience for the truly foundational role of revelation. It is, then, to explore that role in Wesley that we now turn.

Experience as A Priori to Scripture

Even though Scripture serves as the only reliable *source* of knowledge about trans-sensory reality, there is yet a role for experience to play in getting to that source. Given what we have seen of the hermeneutical functioning of reason, experience and Scripture, this is something we might almost expect, and Wesley's own work bears it out quite well.

Wesley will appeal to experience in order to help other people realize what he himself had come to realize, namely that a thorough, experience-based, rational understanding of physical reality opens up the possibility for or—even stronger—demands that we recognize the ultimate insufficiency of knowledge confined solely to that reality. One can use one's experience of this world as evidence that something more than this experience is needed. This can be seen at the general level, in appeals concerning the need for Scripture or for religion in general, or on more particular levels, concerning the need for religious explanations of natural phenomena or human behavior.

In his *Earnest Appeal*, after introducing the idea of spiritual senses (which we saw in the previous chapter), Wesley appeals to the experience of his reader to establish that such faith as he expounds is not—indeed cannot be—a humanly produced or otherwise this-worldly thing. He asks,

> May not your own experience teach you this? Can you give yourself this faith? Is it now in your power to see, or hear, or taste, or feel God? Have you already, or can you raise in yourself, any perception of God, or of an invisible world?...[I]s there any power in your soul whereby you discern either these, or Him that created them? Or, can all your wisdom and strength open an intercourse between yourself and the world of spirits? Is it in your power to burst the veil that is on your heart, and let in the light of eternity? You know it is not. You not only do not, but cannot, by your own strength, thus believe. The more you labour so to do, the more you will be convinced 'it is the gift of God.'"[9]

Here Wesley appeals to experience to open up a place for the idea of faith as "a gift of God." Note that his appeal to experience in this case is not designed to give content to a religious or theological idea but merely to open up the space in this life for scriptural content (which here comes from Eph 2:8). Experience gives us sufficient knowledge of this world to point to a world beyond, but it does not serve as a source for knowledge of that world. All that experience can do, and indeed must do, in cases like this is point to the gap, to the inadequacy of purely human thought and endeavor, and thus to the necessity of God's work. In terms of our knowledge, experience here functions to point out ignorance, not to provide content. It clears the way for an appreciation and apprehension of the truth of Scripture.

Much the same idea can be seen in the sermon "The Case of Reason Impartially Considered." Wesley appeals to experience, both his and that of his reader, to establish that reason cannot produce faith, which means it must come from some other source.

> Many years ago I found the truth of this by sad experience. After carefully heaping up the strongest arguments which I could find, either in ancient or modern authors, for the very being of a God, and (which is nearly connected with it) the existence of an invisible world, I have wandered up and down, musing with myself: "What, if all these things which I see around me, this earth and heaven, this universal frame, has existed from eternity?...How am I sure that this is not the case; that I have not followed cunningly devised fables?" — And I have pursued the thought, till there was no spirit in me, and I was ready to choose strangling rather than life. But in a point of so unspeakable importance, do not depend upon the word of another; but retire for awhile from the busy world, and

make the experiment yourself. Try whether your reason will give you a clear satisfactory evidence of the invisible world. After the prejudices of education are laid aside, produce your strong reasons for the existence of this. Set them all in array; silence all objections; and put all your doubts to flight. Alas! you cannot, with all your understanding...[10]

Experience forms an important part of Wesley's general appeal concerning the necessity of faith, and he believes in the public nature of experience strongly enough to encourage his readers to seek in their own experience what Wesley learned from his. Here, as above, all that experience can do is point out a lack. Throughout that sermon, Wesley will counterpoise that lack with biblical phrases describing the reality of faith (as well as hope and love). Experience can provide none of the content, but it seems to be an important part of opening up the individual to receive the content of Scripture. In other words, experience is allowed to point to the questions for which Scripture will give the answers, and so it does and must have an important function in admitting Scripture into one's circle of knowledge. Of course, this does not mean we start with experience, since, unaided by the Holy Spirit (about whom we learn from Scripture), experience might not lead us to ask the right questions.

In his *Journal*, Wesley will employ a similar technique, using experience to open up questions regarding the sufficiency of a simply materialistic worldview. He enjoys relating phenomena that science is unable to explain. In this way, experience points out the inadequacy of mere experience for true knowledge of reality.

One Christmas, Wesley records an incident of a miraculous healing as a result of prayer. He writes,

The Physician told me he could do no more; Mr. Meyrick could not live over the night. I went up, and found them all crying about him; his legs being cold, and (as it seemed) dead already. We all kneeled down, and called upon God with strong cries and tears. He opened his eyes, and called for me; and, from that hour, he continued to recover his strength, till he was restored to perfect health. — I wait to hear who will either disprove this fact, or philosophically account for it.[11]

Here Wesley's closing appeal points both to the certainty of the experience (i.e., no one can disprove it) and the inadequacy of philosophical or non-supernatural explanations for that experience.

The same approach can be seen in the following account of something that happened while Wesley was preaching in Bristol.

About the middle of the discourse, while there was on every side attention still as night, a vehement noise arose, none could tell why, and shot like lightning through the whole congregation. The terror and confusion were inexpressible. You might have imagined it was a city taken by storm. The people rushed upon each other with the utmost violence; the benches were broke in pieces; and nine-tenths of the congregation appeared to be struck with the same panic. In about six minutes the storm ceased, almost as suddenly as it rose; and, all being calm, I went on without the least interruption. It was the strangest incident of the kind I ever remember; and I believe none can account for it, without supposing some preternatural influence. Satan fought, lest his kingdom should be delivered up.[12]

Again, Wesley records an experience and draws attention to the inability of natural categories to explain it. In this case, he deliberately follows this up with his own, Scripture-based explanation, that Satan was at work. He expects that his readers will be more receptive to his supernatural explanation when they perceive, on the basis of experience, the inadequacy of a natural one.

Wesley's reliance on experience in these cases, as well as in others, points yet again to his strong faith in the objective and public nature of reality. He is willing to wager, as it were, that the outcome of any individual's experience or analysis of experience will match his own. In many of these cases, he immediately juxtaposes the results of that experience (i.e., the realization of one's ignorance) with the content of Scripture. In Wesley's appeal, experience provides the space, Scripture the content to fill it up. He uses the experience of this world to open up the possibility of an encounter with the world beyond. The two dovetail so neatly in Wesley's thought that it is difficult to drive a wedge between them. Experience and Scripture in these cases are essentially complementary. Just as we saw in Part Two that experience is bounded by an a priori faith in Scripture, so an encounter with the truth of Scripture is conducted in the space created by experience. But of course, Wesley is only aware of the need to create such a space in the experience of others because of what he has read in Scripture, which had shaped his own experience—the hermeneutical circle at work.

In addition to these general appeals, Wesley will also appeal to experience to open up the space for biblical content in specific matters of doctrine. Wesley will use this kind of appeal particularly in those cases where he feels that Scripture has not been given enough space or where a doctrine he feels to be scriptural is being discounted or challenged. In these cases as well, he will appeal to experience prior to his appeal to Scripture but only for the purpose of clearing away obstacles to belief and establishing the need for revealed truth on the subject.

Perhaps the best example of this kind can be seen in Wesley's treatment of the doctrine of original sin. It is one of the doctrines that Wesley believed to be foundational to Christian understanding,[13] and so when it was challenged, particularly by Dr. Jeremy Taylor's *Doctrine of Original Sin*, Wesley felt it his duty to respond. His responses take the form of both a tract and a sermon, and in both of these the interplay between experience and Scripture is instructive. The tract is more relevant to our present exploration of the way in which experience pre-informs the reading of Scripture, while the sermon focuses on how experience confirms what Scripture teaches (which we will examine below).

Wesley entitles his response to Dr. Taylor as *The Doctrine of Original Sin According to Scripture, Reason, and Experience*, the subtitle placing Scripture before reason and experience. The tract itself, however, begins with an analysis that focuses on experience. Wesley is concerned to trace the history of humankind in such a way that humanity's propensity to evil is set in the strongest light and so cast doubts on Taylor's assertion that humanity is essentially good. He does begin with Scripture, but only because Scripture provides the only historical account we have of what people were like before the Flood. He then moves on to analyses of ancient history, both of Israel (again from Scripture) and of other parts of the ancient world, proceeding thence to an analysis of the current state of humankind (non-religious, Muslim, and Christian) and ultimately making inquiries about his readers' own individual human experience. All along he reinforces the idea that experience points to the pervasively wicked state of the human race.[14] He sums up the obviousness of this wickedness, along with a few choice Latin quotes, by saying,

> It may be remarked, that this is the plain, glaring, apparent condition of human kind. It strikes the eye of the most careless, inaccurate observer, who does not trouble himself with any more than their outside...This is the plain, naked fact, without any extenuation on the one hand, or exaggeration on the other. The present state of the moral world is as conspicuous as that of the natural.[15]

While Wesley himself would not deny (as his sermon on the subject makes clear[16]) that his perception of the wickedness of the world is pre-informed by his understanding of the scriptural doctrine of original sin, it is interesting to note in this account that Wesley uses the religious language of sin very sparingly. It crops up in a couple of biblical references, and perhaps a couple of other places, but for the most part he uses moral rather than religious language in his description of the state of the world. In that, he is asking his reader to agree with his moral analysis of human experience first. Only then, once this moral ground is established, does Wesley move his reader to the scriptural (i.e., religious) explanation of the phenomenon, which is the subject of Part Two of his tract.

Wesley's arrangement of this tract is both a rhetorical and a methodological move and needs to be understood as such.[17] It is a rhetorical move because he is addressing an audience that may not fully accept the authority of Scripture to decide the truth or falsity of the doctrine of original sin. And so he begins with an authority that they would accept—namely experience—even though he feels that his own views on the subject were grounded in Scripture. However, to dismiss this arrangement as simply rhetorical and thus not informative for Wesley's theological method is to ignore the way in which he employs experience in the construction of knowledge. Wesley uses experience to open up the space for his interpretation of the scriptural doctrine of original sin. While it is true that he deliberately and rhetorically moves his audience in that direction, the very fact that he *can* do so reveals his faith in the power and importance of experience. Wesley might prefer that his readers accept the veracity of Scripture a priori, but if they will not, he can use their experience to prepare them to do so.

This same technique is found in several other places with much the same results.[18] Even Wesley's rhetorical moves are based on his implicit understanding of the dynamic of knowledge. Scripture and experience seem to be inextricably linked in his thought, since he can, in his didactic writing, use one to influence the other. In all these cases, a scriptural doctrine or understanding is the clear goal of Wesley's pedagogy, but in each of them experience plays a significant role in getting to that goal.

That this is not just a theoretical but also a practical matter for Wesley can be seen by tracing Wesley's own spiritual journey, especially the part leading up to what happened at Aldersgate. It was part of Wesley's own experience that he could not produce a fully effective Christian faith in his own life by merely working at it, and he offers up this experience in his *Journal* so that others may reflect on it as well. No matter what he tried, as he notes of his life at Oxford before going to Georgia, he could not bridge the gap between his experience and the kind of faith he desired.

> I began observing the Wednesday and Friday Fasts, commonly observed in the ancient Church; tasting no food till three in the afternoon. And now I knew not how to go any farther. I diligently strove against all sin. I omitted no sort of self-denial which I thought lawful: I carefully used, both in public and in private, all the means of grace at all opportunities. I omitted no occasion of doing good: I for that reason suffered evil. And all this I knew to be nothing, unless as it was directed toward inward holiness. Accordingly this, the image of God, was what I aimed at in all, by doing his will, not my own. Yet when, after continuing some years in this course, I apprehended myself to be near death, I could not find that all this gave me any comfort, or any assurance of acceptance with God. At this I was then not a little surprised; not imagining I had been all this time building on the sand, nor considering that 'other foundation can no man lay, than that which is laid' by God, 'even Christ Jesus.'[19]

All that Wesley's own experience could provide for him was insufficient, and he articulates his experience as an experience of *lack,* of *want.* This reaches a low-point after he returns from his abortive mission to Georgia, where we find Wesley in a state of near despair over what he *lacked* in his Christian life. The closing entry of his first *Journal* typifies his feelings.

> If it be said, that I have faith, (for many such things have I heard, from many miserable comforters,) I answer, So have the devils, — a sort of faith; but still they are strangers to the covenant of promise. So the apostles had even at Cana in Galilee, when Jesus first 'manifested forth his glory;' even then they, in a sort, 'believed on him;' but they had not then 'the faith that overcometh the world.' The faith I want is, 'a sure trust and confidence in God, that, through the merits of Christ, my sins are forgiven, and I reconciled to the favour of God.' I want that faith which St. Paul recommends to all the world, especially in his Epistle to the Romans: That faith which enables every one that hath it to cry out, 'I live not; but Christ liveth in me; and the life which I now live, I live by faith in the Son of God, who loved me, and gave himself for me.' I want that faith which none can have without knowing that he hath it; (though many imagine they have it, who have it not).[20]

That was the end of January 1738. Over the next few months, Wesley's continued encounters with Peter Böhler convinced him more and more of a lack that he had in his own experience. This lack both drove him to the Scriptures and made him receptive to Böhler's interpretation of them. His entry for 23 March 1738 makes this very clear.

I met Peter Böhler again, who now amazed me more and more, by the account he gave of the fruits of living faith, — the holiness and happiness which he affirmed to attend it. The next morning I began the Greek Testament again, resolving to abide by 'the law and the testimony;' and being confident, that God would hereby show me, whether this doctrine was of God.[21]

Once Wesley is convinced of the reality of such faith, he begins to investigate the particulars of it, such as its instantaneous nature.[22] In each case, his experience compels him to search again the Scriptures, until at last his experience *confirms* that which he had already become *convinced* Scripture taught. This was how Wesley found his faith, and because he believed that the realities he so encountered were the same for everyone, it was natural for him to believe that others could find faith in the same way as well. He encourages this interplay between experience and Scripture not by making his own experience at Aldersgate paradigmatic for his followers—he hardly refers to it again after his initial reflection in the *Journal*—but by faithfully employing in his ministry the preparatory work of experience to Scripture that he found to be fruitful in his own life.

Seeing that Wesley uses experience to open the door for Scripture does not, however, prove that experience is always necessary for the construction of theology. It could be that this first-order move is only a stop-gap measure, needed only where Wesley encounters people who do not come with an already functioning faith in Scripture. However, since no one is born with a faith in Scripture, that faith can only arise in one place—experience. And so recognizing this first-order move is important even when one is doing theology in context where everyone begins the discussion by accepting a faith in Scripture. What kind of faith that is and how far it extends can be understood—in some measure at least—as a product of experience. Wesley understands and practices this well, and he sets an example for his theological inheritors to take seriously. Having a theological conversation need not mean beginning with Scripture, but we can confidently offer the truth that we believe God has revealed only if we get there eventually.

This first-order move, however, shows only half of the relationship between experience and Scripture in Wesley. It is in examining the second-order move, the move which takes reasoned interpretations of Scripture and deploys them back into experience, that we see the real power that experience plays in Wesley's theological method, and so it is to that exploration that we must now turn.

Notes

1. Cf. Sermon #95 "On the Education of Children" §5 (*Jackson* 7:89), where Wesley notes, "After all that has been so plausibly written concerning 'the innate idea of God;'

after all that has been said of its being common to all men, in all ages and nations; it does not appear, that man has naturally any more idea of God than any of the beasts of the field; he has no knowledge of God at all; no fear of God at all; neither is God in all his thoughts. Whatever change may afterwards be wrought, (whether by the grace of God, or by his own reflection, or by education,) he is, by nature, a mere Atheist."

2. *Farther Appeal—Part Two* §III.21 (*Jackson* 8:197-98).

3. In the same line are many of the other seeming concessions Wesley makes to natural theology, which are made only to reinforce the complete inadequacy of knowledge of the invisible world without revelation. The following quote from his sermon "On Faith," is another typical example: "And without revelation, how little certainty of invisible things did the wisest of men obtain! The small glimmerings of light which they had were merely conjectural. At best they were only a faint, dim twilight, delivered from uncertain tradition; and so obscured by heathen fables, that it was but one degree better than utter darkness" (Sermon #122 "On Faith" §15 [*Jackson* 7:334]). One could argue that this is an admission of some kind of light, however dim, from experience or reason alone, but that would be to misinterpret Wesley's point, which is precisely to show how useless such dim light is for real knowledge. For more on this point, cf. Williams, *Wesley's Theology*, 30-32.

4. Sermon #26 "Upon Our Lord's Sermon on the Mount—Discourse VI" §III.7 (*Jackson* 5:334-35).

5. Cf. Maddox, *Responsible Grace*, 30.

6. Maddox, *Responsible Grace*, 35. The possibility of "natural theology" or "scientific information" about God in Wesley is also clearly implied by those who see Wesley's experimentation with "spiritual reality" as a theological *source* of knowledge about that reality (so Thorsen, *Wesleyan Quadrilateral*, 59, 62).

7. "Letter to Dr. Robertson" [24 September 1753] (*Jackson* 12:211).

8. So Williams (*Wesley's Theology*, 31) and Runyon (*New Creation*, 244 n. 22). Williams, however, provides no space for experience to influence the approach to Scripture, and Runyon uses Wesley's idea of "prevenient grace" to re-open the possibility of a "natural theology" (moving a bit from Barth to Brunner, as he puts it). Runyon's idea is not without merit, so long as an appropriate role for Scripture is maintained (see below). In the end Maddox himself affirms that Wesley's primary "use" for natural theology is to confirm believers in their belief in God the Creator and not to provide proof independent of Scripture what God the Creator is like. This move, however, empties the idea of natural theology of its content, making it, in the end, dependent on an already existing faith grounded in revelation.

9. *Earnest Appeal* §10 (*Jackson* 8:5-6).

10. Sermon #70 "The Case of Reason Impartially Considered" §II.2,3 (*Jackson* 6:356). In the same sermon, Wesley will also appeal to experience to establish that reason cannot produce hope, in §II.5 (*Jackson* 6:357), or love, in §II.8 (*Jackson* 6:359).

11. *Journal* 25 December 1742 (*Jackson* 1:406).

12. *Journal* 3 March 1788 (*Jackson* 4:408).

13. Concerning the doctrine, Wesley will go so far as to say, "Allow this, and you are so far a Christian. Deny it, and you are but an Heathen still" (Sermon #44 "Original Sin" §III.2 [*Jackson* 6:63]).

14. *The Doctrine of Original Sin According to Scripture, Reason, and Experience—Part One* (*Jackson* 9:196-238).

15. Ibid. (*Jackson* 9:234).

16. Sermon #44 "Original Sin" (*Jackson* 6:54-65).

17. Thorsen (*Wesleyan Quadrilateral*, 104-108) recognizes the move as a methodological one, but he seems to ignore the rhetorical component of Wesley's move. On the other hand, Maddox (*Responsible Grace*, 45) and M. L. Horst ("Christian

Understanding and the Life of Faith in John Wesley" [Ph.D. diss., Yale University, 1985], 285, 287-92) seem to begin by assuming that the placement of experience first is *merely* a rhetorical move and that Wesley's *real* theological methodology was always to begin with Scripture. Both of these interpretations struggle with trying to resolve the tension between Scripture and experience in Wesley, a tension that, in the end, is perhaps better left unresolved as a hermeneutical circle, as we have been suggesting.

18. Cf. Wesley's discussion of the presence of sin the believer (Sermon #14 "The Repentance of Believers" §19 [*Jackson* 5:164]) or his analysis of the origin of power (*Thought Concerning the Origin of Power* [*Jackson* 11:46-53]). In the latter tract, Wesley tips his hand at the beginning (§7), acknowledging his biblical bias, but he then proceeds, through reason and an analysis of experience to show the absurdity of the democratic principle before concluding, "So common sense brings us back to the grand truth, 'There is no power but of God'" (*Jackson* 11:53).

19. *Journal* 23 May 1738 §6 (*Jackson* 1:99-100).

20. *Journal* 29 January 1738 (*Jackson* 1:77).

21. *Journal* 23 March 1738 (*Jackson* 1:89).

22. *Journal* 22 April 1738 (*Jackson* 1:90-91). Wesley also relates some more particulars in the narrative leading up to the events at Aldersgate in his *Journal* 24 May 1738 (*Jackson* 1:98-104).

12

From Scripture to Experience: Experience as "Crucible of Life"

As we saw in Part Two, Wesley's view of knowledge is best described as practical. Knowledge in its best form is not just dependent upon experience as a source, but it is also dependent upon experience because it is the arena in which reasoned constructions of data are made meaningful. Knowledge must impact experience as well as be impacted by it. This is what Wesley wants when he looks for "experimental knowledge." What is true for knowledge in general is true for theological knowledge in particular, and it is not enough to acquire data about God and reason about it. If that is all theology was, then Christian faith would simply be a matter of *assent* to propositions, acknowledging them as true. In addition to "experimental knowledge," Wesley wants "experimental religion." For constructs of theological knowledge to be meaningful, they must then be re-applied back into the crucible of life in which all constructs of knowledge—theological or otherwise—are tested.

Experience in Wesley: The Historic Debate

Like many a good Anglican of his day, Wesley began his intellectual career with an understanding of faith as the mere assent to certain truths about God. This position is clear and explicit in an early letter exchange he has with his mother while at Oxford, during which he notes, "Faith is a species of belief, and belief is defined, 'an assent to a proposition upon rational grounds.'"[1] However, Wesley's mother quickly disabuses him of this notion and helps him to realize that more must be needed for true faith. Thereupon follows a maturing in Wesley's understanding of faith, which culminates in Wesley's "heart strangely warmed" encounter with God at Aldersgate.[2]

What is important in this historical development is not, as many following George Croft Cell have supposed, a transition through various stages in the development of Wesley's concept of faith, allowing him to, in Cell's words, "substitute experiential thinking for the purely logical use of the intellect."[3] This would imply that Wesley left the idea of faith as assent behind him sometime around 1738 and operated on some other understanding for the rest of his life. A better way to see this development is that Wesley's concept of faith matures enough to allow him, to use the terminology we've used thus far, to complete the hermeneutical circle. It is not that the assent to religious propositions (the first-order move) does not belong to the domain of faith, it is merely that faith and theology must be more than that. To stop with the first-order move is to stop short of true knowledge of God.

Wesley will continue to use the language of faith as assent throughout his career, but once he reaches his own mature understanding, he constantly urges people not to stop here. He encourages them to move beyond the point of accepting religious data as true to the point of applying that data back into their experience. Assent is only as a first step. Here a quote from the sermon "The Marks of the New Birth" is typical of the way Wesley affirms the first-order move while always tying it explicitly to the second-order one.

> The true, living, Christian faith which whosoever hath, is born of God, is not only assent, an act of the understanding; but a disposition, which God hath wrought in his heart; 'a sure trust and confidence in God, that, through the merits of Christ, his sins are for given, and he reconciled to the favour of God.'[4]

Where "assent" refers to the first-order move that apprehends the truth of Scripture, "a sure trust and confidence" refers to the second-order move, in which one's experience is shaped by this truth and one's faith becomes an active and not merely passive reality.

Note that the first-order move is not condemned. Wesley knows full well that something like this assent must be involved in any faith or theology. Indeed, he says explicitly in one of his letters to "John Smith," "I believe that a rational assent to the truth of the Bible is one ingredient of Christian faith."[5] However, this is judged to be wholly inadequate if not followed by the second-order move, just as merely speculative scientific theory is dismissed by Wesley if it has no bearing on one's experience. Merely notional faith, which could be extended to include merely notional theology, is what Wesley describes as the faith of devils, the key text here being James 2:19, which in Wesley's Authorized Version would have read: "Thou believest that there is one God; thou doest well: the devils also believe, and tremble."[6]

Wesley does not simply allow that faith *can* be more than the proper acceptance of spiritual data; he demands that it *must* be more. In other words, he points to the hermeneutical relationship between Scripture, reason and experience that we have been exploring, a dynamic in which revealed data come from Scripture (the "rational assent to the truth of the Bible") but then are made truly meaningful and effective when they are directed back into the believer's life. This dynamic of faith, which is found throughout the Wesleyan corpus, is particularly emphasized in those sermons that Wesley himself placed in the first part of his collected sermons.[7]

That this second order move is not just a matter of Christian faith and life but also a matter of Christian understanding (i.e., theology) can be seen most clearly in the way in which Wesley implies the necessary connection between Scripture and experience. Here we encounter the widely recognized role that experience has in Wesley for confirming Scripture.

As we have already noted, many scholars have recognized that experience plays a role in confirming Scripture in Wesley's theological method. Some, such as Colin Williams have made this the only role that experience plays,[8] not allowing anything to compromise the primacy of the authority of Scripture in Wesley's thought. Others have historically given experience a wider role, allowing it to be a source of more or less *independent* confirmation of the truth of Scripture, even if most see Wesley as assuming that experience would never contradict Scripture.[9] Such authors also will allow that experience is a necessary part of Christian theology in that certain *experiences* (in the modern and psychological sense of the word) serve as the goal of the Christian life, toward which Wesley saw Scripture pointing. However, neither a complete subordination of experience to Scripture nor a complete (even if complementary) independence between experience and Scripture can adequately account for the way in which Scripture and experience interact in Wesley's thought.

A complete subordination of experience to Scripture, however well intentioned, is problematic for several reasons. First, it invalidates the theological value of any experience prior to one's encounter with Scripture. Second, it ignores the fact that one always approaches Scripture from the perspective of one's own experience. Neither of these conclusions accords with what we have seen in Wesley thus far. Giving Scripture such clear priority might also make it appear as if Wesley was fundamentally concerned with the proper interpretation of Scripture—with right doctrine and the certainty of knowledge—rather than with the proper living of the Christian life, which is a matter of experience.

A complete subordination of experience to Scripture also ignores Wesley's explicit awareness of extreme differences in the interpretation of Scripture, which means Scripture cannot—in and of itself—be sufficient for true knowledge. How does one adjudicate between competing interpretations? There must be an arena in which good and bad interpretations of Scripture can be seen for what they are, and that arena must have some weight. Wesley, both explicitly in words and implicitly in practice, makes experience this very arena, so that however clever one may be in the interpretation of Scripture, it is meaningless until it can be lived out. So experience cannot be completely subordinated to Scripture and still function as it does in Wesley.

There is likewise trouble with an assumed independence between experience and Scripture, as that opens up the real possibility—however much one may want to assume otherwise—that some facets of experience could (and in some people's mind *do*) contradict Scripture. This forces a choice between Scripture and experience as authorities, which Wesley would have hardly allowed. Any assumed congruence between a functionally independent Scripture and autonomous experience will only last as long as one is willing to ignore or explain away contradictions. In the end, if experience and Scripture are assumed to be independent, one must either subordinate one to the other or eliminate one in favor of the other—and one could argue that this is precisely what happens in the rise of modern science and modern atheism, and in the conservative reactions to both.[10]

Another problem with an assumed independence between Scripture and experience is that if a form of experience is the goal of the Christian life, then one could eliminate the role of Scripture once the goal is achieved. We have already seen how Wesley explicitly rejects this possibility in his use of Scripture to contradict enthusiastic experiences and in the way he uses it as the norm for measuring the description of proper and healthy experience as well.

Another explanation of the interrelationship of experience and Scripture in Wesley is therefore needed, a relationship that recognizes the mutual dependence of each on the other. Randy Maddox strikes very close to such a recognition when he notes that Wesley used experience "to *test* proposed *interpretations* of Scripture," noting that "Wesley's most frequent appeals to experience were on issues where his distinctive interpretation of Scripture was being challenged."[11] Unfortunately, Maddox does not pursue the methodological implications of these hints.

Wesley's implicit Aristotelian understanding of knowledge, the hermeneutical circle between reason and experience aided by Scripture for data about the trans-sensory world, offers a way of balancing the interdependent roles of Scripture and experience in a way that still has relevance for today. Just as experiments are needed to prove scientific constructions to be useful, so experience must confirm reasoned and scriptural constructions of theological knowledge for them to have true meaning. That is what our model of Wesley's dynamic of knowledge would lead us to expect. Turning to Wesley himself, we find this expectation confirmed.

Several times in his writings, Wesley will explicitly articulate a mutual and necessary relationship between experience and the understanding of Scripture. Some of these incidents we have looked at under other headings, but it will be good for us to examine them here again and mine them for what they say about Wesley's theological method. Since this dynamic is most clearly seen in detailed analyses of specific texts, we will conduct our investigation of this idea in Wesley as a series of four case studies: one focused an important theological issue, and then one each from a tract, a sermon, and the *Journal*.

Wesley's Arminianism:
Scripture, Experience and the Calvinist Controversy

One of the best places to see the important role Wesley gave to experienced in the interpretation of Scripture—how necessary it was to have an arena in which various interpretations of Scripture could be evaluated for their validity—is in the long-running Calvinist controversy, in which Wesley engaged off and on throughout his life.[12]

Within the Protestant movement, the questions of the nature of God's election and the operation of God's grace were highly controversial. What was at issue in both of these questions was ultimately the weight of human will or human decision (however minimally conceived). Does God overpower or empower the will? Is God's election in any way conditioned (by God's foreknowledge or anything else), or does God just choose who will be saved and who will not. While Calvin maintained that only unconditional election and irresistible grace were consistent with God's sovereignty as portrayed in Scripture, those who followed Arminius felt that Scripture taught a conditional election and a view of grace that allowed human beings to refuse it. Since Wesley engaged the debate within the Protestant movement, it is not surprising that the debate comes down to a debate over the interpretation of Scripture. Here Wesley sides strongly with Arminius against Calvin.

In his own approach to these questions, Wesley had, as Maddox notes, two main concerns, both of them practical (or we may better say *experiential*). The first concern is the effect the doctrine of unconditional election has on the lived Christian life, and the second concern is the effect the handling of that doctrine has on the integrity and unity of the Methodist movement.[13] Wesley was thus attempting to fight on two fronts—combating an interpretation of Scripture that he (at least initially) believed to be dangerous to Christian living but not combating it so strongly that he ran the risk of fracturing the movement he was trying to lead. His method for walking that very tight line (in which he was not, admittedly, always successful) points to the way in which experience serves as the arena in which interpretations of Scripture (as reasoned constructions of knowledge) can be tested.

Wesley published a number of works on the question of election and almost all of them contain the same basic objections. The order of these objections varies with the publication, but they are nonetheless consistently present. We can see what these objections are, and their importance to our investigation, by looking at Wesley's early sermon "Free Grace" (1739) and the tract *Predestination Calmly Considered* (ca. 1749).

Although George Whitefield and John Wesley both had an important share in the so-called Evangelical Revival in eighteenth century England, they clashed early on the question of unconditional election. Wesley felt it his reluctant duty (which he performed only after casting lots to determine if it were God's will) to publish the sermon "Free Grace"[14] in order to oppose Whitefield's more typically Calvinist ideas. The sermon is ostensibly based on Rom 8:32, but it is much more of a logical argument than it is an exegesis of that scripture. Wesley begins by showing that positive and negative predestination must be held together (in opposition to those who claim to hold election without holding reprobation) and then launches into a series of objections to both unconditional election and reprobation. The first four objections stem from the arena of experience and attempt to show that experience and Scripture would clash if the doctrine of unconditional election were true.

Wesley's first objection against unconditional election is that is nullifies the efficacy of preaching, which Wesley held to be a scriptural command,[15] or what he calls in the sermon an "ordinance of God."

> But if this [unconditional election] be so, then is all preaching vain. It is needless to them that are elected; for they, whether with preaching or without, will infallibly be saved…and it is useless to them that are not elected, for they cannot possibly be saved: They, whether with preaching or without, will infallibly be damned. The end of preaching is therefore void with regard to them likewise; so that in either case our preaching is vain, as your hearing is also vain. [11.] This, then, is a plain proof that the doctrine of predestination is not a doctrine of God, because it makes void the ordinance of God; and God is not divided against himself.[16]

Although Wesley does not explicitly point it out, the clear implication of this is that the holders of predestination (such as Whitefield) still preach, and so their experience and their scriptural practice contradict their doctrine.

Wesley's second objection is that unconditional election saps the initial motivations people have to turn to God and reform their lives.

> [The doctrine of predestination] directly tends to destroy that holiness which is the end of all the ordinances of God…for it wholly takes away those first motives to follow after it, so frequently proposed in Scripture, the hope of future reward and fear of punishment, the hope of heaven and fear of hell. That these shall go away into everlasting punishment, and those into life eternal, is no motive to him to struggle for life who believes his lot is cast already; it is not reasonable for him so to do, if he thinks he is unalterably adjudged either to life or death.[17]

Here again Wesley uses experience to contradict his opponents' interpretation of Scripture. He believes that Scripture teaches ("frequently," at that) that the hope of heaven and fear of hell are motivations to begin living the Christian life and to holiness. Unconditional election takes these scriptural motivations away, and thus leaves a person without any initial motivations at all. Since this interpretation of Scripture would harm the experience of a would-be believer, it cannot be valid.

Wesley's third objection is that unconditional election disrupts Christian assurance, which is provided by the "witness of the spirit," God's direct witness to us that we are His children. Here Wesley explicitly invokes the criterion of experience. "Now, this witness of the Spirit experience shows to be much obstructed by this doctrine; and not only in those who, believing themselves reprobated, by this belief thrust it far from them, but even in them that have tasted of that good gift, who yet have soon lost it again, and fallen back into doubts, and fears, and darkness."[18] Where those who believe that God can save anyone and everyone can trust this experiential witness to assure them of their salvation (as Wesley believes is scriptural), those who hold unconditional election must always be in doubt, lest they might actually be among the damned no matter what they do or feel.[19]

Wesley's fourth objection is that unconditional election destroys an important motivation for doing good works, namely that we would tend to others' physical needs in the hope that it would open doors to allow us to help them with their spiritual needs. However, if we believe that the other may be damned no matter what we would do, we may not even want to help them, let alone feel that our helping them would do any eternal good. And, of course, since the doing of good works is mandated by Scripture, this causes yet one more disconnect between it and our experience.

In all of these objections, the theme is the same. The doctrine of unconditional election cannot be true because if it were to be true, it would lead us *in our experience* into direct conflict with other, more clear and uncontested scriptural truths. Thus the arena of experience is where the doctrine is tested and found wanting because it cannot uphold true Christian experience, at least as Wesley sees it.

It is only with Wesley's fifth and following objections that he finally turns the question back to the issue of Scripture. His main point is that this doctrine makes Scripture self-contradictory. This contradicts one of Wesley's firm hermeneutical rules, that no single passage of Scripture can be interpreted in such a way as to bring it into direct contradiction with other passages of Scripture[20] or with what Wesley calls "the whole scope and tenor of Scripture." Although this scriptural argument is very important to Wesley, it is interesting to note that even in his sermon, it follows the other, experience-based arguments and leads back to experience by the end. There, Wesley concludes by emphasizing again the free grace of God available to all and the necessity of each and every hearer/reader to accept this grace to receive salvation. In other words, he uses what he sees as the proper scriptural interpretation to open up the real possibility for redemption in the experience of all of his hearers and readers (not just those who might happened to be predestined).

Throughout the sermon, Wesley uses the two together—Scripture and experience—not as independent arguments against unconditional election, either one of which could be seen as conclusive, but as two prongs of a single attack. The interpretation of Scripture that affirms unconditional election cannot be true because it leads to experiential contradictions with other truths of Scripture. However, the interpretation of Scripture that affirms free grace leads to scripturally affirmable possibilities for experience. The sermon concludes with an invitation to the hearer/reader to *confirm* in his or her own experience the promise of free grace that Scripture offers, and Wesley can offer this because he believes experience will confirm his interpretation of Scripture just as it disproves the alternative.

In turning to Wesley's tract *Predestination Calmly Considered*,[21] we find a very different focus and order of presentation but with the same intended result. Perhaps Wesley's experience with the publication of the above sermon and the subsequent rift it generated between him and Whitefield caused him to rethink his rhetoric, but it did not change his method. The mutual link between the meaning of Scripture and its validation in experience still shines through.

Wesley begins the tract with an explicit affirmation that his opponents in this debate are truly Christian. However, he claims that they have been carried away in their understanding of what Christianity means by an inappropriate analysis of their own spiritual experience. Their own coming to Christ teaches them justification comes only by faith and that faith itself is a gift of God. Wesley continues,

How easily then may a believer infer from what he hath experienced in his own soul, that the true grace of God always works irresistibly in every believer! that God will finish wherever he has begun this work, so that it is impossible for any believer to fall from grace! and, lastly, that the reason why God gives this to some only and not to others, is, because, of his own will, without any previous regard either to their faith or works, he hath absolutely, unconditionally, predestinated them to life, before the foundation of the world![22]

In a tone much more irenic than that of his sermon, Wesley generously allows his opponents the authenticity of their own experience and something of the reasonableness of their interpretation of it. He further reinforces their position by showing it to be in line with much of Reformed tradition, explicitly quoting the Protestant Confession of Paris (1559), the Synod of Dort (1618) and the Westminster Assembly (1646), as well as with the words of the great John Calvin himself. In other words, he gives them all the ground he can (i.e., their experience and the Reformed tradition) before launching into his arguments.

His first argument, which is really a precursory one, addresses the same problem he addresses at the beginning of "Free Grace," namely the problem of separating unconditional election and reprobation. He affirms to his readers "the uprightness of your hearts"[23] and attempts to persuade them of the fact that unconditional election and reprobation can only be held together, explicitly hoping that the repugnance of the latter will lead them to abandon the former. In these arguments as well, Wesley constantly pushes the question into the arena of experience.

Try whether it be possible in any particular case, to separate election from reprobation...Let me intreat [sic] you to make this case your own. In the midst of life, you are in death; your soul is dead while you live if you live in sin, if you do not live to God. And who can deliver you from the body of this death? Only the grace of God in Jesus Christ our Lord. But God hath decreed to give this grace to others only, and not to you...an unchangeable, irresistible decree standeth between thee and the very possibility of salvation. Go now and find out how to split the hair between thy being reprobated and not elected; how to separate reprobation, in its most effectual sense, from unconditional election![24]

Wesley's argument for the unity of election and reprobation is rooted in an analysis of the supposed experience of one not elected. Again, whatever may be the theoretical difference between passive non-election and active reprobation, Wesley contends that *in experience* they function exactly the same and should be treated as such, meaning that unconditional election and reprobation can only be held together.

Having settled that preliminary question, Wesley moves on to the main question that will occupy the bulk of the tract—the scriptural foundation of election. From section 16 of the tract through section 83, he adduces about a hundred explicit citations of Scripture and as many again implied ones to build his scriptural case against unconditional election. The details of this case need not concern us here, except that occasionally within building those arguments

Wesley will refer the matter to experience when certain understandings of Scripture are in doubt.

One issue raised is the compatibility of our "working out our own salvation" and the idea that God should receive all the glory for our salvation, since the promotion of the glory of God is one of the chief arguments for unconditional election and against any sort of free will. To decide their compatibility, Wesley puts the question to experience:

> Has not even experience taught you this? Have you not often felt, in a particular temptation, power either to resist or yield to the grace of God? And when you have yielded to 'work together with Him,' did you not find it very possible, notwithstanding, to give him all the glory? So that both experience and Scripture are against you here, and make it clear to every impartial inquirer, that though man has freedom to work or not 'work together with God,' yet may God have the whole glory of his salvation.[25]

With this move, Wesley uses his readers' own experience to settle the question of scriptural interpretation, allowing them to see the essential compatibility between our work and God's glory in experience, which would invalidate any interpretation of Scripture that says that the two are ultimately incompatible.

Addressing the supposed use of the doctrine of unconditional election to "exalt God and debase man," Wesley offers scriptural arguments against the first assertion but experiential ones against the second.

> And as to the debasing man; if you mean, this opinion truly humbles the men that hold it, I fear it does not: I have not perceived (and I have had large occasion to make the trial,) that all or even the generality of them that hold it, are more humble than other men. Neither, I think, will you say, that none are humble who hold it not...The truth is, neither this opinion nor that, but the love of God, humbles man, and that only.[26]

Wesley here offers his own experience, but his aim is still to show that an erroneous doctrine will not prove true in experience, not matter how convincing the arguments put forward for it may be.

The mutual interaction between Scripture and experience can also be seen in the way Wesley will explicitly limit the authority of experience, pointing out that our physical experience is of no use in speaking of that which lies beyond it. The point in question is the Reformed conception of the "perseverance of the saints," that if one is "once saved," one is "always saved." Wesley asserts:

> Whatever assurance God may give to particular souls, I find no general promise in holy writ, 'that none who once believes shall finally fall.' Yet, to say the truth, this is so pleasing an opinion...that I see nothing but the mighty power of God which can restrain any who hears it from closing with it. But still it wants one thing to recommend it, — plain, cogent scripture proof. Arguments from experience alone will never determine this point. They can only prove thus much, on the one hand, that our Lord is exceeding patient...and that he does actually bring back many lost sheep, who, to man's apprehensions, were irrecoverable: But all this does not amount to a convincing proof, that no believer can or does

fall from grace. So that this argument, from experience, will weigh little with those who believe the possibility of falling. And it will weigh full as little with those who do not; for if you produce ever so many examples of those who were once strong in faith, and are now more abandoned than ever, they will evade it by saying, 'O, but they will be brought back, they will not die in their sins.' And if they do die in their sins, we come no nearer; we have not gained one point still: For it is easy to say, 'They were only hypocrites; they never had true faith.' Therefore Scripture alone can determine this question.[27]

What is interesting about this reflection is that Wesley recognizes that there are cases where multiple interpretations of the same experience could be valid. One could interpret the life of a former Christian either in Arminian terms (saying that the person has "backslidden") or in Calvinistic ones (saying that the person never had faith in the first place). Experience cannot prove the question because the final perseverance of the believer and the current state of his or her life with God are not part of our sensory experience. They are part of trans-sensory reality, of which the only authoritative description we have is Scripture. And so just as experience serves as arena in which interpretations of Scripture are tested, so also does Scripture serve as the benchmark against which interpretations of experience are tested. Neither stands above the other, but both stand together. There is a mutuality here which is difficult to miss.

For all the important role experience plays in these arguments, the large middle section of this tract still rests largely upon the Scriptural evidences against unconditional election. However, as Wesley begins to close the tract, he shifts from Scripture back to the arena of experience. He is aware of the shift, and he makes it explicitly. And this shift affirms that Wesley's real concern in the debate is not proper understanding of Scripture but proper experience in the Christian life.

> This is my grand objection to the doctrine of reprobation, or (which is the same) unconditional election. That it is an error, I know; because, if this were true, the whole Scripture must be false. But it is not only for this — because it is an error — that I so earnestly oppose it, but because it is an error of so pernicious consequence to the souls of men; because it directly and naturally tends to hinder the inward work of God in every stage of it.[28]

In voicing his concerns this way, Wesley implies that there may be errors or erroneous interpretations of Scripture that are not "pernicious" and so do not need to be so vehemently opposed.[29] But at this point in his life, he does not feel that predestination is one of those. What distinguishes the two is the way interpretation affects experience, and following this quote Wesley will then list some of the same consequences that he adduced in the sermon we looked at above—the lack of motivation to holiness, the lack of assurance of salvation or the foolish assertion of a false assurance. Wesley posits these consequences not as matters of theory but as matters of fact.

> The observing these melancholy examples day by day, this dreadful havoc which the devil makes of souls, especially of those who had begun to run well, by

means of this anti-scriptural doctrine, constrains me to oppose it from the same principle whereon I labour to save souls from destruction...I speak the truth, before God my Judge; not of those who were trained up therein, but of those who were lately brought over to your opinion. Many of these have I known; but I have not known one in ten of all that number, in whom it did not speedily work some of the above-named effects, according to the state of soul they were then in. And one only have I known among them all, after the closest and most impartial observation, who did not evidently show, within one year, that his heart was changed, not for the better, but for the worse.[30]

It is Wesley's own sad experience that leads him to combat this doctrine, his observation of how misinterpretation of Scripture misshapes Christian experience. As far as Wesley is concerned, no interpretation of Scripture can be true which has proven so false in the lives of Christians, particularly new Christians, "those who had begun to run well." Despite his convictions as to the rightness of his opinion, however, Wesley does not simply conclude with this resounding experiential vindication. He is yet concerned of the effect his own tract would have in the experience of his opponents. And so he closes in a conciliatory manner, once again making Christian experience—*not* agreement on the interpretation of Scripture—the ground on which he and his opponent might yet stand together.

I know indeed, ye cannot easily believe this [i.e., all of Wesley's arguments against unconditional election]. But whether ye believe it or no, you believe, as well as I, that without holiness no man shall see the Lord. May we not then, at least, join in this, — in declaring the nature of inward holiness, and testifying to all the necessity of it?...Of whatever opinion or denomination we are, we must serve either God or the devil. If we serve God, our agreement is far greater than our difference. Therefore, as far as may be, setting aside that difference, let us unite in destroying the works of the devil, in bringing all we can from the power of darkness into the kingdom of God's dear Son. And let us assist each other to value more and more the glorious grace whereby we stand, and daily to grow in that grace and in the knowledge of our Lord Jesus Christ.[31]

That is how Wesley finishes the tract—not, as we said, with vindication but with an exhortation to make real in experience the essentials of faith that he believes himself and his opponents to share.

Wesley's fundamental orientation toward experience as the arena in which interpretations of Scripture must be confirmed—which does nothing to minimize Scripture's authority—is also what allows him to moderate his opposition to this doctrine latter on in his life. Further experience, such as his encounter with a group of young Predestinarians at Neath,[32] helped him to realize that a belief in unconditional election was perhaps not as "pernicious" as he once had thought. In a letter that Wesley records in his *Journal*, Wesley compares his combating of predestination with another's opposition to his preaching on Christian perfection. There he records a much more open attitude:

Just so my brother and I reasoned thirty years ago, 'as thinking it our duty to oppose Predestination with our whole strength; not as an opinion, but as a dangerous mistake, which appears to be subversive of the very foundation of Christian experience; and which has, in fact, given occasion to the most grievous offences.' That it has given occasion to such offences, I know; I can name time, place, and persons. But still another fact stares me in the face. Mr. H— and Mr. N— hold this, and yet I believe these have real Christian experience. But if so, this is only an opinion: It is not 'subversive' (here is clear proof to the contrary) 'of the very foundation of Christian experience.' It is 'compatible with love to Christ, and a genuine work of grace.' Yea, many hold it, at whose feet I desire to be found in the day of the Lord Jesus.[33]

So even though Wesley's opinion of the dangers of the doctrine of unconditional election might waver, we still see him giving a substantial place to "Christian experience" as the arena in which interpretations of Scripture are tested for their veracity and their effectiveness—if, indeed, any distinction can even be made between the two. The lives of the two people he mentions are enough to show that people can believe in unconditional election and still be good Christians, and that, Wesley feels, ought to be enough. His whole reason for offering that example was to encourage his own opponent to give him the same space concerning Christian perfection that he wants to give to others concerning Predestination. Let experience judge what is important and true in the Christian life, pleads Wesley. Let us judge those to be the true understandings of Scripture which pass the test of the crucible of life.

In the Calvinist controversy, Wesley uses experience to challenge his opponents interpretation of Scripture, suggesting that it cannot be correct because of its negative experiential consequences. As we will see in turning to Wesley's own favorite doctrine, the doctrine of Christian Perfection, experience must do more than contradict improper ideas. It must also affirm good ones for them to have any real significance.

The Necessity of Experience:
A Plain Account of Christian Perfection

The necessary role for experience in confirming scriptural interpretations is seen most clearly in Wesley's important and oft re-printed tract *A Plain Account of Christian Perfection*. The document is Wesley's central reference point for one of his most treasured doctrines, but in the middle of discussing the doctrine of "Christian Perfection," he drops an intriguing hint about how he sees the relationship between Scripture and experience. Near the end of an extended "question and answer" dialogue about the possibility of being made perfect in love in this life, come these two concluding questions:

Q[uestion]. But what, if none have attained it [Christian Perfection or perfection in love] yet? What, if all who think so are deceived?
A[nswer]. Convince me of this, and I will preach it no more. But understand me right: I do not build any doctrine on this or that person. This or any other man may be deceived, and I am not moved. But, if there are none made perfect yet,

God has not sent me to preach perfection. Put a parallel case: For many years I have preached, 'There is a peace of God which passeth all understanding.' Convince me that this word has fallen to the ground; that in all these years none have attained this peace; that there is no living witness of it at this day; and I will preach it no more...

Q. But what does it signify, whether any have attained it or no, seeing so many scriptures witness for it?

A. If I were convinced that none in England had attained what has been so clearly and strongly preached by such a number of Preachers, in so many places, and for so long a time, I should be clearly convinced that we had all mistaken the meaning of those scriptures; and therefore, for the time to come, I too must teach that 'sin will remain till death.'[34]

Although Wesley does not explicitly employ the language of experience in this passage, the idea of our life as the proving ground for ideas is nevertheless present. Aside from his explicit disavowal of over-valuing *individual* experience (thereby affirming once again the public nature of the concept), there are three important features of the passage that shed light on the mutual role of experience and Scripture in theology.

First of all, both of the answers above assume a necessary role for experience in the confirmation of Scripture. In theory at least, Wesley claims that he would give up his doctrine of Christian perfection and his idea of a "peace that passeth understanding" if it could be proven that no one *actually* experienced such things. Of course, there is a rhetorical element in this claim because Wesley is already convinced that people *have* experienced both peace and Christian perfection and so considers those matters settled. However, the very fact that issue is raised at all is an affirmation of experience's inescapable role. Wesley wants to go on record saying that it is in experience, here represented by "living witnesses," that any doctrine rises or falls. The fact that he will allow these conditions of falsification for even his most treasured doctrinal understanding underscores the seriousness with which Wesley treats his theological method.

A second salient feature of this exchange concerns the kind of role living experience takes in the confirmation of Scripture. Wesley is clear that he does not build doctrine on experience, particularly on individual experience, and it is Scripture, and not experience, which is seen as a given here. What is being tested by experience is not the truth or falsity of Scripture itself, as if experience needs to verify *that* Scripture is true. The veracity of Scripture is something that Wesley just assumes and is not, as we have already seen, open in any way to question. What is being tested here is the *interpretation* of Scripture, *how* Scripture is true, or in Wesley's words, the "meaning of those scriptures." This keeps Scripture from being entirely dependent upon experience, however closely they are tied in practice. Each is independent enough to allow it to challenge the other, but neither is so independent that it can be understood on its own terms.

A final noteworthy, if implicit, feature of this move of Wesley's to test interpretations of Scripture by experience is that Wesley offers his theological method as well as his theology to his readers for their adoption. At the end of this section, Wesley points to the place where he will allow his doctrine of Christian perfection to be vulnerable. As far as Wesley was concerned, the doctrine of Christian perfection has been given a sufficient trial ("clearly and strongly preached by such a number of Preachers, in so many places, and for so long a time") to determine whether or not it is valid, and so he doesn't hide behind a plea to give the doctrine more time. He also allows (even if only rhetorically) the possibility that he himself has misinterpreted the experiences of those perfected in love by offering the reader the possibility of convincing him otherwise.

In allowing for this vulnerability and in being explicit about the terms of that vulnerability, Wesley shifts attention away from the substance of his doctrine to his theological method. By providing these clear terms of falsification, Wesley thus not only invites his readers to accept his doctrine as true (in light of the scriptural and experiential evidence for it adduced in the other parts of the tract), he also invites (perhaps even tempts) them—particularly those who might be opposed to his doctrine—into his theological method, asking them to accept as reasonable the conditions under which he himself had come to affirm that doctrine. This type of a move, which is actually quite common in Wesley, shows that he is concerned with more than vindication, more than convincing his readers that his doctrine is true. He is also concerned with shaping the experience of his reader, attempting to establish the conditions under which his reader can experience what it means for his doctrine to be true. This will become more clear as we turn to our next case study.

The Inextricability of Theory and Practice: "The Witness of the Spirit"

The move to demand or encourage the experimental application of Scripture to life is a very common move in Wesley, and it shows just how inextricable theory and practice are in his mind. One of the best places to see this is in his sermons on another of his more controversial and experiential doctrines—"The Witness of the Spirit." Wesley publishes two discourses on this doctrine, written twenty-two years apart but printed together in the first volume of sermons. Both of them evince a similar method in dealing with the interplay between Scripture and experience as it concerns this witness, even if Wesley is more explicit about that method in the second sermon.

Both sermons are concerned with the exegesis and application of Romans 8:16: "The Spirit itself beareth witness with our spirit, that we are the children of God" (KJV). The issue is whether or not there is some kind of *direct* experience of God that is expressed or implied by this verse, which Wesley calls "the witness of the spirit." Wesley is anxious, in both sermons, to secure the idea that there is such an internal witness and to protect that witness from being confused with *enthusiasm*.

Wesley divides his first sermon on "The Witness of the Spirit" into two main parts, along with a suitable introduction. The first part discusses the nature of both "the witness of our spirit" and "the witness of The Spirit". Typically, Wesley begins with some exegetical notes based on the Greek text of the

Romans 8:16 and adduces a number of other citations to conclude that the Scripture gives us sufficient standards ("so plain, that he which runneth may read them") for us to judge whether or not we have been accepted by God, and we may logically deduce from these grounds whether or not we God's children. Wesley states, "Yet all this is no other than rational evidence, the witness of our spirit, our reason or understanding. It all resolves into this: Those who have these marks are children of God: But we have these marks: Therefore we are children of God."[35]

It is important to note that the content of our understanding—the marks of the new birth in this case—from which we will draw our conclusions must come from Scripture. Scripture provides us with the only adequate description we have of that reality beyond our senses and thus it is only from Scripture that we can learn what it means to be a "child of God." However, this scriptural analysis is not sufficient for Wesley. It can give, as it were, only speculative or theoretical knowledge of what it means to be a child of God, and Wesley is concerned with more than that. He is after practical knowledge, and so once he establishes his scriptural point, he must, of necessity it seems, move to the question of experience. And so, from the quote above, Wesley moves immediately to this:

> But how does it appear, that we have these marks? This is a question which still remains. How does it appear, that we do love God and our neighbour, and that we keep his commandments? Observe, that the meaning of the question is, How does it appear to *ourselves*, not to *others*? I would ask him, then, that proposes this question, How does it appear to you, that you are alive, and that you are now in ease, and not in pain? Are you not immediately conscious of it? By the same immediate consciousness, you will know if your soul is alive to God; if you are saved from the pain of proud wrath, and have the ease of a meek and quiet spirit. By the same means you cannot but perceive if you love, rejoice, and delight in God.[36]

As far as Wesley is concerned, the question of the testimony of one's own spirit *cannot* be resolved by a notional understanding of Scripture. Scripture merely tells us what to look for in our own experience. And he will venture to say that these marks (and he later goes on to list many of them) are things that we are as aware of in our life as we are aware of pain or ease. Once Scripture tells us what marks to look for in our experience, we know immediately if they are to be found or not. And so Scripture provides the information, but our experience provides the only arena in which that information is actually made *meaningful*.

The same dynamic occurs when Wesley shifts his attention to the testimony of God's Spirit in the Christian's life. The Scripture (at least in Wesley's analysis) provides the content, the assurance that there is such a testimony, but the mere knowing *about* it from Scripture is ineffective and insufficient. Here he admittedly begins to struggle with words to describe the experience of the witness of God's Spirit, but the indispensable role of experience as the crucible of life is nevertheless clear.

> But what is that testimony of God's Spirit, which is superadded to, and conjoined with, this [the testimony of our spirit]? How does he 'bear witness with our spirit that we are the children of God?' It is hard to find words in the language of men to explain 'the deep things of God.' Indeed, there are none that will adequately express what the children of God experience. But perhaps one might say, (desiring any who are taught of God to correct, to soften, or strengthen the expression,) The testimony of the Spirit is an inward impression on the soul, whereby the Spirit of God directly witnesses to my spirit, that I am a child of God; that Jesus Christ hath loved me, and given himself for me; and that all my sins are blotted out, and I, even I, am reconciled to God.[37]

Wesley is tentative here in his descriptions. He feels it important to notify his reader that his language will not (indeed cannot) be precise, and that alone ought to warn us away from taking this statement as a strong epistemic affirmation. However, he still asserts that there is something discussed in Scripture to be experienced by Christians, a direct witness of God that forms an "inward impression" on the soul. Proper interpretation of Scripture alerts one to this possibility in experience, but one must nevertheless move from understanding *that* Scripture teaches such a thing to the confirmation of that truth in one's own experience for that truth to have real meaning.[38]

In the last section of this sermon, Wesley raises the very legitimate question of how one may distinguish this *real* experience of God from "the presumption of a natural mind, and from the delusion of the devil."[39] He is very aware of the epistemological questions at stake, and once again his method is to cycle between Scripture and experience, giving to each an important role in answering those questions. The entire last part of the sermon is constructed very much like a dialogue, in which Wesley poses Scriptural content and then questions whether or not this content has been realized in the experience of his hearer or reader.

> How may the real testimony of the Spirit with our spirit, be distinguished from this damning presumption [of fleshly self-delusion]? I answer, the Holy Scriptures abound with marks, whereby the one may be distinguished from the other. They describe, in the plainest manner, the circumstances which go before, which accompany, and which follow, the true, genuine testimony of the Spirit of God with the spirit of a believer. Whoever carefully weighs and attends to these will not need to put darkness for light. He will perceive so wide a difference, with respect to all these, between the real and the pretended witness of the Spirit, that there will be no danger, I might say, no possibility, of confounding the one with the other.[40]

Upon that assertion, Wesley follows with a list of these marks, posing each from Scripture and then pointing out that the one who would presume to claim this witness of the spirit without actually having it would be void of these marks. They include repentance, a change of life, humility, and obedience to the commandments of God. The first two he categorizes as more or less internal, and he claims that a pretender to the witness could examine his or her own heart and find sufficient proof of his pretension. If he finds no repentance from sin in his or her life, "he hath too great reason to believe that he hath grasped a mere shadow, and never yet known the real privilege of the sons of God."[41] Without a true change in his life from light to darkness, "By this also, if he give himself leave to think, may he know, that he is not born of the Spirit; that he has never yet known God; but has mistaken the voice of nature for the voice of God."[42] In other words, an honest self-appraisal of one's own experience is sufficient, *on the basis of Scriptural criteria*, to let people know that they have deceived themselves.

In discussing the other two marks, humility and obedience, Wesley seems to shift his focus from internal to external experience, or from experience that only the person in question could evaluate to experience that is more public and could be evaluated by any observer. Humility, according to Wesley, is a necessary attendant to the true witness of the spirit, whereas those who presume the witness are likely to exhibit pride. In the same way, a love of following God's commandments attends the true witness, whereas a kind of antinomianism attends those who may think they have the witness where they have not. Wesley concludes those sections by saying,

> It follows, with undeniable evidence, that he has not the true testimony of his own spirit. He cannot be conscious of having those marks which he hath not; that lowliness, meekness, and obedience: Nor yet can the Spirit of the God of truth bear witness to a lie; or testify that he is a child of God, when he is manifestly a child of the devil.[43]

All of this is consistent with Wesley's position on enthusiasm, as we glimpsed in the Chapter 8. While one's internal experience is allowed some say, that experience is constantly hedged in by both the Scripture and the external or public experience that others might have. Wesley says, in essence, that it doesn't matter what a person feels he or she has experienced, if the public evidence that must—according to Scripture—accompany such experience is lacking. At the same time, in cases such as this, the Scripture *must* be applied to experience for it to have meaning. In fact, his use of Scripture in this sermon shows that his ultimate concern is with the believer's experience—not with vindicating the truth of Scripture (which he merely assumes on faith). Scripture does serve as the infallible guide, which, rightly handled, leads to "undeniable evidence," but it only serves that role when applied to actual experience.

Wesley concludes the sermon by moving the question from falsifying improper claims to the witness of the spirit to verifying proper ones. He is still concern with the epistemic question, and the grounds for answering it are still those of the continuous interplay between Scripture and experience. It is at this point that Wesley brings in his idea of "spiritual senses," which we looked at in Chapter 10.

Beginning with a hypothetical question from his reader, Wesley asks,

> 'But how may one who has the real witness in himself distinguish it from presumption?' How, I pray, do you distinguish day from night? How do you distinguish light from darkness; or the light of a star, or a glimmering taper, from

the light of the noon-day sun? Is there not an inherent, obvious, essential difference between the one and the other? And do you not immediately and directly perceive that difference, provided your senses are rightly disposed? In like manner, there is an inherent, essential difference between spiritual light and spiritual darkness; and between the light wherewith the Sun of righteousness shines upon our heart, and that glimmering light which arises only from 'sparks of our own kindling:' And this difference also is immediately and directly perceived, if our spiritual senses are rightly disposed. To require a more minute and philosophical account of the manner whereby we distinguish these, and of the *criteria*, or intrinsic marks, whereby we know the voice of God, is to make a demand which can never be answered; no, not by one who has the deepest knowledge of God.[44]

The distinguishing of the true testimony of the Spirit seems, according to Wesley, to be a matter of simple apprehension, a matter of simple experience. One knows the "inward impression on the soul" that comes from God in the same way that one knows light from darkness. It is "immediately and directly perceived." Although Wesley rhetorically eschews the question of philosophical criteria of evaluation, he has himself already provided one important criteria which is necessary for proper apprehension of God's work in the soul: one's spiritual senses must be "right disposed." This raises one final question, which Wesley undertakes to answer in the closing paragraphs of the sermon.

'But how shall I know that my spiritual senses are rightly disposed?' This also is a question of vast importance; for if a man mistake in this, he may run on in endless error and delusion. 'And how am I assured that this is not my case; and that I do not mistake the voice of the Spirit?' Even by the testimony of your own spirit; by 'the answer of a good conscience toward God.' By the fruits which he hath wrought in your spirit, you shall know the testimony of the Spirit of God. Hereby you shall know, that you are in no delusion, that you have not deceived your own soul. The immediate fruits of the Spirit, ruling in the heart, are 'love, joy, peace, bowels of mercies, humbleness of mind, meekness, gentleness, long-suffering.' And the outward fruits are, the doing good to all men; the doing no evil to any; and the walking in the light, — a zealous, uniform obedience to all the commandments of God.[45]

And so the matter is brought full circle. The testimony of one's own spirit is confirmed by internal and external scriptural marks, and the true—as opposed to presumed—testimony of God's Spirit ends up being established by the same criteria, as those are the same criteria that ensure one's "spiritual senses" are "rightly disposed." The doctrine itself is intimately concerned with the question of experience, and its truth is determined by a *necessary* interplay between scriptural marks and experiential confirmation.

In Wesley's second sermon on this witness, he handles the question in much the same way, but in the last sections he adds some further explicit reinforcement of the way in which Scripture and experience interact. In the first sermon, one could argue that Wesley's presentation of the interplay between the two is a matter of rhetoric (i.e., a way of convincing his readers of his opinion) and not a matter of theology (i.e., a way of forming that opinion). In the second sermon, he explicitly puts the issue as one of theological method.

Once Wesley has again established the scriptural basis for this doctrine, he continues on to experience by saying,

> And here properly comes in, to confirm this scriptural doctrine, the experience of the children of God; the experience not of two or three, not of a few, but of a great multitude which no man can number. It has been confirmed, both in this, and in all ages, by 'a cloud' of living and dying 'witnesses.' It is confirmed by *your* experience and *mine*.[46]

There follows a set of arguments that attempt to show how the shape of this doctrine is confirmed by the experience not just of mature Christians but also of those suffering under the conviction of sin and of the children of the world. Those suffering intense conviction of sin are convinced by their own testimony that they are *ungodly*, and nothing less that God's own testimony in their hearts could convince them that they are justified. Those whom Wesley calls "children of the world" may at times desire to please God, but they would not claim to have such a thing as forgiveness of sins based on the testimony of their own spirit. And so their argument, even if it is one from silence, still points to the necessity of a witness of God's Spirit if there is to be anything like assurance of forgiveness.

In those sections, Wesley is attempting to work out the implications of what this witness of God means, not just that it exists (which he knows from Scripture) but what it means in the lives of Christians, "almost Christians," and "children of the world." He is doing theology in a way that consciously weaves together the truth of Scripture and its impact on experience, and he is quite insistent that this is the proper method. The best evidence for this is that Wesley undertakes to answer a number of objections against the use of experience as a theological category in the penultimate section of the sermon.

> It is objected, First, 'Experience is not sufficient to prove a doctrine which is not founded on Scripture.' This is undoubtedly true; and it is an important truth; but it does not affect the present question; for it has been shown, that this doctrine is founded on Scripture: Therefore experience is properly alleged to confirm it. 'But madmen, French prophets, and enthusiasts of every kind, have imagined they experienced this witness.' They have so; and perhaps not a few of them did, although they did not retain it long: But if they did not, this is no proof at all that others have not experienced it; as a madman's imagining himself a king, does not prove that there are no *real* kings.[47]

In the first objection, Wesley insists on a proper place for experience in the confirmation of Scripture. He admits that experience cannot alone establish a spiritual truth outside of Scripture, but he contends that it has a role to play once Scripture has been consulted. In the second objection he maintains a place for true experience even while reaffirming that experience *alone* is not an infallible criterion for truth.

Just a few sections later, Wesley defends himself against the opposite objection, namely that if the witness of the spirit and the marks attendant to justification are given in the Bible, there is no need for experiential confirmation. Wesley replies by saying that it is the very Scripture under examination (Rom 8:16) that points to experience. When a further objection is adduced, claiming that the "testimony of our spirit" has more solid grounding in Scripture than a direct testimony from God, Wesley does not object but merely uses that fact to reinforce his own position: "'But the testimony arising from the internal and external change is constantly referred to in the Bible.' It is so: And we constantly refer thereto, to confirm the testimony of the Spirit."[48] So not only does experience confirm Scripture, but Scripture is used to affirm experience (i.e., the testimony of the Spirit). We are once again come full circle.

Given the multivalent way in which Wesley uses the terminology of experience in these two sermons, it is easy to see why some[49] would feel the need to clarify his thinking on the subject by positing a distinction between experience as the goal of the Christian life (the *experience* of the testimony of the Spirit) and experience as a tool for theological method (helping to prove the doctrine of the testimony of the Spirit). Wesley, however, does not do this. In fact, he interweaves the two supposed types or uses of experience in answering objections against his doctrine, as we saw above, and that could indicate that Wesley thought of them as of a piece. If that is the case, then pulling apart these two facets of experience might cause one to miss something crucial about Wesley's understanding of it.

For Wesley, one does not need to separate a supposed objective component of experience (experience as a criterion for theology) from a supposed subjective component (experience as a goal for the Christian life) because the two roles are only meaningful as they relate to each other. In Wesley's epistemology, the objective and subjective features of experience (so easily separated in our modern psychology) both refer to facets of that second-order move of the application of reasoned interpretations of Scripture back to life. It is one and the same *experience* that confirms our constructions of knowledge and allows us to feel or makes us conscious of that confirmation.

Unless we want to import our modern psychological presumptions back into Wesley, there is little need to create a space for separate, internal experience disconnected from experience as objective criterion. Experience is useful in the construction of knowledge—in this case, theological knowledge—because that knowledge is useful when it impacts people's experience. It is not as if we have notional ideas which are secure and certain in themselves but are somehow helped along by having independent experiential confirmation of them. For a practical person like Wesley, our notional ideas are ideas about what can be experienced in life and so don't mean anything *until* they are applied there. And this fits neatly with Wesley's own concerns about "experimental religion." To separate out the subjective side of experience and focus on it without regard to ideas of Scripture is to run the risk of enthusiasm. The reverse—focusing on the correctness of one's understanding of Scripture without caring how or if it affects lived human life—runs the risk of making religion a dry and lifeless orthodoxy. Both of which, in Wesley's mind, are antithetical to true religion.

The interweaving of experience as confirmation of Scripture and of experience as the direct witness from God also brings up another important feature of Wesley's view and use of experience and its relationship to theology. The dialogical nature of theology, flowing out of Scripture-in-experience and flowing back to re-shape experience, reinforces the active and public nature of experience, to which we have already seen Wesley committed. Given this, it is hard to find room in his understanding for the pursuit of experience-for-experience's-sake. Wesley does not appear to be interested in helping his readers or hearers *have experiences* (in the sense of psychological events). He does, however, seem to be interested in opening up their experience to encounters with God and the world. Where previously we say this idea as a function of Wesley's epistemology, it takes on a new dimension when placed in the framework of his theological method. Understanding this becomes even more important when we turn to our last case study, which concerns Wesley's analysis of that well-known encounter he had with God in 1738.

Wesley's Own Experience: Aldersgate

One of the most fascinating, oft cited and much debated sections of Wesley's entire corpus is his record and analysis of the events leading up to and immediately following what history calls his "Aldersgate experience." We have already noted that Wesley himself does not use this terminology, but that does not change the fact that something happened in Wesley's life on 24 May 1738, and most commentators on Wesley are comfortable with giving the event of that evening a pivotal role in his life.[50] Wesley's descriptions of those events also serve as an interesting and informative test-case in his own life for the ideas about the interplay of Scripture and experience, particularly the way in which the former is applied to the latter.

We will pick up the narrative just before its climax, where Wesley is having an extended debate with the Moravian Peter Böhler over the possibility of an instantaneous saving faith that is a gift of God and that includes the *sense* of pardon for all sins (i.e., the witness of the spirit). The entire section is somewhat lengthy, but it is worth quoting in detail, because it is the clearest and most detailed expression we have in Wesley of how experience and Scripture mutually interacted in his own experience.

> 12. When I met Peter Böhler again, he consented to put the dispute upon the issue which I desired, namely, Scripture and experience. I first consulted the Scripture. But when I set aside the glosses of men, and simply considered the words of God, comparing them together, endeavouring to illustrate the obscure by the plainer passages; I found they all made against me, and was forced to retreat to my last hold, 'that experience would never agree with the *literal interpretation* of those

scriptures. Nor could I therefore allow it to be true, till I found some living witnesses of it.' He replied, he could show me such at any time; if I desired it, the next day. And accordingly, the next day he came again with three others, all of whom testified, of their own personal experience, that a true living faith in Christ is inseparable from a sense of pardon for all past, and freedom from all present, sins. They added with one mouth, that this faith was the gift, the free gift of God; and that he would surely bestow it upon every soul who earnestly and perseveringly sought it. I was now thoroughly convinced; and, by the grace of God, I resolved to seek it unto the end, 1. By absolutely renouncing all dependence, in whole or in part, upon *my own* works or righteousness; on which I had really grounded my hope of salvation, though I knew it not, from my youth up. 2. By adding to the constant use of all the other means of grace, continual prayer for this very thing, justifying, saving faith, a full reliance on the blood of Christ shed for *me*; a trust in Him, as *my* Christ, as my sole justification, sanctification, and redemption.

13. I continued thus to seek it, (though with strange indifference, dulness, and coldness, and unusually frequent relapses into sin,) till Wednesday, May 24. I think it was about five this morning, that I opened my Testament on those words, *Ta megista emin kai timia epaggelmata dedoretai, ina genesthe theias koinonoi phuseos.* 'There are given unto us exceeding great and precious promises, even that ye should be partakers of the divine nature.' (2 Pet. i. 4.) Just as I went out, I opened it again on those words, 'Thou art not far from the kingdom of God.' In the afternoon I was asked to go to St. Paul's. The anthem was, 'Out of the deep have I called unto thee, O Lord: Lord, hear my voice. O let thine ears consider well the voice of my complaint. If thou, Lord, wilt be extreme to mark what is done amiss, O Lord, who may abide it? For there is mercy with thee; therefore shalt thou be feared. O Israel, trust in the Lord: For with the Lord there is mercy, and with him is plenteous redemption. And He shall redeem Israel from all his sins.'

14. In the evening I went very unwillingly to a society in Aldersgate-Street, where one was reading Luther's preface to the Epistle to the Romans. About a quarter before nine, while he was describing the change which God works in the heart through faith in Christ, I felt my heart strangely warmed. I felt I did trust in Christ, Christ alone for salvation: And an assurance was given me, that he had taken away *my* sins, even *mine*, and saved *me* from the law of sin and death.[51]

There are several noteworthy features in this extended passage that speak to the interplay between experience and Scripture. First of all, Wesley himself makes that the issue at the beginning of the quote. Here we see Wesley living out the method that we have been ascribing to him throughout Part Three. He begins (having, as we noted already, been compelled again by his experience to do so) by searching the Scripture in as impartial a manner as he can. Doing so convinces him of the reasonableness of Böhler's interpretation of it. Wesley, however, is not yet convinced. Although he sees that Böhler could very well be right, he demands a test. So he "retreats" to what he identifies as his "last hold," i.e., that such an interpretation would not prove true in experience, which would justify interpreting those Scriptures in a non-literal way. He does not *want* to admit that Böhler is right about the interpretation of Scripture, but he throws open the determination of that, not to further rational arguments, but to experience, the crucible of life. Once he has done so, he has locked himself into the hermeneutical circle that we have described. So when Böhler does produce his "living witnesses," Wesley is forced—against his will as it were—to capitulate. Böhler's interpretation of Scripture has proven true in life, and Wesley has no other arguments.

But the process at this point is only just beginning. Now that Böhler's interpretation of Scripture (first-order move) has proven true in experience (second order move), Wesley must *assent* to Böhler's view (first-order move again). But it is not enough for Wesley that he admit *that* Böhler is correct. Now he wants to "seek" and "pray for" this faith in his own life (second order move again). In other words, Böhler's knowledge is only potential for Wesley until he can actualize it in his own experience. However, Wesley only fully relates this increased *notional* understanding as part of the narrative of an event in his experience, so it seems that the two are—in Wesley's life as well as in his theory—intimately connected. It is as if Wesley can concede to the *truth* of Böhler's idea, but that truth is not *meaningful* until he can experience it for himself.

The events noted in §12 of the *Journal* for 24 May 1738 are probably the same ones that Wesley narrates earlier in the entries for 22-23 April 1738, and so when Wesley "continues to seek" this faith, he seems to be doing so for about a month. It is interesting to note that Wesley describes his experience of that month in negative terms—"strange indifference, dulness, and coldness, and unusually frequent relapses into sin". In other words, Wesley wants to be clear with his readers that his mere notional acceptance of Böhler's interpretation of Scripture, his *assent*, does not—in and of itself—change his spiritual experience for the better. If anything Wesley's new-found understanding only made matters worse, as he knew there was supposed to be more to Christianity than what he currently had.

Then comes the fateful day of 24 May. Rather than just discussing what happened in the evening, Wesley includes a few particulars of the day. All of them refer either to Scripture or to compilations of scriptural thoughts or themes. He cites his reading of 2 Peter 1:4 and Mark 12:34 and the anthem from St. Paul's, which contains references to several passages of Scripture. No other particulars of the day are deemed relevant except these encounters with Scripture, which means that Wesley is directing his reader to pay attention to what we might called the *scriptural expectation* that pre-informed his experience of that evening.

When that evening comes, Wesley is careful to note that he went "very unwillingly" to the society meeting being held in Aldersgate street. There he had his famous "heart warming" experience, which he describes in terms of two feelings. The first was his own feeling of trust: "I felt I did trust in Christ, Christ alone for salvation". This sounds like what we heard Wesley earlier describing as the "testimony of our spirit," and it seems to be active concern. The second feeling he describes, however, does not come from him, and he more or less receives it in a passive way: "And an assurance was given me, that he had taken away *my* sins, even *mine*, and saved *me* from the law of sin and death."

All of this points to an intriguing feature of Wesley's experience that goes beyond the idea of the necessary confirmation of Scripture in life or the mutuality between theory and practice in Wesley's understanding of the connection between Scripture and life—even though these two elements are clearly present. What appears to be happening, at least in the way that Wesley has chosen to relate these events, is that his understanding of Scripture *opens a space of encounter in his experience*, an encounter of a deeply personal nature. Aldersgate is, in the words of Frances Young, a "'scripture-shaped' experience."[52]

All of the preparatory work in Wesley's life that led up to Aldersgate involved an ever-greater appreciation of what Christianity actually entailed. His old understandings are broken down through the events in Georgia and his encounters with Moravians like Peter Böhler, and new understandings come in to take their place. But the real change in Wesley's experience does not subsist in the acquisition of new ideas. He makes that very clear. Rather, these ideas open up the space for an encounter, which he believed to be an encounter with God, that previously did not exist in Wesley's life.

That Wesley believes this encounter to be an encounter with an Other, and not simply the product of his mind, is brought out by the way he relates the events. His experience leading up to Aldersgate was worse for his knowledge, and he only went to the society meeting there "very unwillingly." Thus, he cannot conceive that he created these feelings in his head or that he invented this event himself. His only explanation was that this new-found assurance of salvation (and power for living the Christian life, as he will relate in the sections following) could have only come from the outside. He sought it; he had prepared for it; but as far as he seems to be concerned he did not make it happen. It came to him.

When this encounter occurs, Wesley underlines its radically personal nature. He uses singular personal pronouns, some of which he emphasizes himself, and he speaks of what Christ had done. He does not reflect primarily on a new understanding (as if the event were a type of "Aha! moment") or a new-found intellectual appreciation for a previously learned truth. Instead, the tone of his descriptions is the tone of personal encounter. Wesley was convinced that he had met God in the space provided by his understanding, and that encounter changed him.

This was the heart of the matter, at least as far as Wesley was concerned. All that we have seen thus far about the epistemic role of experience in confirming Scripture—the necessary, mutually informative connection between experience and the interpretation of Scripture—points eventually beyond the hermeneutical functioning of his epistemology toward something else. That something else is a personal encounter between the believer and God and the change this encounter makes in the life or experience of that believer. Wesley's theological method is, thus, driven by something external to it, by a goal which is more than an epistemological one. Wesley, then, is not a "practical theologian" simply because of his subject matter, because he prefers to discuss the realities of Christian living over *philosophical* speculations about the nature of God.

Wesley is a practical theologian because his theological method will support no other kind of theology.

Ultimately, that theology must be understood as a theology of encounter. It is Scripture—and only Scripture—which provides the raw material, the description of trans-sensory reality, out of which that space for encounter is constructed. But that space is only constructed in our lived experience—not just in our understanding. Wesley's increasing appreciation for the truth of Scripture led him to seek in his own life the experience of faith that Scripture described. But that faith was not something produced by understanding, or even by the diligent application of certain means or by a set of ritual actions. All that understanding or means of grace or the performance of worship and good works can do—which indeed they must do—is contribute to creating the space for encounter. But since that encounter depends on an Other as much as it depends on the believer, it cannot be forced or controlled or dictated a priori.[53] Wesley wanders for a month before he experiences it. He records in his *Journal* the experiences of others that took much longer. Whatever these delays might mean for spiritual formation, as questions of methodology, they reinforce the idea that there is more to Christian experience than mere Christian understanding, and for Wesley the latter serves the former.

Conclusion

It should now be apparent, in these more detailed textual investigations, that Wesley conceived of experience (or life) as the necessary crucible in which all interpretations of Scripture must be tested for them to have real meaning. Scripture is assumed without question to be true, but one cannot know *how* it is true until one applies various constructions of that truth to experience. This is the case for essential doctrines of faith—such as the facets of the doctrine of God or salvation discussed above—and for more peripheral matters, areas of life that are not directly addressed by Scripture. There is always some part of Scripture that would apply, and the question of how it applies is determined by experience (aided, of course, by reason).[54]

The role that experience takes in confirming these interpretations of Scripture has intertwining objective and subjective facets. Objectively, experience confirms the truth of interpretations of Scripture by affirming that they "work," meaning they are effective in shaping a Christian life toward scriptural ends. Subjectively, experience confirms the truth of interpretations of Scripture by providing the arena in which one encounters the reality that Scripture represents—namely, God—and that this encounter also has a subsequent effect on the way one lives one's Christian life.

The admission of experience to the theological debate under these terms may raise some questions, however. We noted at the beginning of this project that there is a clear and evident danger in emphasizing experience in theology. If it is one's experience that guides one's interpretation of Scripture and one's interpretation of Scripture that shapes one's experience, then it would be very easy to conceive of Christian life and thought as a highly individualistic affair, with each believer engaging this hermeneutical circle in his or her own way, subject to the various whims and vagaries of individual experience that we know to exist. Indeed, looking at the history of how Wesley was received, we see that was often misunderstood on this point by many, if not most, of his early followers and that the charge of *enthusiasm* and the over-emphasis on experience, was commonplace against the Methodists in Wesley's day.[55]

The picture of an enthusiast, however, is not at all the picture of Christian life and thought that we get from Wesley's writings, however his teaching and preaching might have been taken by his followers or opponents. We have already seen that experience in Wesley's mind was not the sole province of the individual, that it is consistently public, something accessible to all, and thus not about subjective states, private revelations or direct knowledge of God apart from Scripture. It is also not primarily an internal or psychological reality but one that is geared toward encounters, encounters with reality in general and with the ultimate Other in particular.

Nevertheless, given that Wesley's "experimental religion" was so easily misunderstood, we ought to give some further attention to the larger question of religious experience before turning to a comprehensive synthesis of his theological method. We have seen that there is a subjective side to experience and encounter, and that means that there must be some role for individual religious experience, and we cannot do away with it just because some of Wesley's followers abused it. If the subjective and objective components of experience cannot in reality be pulled apart, then this subjective and individual side of experience must be given some attention in the production of theological knowledge. At the same time, Wesley's appeals to religious experience were, like his other appeals, consistently public, referring to that sphere of communal religious experience, to which he provided some access to his readers through various activities and publications. So, it is to a closer investigation of these individual and communal sources that we now turn.

Notes

1. "Letter to Susanna Wesley" [29 July 1725] (*Telford* 1:22).
2. On the finer points of this development, see the excellent analysis of "John Wesley's Changing Concept of Faith" in Matthews, "Reason and Religion," 184-246.
3. Cell, *Rediscovery*, 84.
4. Sermon #18 "The Marks of the New Birth" §I.3 (*Jackson* 5:213).
5. *Letter to John Smith* [28 September 1745] §[III].11 (*Jackson* 12:60).
6. A few typical references to this text can be found in *Journal* 29 January 1738 (*Jackson* 1:77); Sermon #2 "The Almost Christian" §II.3 (*Jackson* 5:22); Sermon #18 "The Marks of the New Birth" §I.2 (*Jackson* 5:213); *Earnest Appeal* §56 (*Jackson* 8:23); *The Principles of a Methodist* §8 (*Jackson* 8:363), and *The Principles of a Methodist Farther Explained* §VI.5 (*Jackson* 8:473).

7. Cf. especially Sermon #1 "Salvation by Faith" §I.4 (*Jackson* 5:9); Sermon #2 "The Almost Christian" §II.5 (*Jackson* 5:23); Sermon #5 "Justification by Faith" §IV.2 (*Jackson* 5:60-61); Sermon #7 "The Way of the Kingdom" §II.10 (*Jackson* 5:85).

8. Williams, *Wesley's Theology*, 32-36.

9. Cf. Cell, *Rediscovery*, 72-93; Paul W. Hoon, "The Soteriology of John Wesley" (Ph.D. diss., University of Edinburgh, 1936), 343; Scott Jones, *Conception and Use*, 179-183; Edward Sugden, ed., *Wesley's Standard Sermons*, vol. 1 (London: Epworth, 1921), 196 n. 2; Thorsen, *Wesleyan Quadrilateral*, 202, 208, 222.

10. Cf. John Hedly Brooke, "Science and the Fortunes of Natural Theology: Some Historical Perspectives," *Zygon* 24 (1989): 3-22; and Michael J. Buckley, *At the Origins of Modern Atheism* (New Haven, CT: Yale University Press, 1987).

11. Maddox, *Responsible Grace*, 46. Emphasis in original.

12. For a more detailed analysis of the *theological* debate here (as opposed to our *theological-methodological* investigation), cf. Allen Coppedge, *Shaping the Message: John Wesley in Theological Debate* (Nappanee, IN: Evangel, 1987); W. Stephen Gunter, *The Limits of 'Love Divine'* (Nashville: Kingswood, 1989), 227-66; Irwin W. Reist, "John Wesley and George Whitefield: A Study in the Integrity of Two Theologies of Grace," *Evangelical Quarterly* 47 (1975): 26-40; and Jerry L. Walls, "The Free Will Defense, Calvinism and Wesley, and the Goodness of God," *Christian Scholar's Review* 13 (1983): 19-33.

13. Maddox, *Responsible Grace*, 55-58.

14. Sermon #128 "Free Grace" (*Jackson* 7:373-86).

15. Cf. *Journal* 2 April 1739 (*Jackson* 1:185) and 11 June 1739 (*Jackson* 1:201).

16. Sermon #128 "Free Grace" §10-11 (*Jackson* 7:376).

17. Ibid.

18. Ibid. §15 (*Jackson* 7:377-78).

19. There is an irony in this objection, though it is not without merit. Predestination was conceived as "comforting" doctrine by both Calvin and Luther, but Wesley wants to point out that it is not always (or even often) so in actual experience, however good the theory may be. On this point, cf. John Calvin, *Institutes of the Christian Religion*, trans. Henry Beveridge, vol. 2 (Grand Rapids: Eerdmans, 1953), 203; and Martin Luther, *Luther's Works*, vol. 5, *Lectures on Genesis*, ed. Jaroslav Pelikan (St. Louis: Concordia, 1968), 45 and vol. 25, *Lectures on Romans*, 371.

20. Cf. Scott Jones, *Conception and Use*, 191-204.

21. *Predestination Calmly Considered* (*Jackson* 10:204-259).

22. Ibid. §4 (*Jackson* 10:205).

23. Ibid. §8 (*Jackson* 10:207).

24. Ibid. §11-12 (*Jackson* 10:208).

25. Ibid. §46 (*Jackson* 10:230).

26. Ibid. §83-84 (*Jackson* 10:255-56).

27. Ibid. §67 (*Jackson* 10:242).

28. Ibid. §86 (*Jackson* 10:256).

29. On this point, cf. Sermon #55 "On the Trinity" §2 (*Jackson* 6:199), in which Wesley says, "There are ten thousand mistakes which may consist with real religion; with regard to which every candid, considerate man will think and let think."

30. *Predestination Calmly Considered* §88-89 (*Jackson* 10:257-58).

31. Ibid. §90 (*Jackson* 10:258-59).

32. *Journal* 18 August 1746 (*Jackson* 2:22).

33. *Journal* 14 May 1765 (*Jackson* 3:212). These sentiments are echoed in "A Letter to the Rev. Mr. Plenderlieth" [23 May 1768] (*Jackson* 12:246). Of course, this does not tell the whole story, as just a few years after this is when Wesley publishes his rather uncharitable "translation" or parody of Augustus Toplady's predestinarian position and

Wesley's own "response" thereto (cf. *The Doctrine of Absolute Predestination: Stated and Asserted by the Reverend Mr. A—T— [Jackson 14:190-98] and The Consequence Proved [Jackson 10:370-74]*). However, even though his attitude on this point is not always *theologically* consistent, we can still see a consistent *method* in Wesley's attempt to allow his understanding of Scripture and his experience to mutually interact.

34. *A Plain Account of Christian Perfection* §19 (*Jackson* 11:405-06). In the original, this "dialogue" is quoted from Wesley's previously published tract on Christian Perfection, but we have simplified the quotation structure to avoid the cumbersome quotes within quotes within quotes.

35. Sermon #11 "The Witness of the Spirit—Discourse II" §I.4 (*Jackson* 5:114).

36. Ibid. §I.5.

37. Ibid. §II.7 (*Jackson* 5:115).

38. The exact shape of this "experience" of the witness of the spirit is something that Wesley himself only came gradually to understand. While immediately after Aldersgate, he preached that it was a necessity in the true Christian life (cf. Sermon #2 "The Almost Christian" §II.[III].9 [*Jackson* 5:24]), he later came to understand that, though it was the "common privilege" of all Christians to have this witness, it was nevertheless *not* to be identified with saving faith itself. (cf. "Letter to Charles Wesley" [31 July 1747] [*Jackson* 12:112-13]). Interestingly enough, it is Wesley's own experience and his analysis of the experience of others that leads him to realize that his original interpretation of the Scripture (indicating the necessity of that witness) was erroneous; it failed the test in the crucible of life. Note, however, that though Wesley's understanding of the content of what is experienced by the believer in this case changes, the fact that *something* must be experienced does not. For more on this doctrine, cf. the studies of Richard Heitzenrater (*Mirror and Memory,* 106-49); Arthur Yates (*The Doctrine of Assurance with Special Reference to John Wesley* [London: Epworth, 1952]); and Lycurgus M. Starkey (*The Work of the Holy Spirit: A Study in Wesleyan Theology* [New York: Abingdon, 1962]).

39. Sermon #10 "The Witness of the Spirit—Discourse I" §II.1 (*Jackson* 5:117).

40. Ibid. §II.2-3 (*Jackson* 5:117-18).

41. Ibid. §II.4 (*Jackson* 5:118).

42. Ibid. §II.5 (*Jackson* 5:119).

43. Ibid. §II.7 (*Jackson* 5:120).

44. Ibid. §II.9-10 (*Jackson* 5:121).

45. Ibid. §II.12 (*Jackson* 5:122).

46. Sermon #11 The Witness of the Spirit—Discourse II" §III.6 (*Jackson* 5:127).

47. Ibid. §IV.1-2 (*Jackson* 5:129).

48. Ibid. §IV.7 (*Jackson* 5:131).

49. E.g. Maddox, *Responsible Grace*, 45; and Scott Jones, *Conception and Use*, 179-83.

50. For an excellent summary of the debate about the importance of Aldersgate, including some dissenting views to this opinion, cf. Randy Maddox, "Aldersgate: A Tradition History," in *Aldersgate Reconsidered*, 133-46.

51. *Journal* 24 May 1738 §12-15 (*Jackson* 1:102-03). Emphases in original.

52. Frances Young, "The Significance of John Wesley's Conversion Experience," in *John Wesley: Contemporary Perspectives*, ed. John Stacey (London: Epworth, 1988), 41.

53. Here is the appropriate place to note the interesting parallels between Wesley and the Christian Mystical Tradition. While there are certainly good arguments to be made for the influence of some strands of that tradition on Wesley, the connection between Wesley and the mystics is better appreciated through their *theology* rather than though an immediate focus on the issue of so-called "mystical experiences." (Cf. Albert Deblaere, "Christian Mystic Testimony," *Ons Geestelijk Erf* 72 [1998]: 129-53, esp. 129-30 and 141-44.)

54. A very good example of this can be found in Wesley's sermon on "The Nature of Enthusiasm" concerning the question of the "will of God". "'But how shall I know what is the will of God, in such and such a particular case? The thing proposed is, in itself, of an indifferent nature, and so left undetermined in Scripture.' I answer, The Scripture itself gives you a general rule, applicable to all particular cases: 'The will of God is our sanctification.'...In order, therefore, to know what is the will of God in a particular case, we have only to apply this general rule. Suppose, for instance, it were proposed to a reasonable man to marry, or to enter into a new business: In order to know whether this is the will of God...he has only to inquire, 'In which of these states can I be most holy, and do the most good?' And this is to be determined, partly by reason, and partly by experience. Experience tells him what advantages he has in his present state, either for being or doing good; and reason is to show, what he certainly or probably will have in the state proposed. By comparing these, he is to judge which of the two may most conduce to his being and doing good; and as far as he knows this, so far he is certain what is the will of God. Meantime, the assistance of his Spirit is supposed, during the whole process of the inquiry." (§23-25 [*Jackson* 5:474]).

55. The best summary of those historical circumstances and how they shaped Wesley's refinement of his theology is Gunter, *'Love Divine'*.

13

Wesley's Sources for Religious Experience

From the perspective of any individual person, there are only two types, categories or sources of experience: one's own experience and the experience of others. Empiricists like Wesley would affirm that our own experience comes to us through our senses and through our memory of past sensations, while the experience of others comes to use through what we usually call *testimony*. While we normally consider our personal experience more reliable than testimony, there are sufficient times when we doubt our own experience or when we credit another's interpretation of experience above our own (as children do quite often) to ensure that the question of reliability is not always easy to answer. In any case, most of us are more comfortable with our own interpretations of experience when they are confirmed by the testimony of others. So however much we may affirm the need to experience things for ourselves in order to have true knowledge of them, we are usually aware, however implicitly, that our individual experience fits into the context of what others experience as well.

This is true for all experience, but it is particularly relevant when it comes to the question of religious experience, since in that arena individual experience is often inappropriately divorced from the communal. This happened among Wesley's followers and continues to happen with people who misunderstand and misuse the Christian mystical tradition. Since Wesley was concerned to balance both the individual and communal aspects of experience when it came to religion, his method is useful in addressing many contemporary concerns about religious experience.

In turning our attention to religious experience, we must also not forget that this is in no way a turn away from the authority or role of Scripture. In one sense, Wesley's understanding of Scripture falls under the category of testimony. It is a testimony of human writers who, guided by the Holy Spirit, have articulated their experience of the trans-sensory world in a way that has been affirmed by the community as reliable (i.e., canonized). This also means that much of what we have been exploring above concerning the interplay (the essential interplay at that) between Scripture and experience could be applied to any interaction between our own experience and the testimony of others. However, scriptural testimony is given substantially more weight than non-scriptural testimony in Wesley, and it has an element of absolute authority that no other testimony is given. Even so, Wesley relies heavily on non-scriptural testimony in his doing of theology—particularly in matters of religious experience where the interpretation of Scripture or the implications of Scripture might be in doubt, as we have seen numerous times above. At the same time, Wesley's affirmation of the value of testimony does not devalue an individual's own experience. We see this as he consistently affirms the need for a more-or-less personal experience of (or encounter with) the truths that Scripture teaches and that are communally affirmed, but he is careful never to make individual experience the ultimate determining factor in establishing truth.

It is, therefore, necessary for us to investigate in a bit more detail some of the non-scriptural sources of religious experience from which Wesley draws when making his appeal to experience. In so doing, we will see how both individual experience and testimony have their role to play in the construction and application of theology. We have already seen some of the important factors related to individual experience earlier in this investigation—such as the fact that even appeals to individual experience are based on the ultimately public nature of experience and that much of experience, at least, has to do with an encounter with an external reality and not with internal psychological events. We have not, however, explored that facet of individual religious experience whose truth appears self-evident and in which the public nature of experience is obscure or even irrelevant—the area of religious feelings.

When it comes to the establishment of communal experience, we have already seen that this is what Wesley refers to most often when appealing to experience, but we have not yet explored the way in which he makes certain religious experiences available to people through his publications and practices, such his *Journal*, "experimental letters," his use of "testimony services," his preaching of biographical sermons and his editing and republishing of biographies as devotional material. All these become important ways for Wesley of making so-called *private* experience public.

Individual Religious Experience: The Value of *Feelings*

In an early and unguarded moment, John Wesley recorded an entry about "inward feeling" in his very first *Journal* that he probably had later occasion to regret. Although his statement is just, especially in light of the later clarifications he gives it, it was misinterpreted by both his contemporaries and later commentators. In describing his spiritual state as he approached England after his abortive mission to Georgia, Wesley writes,

> In the fulness of my heart, I wrote the following words: — 'By the most infallible of proofs, inward feeling, I am convinced, 1. Of unbelief; having no such faith in Christ as will prevent my heart from being troubled; which it could not be, if I believed in God, and rightly believed also in him: 2. Of pride, throughout my life past; inasmuch as I thought I had what I find I have not: 3. Of gross irrecollection; inasmuch as in a storm I cry to God every moment; in a calm, not: 4. Of levity and luxuriancy of spirit, recurring whenever the pressure is taken off, and appearing by my speaking words not tending to edify; but most by my manner of speaking of my enemies. Lord, save, or I perish![1]

Wesley here is quoting his unpublished diary into his published *Journal*, and he admits that the sentiments are more emotive than reflective (coming, as they do, from the "fulness" of his heart). However, by using the phrase "By the most infallible proofs, inward feeling," Wesley opened himself up to the charge of enthusiasm, the idea that he claimed to be led by direct and internal experience rather than by mediate and external authority.[2] Looking at how he handled the misinterpretation of this *Journal* entry provides us a good starting point to see what role Wesley allowed this facet of experience to play in theology and the Christian life.

This entry in the *Journal* is used by Dr. George Lavington, then Bishop of Exeter, in his anonymously published tract *The Enthusiasm of Methodists and Papists Compared*. Wesley undertakes a brief explanation of what he intended by that statement in a second response he writes to that tract. He takes on Bishop Lavington's argument in this way.

> To prove my art, cunning, and evasion, you instance next in the case of impulses and impressions. You begin, 'With what pertinacious confidence have impulses, impressions, feelings, &c., been advanced into certain rules of conduct! Their followers have been taught to depend upon them as sure guides and infallible proofs.' To support this weighty charge, you bring one single scrap, about a line and a quarter, from one of my Journals. The words are these: 'By the most infallible of proofs, inward feeling, I am convinced.' Convinced of what? It immediately follows, 'Of unbelief, having no such faith as will prevent my heart from being troubled.' I here assert, that inward feeling or consciousness is the most infallible of proofs of unbelief, — of the want of such a faith as will prevent the heart's being troubled. But do I here 'advance impressions, impulses, feelings, &c., into certain rules of conduct?' or anywhere else? You may just as well say, I advance them into certain proofs of transubstantiation. Neither in writing, in preaching, nor in private conversation, have I ever 'taught any of my followers to depend upon them as sure guides or infallible proofs' of anything.[3]

In answering Bishop Lavington's charge of enthusiasm, Wesley points out two features of his statement that help us to understand the role that any such "inward feelings" can play in Christian life and thought. First of all, Wesley attempts to narrow the focus of the discussion. Where Lavington wants to use the passage to claim that Wesley used feelings to support all manner of belief and behavior, Wesley points out that the passage refers solely to "unbelief" (along with pride, "irrecollection" and laxity, as we saw above). The passage, however, goes on plead with the Lord to fill up these wants with faith, humility, recollection and seriousness. In other words, Wesley indicates that what is proven by these inward feelings is merely lack or want of something. And so feelings, in this way, function as that part of experience, referred to in Chapter 11 above, which can point to ignorance or insufficiency. Of themselves, they would be unable to point to that knowledge which might be able to fill up that lack.

Secondly, we find that Wesley is attempting to distinguish between the fact of such inward feelings and their epistemological value. He does not say that such "inward feelings" do not exist, merely that they cannot be advanced as "infallible proofs" of anything, by which he means anything that resembles positive knowledge, since he has already allowed that they may prove the lack or want of belief.

This distinction between the reality of inward feelings and their epistemological weight also helps us to understand the role of positive religious feelings in the Christian life, not just negative ones. One can hardly doubt that Wesley unequivocally affirmed God's work in a person's life to have positive and perceptible effects. He asserts this in a letter he writes to the author of "A Caution Against Religious Delusion," which he transcribes into his *Journal*. There he notes,

> These [love, peace, joy] are some of those inward fruits of the Spirit, which must be *felt* wheresoever they are; and without these, I cannot learn from Holy Writ that any man is 'born of the Spirit.' I beseech you, Sir, by the mercies of God, that if as yet you know nothing of such inward feelings, if you do not 'feel in yourself these mighty workings of the Spirit of Christ,' at least you would not contradict and blaspheme. When the Holy Ghost hath fervently kindled your love towards God, you will know these to be very sensible operations. As you hear the wind, and feel it too, while it strikes upon your bodily organs, you will know you are under the guidance of God's Spirit the same way, namely, by feeling it in your soul: By the present peace, and joy, and love, which you feel within, as well as by its outward and more distant effects.[4]

What is at issue in Wesley's insistence upon the perceptibility of these "inward fruits of the Spirit" is nothing less than the reality of God's inward work in the soul. He knows *from Scripture* that such fruit is a necessary sign of being "born of the Spirit," but he understands that such fruit must be perceived by the believer for it to have any reality. As he notes to "Mr. John Smith,"

> We mean that inspiration of God's Holy Spirit, whereby he fills us with righteousness, peace, and joy, with love to Him and to all mankind. And we believe it cannot be, *in the nature of things*, that a man should be filled with this peace, and joy, and love, by the inspiration of the Holy Spirit, without perceiving it as clearly as he does the light of the sun.[5]

In other words, the perceptibility of God's inspiration is a by-product of the nature of that operation. God works in the soul to reform inward tempers, and when those tempers are thus felt, they are known to be the concomitant effects of God's operation. In all this, however, none of these feelings conveys any new data to reason by which any new knowledge may be constructed. Wesley himself confesses as much when he notes, concerning feeling the operations of the Spirit, in his *Farther Appeal*, "By feeling, I mean, being inwardly conscious of. By the operations of the Spirit, I do not mean the manner in which he operates, but the graces which he operates in a Christian."[6] The manner, any knowledge relating to how it is that God works, is yet unknown. The feelings themselves are the products, the graces, of God at work.

The feelings are real, and the privilege of any Christian, but they function more as side effects of God's work than as channels of knowledge. They are, for lack of a better phrase, *evidences of encounter*, evidences that God is, indeed, at work in the heart and experience of a believer. If Scripture has opened up the space for the encounter with God in one's experience, then one will undoubtedly feel the emotions evoked by that encounter. Thus, these feelings do objectively confirm the *fact* that it is God at work—i.e., one may deduce, based on the parameters given in Scripture, that one did not produce these feelings oneself and that they cannot come from diabolical operations, so they must be from God—and they subjectively confirm the encounter with God, much as one's happiness at seeing a lost loved one would confirm the encounter with that person. The feelings, however, do not have any content; they filter no new direct data to reason from which theological constructions of knowledge can be built. To quote again from Wesley's letter to Dr. Rutherforth, "Observe, what he inwardly feels is these fruits themselves: Whence they come, he learns from the Bible."[7]

More than anything else, Wesley's affirmation of the perceptibility of the love, peace, and joy produced by the Holy Spirit in the life of a believer is simply a result of his belief that Christianity is ultimately experiential (i.e., it affects experience) and that human emotions are part and parcel of human experience. To exclude them is to exclude the implications of the gospel for the whole of human experience, as he notes to Mr. Church:

> Do you reject inward feelings *toto genere*? Then you reject both the love of God and of our neighbour. For, if these cannot be inwardly felt, nothing can. You reject all joy in the Holy Ghost; for if we cannot be sensible of this, it is no joy at all. You reject the peace of God, which, if it be not felt in the inmost soul, is a dream, a notion, an empty name. You therefore reject the whole inward kingdom of God; that is, in effect, the whole gospel of Jesus Christ.[8]

If Christianity is to be experiential, then it will at times involve emotions and feelings. Such feelings may serve a confirmatory role provided—as is the case with all experience—that they are linked to Scripture as the only true source of theological data. Feelings of want compel one to seek scriptural fulfillment, and positive feelings confirm that fulfillment when it comes. In both cases, the *experiential* value of feelings is strongly affirmed all the while the *epistemological* value of feelings is constrained to confirming that what is happening in one's own life is, indeed, that which is promised in Scripture.

Communal Experience:
Wesley's Theological Use of the *Journal*

Turning away from the idea of "inward feeling," which has limited epistemological value, we now come to the concept of communal experience, which has far greater epistemological weight in Wesley's opinion. The fact that

Wesley's understanding of experience was public and communal has already been established. However, we have not yet explored the manner in which he provides his followers access to communal religious experience. Here, too, we find some interesting implications for his use of experience for theology, its relationship to Scripture, and its role in the lived Christian life. These can be seen in the two most important sources for communal religious experience that Wesley uses and discusses in his writings: his *Journal*[9] and his biographical reflections—both in sermon and book form. We will explore each of these in turn.

The idea of a journal as a theological tool does not originate with Wesley. Many religious leaders kept and published journals for the instruction or devotional edification of their followers or others. From *The Shepherd of Hermas* to Augustine's *Confessions* to the spiritual diaries of many great mystics of the Church, there have been those who have recorded their religious experiences (or purported experiences) in the hope that someone else could learn something from them. What is interesting, although not unique, about Wesley's *Journal* is that it is entirely not a personal spiritual journal in the sense of a record of private or inner experience, as would be the case for someone recording visions or the like. It is, rather, a religious interpretation of the events of his life, a record of the impact of spiritual issues on the visible or physical world. This is quite consonant with what we have seen Wesley's understanding of experience to be, and, as such, it serves as an important indicator of the value and role in the Christian life of the *religious* as a facet of all experience and not just a subdivision of it.

Wesley's *Journal,* by his own admission, is substantially an edited version of his own personal diary.[10] However, his purpose in publishing the *Journal* appears to be quite different from his purpose in keeping the diary. The diary Wesley kept pursuant to Jeremy Taylor's advice (in *Rule and Exercises for Holy Living and Dying* [1650-51]) that such an activity would help one be more accountable for, and thus a better steward of, one's time. The diary was a tool Wesley used for his own spiritual growth. The *Journal*, however, was published for very public reasons, and theological ones at that.

Wesley appends a "Preface" to four of the twenty parts of the *Journal* that he published himself,[11] explaining in some measure why he was airing his experience to the world. For the first section of the *Journal*, the reason is explicitly to serve as an *apologia*, a defense of his conduct in Georgia against accusations against him published by one Capt. Williams. However, Wesley gives what may be called a theological reason for offering such a defense, couched in terms of scriptural quotations. Wesley writes,

> Indeed I had no design or desire to trouble the world with any of my little affairs: As cannot but appear to every impartial mind, from my having been so long 'as one that heareth not' [Psalm 38:14]; notwithstanding the loud and frequent calls I have had to answer for myself. Neither should I have done it now, had not Captain Williams's affidavit, published *as soon as he had left England*, laid an obligation upon me, to do what in me lies, in obedience to that command of God, 'Let not the good which is in you be evil spoken of' [Romans 14:16]. With this

view I do at length 'give an answer to every man that asketh me a reason of the hope which is in me'[1 Peter 3:15] that in all these things 'I have a conscience void of offence toward God and toward men'[Acts 24:16].[12]

The "Preface" to the second section of the *Journal* offers a partly apologetic, partly theological defense for its publication,[13] and the "Prefaces" to the third and twelfth sections of the *Journal* offer almost purely theological defenses for their publication.[14]

So even though there were personal reasons for Wesley's publication of the *Journal*, the theological reasons seem eventually to come to the fore, particularly if we allow Wesley's stated indifference to the opinions of men to stand unchallenged. The *Journal* must be read, therefore, as a theological work. As a theological work, it both reinforces the importance of experience for Wesley's theology and provides a number of illustrations of how Wesley used descriptions of religious experience to further what he considered to be the proper interpretation of Scripture.

First of all, the sheer fact that Wesley publishes his *Journal* with theological motivations speaks to the importance of experience for theology. In relating both his own experience and the experience of others, Wesley is offering testimony—communally accessible data concerning experience—about the shape of the Christian life and the effect that his interpretation of Scripture can have on it. He offers that testimony in the belief that it can help shape the lives of those who would read the *Journal* so that they might become receptive to God's work. By relating incident after incident in which his interpretation of Scripture (concerning such things as radical conversions, felt forgiveness of sins or perfection in love) are confirmed in the experience of people, Wesley's *Journal* provides experiential *proof* that his interpretations are valid. When tested in the crucible of life, they work.

The incidents related in the *Journal* also serve to offer the experience of others to the experience of his reader. By relating what happens to his Methodists, Wesley invites his readers into the same experience.[15] This theological validation and invitation—not the mere relating of personal facts about himself—is one central purpose of the *Journal*, and this can be seen in the numerous times that Wesley relates the experience of those other than himself.[16]

Wesley's testimony (both of himself and of others) has power because, as we have already seen, he believes in the public nature of experience. In fact, testimonies are the only access we have to what is possible to be experienced but which we ourselves have not yet experienced. Religious testimonies are, as we said, invitations to experience. This is particularly noticeable when Wesley relates two kinds of experiences that are, by nature, unique in an individual's life and so are places where we cannot learn from our own experience but must trust the testimony of others—the experience of "new birth" found in conversion and the experience of death.

Wesley's Use of Conversion Stories

At the beginning of the so-called Evangelical Revival, of which Wesley was one of the chief leaders, many people experienced strange epiphenomena (such as violent fits or great tears or strange visions) when confronted by the message of the gospel as Wesley was relating it—that all are concluded under original sin, that any who will can be justified by faith, and that God would work in those so justified to bring them to perfection in love. In defending this revival as a work of God, Wesley articulates the value that relating the testimonies to converted lives has—in whatever manner they occurred, however bizarre some might think it—for verifying or confirming the gospel. He notes in a letter to one of his detractors,

> The question between us turns chiefly, if not wholly, on matter of fact. You deny that God does now work these effects: At least, that he works them in this manner. I affirm both; because I have heard these things with my own ears, and have seen them with my eyes. I have seen (as far as a thing of this kind can be seen) very many persons changed in a moment from the spirit of fear, horror, despair, to the spirit of love, joy, and peace; and from sinful desire, till then reigning over them, to a pure desire of doing the will of God. These are matters of fact, whereof I have been, and almost daily am, an eye or ear witness...These are my living arguments for what I assert, viz., 'That God does now, as aforetime, give remission of sins, and the gift of the Holy Ghost, even to us and to our children; yea, and that always suddenly, as far as I have known, and often in dreams or in the visions of God.'[17]

After defending himself in this transcribed letter, he offers, just a paragraph later, further experiential testimony.

> To-day, *Monday*, 21 [May 1739], our Lord answered for himself. For while I was enforcing these words, 'Be still, and know that I am God,' He began to make bare his arm, not in a close room, neither in private, but in the open air, and before more than two thousand witnesses. One, and another, and another was struck to the earth; exceedingly trembling at the presence of His power. Others cried, with a loud and bitter cry, 'What must we do to be saved?' And in less than an hour seven persons, wholly unknown to me till that time, were rejoicing, and singing, and with all their might giving thanks to the God of their salvation.[18]

Stories touching on such conversions, sometimes in passing, sometimes in great detail, teem throughout the *Journal*. Sometimes they are related with a strong tone of vindication,[19] sometimes with humor,[20] and sometimes with bewilderment.[21] In every case, however, Wesley attempts to offer "what happened," using his own testimony and the testimony of others in the hope of establishing both the veracity of his scriptural message and the reality of such a thing as true forgiveness of sin and perfection in love. In this way, these testimonies of conversion serve to reinforce Wesley's interpretation of Scripture. He never contends that such testimonies prove his interpretation of Scripture to be the only possible one, but he does contend that his interpretation of Scripture works. It affects reality in ways that anyone ought to be able to approve of. Again we see how truth for Wesley is ultimately experiential and practical and not just imaginative speculation.

The *Journal* also uses these testimonies of conversion to reinforce the space for a similar spiritual encounter, a similar conversion, within the experience of those who may read it. While this space is, of course, grounded in Scripture, Wesley uses the experience of others to show that this is how Scripture ought to be understood. Just as the testimonies would mean nothing if not interpreted in accordance with Scripture, so the Scripture would not mean anything if it never affected anyone's life is such a way that they could testify about it. Wesley's confidence in the power (perhaps even the necessity) of these testimonies can also be seen from the fact that he not only records such things in his *Journal* but that he organizes "love-feasts," which were, at least in part, testimony services where people could hear these stories first hand. Wesley would often comment on how these testimonies positively affected those who heard them, including himself, offering, as it were, testimonial support for the power of testimonies.[22]

Wesley's Use of Stories of "Dying Well"

Another set of experiences that Wesley enjoys relating in his *Journal* is that of people who "died well," people who had such confidence and assurance in their faith and in God that they could face death with equanimity, sometimes even eagerness. Wesley found this type of testimony particularly powerful. One reason for this was, no doubt, that it was the Moravians' calmness in the face of death that first stirred his own suspicion of the inadequacy of his faith. Wesley had a strong apprehension of the tenuous nature of life,[23] and any faith that did not affect the way one approached death was not a faith that Wesley was interested in.

Another reason for Wesley's fascination with stories like this may stem from the nature of such experience. In this area all of us are forced to rely on the experience of others to tell us what it is like, as our own experience of the matter comes too late to be of any use. Testimonies regarding the deaths of others is the closest we can come to learning from experience about this universal fact of human life. In Wesley's work (unlike many contemporary accounts of so-called *near-death experiences*), these testimonies provide us no information, no data, concerning the trans-sensory world, whatever might come after death. That data can only be gotten from Scripture. But testimonies to dying in full confidence of faith do demonstrate that such faith is possible within this sensory world, and they are all the more powerful for being largely inarguable. One cannot contradict them from one's own experience, and so one must simply believe them or reject them—and rejecting them entails, in some sense, a rejection of the power of testimony altogether. So if any testimonies have value, surely such testimonies as these will.

Wesley relates the stories of the deaths of a whole host of people, some of whom he had personal acquaintance with, others he had only heard about. While he will relate a few stories of the deaths of those who refused to believe in the gospel as cautionary tales,[24] Wesley is much more concerned to related the stories of those in whom he believed God's work to be clearly and powerfully evident. The persons and circumstances vary, but the main point of relating these stories is always the same: the idea that someone can meet death with equanimity or eagerness can only be explained by the reality of some assurance of faith. Wesley contended that this was the clear teaching of Scripture, and that even before he had experienced it himself. A few brief examples are sufficient to make this clear.

Just a few months before Wesley had his own experience of assurance, he recorded the following incident in his *Journal*:

> Mr. Kinchin went with me to the Castle, where, after reading prayers, and preaching on, 'It is appointed unto men once to die,' we prayed with the condemned man, first in several forms of prayer, and then in such words as were given us in that hour. He kneeled down in much heaviness and confusion, having 'no rest in' his 'bones, by reason of' his 'sins.' After a space he rose up, and eagerly said, 'I am now ready to die. I know Christ has taken away my sins; and there is no more condemnation for me.' The same composed cheerfulness he showed, when he was carried to execution: And in his last moments he was the same, enjoying a perfect peace, in confidence that he was 'accepted in the Beloved.'[25]

Wesley comments no more on the incident, but the mere way he describes it focuses the reader's attention on the question of assurance.

In one of the more extended accounts of this type in the *Journal*, Wesley relates the experience of one Sarah Peters, not so much for her own death (which was as Wesley felt a Christian's should be) but because she had worked with a group of condemned prisoners in Newgate prison. A number of these prisoners received such an assurances of the forgiveness of their sins that they could rejoice at the thought of being executed. Even their executions had a pronounced affect on those who observed them, the whole event (from Wesley's second-hand description in any case) taking on something of the character of a worship service.[26] As with many other such executions that Wesley describes, he does not comment on the events but attempts to let them speak for themselves. As far as Wesley seems concerned, it is the events, the experience itself, which is the argument for the reality of assurance, and his faith in that is sufficient enough for him to merely relate the events without sermonizing on them.

At other times, however, Wesley will explicitly connect the death of saints with the reality of Christian assurance. Commenting on the life and death of Rebecca Mills, Wesley notes,

> She found peace with God many years since, and about five years ago was entirely changed, and enabled to give her whole soul to God. From that hour she never found any decay, but loved and served him with her whole heart. Pain and sickness, and various trials, succeeded almost without any intermission: But she was always the same, firm and unmoved, as the rock on which she was built; in life and in death uniformly praising the God of her salvation. The attainableness

of this great salvation is put beyond all reasonable doubt by the testimony of one such (were there but one) living and dying witness.[27]

Many such stories appear through the *Journal*, but these brief examples show why Wesley relates them. As with the stories of conversion, stories like these both validate his understanding of Scripture and encourage his readers to seek in their own experience the assurance demonstrated by the lives of these people. These experiences can be read as both arguments and invitations, and they are often allowed to stand alone as such, unaided by scriptural commentary. As with the stories of conversion, the stories of "dying well" also illustrate the dynamic interplay between Scripture and experience. These dying saints had believed the scriptural message and so had the faith to encounter death as they did. Their encounters, in turn, afford Wesley's readers with compelling arguments to open their own lives to the same scriptural message. As before, neither Scripture nor experience functions without the other, both being necessary in the understanding and living out of truth.

Wesley's Theological Use of Biography

In addition to direct and indirect testimonies about religious experience, discreet incidents of conversion or dying in the full assurance of one's faith, Wesley will also use extended biographical treatments to bring experience to bear on the truths of Scripture and the truths of Scripture to bear on common experience. His concern in doing this does not seem to be the validation of or invitation to specific encounters of faith but rather to show the general consonance between the world as people experience it and the trans-sensory world that Scripture describes. He does this in preaching biographical sermons and in compiling or editing biographies of Christians from whose lives Wesley feels his readers can learn.

Wesley preaches two important biographical sermons, both more or less funeral sermons, that eventually find their way into his published collection. The first one was at the occasion of the death of George Whitefield, and the second on the death of John Fletcher.[28] Although each of these is given a scriptural epigraph,[29] it is clear that in both of these sermons that it is the life of the person in questions—and not the Scripture—that is the primary *text* of the discourse. Each life is evaluated in terms of its clear demonstration of scriptural truths, but it is the experience of each person and not the scriptural truths they represent that forms the basic argument of the sermon. Naturally, such biographical sermons are not unique to Wesley, and Wesley's sermon on John Fletcher follows a well established and accepted Puritan funeral sermon form. However, in light of the important role we have seen experience to play in Wesley, his use of this more or less conventional form is still instructive.

In his sermon on Whitefield, Wesley begins by admitting that he will not spend his time commenting on the chosen text. He turns immediately to an overview of Whitefield's life, the circumstances of which he explicitly takes from Whitefield's journals. As with his own *Journal*, Wesley focuses on the exterior rather than the interior details of Whitefield's life, confining himself in the main to Whitefield's indefatigable ministerial activity. In the second part of the sermon, Wesley attempts to bring out the Christian attitudes and actions that Whitefield embodied, things like modesty, courage, gratitude and zeal. All these are explicitly tied to Whitefield's "faith in a bleeding Lord; 'faith of the operation of God'" and to "the love of God shed abroad in his heart by the Holy Ghost which was given him." "From this source," Wesley affirms, "arose that torrent of eloquence, which frequently bore down all before; from this, that astonishing force of persuasion, which the most hardened sinners could not resist."[30] Wesley, thus, does not praise Whitefield for being a great orator so much as he praises him for being a representative of the type of evangelical Christianity that Wesley himself preached. His oratory skills, impressive as they were, are nonetheless seen as a by-product of his greatness, not its cause.

Whitefield's life is, thus, interpreted in terms of the doctrines of faith and love that Wesley felt were taught by Scripture, and that life in turn becomes an argument for the reality of that faith and love and for the validity of an interpretation of Scripture that highlights them. In the final section of the sermon, Wesley turns his attention to his hearers, exhorting them to follow Whitefield's example, both in terms of the essential doctrine's he preached and in the spirit with which he preached them.[31]

Wesley's sermon on John Fletcher follows a similar pattern, but he spends more time in this sermon, following Puritan conventions, explicating the meaning of an "upright man" from Psalm 37. Still, the bulk of this sermon, too, is occupied with a description of and theological reflection on Fletcher's life, mostly by means of a testimony from the pen of Fletcher's wife. Wesley describes in brief Fletcher's ministry, approving his spirit and his conduct, and Mrs. Fletcher describes other details of his life and the graceful way in which he died. Again, at the end, Wesley urges his hearers to follow Fletcher's example in holiness, as remarkable as that example was. "So unblamable a character in every respect I have not found either in Europe or America; and I scare expect to find another such on this side of eternity. But it is possible we all may be such as he was: Let us then endeavour to follow him as he followed Christ!"[32] And so the sermon ends.

In these biographical sermons, the experience of a person—conceived of as the external and publicly accessible account of their life—serves as the text of the sermon. Each life is interpreted as an example of scriptural experience and offered to his hearers as both an argument for the reality of such experience and as an invitation to make that experience their own.

Although the experience discussed in each case is the experience of an individual person, it is nonetheless communally-oriented in that it is related in terms of its publicly accessible features. It that sense, it is not just the private experience of a George Whitefield or a John Fletcher as individuals that is important, it is also the community's experience of a George Whitefield or a John Fletcher that Wesley seeks to make available. The community's experience of their lives, seeing the way they conducted their ministry and died in full in assurance of their faith, is a much more effective argument for the efficacy of

Wesley's interpretation of Scripture than would be even a first-hand testimony of their private religious feelings. As with the *Journal*, Wesley portrays lives shaped by Scripture so that those lives will, in turn, shape other lives and create a responsiveness to the same Scripture. Such a mutuality between Scripture and experience is one reason why Wesley can use an explicitly (for him, in any case) Scripture-dependent literary form like a sermon as a vehicle for describing experience.

Wesley will, of course, use other literary forms to achieve the same ends as these sermons, but most of the time he is merely responsible for their editing (usually condensing) and publishing and is not himself the author. However, as his concern is to make available the experience of Christian exemplars for the benefit of others, the fact that he does not himself author many biographies in no way detracts from the importance of their publication. A few exemplary statements from the prefaces that Wesley attaches to his (re)publications or redactions of biographical works are sufficient to show how important he considered these experiences.

First of all, Wesley's intention in referring to biographies and making them available to the public is didactic—and religiously didactic at that. Learning about life (the Christian life in particular) can only be done, apparently, from life itself, as is evident in his expressed preference for history and biography over novels.[33] He will, therefore, edit and produce works about lived examples of the Christian life on the basis of what those representative lives might teach us. Here Wesley's introduction to Fox's *Acts and Monuments of the Christian Martyrs* represents his concern:

> After the venerable remains of Ignatius and Polycarp, closed with the artless, yet lively, discourses of Macarius, and John Arndt's nervous account of true Christianity, worthy of the earliest ages, I believed nothing could be more acceptable to the serious reader, than to see this Christianity reduced to practice. I was therefore easily determined to subjoin to these, 'The Acts and Monuments of the Christian Martyrs.' Here we see that pure and amiable religion evidently set forth before our eyes; assaulted, indeed, by all the powers of earth and hell, but more than conqueror over all. In abridging this vast work I have purposely omitted, not only all the secular history, but likewise those accounts, writings, and examinations of the martyrs, which contained nothing particularly affecting or instructive...May we all learn from these worthies, to be, not almost only, but altogether, Christians! to reckon all things but dung and dross for the excellency of the experimental knowledge of Jesus Christ! and not to count our lives dear unto ourselves, so we may finish our course with joy![34]

As with his sermons, Wesley here interprets these lives as "Christianity reduced to practice." He points to the importance of "experimental knowledge of Jesus Christ" and exhorts his readers not simply to learn from the data of the these lives but to engage the same reality which guided them.

A second point concerning Wesley's theological use of biography concerns the way in which he deliberately interacted Christian life with Scripture. That is perhaps most clearly portrayed in the "Preface" he writes to his redaction of a life of Madam Guyon (which he spells "Guion"). In that preface, Wesley unashamedly avows that Scripture (at least his understanding of it) is what guides his editing of the book. After noting that someone was needed to separate the "dross from the gold" in the telling of her life, he continues by saying, "This I have endeavoured to do in the following tract, which contains all that is truly excellent, all that is scriptural and rational in her Life; all that tends to the genuine love of God and our neighbour. In the mean time, most of what I judged to be contrary to Scripture and reason is omitted."[35]

It is important to note that Wesley does not engage in any personal-historical research concerning Madam Guyon's life, as if his concern were to have a more accurate *historical* account of her life with God. Instead, he is content with a scriptural hermeneutic which will allow him to remove that which is a priori determined to be false in that it contradicts Scripture. Later on in that preface, he affirms even more explicitly that the interpretation of her life (both by herself and her biographer) exactly turns on this question.

> The grand source of all her mistakes was this, the not being guided by the written word. She did not take the Scripture for the rule of her actions; at most it was but the secondary rule. Inward impressions, which she called inspirations, were her primary rule. The written word was not a lantern to her feet, a light in all her paths.[36]

This mistake, in Wesley's eyes, led her to focus on questions of mystical darkness or *privation*. "This unscriptural notion," says Wesley, "led her into the unscriptural practice of bringing suffering upon herself."[37]

Wesley then sees the improper understanding of Scripture, here basically signaled by its lack of use, as the chief reason for what was improper in her life and practice. This gives a clear priority to Scripture over experience, or to Scripture as determinative of experience. However, at the same time, Wesley recognized in Madam Guyon's life a work of God that ought to be held up as exemplary to other Christians. He notes, "As to Madam Guion herself, I believe she was not only a good woman, but good in all eminent degree; deeply devoted to God, and often favoured with uncommon communications of his Spirit."[38] She did make her mistakes, Wesley claims, but those do not detract from the positive things in her life. "It is true," he affirms, "the anointing of the Holy One taught her of all things which were necessary to her salvation. But it pleased God to leave her to her own judgment in things of a less important nature."[39]

The end result of this analysis by Wesley, while fully acknowledging Madam Guyon's failures and unscriptural practice, is nevertheless a ringing endorsement of her example which places the value of her experience above the problems induced by her failure to properly deal with Scripture. His last words in that preface are these:

> And yet with all this dross, how much pure gold is mixed! So did God wink at involuntary ignorance! What a depth of religion did she enjoy! of the mind that was in Christ Jesus! what heights of righteousness, and peace, and joy in the Holy Ghost! How few such instances do we find, of exalted love to God and our neighbour; of genuine humility; of invincible meekness, and unbounded

resignation! So that, upon the whole, I know not whether we may not search many centuries to find another woman who was such a pattern of true holiness.[40]

Such a paradoxical affirmation, which asserts both the value of Scripture and the value of experience is only comprehensible if the two function together in Wesley's thought in a mutually interactive way that will allow no *absolute* priority of the one over the other.[41]

It thus appears that all of Wesley's explorations of life, in his *Journal*, in sermons and in biographies, serve to make Christian experience as it is actually lived out in the crucible of life accessible to his people. These are the religious experiences that he portrays and exhorts his readers to emulate. While he will not denigrate ideas of any inner life with God (as is clear from his republishing the life of Madam Guyon), neither will he equate that with true religious experience, always situating it in the larger context of life. In all of these explorations, the roles of Scripture and experience are never completely separated. Each informs the other in a dynamic which, in Wesley's understanding at least, results in true, trustworthy and useful knowledge, which in turn enables and enforces genuine Christian living.

Notes

1. *Journal* 8 January 1738 (*Jackson* 1:72).

2. In what can only be described as a severely truncated reading of Wesley, Clifford Hindley rests much of his charge against Wesley as an enthusiast on the claim that these words indicate Wesley's fundamental epistemological assumption. Cf. Hindley, "Philosophy of Enthusiasm," 101.

3. *Letter to Bishop Lavington* [27 November 1750] §21 (*Jackson* 9:33).

4. *Journal* 31 July 1739 §7 (*Jackson* 1:215). Emphasis in original. Virtually the same sentiments are expressed in *An Answer to the Rev. Mr. Church's Remarks on the Rev. Mr. John Wesley's Last Journal* [2 February 1745] §III.6 (*Jackson* 8:407-408); "A Letter to A Gentleman at Bristol" [6 January 1758] (*Jackson* 10:311-12); and "A Letter to the Reverend Mr. Downes" [17 November 1759] §11 (*Jackson* 9:103); "A Letter to the Right Reverend the Lord Bishop of Gloucester" [26 November 1762] (*Jackson* 9:143); and Sermon #45 "The New Birth" §II.4 (*Jackson* 6:70), as well as many other places. For a deeper analysis of the theological question of the perceptibility of grace in John Wesley, cf. Daniel J. Luby, "The Perceptibility of Grace in the Theology of John Wesley: A Roman Catholic Consideration" (Ph.D. diss., Pontifical University of Thomas Aquinas in Urbe, 1984).

5. *Letter to Mr. John Smith* [30 December 1745] §13 (*Jackson* 12:70). Emphasis added.

6. *Farther Appeal—Part One* §V.2 (*Jackson* 8:78).

7. *Letter to Dr. Rutherforth* [28 March 1768] §III.1 (*Jackson* 14:354). In this light, the contentions of Maddox (*Responsible Grace*, 129) and Luby ("Perceptibility of Grace," 154)—that Wesley needed these "experiential proofs" of God's renewal of the believer in love because they were less fallible than deductive proofs—need further nuance. Emotions prove nothing epistemologically outside of the meaning of those emotions given by Scripture. Again, Wesley cannot be read as contending for independent and infallible experiential confirmation of Scripture. Rather, he is bringing

out what he sees to be a necessary implication of the whole idea of being renewed in love. Love is not a deductive enterprise and so, by the nature of the thing, cannot be deductively proven to existence in one's heart. Love is experiential and rooted in the idea of encounter. If it means anything at all, it must be felt. Note, however, that the *content* given to the meaning of love—i.e., that it is a sign of God's work in a believer—is rooted in Scripture, not in experience.

8. *An Answer to the Rev. Mr. Church's Remarks on the Rev. Mr. John Wesley's Last Journal* [2 February 1745] §III.6 (*Jackson* 8:408).

9. The most relevant sections of the *Journal* for our purposes are the sections recording religious testimonies, which also find their way into Wesley's work through his use and publication of "experimental letters," both in class meetings (cf. Cf. *Journal* 27 April 1748 [*Jackson* 2:80], 10 May 1750 [*Jackson* 2:185], 4 August 1760 [*Jackson* 3:12], and 26 December 1769 [*Jackson* 3:385]) and in the *Arminian Magazine* (cf. "Preface" to *The Arminian Magazine, Volume 2* §4 [*Jackson* 14:282]). However, since the dynamic of the testimonies contained in those letters parallels that of the use of testimonies in the *Journal*, we can confine our investigation to the latter.

10. "Preface" to *An Extract of the Rev. Mr. John Wesley's Journal, Number 1* §1 (*Jackson* 1:2).

11. The 21st Journal (*Jackson* 4:339-499) was published after Wesley's death.

12. Ibid. §2 (*Jackson* 1:2). Emphasis in original.

13. "Preface" to *An Extract of the Rev. Mr. John Wesley's Journal, Number 2* §2, 8-10 (*Jackson* 1:79-82).

14. "Preface" to *An Extract of the Rev. Mr. John Wesley's Journal, Number 3* §3 (*Jackson* 1:150) and "Preface" to *An Extract of the Rev. Mr. John Wesley's Journal, Number 12* (*Jackson* 3:2).

15. Wesley himself makes this explicit in his address to the reader at the beginning of that twelfth Journal, wherein he notes, "I have only to desire, that those who think differently from me, will bear with me, as I do with them; and that those who think with me, that this was the most glorious work of God which has ever been wrought in our memory, may be encouraged to expect to be themselves partakers of all the great and precious promises, — and that without delay, — seeing, 'now is the accepted time! now is the day of salvation!'" (Ibid.).

16. Cf. among many examples, the testimony of Mr. Spangenberg (*Journal* 9 February 1736 [*Jackson* 1:23-24]), the numerous testimonies he relates of those he met in Hernhuth (*Journal* 12 August 1738 [*Jackson* 1:120-140]), and the testimonies of John Evans (*Journal* 3 December 1744 [*Jackson* 1:476-78]), Judith Berresford (*Journal* 5 May 1757 [*Jackson* 2:400-06]), and Katherine Murray (*Journal* 21 July 1767 [*Jackson* 3:288:292]).

17. *Journal* 20 May 1739 (*Jackson* 1:195)

18. Ibid. (*Jackson* 1:196).

19. As with the conversions of some who used to oppose Methodism in its earliest days, cf. *Journal* 30 September 1738 (*Jackson* 1:160), 2 March 1739 (*Jackson* 1:174-75), 16 September 1740 (*Jackson* 1:288), 30 December 1740 (*Jackson* 1:294), and 3 March 1748 (*Jackson* 2:86).

20. Cf. *Journal* 9 June 1742 (*Jackson* 1:378). "I rode over to a neighbouring town, to wait upon a Justice of Peace, a man of candour and understanding; before whom (I was informed) their angry neighbours had carried a whole wagon-load of these new heretics [i.e., followers of Wesley]. But when he asked what they had done, there was a deep silence; for that was a point their conductors had forgot. At length one said, 'Why, they pretended to be better than other people: And besides, they prayed from morning to night.' Mr. S. asked, 'But have they done nothing besides?' 'Yes, Sir,' said an old man: 'An't please your worship, they have convarted my wife. Till she went among them, she

had such a tongue! And now she is as quiet as a lamb.' 'Carry them back, carry them back,' replied the Justice, 'and let them convert all the scolds in the town.'"

21. Cf. *Journal* 6 September 1742 (*Jackson* 1:396-97) and 25 September 1748 (*Jackson* 2:117).

22. Cf. among many others, *Journal* 29 April 1739 (*Jackson* 1:189), 26 October 1741 (*Jackson* 1:343), 18 February 1750 (*Jackson* 2:173), 21 September 1760 (*Jackson* 3:21), 6 February 1763 (*Jackson* 3:128), 1 July 1766 (*Jackson* 3:255), 29 August 1770 (*Jackson* 3:407), 14 July 1776 (*Jackson* 4:81), 17 June 1778 (*Jackson* 4:129), 1 June 1780 (*Jackson* 4:183), 8 July 1787 (*Jackson* 4:387).

23. In the "Preface" to his volumes of sermons, Wesley makes this theme a grounding one for his production of these sermons and others' reading of them. "To candid, reasonable men, I am not afraid to lay open what have been the inmost thoughts of my heart," Wesley confesses. "I have thought, I am a creature of a day, passing through life as an arrow through the air. I am a spirit come from God, and returning to God: Just hovering over the great gulf; till, a few moments hence, I am no more seen; I drop into an unchangeable eternity! I want to know one thing, — the way to heaven; how to land safe on that happy shore" (*Preface to Sermons on Several Occasions* §5 [*Jackson* 5:1]).

24. *Journal* 3 August 1755 (*Jackson* 2:338), 5 May 1757 (*Jackson* 2:406), and 6 July 1762 (*Jackson* 3:99).

25. *Journal* 27 March 1738 (*Jackson* 1:90).

26. *Journal* 13 November 1748 (*Jackson* 2:119-126).

27. *Journal* 15 November 1767 (*Jackson* 3:303).

28. Sermon #53 "On the Death of the Rev. Mr. George Whitefield" (*Jackson* 6:167-82) and Sermon #133 On the Death of the Rev. John Fletcher" (*Jackson* 7:431-49).

29. Whitefield's was Num 23:10, "Let me die the death of the righteous, and let my last end be like his!" while Fletcher's was Ps 37:37, "Mark the perfect man, and behold the upright: For the end of that man is peace."

30. Sermon #53 "On the Death of the Rev. Mr. George Whitefield" §II.8 (*Jackson* 6:177).

31. Wesley, of course, controversially leaves out from those "essentials" the doctrine of Predestination, which was the major point of contention between Wesley and Whitefield during their earliest years together, and this causes not small bit of consternation among Whitefield's followers. However, this, too, is simply a clear indication of Wesley interpreting Whitefield's life according to Scripture (which Wesley felt did not support Calvinistic Predestination) and so relegating that doctrine to unimportance, despite Whitefield's own well-known views on the matter.

32. Sermon #133 "On the Death of Mr. Fletcher" §12 (*Jackson* 7:449).

33. Cf. *Journal* 30 March 1769 (*Jackson* 3:357) and "Letter to Miss Bishop" [18 August 1784] (*Jackson* 13:39).

34. "Preface" to *Fox's Acts and Monuments of the Christian Martyrs* (*Jackson* 14:227-28). Virtually the same sentiment guides both his omissions from and personal additions to Samuel Clark's *Lives of Eminent Persons* ("Preface" to *Clark's Lives of Eminent Persons* [*Jackson* 14:232]).

35. "Preface" to *An Extract of the Life of Madam Guion* §3 (*Jackson* 14:276).

36. Ibid. §7 (*Jackson* 14:277). Note that Wesley even describes the "interpretive" function of Scriptural in scriptural terms (cf. Ps 119:105).

37. Ibid. §8.

38. Ibid. §4 (*Jackson* 14:276).

39. Ibid.

40. Ibid. §9 (*Jackson* 14:278).

41. Similar concerns are in evidence in Wesley abridgement of the life of Henry Earl of Moreland (Cf. "Preface" to *The History of Henry Earl of Moreland* [*Jackson* 14:295-96]).

14

Wesley's Theological Method

Now that we have seen how Wesley treats his various sources for experience and how Scripture and experience mutually interact in the construction and confirmation of theological knowledge, knowledge which is directed toward a personal encounter with God, we are now ready to turn our attention to a brief synthesis of Wesley's theological method. Our purpose in this section is not to engage in a detailed analysis of those other factors that contribute to Wesley's theology so much as to show how they may be comfortably situated within the basic framework of the Scripture-Experience circle that we have been describing.

It should be clear at this point that a static conception of Wesley's theological method is not entirely adequate. The typical and now traditional short-hand description of Wesley's method as the so-called Wesleyan Quadrilateral does not convey what we have seen to be essential features of Wesley's approach. The motionless impression conveyed by a metaphor like a quadrilateral could lead one to think of a set of non-interacting, even independent epistemic criteria for theology. Each *side* of the quadrilateral is interpreted on more or less the same terms as a *source* for theology and brought into a more or less equal epistemic partnership, at which point the trick becomes balancing those sources in such a way that they do not end up contradicting one another.[1] To solve this problem, Scripture is given an absolute (again static) priority over the other sources (and the metaphor now shifts to something like a three-legged stool, with Scripture as the seat and the other three components as legs). Unfortunately, this approach cannot deal with the deeper epistemological question of how one knows that one has interpreted Scripture aright.

Secondly, in putting each of the components of the quadrilateral on more or less equal epistemic footing, that construction ignores the philosophical convictions with which we have seen Wesley consistently operate. If, on the other hand, the picture of Wesley's interaction between Scripture and experience that we have sketched is accurate, then Scripture and experience are the only possible sources of data, and they each have their own (even if mutually dependent) kinds of data to offer. This is not to say that the other parts of the quadrilateral—reason and tradition—do not contribute to theology, but merely that they cannot serve the role of *authorities* or sources in the same way that Scripture and experience do. If we have adequately described Wesley's functional epistemology—both general and theological—in terms of the dynamic between Scripture and experience, then we should understand reason and tradition more as *tools* than sources. They assist the dynamic interplay between experience and Scripture; they offer no new data not already present on one of those two places. We have already seen how, in Wesley's implicit Aristotelian conception of knowledge, that reason functions this way for experience—processing the data given it in order to re-address the empirical world of experience. It now remains for us to show how this works for the Scripture-Experience interplay, and to show how tradition provides its assistance as well.

The Scripture-Experience Circle and Reason

We have already outlined the important and irreplaceable role that reason plays in Wesley's thought, and so we shall be able to deal with reason here briefly and in terms of review. As a good Aristotelian, Wesley sees reason as a means of processing the data of experience (and so of Scripture) into usable knowledge. It cannot function as a source because it is completely dependent upon something else to provide it data. It is still important, however, in that without reason's processing work, neither experience nor Scripture are comprehensible. And so, in the dynamic functioning between Scripture and experience, reason (with the emphasis on logic and so as distinct from intuition) is best seen as the chief means by which data from either source is processed so as to effectively impact the other. Reason allows us more experientially informed readings of Scripture and more scripturally informed engagements with our experience and our life. To use another metaphor, if Scripture and experience are the sources of data, reason is the indispensable pump that keeps the data flowing productively in the system.

Any authority, then, that reason would have for theology would, therefore, be tied to one's faith in its ability (once properly trained, of course) to process the data it is given. Wesley's theological convictions about the nature of sin and his continued endorsement of the importance of the study of logic indicate that this proper processing of data by reason cannot simply be taken for granted. However, because Wesley's epistemology is dynamic in nature, the trustworthiness of reason as a processor of information is decided in the same arena as the trustworthiness of one's understanding of Scripture or experience— i.e., in the crucible of life. The kind of thinking that can be trusts, in the end, is the kind that produces genuine understanding, which in turn leads to effective Christian living.

The Scripture-Experience Circle and *Tradition*

The question of the role of "tradition" in Wesley's thought has already undergone much analysis and raises many important issues that do not relate directly to our present investigation. However, a brief sketch can be made to show how tradition functions in Wesley's theological method. There is a rather wide consensus that Wesley's understanding of tradition does not include everything that has happened in the Christian church's life and thought since the apostolic times. His affirmation of tradition is more or less confined to the earliest post-apostolic church, which Wesley will often label "antiquity," and the Church of England.[2] In the end, both of these important loci of tradition function in Wesley's theological method not as independent sources of thought but as important tools in the understanding of the message of Scripture and its application to experience or the lived Christian life.

Wesley affirms the witness of the earliest post-apostolic church to be valuable because of the relationship those early Fathers had both to the Apostles themselves and to the very Spirit which inspired the Apostle's writings in Scripture. In a somewhat romantic portrayal of history, Wesley affirms that these Apostolic Fathers (specifically Ignatius, Polycarp and Clement of Rome, whose work he reproduces in the very first volume of his *Christian Library*) were personally entrusted by the Apostles with the furtherance of the Gospel in their respective sees after the Apostles themselves had passed on.[3] When one adds to this their own piety and devotion to the Gospel and the fact that the Spirit was still extraordinarily active in their times, "We cannot with any reason," claims Wesley, "doubt of what they deliver to us as the Gospel of Christ; but ought to receive it, though not with equal veneration, yet with only little less regard than we do the sacred writings of those who were their masters and instructers."[4]

It is, thus, their proximity to the very sources of Scripture—the Apostles and the Holy Spirit—that gives their own work the high level of credibility it has. Wesley would have, of course, imbibed much of his interest in Christian antiquity from his Augustan age,[5] but the fact that he links his apology for this interest to Scripture is significant. This raises a couple of important issues concerning theological use of this part of tradition in light of the interplay between Scripture and experience that we have been examining.

First of all, whatever the amount and kind of theological weight Wesley will give to antiquity—and this changes during the course of his life—it is clear that the authority of Christian antiquity is derivative. To the extent that it illuminates the teaching and spirit of the Scriptures and demonstrates the practical application of that teaching in life, it is beneficial and productive. However, once the church begins to drift away from that teaching and Spirit—and for Wesley this seems to have happened with Constantine—the tradition loses touch with spiritual life and with Scripture and so diminishes in authority.[6]

In consequence to this, it seems that antiquity has an ancillary role in theology, aiding the role of Scripture in testifying to the truth of the Christian message but not serving as an independent criterion for truth. When one has access to the primary source of spiritual data—i.e., Scripture—one only uses secondary sources as necessary. This seems to be what Wesley implies when he claims that "We prove the doctrines we preach by Scripture and reason, and, if need be, by antiquity."[7] The first two are indispensable, the latter is called upon at need, and only to the extent that it reinforces and does not contradict what is said by the other two.

One brief example of how this works out in Wesley's life can be seen in a matter upon which Scripture is not exactly clear: the question of ordination and its relationship to the offices of bishop and elder. It seems on first sight that Wesley becomes convinced of the right of any elder (and not just a bishop) to ordain someone to ministry through the historical investigations of Lord Peter King and Bishop Edward Stillingfleet,[8] both of whom contend against the sole right of diocesan bishops to ordain on the basis of the practice of the earliest church. He reads both of their works in the 1740s and even at the end of his life is confirmed in his agreement with them.[9]

However, this is not just a matter of the theological weight of Christian antiquity, as one can see in looking at the context in which Wesley raises this issue. First of all, his initial reaction to King's work, recorded in his *Journal*, strikes the reader as somewhat incredulous:

> On the road I read over Lord King's Account of the Primitive Church. In spite of the vehement prejudice of my education, I was ready to believe that this was a fair and impartial draught; but if so, it would follow that Bishops and Presbyters are (essentially) of one order; and that originally every Christian congregation was a Church independent on all others![10]

The historical case is there, but the "vehement prejudice" of Wesley's high church education does not seem to accommodate itself to this new evidence right away.

Ten years later, however, in commenting on Bishop Stillingfleet's work, Wesley makes it clear that the real issue is scriptural, not historical. He says,

> As to my own judgment, I still believe 'the Episcopal form of church government to be scriptural and apostolical.' I mean, well agreeing with the practice and writings of the Apostles. But that it is prescribed in Scripture, I do not believe. This opinion, which I once zealously espoused, I have been heartily ashamed of ever since I read Bishop Stillingfleet's 'Irenicon.' I think he has unanswerably proved, that 'neither Christ nor his Apostles prescribe any particular form of church government; and that the plea of divine right for diocesan Episcopacy was never heard of in the primitive church.'[11]

Here one can see that the issue is not the independent weight of antiquity, but the way in which antiquity bears out the teaching of Christ and his apostles—i.e., Scripture—in the life of the Church.

Finally, in Wesley own ministry, the matter only comes to a head when circumstances—i.e., experience and the crucible of life—dictate that he do something to aid the churches in North America once they were freed from the secular (and so also the sacred) rule of the King of England. Since they need ministers and have no bishop to ordain them, Wesley takes it upon himself to fulfill that role. He states as much in a letter that he sends with his new ordinands to the Methodists in America. The account is relevant enough to quote at some length:

Lord King's 'Account of the Primitive Church' convinced me many years ago, that Bishops and Presbyters are the same order, and consequently have the same right to ordain. For many years I have been importuned, from time to time, to exercise this right, by ordaining part of our Travelling Preachers. But I have still refused, not only for peace' sake, but because I was determined as little as possible to violate the established order of the national Church to which I belonged. But the case is widely different between England and North America. Here there are Bishops who have a legal jurisdiction: In America there are none, neither any parish Ministers. So that for some hundred miles together, there is none, either to baptize, or to administer the Lord's supper. Here, therefore, my scruples are at an end; and I conceive myself at full liberty, as I violate no order, and invade no man's right, by appointing and sending labourers into the harvest...If any one will point out a more rational and scriptural way of feeding and guiding those poor sheep in the wilderness, I will gladly embrace it. At present, I cannot see any better method than that I have taken.[12]

Wesley then answers the objection of why he did not have these men ordained by an English bishop, all of which are owing to the circumstances, and concludes by affirming of the American Methodists that "They are now at full liberty, simply to follow the Scriptures and the primitive church. And we judge it best that they should stand fast in that liberty wherewith God has so strangely made them free."[13]

Here, it is experience which is forcing Wesley to address the theological issue of ordination, and he wishes to do so in a "rational and scriptural way." Reason and Scripture, then, are his main criterion. But it does matter to him that he finds corroborating support for his actions in the practice of the earliest church. So, Christian antiquity does have an important contribution to make to theology in Wesley's mind, but it is one that seems solidly dependent upon the functioning of the Scripture-experience circle that forms the core of his theological method.

The issue of ordination brings us to the other of Wesley's loci of tradition, namely the Church of England. Here, Wesley is quite clear that he can affirm the authority of that church because it affirms what Scripture teaches. Wesley was *traditional*, in the sense that he operated from his tradition and valued what it had to say. He found it important that he could demonstrate the doctrine of justification by faith from the official *Homilies* of the Church of England[14] and could even affirm that his Methodist movement was really just the "plain, old religion of the Church of England."[15] But at the same time, as we have already seen, he felt free to challenge the Church of England's practice in a number of areas—such as in the use of field preaching, lay preachers, or even himself taking on the powers of a bishop—when his dynamic of Scripture-in-experience dictated otherwise. Lay preaching arises when the scriptural need of having preachers outweighs the Church of England canon allowing only ordained persons to preach. Wesley engages in field preaching—much to his own chagrin—when Scripture and experience convince him that it is more important to save souls where they can be found that to follow any supposed Church of England tradition about only preaching within consecrated walls.[16]

Wesley's willingness to violate his tradition arises from the way he understands Scripture and experience. His clearest expressions of the direct relationship of his tradition to Scripture are found in his tract "Ought We to Separate from the Church of England" and in his sermon "On Schism." In the latter he affirms the value of tradition (and of loyalty to tradition) but only in terms of the way in which that tradition upholds or at least does not contradict Scripture. "Suppose," Wesley reflects, "the Church or society to which I am now united does not require me to do anything which the Scripture forbids, or to omit anything which the Scripture enjoins, it is then my indispensable duty to continue therein."[17] And so even the Church of England must function within the parameters defined by Wesley's dynamic of Scripture and experience, and when those sources dictate otherwise, he can with good conscience follow them even in opposition to his church. Tradition, then, holds no independent claim over his thinking, nor can it be trusted to offer new data not already affirmed by experience or Scripture.[18]

Putting the Pieces Together

The model of Wesley's theological method as a quadrilateral has proven useful to Wesley's inheritors for keeping them mindful that theology is much more than cutting and pasting from Scripture into life. It has reminded them that reason and tradition ought to have their place, and it has kept them aware that experience plays a vital role. However, that model cannot preserve what we have seen to be the central feature of Wesley's theological method, and that is the dynamic interplay between his understanding of Scripture and his understanding of experience. We need another model that preserves the good but add this essential piece.

What we have here proposed is the idea of a hermeneutical circle, and interactive dynamic between two *sources* aided by two *tools*. The first source is the revelation from God about the trans-sensory world, the testimony to which is found in the pages of Scripture. The second source is the everyday world, about which we learn from our senses and from the testimonies of others around us. These two function to interpret each other, and each is made most meaningful when it is seen in the light of the data offered by the other. To aid this connection, we have the patterns and rules of proper thinking, reason, which helps us process the data of experience in ways that enable Scripture make more sense and also help us to interpret Scripture in ways that positively shape our experience. We can also take advantage of the fact that this circling dynamic has a history, a tradition of others who have sought to build the same connection between experience and Scripture and who have left to us the record of their attempts.

Such a conception, exemplified in a simple way in Figure 1, allows us to see the central thrust of Wesley's approach to theology, showing the primary roles of Scripture and experience and the secondary roles of reason and tradition. It also portrays Wesley's method as the dynamic that it is rather than as a static list

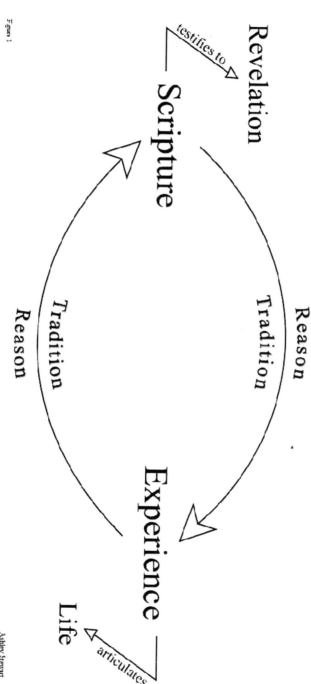

Figure 1

Ashley Stewart

of four, more-or-less independent sources of data which we must somehow balance. The central role of Scripture is not compromised by its engagement with experience because one is only allowed to interpret one's experience in ways that cohere with scriptural testimony. This seems to be the method Wesley evinced throughout his life, and it may be one of his most lasting gifts to the church.

Conclusion to Part Three

Throughout Part Three, we have been examining the central dynamic of Wesley's theological method. We have seen in the arena of theology a natural outworking of a basic epistemological stance which values both experience and Scripture in an ever-circling dynamic (aided by reason and on occasion assisted by tradition). Both divine revelation and human experience of the world are valued, and each are employed to comprehend the other and to create scriptural space in experience for an encounter with divine reality. In that, human experience of the physical world is insufficient to provide us reliable data about God, but that it can serve the role of opening us up to the only true source for that data. Once theological knowledge is constructed from Scripture, however, it *must*, according to Wesley, be placed back into the crucible of life to be tested and further refined. This, in turn, drives the theologian back to the Scripture on the basis of the results of this new experience, and so the circle goes on.

To aid the functioning of that circle in the lives and minds of his followers and readers, Wesley provided means by which people might evaluate the weight of their own experiences, and he also provided access, through various media, to the experience of other people. The criteria for evaluating one's own experience and the yardstick provided by the experience of others function together to allow one to "do theology": to interpret Scripture aright, think well about theological truth and meaningfully apply that truth in one's own life. Thus we have the means of balancing the four most often recognized components of Wesley's theology (i.e., the so-called Wesleyan Quadrilateral) within the framework of Wesley's twin and mutually reinforcing commitments to Scripture and experience.[19] We also have the means for describing how and why his theology underwent some change, possibly even significant change, over the course of his life. Indeed, given what we have seen of his method, it would have been extraordinary if Wesley's thought on many issues did not refine itself. That would mean that his experience did not make any difference to his thought, which it surely did.

Our investigation into Wesley's theological method is, however, not yet complete. While we have explored the basic functioning of the dynamics involved, we have not yet explored the implications of that functioning. In Part Four, we will turn to the question of the difference Wesley's theological method makes for his theology in general and begin to sketch out a few possible implications for reckoning with Wesley's method in contemporary theology.

Notes

1. Which is the main thrust of Thorsen's major work on the subject. Cf. Thorsen, *Wesleyan Quadrilateral.*

2. On this point, cf. Frank Baker *John Wesley and the Church of England* (Nashville: Abingdon, 1970); Campbell, *Wesley and Christian Antiquity*; Scott Jones, *Conception and Use*, 62-65; Luke L. Keefer, "John Wesley, Disciple of Early Christianity" (Ph.D. diss., Temple University, 1982); Maddox, *Responsible Grace*, 42-44; and Arthur C. Meyers, Jr., "John Wesley and the Church Fathers" (Ph.D. diss., St. Louis University, 1985).

3. "Preface" to *The Epistles of the Apostolic Fathers* (*Jackson* 14:223-26).

4. Ibid. §3 (*Jackson* 14:224). Wesley's comments substantially depend on the introduction to the Apostolic Fathers given by Archbishop William Wake in *The Genuine Epistles of the Apostolical Fathers* 4th edition, ed. William Wake (London 1693) [1]:175, cited in Campbell, *Wesley and Christian Antiquity*, 13.

5. Cf. Campbell, *Wesley and Christian Antiquity*, 7-22.

6. On this point, see Wesley's comment on "The Mystery of Iniquity," claiming, "Persecution never did, never could, give any lasting wound to genuine Christianity. But the greatest it ever received, the grand blow which was struck at the very root of that humble, gentle, patient love, which is the fulfilling of the Christian law, the whole essence of true religion, was struck in the fourth century by Constantine the Great, when he called himself a Christian, and poured in a flood of riches, honours, and power, upon the Christians; more especially upon the Clergy...Then, not the golden but the iron age of the Church commenced" (Sermon #61 "The Mystery of Iniquity" §27 [*Jackson* 6:261-62]). Cf. similar comments in, among others, Sermon #64 "The New Creation" §4 (*Jackson* 6:289), Sermon #89 "The More Excellent Way" §2 (*Jackson* 7:26-27), and Sermon #102 "Of Former Times" §15-19 (*Jackson* 7:163-65).

7. *Farther Appeal—Part Three* §III.28 (*Jackson* 8:233).

8. Peter King's *An Inquiry into the Constitution, Discipline, Unity, and Worship of the Primitive Church that Flourished within the First Three Hundred Years after Christ*, published in 1712; and Edward Stillingfleet's, *The Irenicum, or Pacificator: Being a Reconciler of Church Differences*, published in 1659.

9. In addition to the citations from Wesley, listed below, see also Cambpell, *Wesley and Christian Antiquity*, 43.

10. *Journal* 20 January 1746 (*Jackson* 2:6-7).

11. "A Letter to the Rev. Mr. Clarke" [3 July 1756] (*Jackson* 13:211).

12. "Letter to Dr. Coke, Mr. Asbury, and our Brethren in North America" [10 September 1784] §2-6 (*Jackson* 13:251-52).

13. Ibid.

14. *Journal* 12 November 1738 (*Jackson* 1:164).

15. *Journal* 16 October 1739 (*Jackson* 1:239).

16. On the issue of lay preaching, cf. Sermon #38 "A Caution Against Bigotry" §III.7-10 (*Jackson* 5:488-89); *Journal* 27 December 1745 (*Jackson* 2:3-6) and 3 August 1788 (*Jackson* 4:432-33), and "Letter to Mr. N." [3 September 1756] (*Jackson* 13:218-19). Concerning field preaching, cf. *Journal* 29 March-2 April 1739 (*Jackson* 1:185), 30 September 1767 (*Jackson* 3:301, and 6 September 1772 (*Jackson* 3:479); as well as *Farther Appeal—Part One* §VI.4-6, (*Jackson* 8:113-16) and *Farther Appeal—Part Three* §III.23-24 (*Jackson* 8:230-31).

17. Sermon #75 "On Schism" §17 (*Jackson* 6:408).

18. This is further confirmed by looking at how Wesley critiqued the over-valuing of tradition in the Roman Catholic community, cf. *Popery Calmly Considered* §I.3 (*Jackson* 10:141).

19. We mention "most often recognized" components of Wesley's theology because there are obviously other factors at work which have not, up to this point, been sufficiently explored. Wesley's insistence, for example, on the importance of sacraments and his call to his Methodists to continue to partake of them in established Anglican churches also seems to have an influence on his theology, and it would be interesting to see how such "embodied rituals" might interact with the Scripture-experience circle that we have been describing.

Part Four

15

Implications of Wesley's Experiential Theology

As we have seen, Wesley weaves together experience and Scripture in the doing of theology, giving a large and important role to experience but never surrendering or compromising biblical authority. Experience and Scripture work together to point one in the direction of theological truth. They provide a comfortable degree of reliability to one's theological constructions but do so without cutting short a process which is always open to new insight and new discovery. While requiring some minimal faith commitments at the outset—a moderate realist approach to sensory reality, a trust in the mind's ability to process it, and at least a suspicion that Scripture could be trusted to point toward any trans-sensory reality—Wesley's method derives its strength much more from the process it represents than the grounds upon which it is built. It now remains for us to draw out a few implications for doing theology in the way Wesley models and begin to sketch out a few benefits we may derive from emulating Wesley's theological method in our contemporary theological environment.

In looking at the implications of Wesley's theological method, we are looking for the ways in which that method impacts his theological in general. What differences does it make for Wesley to have taken experience as seriously as he seems to have? What does theology performed in the space created by the hermeneutical circle between Scripture and experience look like? What are its major characteristics, and more importantly how might those characteristics be understood as connected to the theological method that produces them?

In discussing the connection between a few general characteristics of Wesley's theology and his theological method, we are not necessarily looking for direct causal relationships, as if we could prove that Wesley first adopted a method and then that method was solely responsible for producing the kind of theology he embodies. First of all, that implies an easier separation between content and method than is tenable for Wesley. Secondly, it assumes that Wesley's theology developed in a purely methodological way, when it could also be the case that Wesley's prior theological commitments influenced the development of his method.

Nevertheless, it is still a useful exercise to explore the connections between method and theology in Wesley. Even when we cannot prove a causal connection between them, we can still demonstrate a important level of coherence. Even if these characteristics of theology began as content-oriented commitments instead of methodological ones, they are substantially reinforced by Wesley's method and so become more pervasive in his thought than they might otherwise have been. Also, if the features that we will explore in Wesley have a methodological side, then investigating it provides us a way to actualize those features that are positive—and avoid those that are negative—without necessarily demanding an array of content-oriented commitments.

As may already be evident from the course of this investigation, Wesley's theology has a very distinctive shape. It is so different from the kind of theology one might find in theological textbooks—either from Wesley's day or from our own—that, as we noted earlier, the recognition of Wesley as a serious theologian has been a long time in coming. For example, his theology is much more *systemic* than *systematic*, dealing with all areas but never organizing all those results together. It is also exceedingly practical, unconcerned with the types of questions that occupy many monographs on theology, but nevertheless effective, shaping the lives in Britain and America, to some extent affecting the culture of those areas as well.[1] In some ways, his theology crosses some confessional dividing lines with relative ease and yet is not unconcerned with the question of orthodoxy.[2] If these distinctive characteristics are not merely the result of one person's idiosyncratic theology, then perhaps they can be understood in relationship to the distinctive theological method that drove him. And if we should find some of these concerns and orientations congenial to contemporary theology, then perhaps paying serious attention to the way they are connected to Wesley's method is one good way for us to develop them for theology today.

Before discussing in more depth the general characteristics of Wesley's theology, we need to say a bit more about its actual content. Very often, to speak of *Wesleyan Theology* is to speak of a set of content-oriented theological emphases, including such ideas a "prevenient grace," "Arminianism," "entire sanctification," and "perfect love." These emphases in content are then usually contrasted with more typical Reformed or Calvinist theological emphases, either to endorse or condemn them. In one sense, of course, it would be a very natural extension of this investigation to pursue the question of how Wesley's theological method informed or gave rise to his especial theological content rather than exploring these admittedly more vague general theological characteristics. However, while we would affirm that questions of content are extremely important, in our pursuit of the implications of Wesley's experiential theological method we will hold specific questions related to content yet in abeyance. We do this for two main reasons.

First of all, there are broader implications for understanding Wesley's method than for understanding the content of his theology. Likely only Methodists or Holiness churches (and not all of them) would be concerned about being *Wesleyan* in their content, and tying Wesley's theological method too quickly to that content might relegate the method to those parochially defined circles. On the other hand, there may be many theologians who might consider employing a method that could positively inform their own theology and help them to take seriously both a commitment to Scripture and an openness to experience. We believe that Wesley offers just such a method, and that his method may be critically engaged without requiring any of his own specific theological commitments. In this, our concern is not so much to do Wesleyan Theology as merely to do theology well, obtaining the kind of results that are most fruitful or productive for the contemporary church and its engagement with contemporary cultures.

Secondly, Wesley's method itself somewhat relativizes the a priori importance of any specific content. Not that content is unimportant—it is, and methods that cannot produce adequate content are theologically worthless. However, as Wesley's method is grounded in a faith in the *knowability* of reality, it constantly measures the content that it produces against its applicability to the reality it attempts to describe. This measuring is done again by employing the same Scripture-experience hermeneutical circle that gave rise to the content in the first place. Therefore, proper attention to the question of method—in Wesley's schema at least—is one way to address the concerns about the reliability of content. If Wesley's theological method *is* sound, and the content that arises from it reflects something of the way things are, then those who emulate his method may very well find themselves agreeing with his content without any prior commitment to doing so, just as scientists who copy the experiments of other scientists may end up agreeing with their results. Such reaffirmed or rediscovered content, then, should not be called *Wesleyan* but would be much more adequately labeled *Christian*, or, perhaps even more simply, *true*.[3]

By looking at the characteristics of Wesley's theology, then, we are looking beyond the question of specific content and are tracing instead its general shape, a shape that we may describe with four important adjectival descriptions—three of which are positive, one of which is better described as cautionary. Wesley's theology is relational, ecumenical, interdisciplinary, but also overly pragmatic. The first three are characteristics of theology that we may be very interested in advancing today; the fourth is a pitfall that we would be better off avoiding.

We have chosen these four characteristics, among others that might also be chosen, because they are particularly relevant to the contemporary theological scene. The late modern scene is marked by a concern for people and suspicion of institutions, which means that far more people are open to a relational theology than one that is simply about organizing abstract or metaphysical truth. The issues of the relationship between theologies (ecumenism) and between theology and other branches of human leaning (the interdisciplinary question) is also one of extreme importance, whether one ends up affirming a privileged place for theology in general or a particular theology (as "Radical Orthodoxy" does) or ultimately rejecting such a privilege (as reflected in, say, the "Liverpool Statement"). And finally, given that many ecumenical resources are being to devoted to common action even in the absence of theological agreement (as championed by those originally concerned with "Life and Work" over "Faith and Order"), and given the tendency in many corners to reduce Christianity to an ethical program, the specter, which is certainly present in Wesley, of becoming too practical (or overly pragmatic) is also one that always arises from taking experience seriously and ought also to be addressed.

So, while acknowledging the relevance of—and even the ultimate need for—content-oriented theological reflections informed by Wesley's methodological insights, we will conclude our dialogue with Wesley by looking at the way in which his method coheres into a relational, ecumenical, interdisciplinary, but overly pragmatic theology. We will also explore, in a tentative and merely suggestive way, what difference that might make today. In engaging Wesley's theology with more contemporary concerns, we cannot, in the scope of this project, engage those concerns finely or with much detail, but we can offer what might be understood as suggestions for further research or reflection. Under each general heading, we will first explore that characteristic in Wesley and then we will reflect on some ways in which engaging Wesley's theological method might actualize (or in the last case, avoid) that characteristic for contemporary theology.

Notes

1. As in Wesley's encouragement of popular literacy (Clark, *English Society*, 285-95) or with the importance of the Methodists on the American frontier (cf. Edwin Gaustad and Leigh Schmidt, *The Religious History of America: The Heart of the American Story from Colonial Times to Today*, rev. ed. [New York: HarperCollins, 2002], 101-02, 166-68).

2. For more on these general characteristics of Wesley's theology, cf. Maddox, *Responsible Grace*, 15-25. For Wesley as a comprehensive, even if not systematic thinker, cf. Thomas Oden, *John Wesley's Scriptural Christianity: A Plain Exposition of His Teaching on Christian Doctrine* (Grand Rapids: Zondervan, 1994), 19.

3. For the importance of this perspective, cf. John W. Wright and J. Douglas Harrison, "The Ecclesial Practice of Reconciliation and the End of the 'Wesleyan'," *Wesleyan Theological Journal* 37 (2002): 212-214.

16

Experiential Theology as Relational Theology

A *relational theology*, in the sense that we will be using it in this chapter, is a theology that takes seriously both its derivation from relationships and its purpose or goal in shaping relationships. Such a theology would also be organized by categories of personal relationships—as opposed to categories drawn from a philosophical system or institutional structure. From the way Wesley engages experience as both source and goal, this conception of theology fits him very well.

Relational Theology in Wesley

Wesley's theology is relational, or perhaps more precise "communal," because he has a communal understanding of experience. One cannot learn from experience merely on the basis of one individualistic encounters, however important they might be for making things meaningful in one's life. Wesley's theology is also relational he will only allow the theological hermeneutical circle between Scripture and experience to function for some end beyond its own proper functioning. That end is a relationship or an encounter. The priority of this end over the means used to obtain can be seen in that Wesley will only value knowledge as it leads to encounter, but he will value encounter even one cannot do anything with that encounter epistemologically. We will deal with each of these two facets of relational theology in Wesley in turn before turning to the question of their importance for contemporary theology.

Relational Theology as Communally Rooted

Wesley's understanding of experience is fundamentally public and external (as opposed to private and internal). It is the crucible of life from which all ideas derive and in which they all must be tested. If it is such a public arena, and if the value and weight of even our *private* experience is tested in that arena, then a theology that reckons seriously with such a view of experience cannot be done by individuals in isolation. It can only be done relationally and communally.

A theologian following Wesley's model of theology recognizes his or her dependence not just upon other theologians but on the rest of humanity to provide the experiential/ experimental context out of which his or her own investigations flow and in which his or her ideas and interpretations of Scripture can be tested in order to become meaningful. Private religious or theological insights, however cogently argued or internally coherent they might be, are subject to the same strictures as private religious experience. They must prove true in the lived Christian life in order to qualify as meaningful bits of Christian theology. This proof is not just a matter of the theologian privately interpreting his or her own experience in light of his or her own insights. It is also a matter of allowing others to interpret the theologian's experience or their own with reference to those insights. Only in the light of such communal experience can theology be done. Anything short of that will not qualify as true theology in Wesley's scheme because it may bear no relation to the reality it seeks to describe.

Clear indications of the weight of this consideration in Wesley can be found both in his analyses of individualistic theologians and in his affirmation of the communal and relational context for theological learning and debate. Both of these opinions in Wesley can be connected to his theological method, and both might be very useful to contemporary theology.

The two individualistic theologians that take the greatest beating in Wesley's writings are Baron Swedenborg and Jacob Boehme (spelled *Behmen* in Wesley's writings). We have already seen how he critiques these two thinkers for their lack of attention to Scripture, but that is not the only place he faults them. He also faults them for being too individualistic in the way they came up with their theological ideas (i.e., in their theological method). Concerning Swedenborg's "Account of Heaven and Hell," Wesley notes, "Of this work in particular I must observe, that the doctrine contained therein is not only quite unproved, quite precarious from beginning to end, as depending entirely on the assertion of a single brain-sick man; but that, in many instances, it is contradictory to Scripture, to reason, and to itself."[1]

The doctrine in the book is "unproved" and "precarious" because it depends on the word of just one person (and this would explain why it is also unscriptural and irrational). Of course, it does not help that Swedenborg was, in Wesley's opinion, "brain-sick," having lost a firm grip on his understanding from a fever.[2] That, however, merely exacerbates the problems created by a lack of a communal context for coming up with or testing theology; it is not the cause of those problems.

Several times in his tract-length explication and critique of Swedenborg's ideas, Wesley will decry those ideas as contrary to "common sense" or "common understanding." One time, after elucidating how Swedenborg exegetes Scripture, Wesley asks, "Can any person of common understanding defend any of these expositions? Are they not so utterly absurd, so far removed from all shadow of reason, that, instead of pronouncing them the dictates of the Holy Ghost, we cannot but judge them to be whims of a distempered imagination?"[3] The appeal is to common or public judgment, which is opposed to "whims of a distempered imagination." Nowhere does Wesley deny that the Baron believed his own experiences; nowhere does he accuse him of just making up his visions. However, he everywhere points out that his is a completely inadequate way of doing theology, which results in both idiosyncratic expositions of Scripture and completely unscriptural (and downright dangerous) ideas.

Jacob Boehme fares little better in Wesley's estimation and for much the same reasons. Certainly, he believes Boehme to be unscriptural and irrational, but the reason why he is so is that he functions purely out of his own authority. Wesley writes,

> What some seem most to admire in his writings is what I most object to; I mean his philosophy and his phraseology. These are really his own; and these are quite new; therefore, they are quite wrong. I totally object to his blending religion with philosophy; and as vain a philosophy as ever existed: Crude, indigested; supported neither by Scripture nor reason, nor anything but his own *ipse dixit.*[4]

Boehme's ideas are wrong because they are novel, because they are original to him and him alone. They arise out of his own imagination, and so it is unsurprising that they would not prove true when tested by the hermeneutical circle of Scripture and experience. Any such individualistic theology would prove itself inadequate, it seems, the natural consequence of failing to reckon with either Scripture or experience and reason, all of which are only accessible in communal contexts.[5]

On the other side, Wesley strongly insists on a communal context for understanding Scripture or for doing and debating theology. We have already glimpsed this in seeing Wesley's high valuation of the role of tradition, academic learning and the importance he gives to books.[6] This regard he gives to history and the printed pages reinforces the idea that so much of what is needed for doing theology—including even the ability to think well—is acquired from the outside, acquired from others. To those of his lay preachers who would decry the need for learning and proclaim a sole reliance on the Bible, Wesley had this to say:

> 'But I read only the Bible.' Then you ought to teach others to read only the Bible, and, by parity of reason, to hear only the Bible: But if so, you need preach no more. Just so said George Bell. And what is the fruit? Why, now he neither reads the Bible, nor anything else. This is rank enthusiasm. If you need no book but the Bible, you are got above St. Paul. He wanted others too. 'Bring the books,' says he, 'but especially the parchments,' those wrote on parchment. 'But I have no taste for reading.' Contract a taste for it by use, or return to your trade.[7]

Those who have no place in their world for learning—no openness to the community for ideas beyond their own—have no place in ministry as far as Wesley is concerned.

Beyond mere books, however, which one could read alone in one's study, Wesley also affirms the need for a relational context in which to discuss theology and arrive at Christian truth. Time and time again when Wesley is debating a theological issues with his opponents, he affirms that such debate can only be productive if conducted in an environment of love, often invoking the twin biblical phrases about "speaking the truth in love" (Eph 4:15)[8] and loving "not in word but in deed and in truth" (1 John 3:18)[9] to make that link.

For his own part, Wesley will often state his own openness to correction by others. He claims that, if someone understands a theological point better than he, then he is always willing to be instructed, although he pleads that such correction be done in love.[10] Typical in this regard is one of his concluding objections to the author of a pamphlet entitled "Observations on the Conduct and Behaviour of a certain Sect, usually distinguished by the name of *Methodists.*"

> I am grieved at your extreme warmth: You are in a thorough ill-humour from the very beginning of your book to the end. This cannot hurt me; but it may yourself. And it does not at all help your cause. If you denounce against me all the curses from Genesis to the Revelation, they will not amount to one argument. I am willing (so far as I know myself) to be reproved either by you or any other. But whatever you do, let it be done in love, in patience, in meekness of wisdom.[11]

Wesley's opponent's lack of charity and his "extreme warmth" is not just a bother to Wesley; it is an obstacle to the very pursuit of truth.[12] In opposition to such "warm" authors, Wesley defends his Methodists and their manner of correcting the errors of others by claiming, "Do they allow any method of bringing even those who are farthest out of the way, who are in the grossest errors, to the knowledge of the truth, except the methods of reason and persuasion; of love, patience, gentleness, long-suffering?"[13] To show that this is not just a Methodist concern but a Christian one, Wesley will lay the duty of loving reproof on every Christian as a natural outgrowth of even being a Christian.[14]

Relationships or community or love must serve as the foundation for any pursuit of truth, not merely because Wesley believes in the theological importance of love but because his theological method cannot function in any other kind of environment. No true advance in knowledge is even possible if individual theologians either function on their own or work in opposition to others. This does not lessen Wesley's concern for attaining truth, but it affirms that truth is only attainable in a communal context.[15]

Relational Theology as Communally Directed

In addition to functioning in the context of love, Wesley's theological method is also directed at relational ends. As we saw in Part Three, the dynamic of Wesley's method is geared toward more than the mere acquisition and testing of knowledge (in the sense of data). It is about the active engagement with reality, shaping proper experience. One of the natural results of this theological method—regardless of specific issues of content—will be a "theology of encounter," a theology directed at facilitating relationships.

The place in which this implication of Wesley's method is best seen in his own thought is in the intimate connection between truth, knowledge and love in Wesley's mind, a connection that has long been recognized. In 1831, Thomas Jackson, the editor of the third edition of Wesley's works, comments in his "Preface" to that edition that—unlike the work of many authors—"the whole of his [Wesley's] publications are at once designed and calculated, not only to improve the understanding, but also to promote the love of God and man."[16] Wesley's theological method never denigrates the importance of understanding, but it always directs that understanding at relational ends.

The joint phrase "knowledge and love"—usually "knowledge and love of God"—occurs quite frequently in Wesley, always with the implication that these are not just two items in a list but are somehow united. In his sermon on "Spiritual Worship," Wesley will use that phrase to define the essence of *religion*. "Religion, as to the nature or essence of it, does not lie in this or that set of notions, vulgarly called *faith*; nor in a round of duties, however carefully *reformed* from error and superstition. It does not consist in any number of outward actions. No: It properly and directly consists in the knowledge and love of God,"[17] from which then outward manifestations will spring. In his sermon "The General Spread of the Gospel," he equates "pure and undefiled religion" with "the experimental knowledge and love of God."[18] The two are so closely entwined that when Adam sins in the Garden, Wesley cannot conceive of him losing the love of God without losing knowledge as well, and he reads Adam's attempt to hide from God as showing a new ignorance of God's omniscience or omnipresence.[19]

The link in Wesley between knowledge and love is not simply one of concomitance, of two things that naturally occur together. Rather, the latter is an essential goal for the former. The hermeneutical circle between Scripture and experience can cycle around and produce much knowledge, but knowledge is never the end goal, however true it might be. One Sunday, Wesley comments about the sermons he had heard, saying,

> My spirit was moved within me at the sermons I heard both morning and afternoon. They contained much truth, but were no more likely to awaken one soul than an Italian Opera. In the evening a multitude of people assembled on the Green, to whom I earnestly applied these words, 'Though I have all knowledge, — though I have all faith, — though I give all my goods to feed the poor,' &c., 'and have not love, I am nothing.'[20]

The truth contained in the sermons Wesley heard was, in his evaluation, worthless because it was not focused in the right direction. It is likely that reflecting on this is what gave Wesley is own theme about the superiority of love to knowledge, and the need of the latter to move toward the former. Truth, in Wesley's biblical understanding, must be a "truth which is after godliness" (Titus 1:1).[21] And godliness consists mainly in loving God and loving one's neighbor. His favorite phrase for discussing this is again a biblical one, talking of a religion without love as "having a form of godliness, but denying the power thereof' (2 Tim 3:5).[22] Factual bits of knowledge that do not promote love are hardly worthy of the name *truth*.

However, while Wesley gives a clear priority to love over knowledge,[23] there is no positive affirmation of *ignorant love* in Wesley's epistemology. While he affirms that love is the primary reality, he also realizes that knowledge is an important avenue to love. In discussing the naturally atheistic state of humankind, Wesley claims, "Having no knowledge, we can have no love of God: We cannot love him we know not."[24] In diagnosing the progress of what Wesley calls "The Wilderness State," he shows how the loss of love for God proceeds from the loss of faith-as-experimental-knowledge of God.[25] Summing up this connection at the end of his sermon "An Israelite Indeed," Wesley leaves no doubt of the mutuality between truth and love:

> This then is real, genuine, solid virtue. Not truth alone, nor conformity to truth. This is a property of real virtue; not the essence of it. Not love alone; though this comes nearer the mark: For *love*, in one sense, 'is the fulfilling of the law.' No: Truth and love united together, are the essence of virtue or holiness. God indispensably requires 'truth in the inward parts,' influencing all our words and actions. Yet truth itself, separate from love, is nothing in his sight. But let the humble, gentle, patient love of all mankind, be fixed on its right foundation, namely, the love of God.[26]

So, while love is the foundational reality, truth is not to be discounted.

Again, the relationship between Wesley's ideas and his theological method on this point is not casual; this is not just simply a good idea based on the importance of love for the content of his theology. It is how Wesley understands his own theological method to function. Truth that does not move toward love is no truth to be sought, and moving toward love ensures that one will more adequately pursue truth. Wesley will explicitly affirm (perhaps a bit pretentiously) that the Methodists are free from doctrinal error precisely because they are so focused on "love for God and love for neighbour."[27] The pursuit of knowledge in the interplay between Scripture and experience is an empty pursuit if it is not directed beyond itself, nor is it likely to discover the only kinds of truth Wesley finds worth discovering. It is the cycling of the hermeneutical circle between Scripture and experience toward love, of both God and neighbor, that enables it to function at all.

We see, then, that Wesley's theological method functions out of and back into a context of relationships, a context of love. This coheres naturally with the essential functioning of that method, a method that takes seriously a communal view of experience as both source and goal of knowledge. Such a model for theology could offer a powerful and attractive alternative to the fragmentary or individualistic nature of theologies strongly influenced by so-called *post-modern* perspectives.

Implications for Contemporary Theology

There are a number of contemporary theological issues that a relationally-directed theological method might help to address. In this brief section, we will limit ourselves to exploring two: the gap between the academy and the church and the late modern fragmentation of theology. To any theologian who believes these to be problems worth addressing, Wesley's theological method offers a good place to start.

A gap between the popular Christianity embodied in the everyday life of the church and the academic theological reflection on the Christian faith has existed since the creation of the very idea of a theological academy and the relegation of serious theological reflection to the schools.[28] While there have always been theologians who have faithfully served the church and sectors of the church that have looked to the academy for guidance and help, the two domains still tend to function autonomously, each dealing with its own problems and relatively unconcerned about the problems of the other. For those theologians who feel that this situation impoverishes both theology and the church, Wesley's theological method offers a way to bridge the gap without surrendering the ideals of critical thinking on the one side and the concerns over practical applicability on the other. Both of these concerns are held together in Wesley's method by its more or less relational nature.

To someone serious about employing Wesley's theological method, the gap between the church and the academy is not just an inconvenience to be addressed when one has the spare time and energy. Such a gap would be perceived as a threat to the very possibility of doing good theology. It is in the everyday lives of Christian believers—in experience—that Christian truth becomes meaningful, even for theologians themselves. The relational context for doing theology dictated by Wesley's corporate view of experience means that theologians cannot function alone. If they do, they are bound to end up in error and not in truth. Whether the theologian has any personal love for the community or not, following Wesley's method means recognizing the inherently corporate nature of doing *meaningful* theology.

At the same time, the mining of truth from Scripture takes serious, sustained, and disciplined—i.e., academic—work. Any sector of the church that would eschew the value of learning is equally bound to end up in error as they will have little truth by which to shape their experience.[29] This makes the presence of the theologian in the community of faith not a threat to truth but rather a necessary partner in its pursuit. As uncomfortable as this recognition might be in many circles—even some that would call themselves *Wesleyan*—theology, at least in the way that Wesley does it, is not possible without it.

If there is a gap that prevents the church and the theological academy from coming together, then the hermeneutical circle between Scripture and experience is arrested, and theology cannot function. Theology loses is context and its goal and becomes merely a splendid set of interesting mental games. If that situation accurately diagnoses one of the problems theology faces today, then Wesley's prescription might be the way to deal with it.

The same concerns can be used to address our second issue, what we might call the late modern fragmentation of theology. In some sectors of the academy, theology has become pre-occupied with increasingly particular concerns, which could, and sometimes do, become insular concerns.[30] For example, what began as a gender-oriented concern in Feminist theology begins to add on racial and economic concerns in Womanist theology, which is then not seen as addressing the unique concerns of Asian or Latin woman. The academic environment created by such increasing individualism in theology seems to invite and value such increasingly narrow perspectives and assume as a matter of course that highly individuated groups *cannot* function within the parameters of more *general* theology and therefore must have a theology of their own.[31]

In reaction to this, some so-called *conservative* sectors of theology have outright dismissed the uniqueness of such individual perspectives and the value of theological reflection in the context of the experience they represent because they conflict with more *traditional* interpretations of the Bible.[32] Wesley's theological method, however, provides another alternative, one that can both validate the concerns or perspectives of so-called *minority* groups but also properly contextualize them within a larger community. Experience cannot be the unitary whole that Wesley envisions if the experience of one or more sectors of the human community is suppressed or ignored. In that sense, Wesley's theological method demands that one listen to all of experience, not setting a priori limits on what does and does not count as experience nor assuming that one's own experience (or that of one's particular community) is normative for all. At the same time, it is only experience as a whole and not collections of individual interpretations of experience that serves as the crucible of life in which theological constructs become meaningful.[33] Such individual interpretations only become meaningful as they engage themselves with Scripture and with the experiences of others.

Liberation theologies, Feminist theologies, and Third World theologies—to the extent that they could become insular or individual agendas for theology—must, in Wesley's scheme, eventually and inevitably lead off into error as they forsake the concerns of others not represented by their group. They not only lose touch with other groups of believers and the experience they represent, they also consistently distance themselves from traditional sources of authority (such as Scripture) when such authorities are deemed too deeply enmeshed in or determined by the experience of those other groups. This leaves the theological academy as either an arena of competition, with each voice striving to make itself heard, or a place in which all theologies are validated and in which the pursuit of a unified vision of truth becomes untenable or absurd.

However, Liberation theologies, Feminist Theologies or Third World theologies as parts of a larger theological community function very differently. Theology is a complex conversation that continually tests interpretations of Scripture against the experience in the broadest sense and promotes positive relations between people and between people and God. As dialogue partners in this conversation, these varying perspectives are valuable—even necessary. In such a context, these theologies become significant communal resources, even to those who are not driven by their particular concerns. Following Wesley's theological method, engagement with these varying perspectives and the experience they represent is not simply a matter of being tolerant or fair, it is a matter of doing theology well. It is recognizing the inherently communal context for theology and engaging that to the full. To do anything less would be to surrender the pursuit of truth.

These are just a few ways in which Wesley's relationally sensitive theological method might positively impact contemporary theology. There may naturally be many more, but it is time we moved on to our second implication of Wesley's theological method: its inherent ecumenicity.

Notes

1. *Journal* 22 April 1779 (*Jackson* 4:149).

2. Cf. *Journal* 8 December 1771 (*Jackson* 3:450).

3. *Thoughts on the Writings of Baron Swedenborg* §7 (*Jackson* 13:428).

4. *Thoughts upon Jacob Behmen* (*Jackson* 9:509).

5. Cf. Wesley's critique of the theology of one William Dell, about whom he notes, "Here I light upon the works of that odd writer, William Dell. From his whole manner, one may learn, that he was not very patient of reproof or contradiction: So that it is no wonder there is generally so much error mixed with the great truths which he delivers" (*Journal* 12 September 1751 [*Jackson* 2:243]). In his writings, Dell ignores the constructive role of others, the role of the community in other words, and that is the signal reason why he errs so much.

6. For the importance of this in Wesley's own life, cf. Onva K. Boshears Jr., "John Wesley, the Bookman: A Study in His Reading Interests in the Eighteenth Century," (Ph.D. diss., University of Michigan, 1972).

7. *Minutes of Several Conversations Between the Rev. Mr. Wesley and Others* §Q32 (*Jackson* 8:315) [usually called the "Large Minutes"].

8. Cf. among others, *Journal* 18 September 1738 (*Jackson* 1:159), 14 September 1755 (*Jackson* 2:344), 12 June 1767 (*Jackson* 3:282) and 24 October 1784 (*Jackson* 4:291); as well as comments in sermons (Sermon #90 "An Israelite Indeed" §5 [*Jackson* 7:39]) and in tracts (*A Plain Account of the People Called Methodists* §II.7 [*Jackson* 8:254] and *The Principles of a Methodist Farther Explained* §VI.10 [*Jackson* 8:479]).

9. Cf. Sermon #10 "The Witness of the Spirit—Discourse I" §I.3 (*Jackson* 5:113-14); Sermon #39 "Catholic Spirit" §II.7 (*Jackson* 5:501); and Sermon #49 "The Cure of Evil Speaking" §III.5 (*Jackson* 6:124),

10. As he does, for example, in "Preface" to *An Extract of the Rev. Mr. John Wesley's Journal, Number 2* §10 (*Jackson* 1:82); Sermon #10 "The Witness of the Spirit—Discourse I" §I.7 (*Jackson* 5:115); *Principles of a Methodist* §10 (*Jackson* 8:363); but most especially Sermon #39 "Catholic Spirit" §II.4 (*Jackson* 5:500).

11. *Farther Appeal—Part One* §IV.7 (*Jackson* 8:76).

12. Wesley reinforces this point in the "Preface" to his collection of sermons, in which he states, "Nay, perhaps, if you are angry, so shall I be too; and then there will be small hopes of finding the truth. If once anger arise...this smoke will so dim the eyes of my soul, that I shall be able to see nothing clearly" ("Preface" to *Sermons on Several Occasions* §10 [*Jackson* 5:6-7]).

13. *Farther Appeal—Part Three* §I.14 (*Jackson* 8:208). Cf. also Sermon #37 "The Nature of Enthusiasm" §36 (*Jackson* 5:478).

14. Cf. Sermon #65 "The Duty of Reproving Our Neighbour" [esp. §I.2] (*Jackson* 6:296-304 [esp. 297]) and Sermon #107 "On God's Vineyard" §V.6 (*Jackson* 7:213).

15. Of course, this issue in Wesley is thoroughly embedded in the content-oriented question concerning the communal nature of Christian life, not just Christian thought. In his fourth discourse on the Sermon on the Mount, Wesley attacks the idea of "solitary Christianity" as a "grand engine of hell against some of the most important truths of God" [Sermon #24 "Sermon on the Mount—Discourse IV" §4 (*Jackson* 5:296)]. The entire first section of the sermon is designed to show "that Christianity is essentially a social religion; and that to turn it into a solitary religion, is indeed to destroy it...When I say, This is essentially a social religion, I mean not only that it cannot subsist so well, but that it cannot subsist at all, without society, — without living and conversing with other men [*sic*]" (*Ibid.* §I.1). Much the same can be seen in Wesley's sermon "On Schism," which addresses the problem of heresy not as a problem of theological opinions but as a dividing of the community of faith, which Wesley considers to be a serious evil (Sermon #75 "On Schism" [*Jackson* 6:401-410]). For more on how these implications work out in the content of Wesley's theology, cf. Mildred Bangs Wynkoop, *A Theology of Love* (Kansas City: Beacon Hill Press of Kansas City, 1972).

16. Thomas Jackson, *Preface to the Third Edition* (*Jackson* 1:xvi).

17. Sermon #77 "Spiritual Worship" §III.4 (*Jackson* 6:432).

18. Sermon #63 "The General Spread of the Gospel" §18 (*Jackson* 6:283).

19. Sermon #45 "The New Birth" §I.2 (*Jackson* 6:67).

20. *Journal* 15 May 1774 (*Jackson* 4:13).

21. Cf. *Journal* 3 September 1740 (*Jackson* 1:286) and Sermon #22 "Upon Our Lord's Sermon on the Mount—Discourse II" §III.13 (*Jackson* 5:274).

22. Wesley favorite phrase for discussing this is again a biblical one, talking of a religion without love as "having a form of godliness, but denying the power thereof" (2 Tim 3:5) (Cf. esp. *Earnest Appeal* §48 [*Jackson* 8:18-19]).

23. This, too, is one of the themes Wesley feels important enough to raise in the "Preface" to his sermons. Wesley notes, "How far is love, even with many wrong opinions, to be preferred before truth itself without love! We may die without the knowledge of many truths, and yet be carried into Abraham's bosom. But, if we die without love, what will knowledge avail? Just as much as it avails the devil and his angels!" ("Preface" to *Sermons on Several Occasions* §10 [*Jackson* 5:7]).

24. Sermon #44 "Original Sin" §II.5 (*Jackson* 6:59).

25. Sermon #46 "The Wilderness State" §I.1,2 (*Jackson* 6:78-79).

26. Sermon #90 "An Israelite Indeed" §II.11 (*Jackson* 7:45). Cf. also Sermon #100 "On Pleasing All Men" §II.8 (*Jackson* 7:146).

27. Sermon #132 "On Laying the Foundation of the New Chapel" §II.8 (*Jackson* 7:426).

28. For more on the diagnosis of this problem, cf. Andrew Louth, *Discerning the Mystery. An Essay on the Nature of Theology* (Oxford: Oxford University Press, 1984); Hans Urs von Balthasar, "Theology and Sanctity," in *Word and Redemption. Essays in Theology* vol. 2, trans. A. V. Littledale in cooperation with Alexander Dru (New York: Herder and Herder, 1965), 72; and William J. Abraham, *Canon and Criterion in Christian Theology* (Oxford: Oxford University Press, 1998).

29. Again, we are dealing with this question as one of theological method. One may have a content-oriented belief in the operation of the Holy Spirit that would ameliorate this problem to a certain extent, but one cannot build a theological method by pre-programming the Holy Spirit's presence (as in "cue the Holy Spirit here").

30. By *insular* here, we mean theologies that deliberately reject any positive connection to other theologies. This can be seen in such disparate approaches as Carl McIntire's rejection of the *liberalism* of the World Council of Churches (*Servants of Apostasy* [New York: Christian Beacon Press, 1954]), Mary Daly's dismissal of the theological value anything remotely *patriarchal* (*Beyond God the Father. Toward a Philosophy of Women's Liberation*, 2nd edition (Boston: Beason Press, 1985), or James Cone's seeming equation of *white theology* with *white racism* (*Black Theology and Black Power*, [Maryknoll, NY: Orbis, 1997]). This is not to say that theologies cannot be critical of other each—often they must—only that such critical attitudes are only beneficial in dialogues, and not in diatribes or monologues. In fact, the use of such diatribes might be one valuable indicator if a theology is becoming insular.

31. Of course, highly individuated groups must have a place at the theological table, and their experience must be valued for what it is. But such dialogues are difficult to conduct if the environment surrounding them assumes an attitude of *complete* inadequacy of other theologies and focuses on their outright rejection rather than their critical modification. To the extent that individuation increases our perspective on *experience*, it may be valued and celebrated. To the extent that such individuation becomes an excuse to dismiss the experience of others (be they economically disadvantaged Asian women or middle class Caucasian men), it has become insular and ultimately, as we shall see below, destructive.

32. So, for example, the reaction of David L. Smith to Liberation, Feminist and Third World Theologies in his *A Handbook of Contemporary Theology* (Grand Rapids: Baker, 1992), 203-226, 241-258 and 306-317.

33. One could, of course, adopt the contrary assumption to Wesley's and deny the possibility of experience as a "unitary whole," in which case all that one *can* have are individual perspectives. For such people, admittedly, Wesley's theological method will have little, if any, appeal.

17

Experiential Theology as Ecumenical Theology

A theological method that is as relationally embedded as Wesley's ought also to produce an ecumenically sensitive theology. By ecumenical here, we do not simply mean a theology that is committed to the ultimate unity of the church. While Wesley's theology is such, that conclusion is more a matter of ecclesiological content than of theological method. Neither do we mean a theology that is driven toward some kind of ultimate *mega-theology*[1] which could be provide normative content to all sectors of the church. By tracing the ecumenical nature of Wesley's theological method, we mean to imply a way of doing theology that, by its very nature, is open to and profits from engagement with those of differing theological convictions. Conceiving of theology as fundamentally a process rather than a set of static content—which is certainly one of the things Wesley's method implies—forces one to recognize the validity of others who are engaged in that process, even if their content differs from one's own. Additionally, a theology that primarily seeks to engage reality and experience more than merely to understand it (even though that engagement is always on the basis of understanding) will find and value areas of commonality, even if such commonality is not complete.

There is a sense in which this concern is a narrowing of the relational one expressed above, and many of the same basic themes can be heard here again, but in another sense it ought to be treated separately. The problem of ecumenism is not simply a relational problem of everyone getting along (however desirable this is). It is also a problem of how one deals with the whole concept of truth in a pluralistic environment. Wesley's method seeks to maintain a positive role for pluralism while at the same time holding a robust view of truth and normativity.

Ecumenical Theology in Wesley

The ecumenical nature of Wesley's theology has been well-documented and discussed.[2] His sermon "Catholic Spirit" and his "A Letter to a Roman Catholic"[3] are probably the most noteworthy expressions of his desire to have positive communion—and not just a lack of antagonism—between various branches of Christianity. While he may fall short of the ideal of an ecumenical theologian of the 21st century, for his own time his ecumenical sensitivities were remarkable, so much so that in his early ministry he was accused of being everything from a Quaker to a Jesuit in disguise.[4] While this ecumenical orientation cannot be divorced from Wesley's content-oriented understanding of the necessity of Christian love and the essential unity of the church's mission, his ecumenism has a pronounced methodological strand. One can see that in how Wesley deals with the concept of *orthodoxy* and right religious opinions and in how he prioritizes the functioning of the hermeneutical circle over its conclusion.

Orthodoxy and the Weight of Right Opinions

In describing some of the early practices of the Oxford "Holy Club," Wesley makes a statement that he was later forced to defend. That statement was this: "Orthodoxy, or right opinions, is, at best, but a very slender part of religion, if it can be allowed to be any part of it at all."[5] What Wesley means by that, as his later defenses of the statement make clear, is that right opinions can exist even where there is no true religion. If orthodoxy can exist in the absence of true religion, then it does not seem as if the latter follows neatly from the former. Here again, the Devil is Wesley's chief argument, as he claims that the Devil must have perfect orthodoxy, a perfect *understanding* of the truth of the Christian religion, but he is not one whit religious because of it.[6]

It also means that the possession of right opinions is not one of the criteria of the final judgment of one's religion in God's eyes. Wesley will allow for something he calls "invincible ignorance" to permit even those who are in error to obtain final salvation. In his correspondence with the anonymous John Smith, Wesley notes, "Touching the charity due to those who are in error, I suppose, we both likewise agree, that really invincible ignorance never did, nor ever shall, exclude any man from heaven. And hence, I doubt not, but God will receive thousands of those who differ from me, even where I hold the truth."[7] Wesley expresses a similar opinion in his sermon "On Living Without God, where he notes,

> I believe the merciful God regards the lives and tempers of men more than their ideas. I believe he respects the goodness of the heart, rather than the clearness of the head; and that if the heart of a man be filled (by the grace of God, and the power of his Spirit) with the humble, gentle, patient love of God and man, God will not cast him into everlasting fire, prepared for the devil and his angels, because his ideas are not clear, or because his conceptions are confused.[8]

One must always keep in mind in reading statements like this that Wesley is writing in more or less polemic contexts. In such an environment, it is easy to contra-pose a *religion of the heart* (which was Wesley's real concern) with *religion of the head* (which Wesley felt was all that much British Christianity of the time offered). Weighted against genuine, faith-based, grace-enabled love for God and man, orthodoxy would always be found wanting.

This valuation of orthodoxy as *the* set of right opinions can been seen as flowing naturally from Wesley's theological method. Proper theologizing is properly engaging reasoned interpretation of Scripture into experience in order to facilitate relationships with God and fellow human beings. This is a different understanding of theology than one bent on arriving at a perfect (or at least coherent) set of such reasoned interpretations. Given that theology has much more the character of a process than a conclusion, it is not at all surprising to see Wesley deprecating the *absolute* weight of that proper understanding of divine reality that we call orthodoxy.

This does not mean, however, that Wesley believed the idea of truth to be irrelevant. While he never recants what he said above, in actual practice, Wesley did function with a very high regard for proper religious opinions. Much of his own writing is bent on showing the validity of his own interpretation of Scripture and the errors of such folk as the Calvinists and Papists. Upon being accused of theological indifferentism by Rev. James Clarke, Wesley replies quite vehemently that he is guilty of no such thing.

> Am I 'quite indifferent as to any man's opinion in religion?' Far, very far from it; as I have declared again and again in the very sermon under consideration [i.e., "Catholic Spirit"], in the 'Character of a Methodist,' in the 'Plain Account [of Christian Perfection],' and twenty tracts besides. Neither do I 'conceal my sentiments.' Few men less. I have written severally, and printed, against Deists, Papists, Mystics, Quakers, Anabaptists, Presbyterians, Calvinists, and Antinomians. An odd way of ingratiating myself with them, to strike at the apple of their eye! Nevertheless, in all things indifferent, (*but not at the expense of truth,*) I rejoice to 'please all men for their good to edification;' if haply I may 'gain more proselytes' to genuine, scriptural Christianity; if I may prevail upon the more to love God and their neighbour, and to walk as Christ walked. So far as I find them obstructive of this, I oppose wrong opinions with my might.[9]

So Wesley does oppose wrong opinions and that "with his might," but he does so for reasons other than the vindication of truth. He does so because such things are "obstructive" of the love of God and neighbor. As he says in the sermon "The Wedding Garment," "We know, indeed, that wrong opinions in religion naturally lead to wrong tempers, or wrong practices; and that, consequently, it is our bounden duty to pray that we may have a right judgment in all things. But," Wesley is quick to add, "still a man may judge as accurately as the devil, and yet be as wicked as he."[10] Elsewhere, he puts the connection between thought and practice like this: "The religion of a child of God is righteousness, and peace, and joy in the Holy Ghost. Now, if orthodoxy be any part of this, (which itself might admit of a question,) it is a very slender part; though it is a considerable help both [sic] of love, peace, and joy."[11]

So it is not that right opinions are unimportant to Wesley, it is just that they only have relative importance, relative to the promotion of the relational ends we discussed earlier in Chapter 16. It is, of course, easy to see how someone like Rev. Clarke could misunderstand Wesley on this point, as have many others since him, but that comes from paying attention to the parts of Wesley's thought rather than the whole. Wesley is in a sense fighting on two fronts—opposing the erroneous *idea* that orthodoxy is religion but also opposing those other erroneous *ideas* that also damage true religion. Orthodoxy, in Wesley's mind, is not part of the *being* of religion, but it does contribute to its *well-being*. The trick is upholding orthodoxy without allowing it to go too far.

It is in this light that we may recognize Wesley's affirmation that there are such right opinions, such truths of understanding that are very important. There are basic elements of Christian understanding without which one cannot be said to even have a Christian understanding. In Wesley's mind, the doctrines of the Incarnation, salvation by faith, original sin, and the Trinity seem to fall into this category.[12] Wesley's sermon "On the Trinity" illustrates this perhaps most clearly. The first paragraph of the sermon is devoted to enforcing the idea that love is much more important that right knowledge in the final analysis. However, the second paragraph immediately arrests the supposed slide into relativism that could be one consequence of such a de-emphasis on orthodoxy. There Wesley notes,

> Hence, we cannot but infer, that there are ten thousand mistakes which may consist with real religion; with regard to which every candid, considerate man will think and let think. But there are some truths more important than others. It seems there are some which are of deep importance...[S]urely there are some which it nearly concerns us to know, as having a close connexion with vital religion. And doubtless we may rank among these that contained in the words above cited: 'There are three that bear record in heaven, the Father, the Word, and the Holy Ghost: And these three are one.'[13]

Later in that same sermon Wesley will note, "The knowledge of the Three-One God is interwoven with all true Christian faith; with all vital religion."[14]

Wesley, then, is clearly not interested in tolerance for tolerance sake, and he will accept no demeaning of the idea of truth under the guise of the promotion of love. He is also not indifferent to the important role that basic doctrines play in keeping theology on track. Toward the end of the sermon "Catholic Spirit," Wesley explicitly repudiates any kind of complete theological indifference and consciously distances himself from the latitudinarian movements of his day.

> A catholic spirit is not *speculative* latitudinarianism. It is not an indifference to all opinions: This is the spawn of hell, not the offspring of heaven. This unsettledness of thought...is a great curse, not a blessing; an irreconcilable enemy, not a friend, to true catholicism. A man of a truly catholic spirit, has not now his religion to seek. He is fixed as the sun in his judgment concerning the main branches of Christian doctrine. It is true, he is always ready to hear and weigh whatsoever can be offered against his principles; but as this does not show any wavering in his own mind, so neither does it occasion any. He does not halt between two opinions, nor vainly endeavour to blend them into one. Observe this, you who know not what spirit ye are of; who call yourselves men of a catholic spirit, only because you are of a muddy understanding; because your mind is all in a mist; because you have no settled, consistent principles, but are for jumbling all opinions together. Be convinced, that you have quite missed your way; you know not where you are...Go, first, and learn the first elements of the gospel of Christ, and then shall you learn to be of a truly catholic spirit.[15]

Thus, a *relativization* of the importance of orthodoxy to the importance of love in no way *denigrates* the value of proper theological opinions, which are still to be sought as one goal of good theology.

This, too, can be understood as a function of Wesley's theological method. The very fact that he cares at all about how theology ought to be done and has so coherent a theological method as he does is itself proof that proper theology matters. The serious engagement with a normative center for truth such as Scripture and the belief that experience is an experience of something real both entail an understanding of truth as data which *does* correspond to reality and error as supposed data that *does not*. But as we noted earlier, proper theology—in order to be proper theology—must orient its pursuit of proper opinion into the framework of relational experience. Wesley's theological method balances a sincere concern for theological truth, while also continuously trying to keep that truth in its proper place. This balance may be an extremely useful one to strike in contemporary ecumenical discussions, as we shall examine below.

The Priority of Function over Conclusion

The tension between the relativization of orthodoxy and the affirmation of the importance of right opinions brings us naturally to a second consideration of the ecumenical import of Wesley's theological method. He consistently prioritizes the proper functioning of the hermeneutical circle between Scripture and experience over the conclusions that are the various outcomes of that functioning. The restriction of orthodoxy to having only relative importance and the desire to have all the advantages that proper theological reflection can afford are in reality the twin sides of that single coin in Wesley that represents how theology properly functions.

If truth does not matter at all, then there is no reason to engage the theological process. Therefore, some acknowledgement of the superiority of good thinking over bad thinking is necessary for setting up the conscious engagement between Scripture and experience that Wesley's method represents. At the same time, if orthodoxy were the ultimate goal of such a process, then once orthodoxy was achieved (however illusory we might deem such an achievement), there would be no further need of continued engagement in the process. Once the one true set of right opinions is discovered, which perfectly coheres with reality, the need for theological thinking comes to an end and the circle stops. And so, it is only by upholding the value of proper thinking *and* by orienting the value of that thinking toward some other end that a dynamic theological method such as Wesley's has validity.

The priority of the process over the end results in Wesley is best seen in his understanding of the importance of *religious liberty* as the proper environment for religious progress and in his idea of "acting in the light you have." Throughout his life, he always held as an explicit (and ecumenical) principle that, in matters not touching the core of the Gospel, one should "think and let think."[16] Wesley taught that "Religious liberty is a liberty to choose our own religion, to worship God according to our own conscience, according to the best light we have. Every man living, as man, has a right to this, as he is a rational creature...Consequently, this is an indefeasible right; it is inseparable from humanity."[17]

It was, in Wesley's mind, one of the cardinal features of the Methodist Societies that they allowed for this as no one else had for a long time. As he reflects in his Journal:

> The Methodists alone do not insist on your holding this or that opinion; but they think and let think. Neither do they impose any particular mode of worship; but you may continue to worship in your former manner, be it what it may. Now, I do not know any other religious society, either ancient or modern, wherein such liberty of conscience is now allowed, or has been allowed, since the age of the Apostles. Here is our glorying; and a glorying peculiar to us.[18]

This liberty is important, for Wesley, precisely because it provides the proper environment for people to be able to engage experience and Scripture to discover truth. Wesley, of course, had his own ideas of what truth they might discover, and, as we noted above, he wrote on those various bits of truth often and persuasively, and he unashamedly tried to pre-inform people's experience toward those ends. However, he understood that truth could only be discovered by his method in an environment of freedom, only where the process was allowed to continue unimpeded and not a priori constrained into predefined ends. "Never dream of forcing men into the ways of God," Wesley warns. "Think yourself, and let think. Use no constraint in matters of religion. Even those who are farthest out of the way never compel to come in by any other means than reason, truth, and love."[19] Again, this is not just a good theological idea; it is demanded by the nature of Wesley's theological method.

At the same time, the unfettered pursuit of truth was not an academic or theoretical concern for Wesley. The proper pursuit of truth must result in further engagement, and nothing one knows is worth anything unless one can put it to work. This is why he was constantly urging people to *act* according to the light, the understanding, they already possessed. The importance of this cycle of engagement and reflection (which is just another way to describe the process of the hermeneutical circle between Scripture and experience) comes out clearly in one of Wesley's sermons on "The Law Established Through Faith".

> Now then do all diligence to walk, in every respect, according to the light you have received! Now be zealous to receive more light daily, more of the knowledge and love of God, more of the Spirit of Christ, more of his life, and of the power of his resurrection! Now use all the knowledge, and love, and life, and power you have already attained: So shall you continually go on from faith to faith; so shall you daily increase in holy love, till faith is swallowed up in sight, and the law of love is established to all eternity![20]

Engagement leads to more knowledge, which leads to further engagement. It is the cycle that is important, and any conclusions one draws along the way (however much Wesley may insist that some of them are of essential importance) serve in the end primarily to further the process.

This is also reflected in Wesley's idea that, while orthodoxy is *not* one of the criteria for final judgment, active engagement is. Commenting upon the ruins of a Carthusian monastery in Osmotherley, Wesley asks, "Who knows but some of the poor, superstitious Monks, who once served God here according to the light they had, may meet us, by and by, in that house of God, 'not made with hands, eternal in the heavens?'"[21] Wesley may feel that the monks were "superstitious" and did not have proper beliefs, but their acceptance to God is based on their service to Him "according to the light they had." The same concerns come out clearly in the conclusion to the "Large Minutes"[22] and in his sermon "On Charity."[23]

Wesley's concern with religious liberty and engagement, or his prioritization of the freely flowing process over pre-determined doctrinal conclusions, is one more expression of the basic ecumenical tension that his theological method embodies. The liberty must be there if truth is to be found, but liberty makes no sense in the total absence of normative structures. There must be freedom to explore truth but still a recognition that once truth is found it has a commanding authority over us and must be engaged. The freedom is represented by Wesley's valuation of experience, and the concern for truth and normativity by the authority of Scripture. An attempt to balance both of these foundational concerns is one of the things that distinguishes Wesley's theological method as genuinely ecumenical.[24]

Implications for Contemporary Theology

The ecumenical implications for such a theological method are large and varied. Some of them are immediately obvious; others may require deeper reflection. Two that appear immediately relevant to the issues of contemporary theology are the implication such a method has for inter-religious dialogue and the way in which such a method can balance the concerns of so-called *liberals* and *conservatives* in intra-Christian discussions.

The question of how Christianity ought to address other faiths was one that was just beginning to receive attention in Wesley's day, but it has become a major issue for any serious contemporary theological project. The option of complete religious relativism (represented, say, by John Hick) requires extensive re-traditioning of the Christian faith away from its historical self-understanding. On the other hand, the attitude that people of other faiths are simply objects of conversion seems dehumanizing and out of place in a self-consciously pluralist contemporary society. Some mediating position between these two extremes might be very attractive to a large number of theologians, and such a position flows naturally out of Wesley's theological method.

First of all, as a piece of religious epistemology (specifically adapted, of course, to a Christian frame of reference), Wesley's theological method offers a basic approach to authority and reality that may be acceptable to members of other religions. Any genuine ecumenical dialogue can only take place in the tension between conviction and tolerance, between an affirmation of one's own beliefs and an openness to those of others. To approach the ecumenical discussion as a discussion (and not simply a mask hiding an agenda aimed at conversion) requires at least recognizing this much, and this is precisely the tension embodied in Wesley's theological method. That is the meaning of the balance between the *relative* concern for right opinion and the *absolute* concern for the proper functioning of a process that leads to truth and encounter. What is required to engage this method, then, are not theological convictions so much as philosophical ones about the knowability of reality, the usefulness of reason, and the way in which authority and experience mutually interact.

If, then, two people from different religions could agree on experience as the arena of the determination of truth, then they would have at least some bit of intellectually respectable common ground on which to start, ground that does not involve any automatic reductionism or denigration of anyone's ideas about truth. Of course—and this is the crux of the matter—no two members of different religions would agree on the authoritative structure that would be set up as a dialogue partner with experience, be that Scripture or the Q'uran or something must less tangible (as in Taoism or Hinduism). But at least the pattern for such an interaction could be established in such a way that both parties recognize the other as engaged in *a* genuine pursuit of truth, however much they might doubt the efficacy of the other's starting point. That might facilitate the possibility of a dialogue at the outset without threatening a priori anyone's initial convictions or faith.

Secondly, Wesley's theological method could be used as a model for pursuing such a discussion, not merely providing the place to start. Valuing the process of obtaining truth over the data of the explicit truth obtained would have disallowed Wesley *as a Christian* from discouraging even non-Christians in their independent pursuits of truth.[25] If others can agree that such a pursuit is worthy and to be encouraged and even esteemed, then this will foster an appropriate environment for productive ecumenical discussions. This can be so even if each party begins the dialogue convinced of their own understanding of truth, confident that the process will lead their interlocutors over to their opinion. All that is needed is that they allow those convictions to be tested under the same rules as those of their dialogue partners.

Finally, the focus on the interaction between idea (or authority) and reality over the content-oriented results would allow for a role for some bit of *scientific experimentation* with religious reality, or at least with the way such reality impacts the arena of public and sensory experience. In the absence of an agreed authority structure, these experiments would not likely lead one party or the other to change their mind, but it does provide an opportunity for each to understand their own faith better in light of a dialogue with another who is allowed to remain other.

Here's how such a thing might work. In any given dialogue about an issue, there exists an opportunity for each party to present to the other *experimental hypotheses*, along with such criteria of verification or falsification as would show how those hypotheses might be adjudged in experience.[26] Granted, such hypotheses and criteria for evaluation may be very difficult to come up with, but it would not be impossible given two patient and open practitioners of an inter-religious dialogue. For example, a Christian might begin with a belief that all human beings have some latent understanding of God and that this latent understanding is part of universal human experience. She might present as one possible condition of falsification for that belief that all languages must then contain some suitable word for God, just as all languages contain a word or words for other universal human realities like *hunger* or *friendship*. In dialogue with a Chinese Taoist, she might then discover that most Chinese dialects contained no such word originally before contact with Western missionaries, and only then was some attempt made at representing the idea of *God* in Chinese. If the Christian's initial hypothesis and conditions of falsification were well thought through, then she would have to accede to the inadequacy of her original idea.[27] This can only be considered progress in a given dialogue, and it represents the kind of progress that is achievable under the terms of Wesley's theological method.

Wesley's theological method also has import for intra-Christian dialogues, such as one that might be represented between a so-called *liberal* and a *conservative*. Of course, these labels are so often used pejoratively that they have almost ceased to have descriptive meaning. However, they nevertheless represent two basic approaches to the faith that are both widely represented. In a recent book designed to restate and reassert the liberal agenda for theology, Prof. Ian Markham of Liverpool Hope University College articulated the difference between liberals and conservatives in this way: "A 'liberal' believes that faith must be adapted in the light of the broad achievement of European thought and of contemporary culture, while a 'conservative' claims to hold an unchanging faith which is grounded in certain core beliefs that are authoritatively revealed."[28]

Markham's definition involves what he himself identifies as a "methodological difference," but interestingly enough it also highlights the distinct combination of those methodological differences that Wesley's own method seeks to embody. Depending upon one's definition of *faith*, Wesley's theology can be identified with both the liberal and conservative elements of Markham's definition. On the one hand, Wesley's method is clearly conservative in that it holds to the authoritatively revealed beliefs in Scripture. But then he was never comfortable with a content-oriented definition of faith, consistently referring to that idea as a more or less popular misconception. In that sense, then, Wesley's method may also be styled liberal in that it demands the kind of engagement with experience ("thought" and "culture") that Markham himself endorses, and it recognizes that our *understanding* of our faith (although not our *faith* as Wesley understands it) *must* be adapted to our better understandings of experience. Of course, a "pure liberal" might contend that Wesley's appreciation of Scripture inhibits the needed range for adaptation, and a "pure conservative" might fear that any engagement with experience would dilute the "authoritatively revealed" faith, but for those away from the extremes,

Wesley's method represents one way to balance the general concerns of both sides.

As a platform for ecumenical dialogue, Wesley's method also has the advantage of requiring only minimal epistemological commitments either to the reliability of Scripture or to ability of experience to resist our constructions of it. Two parties in an ecumenical dialogue could begin with widely disparate affirmations and yet still engage the same method as a way to find common ground. Wesley, of course, functioned in his method in a strongly conservative way, laying out Scripture as his final authority and not allowing experience the possibility of falsifying Scripture *per se* (however much it must falsify certain understandings of it). However, Wesley himself was open enough to experience to be quite liberal, particularly in matters of practice (such as the use of field preaching, lay preachers, or even ordination of ministers). On the other hand, a liberal could engage the very same method with the opposite set of convictions. So long as the Scripture is given some role—however minimally conceived at first—in the interpretation or pre-informing of experience, then the hermeneutical circle will function. And, if Wesley's method is sound, then both sides would tend to move toward more moderate methodological positions as the general reliability of Scripture and experience are mutually reinforced by the productive functioning of the method.[29]

Of course, we are not supposing that Wesley's theological method could offer a panacea that would quickly and easily solve all the ecumenical problems among Christians today. Nor would it be acceptable to those on the extreme methodological ends who would be threatened by *any* dialogue between Scripture and experience, any supposition that Scripture may be reliable or that experience may be a necessary tool in figuring out what Scripture says. However, to a large number of people who are concerned with the mutual interaction between Scripture and experience, Wesley's method offers a way to treat them both with integrity. Should they seriously engage such a method, they will likely discover that they have more common ground with those with whom they disagree than they might have ever suspected at first.

Notes

1. This term comes from Eugene d'Aquili and Andrew B. Newberg, *The Mystical Mind* (Theology and the Sciences) (Minneapolis: Augsburg, 1999), 195, 198.

2. For some of these discussions, see Henri Daniel-Rops, *The Church in the Eighteenth Century*, trans. John Warrington (London: Dent, 1964), 173-77; B. Kent, "John Wesley: Inspiration," in Stacey, *Contemporary Perspectives*; J. Augustin Leger, "Wesley's Place in Catholic Thought," *Constructive Quarterly* 2 (1914): 329-60; John A. Newton, "The Ecumenical Wesley," *Ecumenical Review* 24 (1972):160-75; Runyon, *New Creation*, 207-221; and John M. Todd, *John Wesley and the Catholic Church* (London: Hodder and Stoughton, 1958). Colin Williams even makes this issue his orienting concern in his approach to Wesley, subtitling his book "A study of the Wesleyan tradition in the light of current theological dialogue" and giving over both his "Preface" and his

first chapter to the question of Wesley's ecumenical importance (cf. Williams, *Wesley's Theology.*, 5-10 and 13-22).

3. Sermon #39 "Catholic Spirit" (*Jackson* 5:492-504) and *A Letter to a Roman Catholic* (*Jackson* 10:80-86).

4. Cf., e.g., *Journal* 27 August 1739 (*Jackson* 1:218) and 30 October 1743 (*Jackson* 1:445).

5. *A Plain Account of the People Called Methodists* §I.2 (*Jackson* 8:249).

6. On these points, see *Journal* 21 June 1766 (*Jackson* 3:353); *Letter to Bishop Lavington* §46 [8 May 1752] (*Jackson* 9:56); "Letter to the Rev. Mr. Clarke" §7 [10 September 1756] (*Jackson* 13:215-16); "A Letter to the Lord Bishop of Gloucester" [26 November 1762] (*Jackson* 9:126); and *Some Remarks on 'A Defense of the Preface to the Edinburgh Edition of Aspasio Vindicated'* §2 (*Jackson* 10:347-48).

7. *Letter to Mr. John Smith* [25 June 1746] §2 (*Jackson* 12:73).

8. Sermon #125 "On Living Without God" §15 (*Jackson* 7:354).

9. "Letter to the Rev. Mr. Clarke" §7 [10 September 1756] (*Jackson* 13:215-16). Emphasis added.

10. Sermon #120 "The Wedding Garment" §15 (*Jackson* 7:316). On the relative weight of right practices and right opinions, cf. Runyon, *New Creation*, 147-49.

11. "Letter to the Rev. Mr. Clarke" §7 [10 September 1756] (*Jackson* 13:215).

12. On this point, cf. Williams, *Wesley's Theology*, 16-17.

13. Sermon #55 "On the Trinity" §2 (*Jackson* 6:200).

14. Ibid. §17 (*Jackson* 6:205). Note that Wesley's Trinitarian understanding is almost entirely directed at the economic Trinity. For the problem this creates, see Chapter 19.

15. Sermon #39 "Catholic Spirit" §III.1 (*Jackson* 5:502).

16. Cf. *Journal* 29 May 1745 (*Jackson* 1:496) and 3 December 1776 (*Jackson* 4:90); as well as Sermon #20 "The Lord Our Righteousness" [conclusion after §20] (*Jackson* 5:246); Sermon #53 "On the Death of the Rev. Mr. George Whitefield" §III.1 (*Jackson* 6:178); *The Character of a Methodist* §1 (*Jackson* 8:340); and *A Short Address to the Inhabitants of Ireland* §15 (*Jackson* 9:177).

17. *Thoughts on Liberty* §16 (*Jackson* 11:37). Cf. also *Some Observations on Liberty* §4 (*Jackson* 11:92).

18. *Journal* 18 May 1788 (*Jackson* 4:419).

19. Sermon #37 "The Nature of Enthusiasm" §36 (*Jackson* 5:478). Cf. also the same sentiments expressed in Sermon #39 "Catholic Spirit" §I.9 (*Jackson* 5:496).

20. Sermon #36 "The Law Established Through Faith—Discourse II" §III.6 (*Jackson* 5:466).

21. *Journal* 17 September 1745 (*Jackson* 1:518).

22. "Once more review the whole affair: (1.) Who of us is now accepted of God? He that now believes in Christ with a loving, obedient heart. (2.) But who among those that never heard of Christ? He that, according to the light he has, 'feareth God and worketh righteousness'" ("Large Minutes" §Q77 [*Jackson* 8:337]).

23. "How it will please God, the Judge of all, to deal with them, we may leave to God himself. But this we know, that he is not the God of the Christians only, but the God of the Heathens also; that he is 'rich in mercy to all that call upon him,' according to the light they have; and that 'in every nation, he that feareth God and worketh righteousness is accepted of him'" (Sermon #91 "On Charity" §I.3 [*Jackson* 7:48]).

24. Of course, this issue, too, is embedded in a content-oriented issue for Wesley. Theologically, Wesley would affirm intellectual life as one location in which the Holy Spirit works, guiding one's reason to right conclusions in order to provoke right actions as much as merely stirring emotions to provoke right actions. Cf. "Letter to a Person Lately Joined with the People Called Quakers" [10 February 1747-8] (*Jackson* 10:181).

25. Wesley would have called this "not grieving those whom God has not grieved," cf. Sermon #13 "On Sin in Believers" §III.10 (*Jackson* 5:150); Sermon #41 "Wandering Thoughts" §III.7 (*Jackson* 6:29); and *A Plain Account of Christian Perfection* (*Jackson* 11:404).

26. Such as the ones Wesley offers his non-Christian readers of *Earnest Appeal* (cf. *Earnest Appeal* §13-18 [*Jackson* 8:6-8]).

27. This is exactly the experience of this writer on this subject, which just happens to reinforce Wesley's own conclusions on the matter, that human beings are, by nature, atheists.

28. Ian Markham, "The Liberal Tradition and its Conservative Successors," in *Theological Liberalism*, ed. J'annine Jobling and Ian Markham (London: SPCK, 2000), 1.

29. This is generally borne out in the lives of many theologians, who began their careers far more on the extremes (either right or left) than they ended them.

18

Experiential Theology as Interdisciplinary Theology

The third and final positive feature of Wesley's experiential theology that we will explore is its interdisciplinary nature. A theology that seriously engages experience in all of its facets must be open to and even seek out interdisciplinary dialogues. To an empiricist, all of human learning—even the most speculative of metaphysics—eventually arises out of human experience. If theology is concerned with that experience, then it naturally finds itself engaged with that learning. Within a hermeneutical circle constructed by Scripture and experience, the distinction between *secular* and *sacred* learning becomes rather tenuous.

Interdisciplinary Theology in Wesley

We have had ample opportunity throughout this exploration to see this dynamic at work in Wesley himself. We have already seen his engagement with history, medicine, philosophy, astronomy, aesthetics, literature, law and economics, so there is little sense in plowing over that territory yet again. What is important to note at this juncture is that Wesley's love of learning and his broad engagement with these various disciplines cannot be explained merely by "general interest" or by his having a scholarly or academic temperament. As he noted early in a letter to his mother,

> I am perfectly come over to your opinion, that there are many truths it is not worth while to know. Curiosity, indeed, might be a sufficient plea for our laying out some time upon them, if we had half a dozen centuries of life to come; but methinks it is great ill-husbandry to spend a considerable part of the small pittance now allowed us, in what makes us neither a quick nor a sure return.[1]

His attitude on this subject does not seem to vary throughout his life,[2] and so Wesley must have believed interdisciplinary intellectual engagement to make that "quick" and "sure" return. This is best explained by recourse to his theological method.

As we noted above, a theological method that seriously engages experience cannot help but be interdisciplinary in its intellectual approach. Wesley himself seems to understand this, as one can see in the way that he endorses a very broad platform of learning for ministry in his *Address to the Clergy*[3] or in the reading list he gives to Miss Lewin in order that she might have "knowledge enough for any reasonable Christian."[4] While affirming that broad learning must never become an end it itself ("without love, all learning is but splendid ignorance, pompous folly, vexation of spirit"[5]), Wesley will nevertheless point out its positive worth. The more one understands about life, the more one is able both to understand and to apply the truths contain in Scripture. It is an easy and natural extension of his general affirmation of the value of experience.[6]

Implications for Contemporary Theology

The contemporary implications of a method that affirms an interdisciplinary approach to theology are most likely to be felt in the formal theological academy. Here the questions of theology's self-understood relationship to other disciplines and the understanding other disciplines have of their relationship to theology is an important question. It affects matters from curriculum development for theology programs to the role of so-called *general education* religion courses in other programs, from the role of Bible colleges and seminaries in the church to the role of departments of religion in research universities. As both a theological method and the reflection of an epistemological orientation, Wesley's approach to theology can inform both the way academic departments of religion see themselves in relationship to other departments and also the way other disciplines may view their relationship to theology.

In the first place, any serious engagement with experience as a necessary partner in the task of doing theology will mean that theologians, perhaps more than practitioners of many other disciplines, must be broadly informed and broadly engaged in order to do their job. Serious reflections on the range of human experience embodied in other departments or faculties of a university is not just a nice idea or one way of fulfilling an aspiration to be a well-rounded person. It is a necessary component of doing theology.

Even though one might, as Wesley did, elevate concerns about personal faith over concerns over proper theology, it is nevertheless impossible to engage his theological method on any basis other than solid learning and broad scholarship. Just as the relational implication of Wesley's method means that it cannot be engaged in an ivory tower divorced from the ordinary lives of men and women, so, too, can it not be engaged in a ivory *ghetto* set amidst a number of other such ghettos. The more one is informed about the broad implications and interpretations of human experience, the more one is prepared to engage that experience in the interpreting the Scripture and in the transforming of human life. In other words, the better an economist, psychologist, sociologist or historian one is, the better a theologian one is prepared to be.

Of course, what makes a theologian a theologian in Wesley's schema is that one's interdisciplinary learning is coupled with equally intense reflections on the content and meaning of Scripture. Broad knowledge of sciences and humanities will not of itself produce any better theology than will the study of Scripture divorced from human life. It is the process of reflection and application between Scripture and experience that produces useful theology, and the neglect of either side results in the collapse of the theological endeavor.

One thing this may mean in the concrete for those who would own Wesley's approach to theology is a serious re-appraisal of how theological education is conducted. For example, while the place of seminaries—as graduate-level centers of learning that build on a university liberal arts foundation—in such a vision is secure, the place of a "Bible school" as a *replacement* for such liberal arts education is not. Particularly in areas of the world where economics makes the question of education difficult, there is the temptation among many sectors of the church—so-called *evangelical* and otherwise—to get ministers trained as quickly as possible so that they can be put to work. However, if Wesley's methodological reflections carry any weight, then such an attitude may lay the seeds for long-term *theological* failure in the field of short-term *ministerial* success. Any system of education that *devalues* learning outside of basic theology, biblical studies and tools for ministry (regardless of whether or not the system has time to inculcate such learning) is a system in which real theology— at least as Wesley sees it—cannot function. In light of this, it is small wonder that the strongest developments in theology outside of the West have come from traditions that enforce the value of broad learning (such as the Roman Catholic Church) rather than from those sectors of the Christian church that would focus on a kind of vocational-technical training for ministry.

On the other side of the question, Wesley's theological method—as a reflection of a basic epistemological project—can also contribute to the way other disciplines view theology and the way in which departments of religion are valued within a university system. This is not to say that Academic Deans and University Presidents have to adopt Wesley's theological method in order to appreciate the role for a theology or religion faculty in their institution, but it is to say that the basic approach to the question of knowledge that Wesley embodies can be instructive even to those who have no concern for his theological or religious views.

Wesley builds his theology on the implicit but quite evident epistemological assumption that knowledge is constructed in the interplay between authority and experience. If this is true for knowledge in general, and not just theological knowledge, then the operation of a department of religion is parallel to—and can be affirmed on the same basis as—any other department in a university. Under this model, all learning consists of partially controlled encounters with reality. Sometimes these encounters are deliberately controlled, as when a chemistry teacher demands a certain experiment or a literature professor the reading of a certain piece of literature. Sometimes they are controlled only by implicit prejudices and pre-understandings.[7] In any case, it is only as these encounters with reality affirm or challenge the pre-informed constructions of it that learning takes place. Wesley's theological method allows for theology to be seen in much the same light, and so faculties and departments of theology are just as justified in their university existence as departments of physics or faculties of letters.[8] All academic disciplines may been seen as functioning in the same way when it comes to the process of learning, and so they all may find a home in the university setting. If we will allow Wesley another of his epistemological assumptions—that there is a unified reality out there to be encountered—then divorcing theology from literature and economics makes no more sense than divorcing psychology from chemistry or physics. If reality is one, then all human learning is necessarily interconnected by virtue of its addressing various facets of that one reality.

Notes

1. "Letter to Susanna Wesley" [January 1727] (*Jackson* 12:9).
2. Cf. Sermon #78 "Spiritual Idolatry" (*Jackson* 6:435-444) and Sermon #93 "On Redeeming the Time" (*Jackson* 7:67-75).
3. Explicitly including original languages, history, science, logic, psychology and sociology ("a knowledge of men, of their maxims, tempers, and manners, such as they occur in real life"), and manners (*An Address to the Clergy* §I.2 (*Jackson* 10:482-86).
4. "Letter to Miss Lewin [n.d.] (*Jackson* 12:260-62).
5. Sermon #4 "Scriptural Christianity" §IV.6 (*Jackson* 5:49).
6. And one, interestingly enough, that reinforces the above point about balancing liberal and conservative elements, as seen in The Liverpool Statement's affirmation of interdisciplinary work as a foundational part of a renewed liberal agenda (*The Liverpool Statement*, in *Theological Liberalism*, ix-xi).
7. Here Wesley's implicit epistemology allows one to engage many of the concerns of Hans Georg Gadamer (cf. *Truth and Method*, trans. Joel Weinsheimer and Donald Marshall (New York: Continuum, 2004).
8. This line of argumentation sounds like, but is actually quite different from, the kind of justification for theology attacked (rightfully) by Kai Nielsen as "Wittgensteinian Fideism" (*Philosophy* 42 [1967] 191-209). "Wittgensteinian Fideism" is the idea that justification is linguistically based and that systems of thought, such as that represented by an academic discipline, are only governed by an interior logic and so all such systems have equal claims for validity. The problem here, as Nielsen points out, is that this idea does away with any question of the evaluation of systems or normativity. What we are claiming here are strong parallels in method between Wesley's vision for theology and other branches of human learning, all of which entail a normative role for interpreted experience and invite a recognition of the interdependence of the various views on experience that each discipline brings to the table.

19

Experiential Theology as
Overly Pragmatic Theology

The final feature of Wesley's experiential theology with which we need to deal is not a positive one, and so it is raised as more of a caution than an encouragement. While we ought to be open to following Wesley whenever he might lead us to new or better understandings, we must maintain a critical stance that will allow us to notice pitfalls that ought to be avoided. Any theology that engages in experience as Wesley's does can fall into a too narrow view of experience. When that happens, the question of the applicability of a piece of data in experience becomes a question of *immediate* applicability. This creates a problem that we call being *overly pragmatic*. In affirming the role of experience in theology, we must guard against any approach that discounts any theoretical or speculative idea just because it cannot be easily or immediately applied. While we may still want to say that all truth is ultimately practical, a short-sighted view of the utility of an idea may be just as much an impediment to truth as a view which seeks only ideas and cares not for their impact on the lived Christian life.

Overly Pragmatic Theology in Wesley

Wesley himself at times sounds like an overly pragmatic theologian, but he falls into this trip with the very best of intentions. Because he is concerned to guide the process of theology toward its ultimate ends (i.e., the love of God and neighbor) and to enforce its relative (as opposed to absolute) value, Wesley has a tendency to undervalue—or even devalue—some parts of both human experience and theology for which he does not see an *immediate* use. This narrows in practice what, in theory at any rate, could be a very broad arena of interplay between Scripture and experience and results in what we can only label as theological distortions. In other words, many of we may be able to attribute many of Wesley's own theological inadequacies to his not being true to the method that is implicit in all of his theological successes. In the realm of experience, we see his overly pragmatic bent coming out in his devaluation of medical theory. In theology, we see this in his under-appreciation (and therefore under-application) of the doctrine of the immanent Trinity.

We begin with the problem of over-pragmatism as an epistemological one rather than a theological one, because it is likely that the latter is grounded in the former. Wesley's attitudes toward the relative value of theory and experience in general are likely to affect the way in which he interacts the two when it comes to Christianity. His attitude toward medicine is the most conspicuous place in which this comes up, but it can also be seen in his approach to the question of literary fiction[1] and even in the way we have seen him approach "speculative philosophy."[2]

Wesley's frustration with medicine and medical theory is in some sense very understandable. Faced with the great medical needs and the great costs of physicians in his own day, Wesley may be partially justified in questioning medicine based on abstruse theory and wanting to reintroduce a common sense, experimental approach to the discipline. His mistake, however, is to move beyond a relative valuation of practice over theory to an actual devaluation of theory itself.

In his *Journal*, Wesley notes reading Dr. Priestley's book on electricity.

> He seems to have accurately collected and well digested all that is known on that curious subject. But how little is that all! Indeed the use of it we know; at least, in some good degree. We know it is a thousand medicines in one: In particular, that it is the most efficacious medicine, in nervous disorders of every kind, which has ever yet been discovered. But if we aim at theory, we know nothing. We are soon 'Lost and bewilder'd in the fruitless search.'[3]

Wesley would be very happy to merely put to use what we already know about electricity to effect "cures" of nervous disorders, but it seems he has little time to waste on theoretical reflection. The pursuit of theory is here styled a "fruitless search" and one that Wesley seems to feel beyond the capacity of human achievement. Much the same attitude comes out in the introduction to *Primitive Physic*. In decrying the complexity of medicine in his day, Wesley lays the root of the problem on "speculative, reasoning men" who would rather think about a medical problem than experiment with a way to fix it. Implicit in his appeal to return to a more pristine and practical view of medicine is that speculation on the subject is vain and will never bear as much fruit as direct experimentation.[4]

The problem with this approach is that experience and history will not support it (i.e., it fails the test of the crucible of life). While medicine has always been in some sense an experimental discipline, the development of medical theory has always been needed to tell the medical experimenter what to look for. Wesley's failure to recognize the value of medical theory is in some sense a failure to give experience its broadest possible rein. While many of the prevalent medical theories of Wesley's day were later disproved and replaced with more adequate constructions, even those failures may be seen as opening the door to future successes.

Any approach to knowledge, then, which will go beyond relative subjection of theory to practice (as in "Eventually a medical theory will need to make a difference in medical practice before we can account it of any worth") to a devaluation of theory itself (as in "Medical theory is worthless") will inevitably foreshorten the range of the hermeneutical circle between experience and authority and so cut off the possibility of new areas of knowledge that apply to things beyond those we presently understand. In focusing on *practical* knowledge (be that scientific or theological), we have to allow for one possible answer to the question "How does it affect experience?" to be "We don't know yet." To do otherwise is to confine our trial of new knowledge to the arena of the already known, and thus limit the range in which experience can challenge the "already known" and open up the possibilities for new knowledge. The recognition of that which is yet unknown is important for the open functioning of the hermeneutical circle we have described. There is an inherent value to mystery, an inherent benefit to acknowledging that what we know of experience is not all there is to experience. We can maintain that and still hold an ultimately practical view of knowledge; it just keeps us from concluding the question of practicality prematurely.[5]

While an epistemological foreshortening of the dialogue between authority and experience is disruptive, a theological foreshortening of the dialogue between Scripture and experience is dangerous. While the demand that all theologizing eventually be consonant with and applicable to experience is a just demand, rightfully aligning theology toward appropriate ends, the devaluation of a theological concept because one cannot see an *immediate* application for it hampers the theological quest for truth-that-leads-to-encounter. There may be particularly important truths whose application to experience is real but mediated to experience by other truths that derive from it. It is a danger that comes from a high valuation of experience, and it is probably best seen in Wesley's treatment of the doctrine of the immanent Trinity, but it is also evident in his tendency toward a monophysite Christology.[6]

First of all, we must begin by reaffirming, as we noted above, that Wesley believes in the Trinity, and he also believes that Trinity is an essential doctrine to Christianity. He defends the doctrine against detractors like Baron Swedenborg[7] and even concludes his sermon "On the Trinity" with an assertion that the belief impinges on one's very salvation.

> Therefore, I do not see how it is possible for any to have vital religion who denies that these Three are One. And all my hope for them is, not that they will be saved during their unbelief, (unless on the footing of honest Heathens, upon the plea of invincible ignorance,) but that God, before they go hence, will 'bring them to the knowledge of the truth.'[8]

He appears to have preached on the topic consistently, particularly on the occasion of Trinity Sunday,[9] and even in his *Notes Upon the New Testament* he highlights the doctrine in several importance places.[10] Wesley will even endorse such explicitly Trinitarian religious experience as represented by the Marquis de Renty and others he has met.[11]

Even admitting this, however, the most casual reader of Wesley can see that his discussions of Trinity are only concerned with the economic Trinity. Wesley affirms *that* the doctrine of the Trinity is true but explicitly disavows any speculation or reflections on the doctrine beyond the ways in which it immediately affects Soteriology. Wesley affirms the essential unity of all of God's creating/saving/sanctifying work,[12] but nothing of the life of God that might lie behind such unity. In fact, he several times renounces any speculation beyond the mere fact of the doctrine, claiming that this is all that Scripture requires. In a letter he writes to Miss Bishop, he notes,

> After all the noise that has been made about mysteries, and the trouble we have given ourselves upon that head, nothing is more certain than that no child of man is required to believe any mystery at all. With regard to the Trinity, for instance; what am I required to believe? Not the manner, wherein the mystery lies. This is not the object of my faith; but the plain matter of fact, 'These Three are One.' This I believe, and only this.[13]

That, for Wesley, settles the matter.

If Wesley had left off there, we may fault him for a serious lacuna in his theology, but not a serious lapse in theological method. However, he does not stop there. More than simply affirming that he himself does not speculate on the Trinity, Wesley also claims that such speculation is inherently destructive and should be shunned. In the beginning of his sermon "On the Trinity," immediately after affirming *that* one must believe the words of 1 John 5:8, Wesley as this to say:

> I do not mean that it is of importance to believe this or that *explication* of these words. I know not that any well-judging man would attempt to explain them at all. One of the best tracts which that great man, Dean Swift, ever wrote, was his Sermon upon the Trinity. Herein he shows, that all who endeavoured to explain it at all, have utterly lost their way; have, above all other persons, hurt the cause which they intended to promote; having only, as Job speaks, 'darkened counsel by words without knowledge.' It was in an evil hour that these explainers began their fruitless work.[14]

The rest of his sermon, then, is not at all spent on *explaining* the Trinity but on proving how one can believe something that one does not understand. Not one thing is said about the Trinity more than that it exists.

The reason for this aversion to speculation is Wesley's inability to see any practical import in such an activity. In fact, Wesley critiques his favorite book on the Trinity (William Jones's *The Catholic Doctrine of the Trinity*) on that very basis. Wesley begins that letter to Miss Bishop cited above by saying, "Mr. Jones's book on the Trinity is both more clear and more strong, than any I ever saw on that subject. If anything is wanting, it is the application, lest it should appear to be a merely speculative doctrine, which has no influence on our hearts or lives; but this is abundantly supplied by my brother's Hymns."[15] While this demonstrates that Wesley does see some practical implications for the doctrine of Trinity, those implications only obtain for the economic Trinity. The fact that Wesley will allow his brother's poetical/liturgical works to supply this doctrinal defect while he would preach sermons and write tracts on "justification by faith" and "Christian Perfection" is enough to reinforce the idea that the practical "uses" of the doctrine of Trinity were limited indeed.

So, while Wesley may have well-developed and well-tested understandings of Pneumatology and a high appreciation and application for some crucial parts of Christology, his doctrine of the Trinity can only be described as anemic. It lies in the background, there mostly because it is supposed to be there, but nowhere is it explored to any degree because such explorations are impractical if not downright dangerous. It is affirmed because it anchors and unites the work of the Son and the Spirit in the doctrine of salvation[16] (which is, of course, *the* eminently practical area of doctrine), but apart from that it has little impact on the whole of Wesley's theology.[17]

Here the specter of an overly pragmatic bent raises its head. Wesley is not just picking and choosing where to expend his theological energies. He is dismissing the value of theological reflection on the immanent Trinity (although he affirms his brother's devotional and liturgical reflections) because he sees no way for it to positively affect Christian experience. While we can agree with Wesley that much theological speculation about the Trinity may be ultimately useless, that it may be tried in the arena of experience and found wanting, we cannot agree that all such speculation *must* be so. While we can agree that all human understanding serves human experience, we cannot limit the possibility of experience to our present understanding of it. To devalue such speculation *per se* is to confine our understanding of experience to what we already understand and so close off the very possibility of any advance in understanding.

In the case of the doctrine of the immanent Trinity, it is a particularly dangerous mistake to make because it ends up making our understanding of God serve our understanding of our salvation. In Wesley's view, our understanding of the Triune God is only there to further our understanding of God's salvation through His Son and sanctification through His Spirit. The result is a tacit theological shift which re-centers Christianity on the Christian rather than on God. Once that is done, Wesley's own relational understanding of theology— aimed at, even *centered on,* love for God and its corollary, love for neighbor—is undercut, and experience becomes a matter of our interpretation of it rather than a matter of a reality out there beyond us, which may either affirm or challenge us.

Part of the reason for Wesley's anemic doctrine of the Trinity is no doubt historical. The Trinitarian controversies of the century previous to Wesley had both damaged the estimation of the importance of the doctrine in the minds of many and also left them with little will to continue to debate the issues that were then raised.[18] This, however, does not excuse Wesley from not engaging in the kind of theological reflection on the issues that may have yielded productive results. After all, Wesley was dissatisfied with much of British Christianity in his day. He challenged many inadequate understandings of faith and practice on the basis of his theological reflection, reasserting in a powerful way the doctrine of justification by faith and the importance of sanctification, as well as broadening the evangelistic mission of the church in significant if highly controversial ways. Here again, the reason why Wesley felt some of these doctrines worth contending for and others allowed to idle in the background of the Christian faith is that he feels that these other ideas are clearly and immediately practical, while the doctrine of the immanent Trinity is not.

The ironic thing is that, as the centerpiece of Christian theology, the doctrine of the Trinity (both economic and immanent) is eminently practical. It has the potential to affect every part of Christian life and thought, including ones about which Wesley himself was very much concerned, such as the doctrine of the church[19] or the problem of predestination.[20] The problem is that these sustained reflections require a bit more *experiential space* to reach their practical potential than Wesley himself allows.

Serious reflection on the Trinity affects thinking in every area of theology, all of which then affect experience. The hermeneutical dialogue between Scripture and life is still intact, and experience is still given a role in affirming or denying the efficacy of any given idea, but it is experience in its broad—as opposed to overly-pragmatic—sense. As a problem of methodology, Wesley's failure to allow for a full dialogue between Scripture and experience on this point is actually impractical, denying to experience some very practical ideas merely because those practical ideas could only be developed from an *impractical* source. So, if the hermeneutical circle between Scripture and experience is to function well, it must be free from inordinate demands that knowledge be immediately practical in experience.

Interestingly enough, this serious lacuna in Wesley's theology has become problematic for some of his contemporary interpreters.[21] The result of affirming a doctrine but not applying it in any serious *theological* way is that the doctrine loses theological efficacy. If Wesley's own method is valid, then not applying an idea is one sure way to deny it. It is, in fact, impossible to maintain Wesley's pneumatological and christological insights without some type of qualitative Trinitarian reflection of the kind that Wesley himself repudiated. In the clearest examples of this, Maddox and Runyon both take pains to point out how consonant Wesley's Pneumatology and Christology are with the Eastern Orthodox idea of *perichoresis*[22] and how that idea can be used to advance Wesley's thought in significant ways. Their reflections on this matter are good, and they are very right to supplement Wesley's own deficiencies in the matter. However, the move to then attribute this idea implicitly to Wesley himself is not warranted.

Wesley's disavowal of Trinitarian speculation prevents us from giving him credit for a better Trinitarian theology than that which he displays. To do that is the end of *reading* Wesley and the beginning of *re-traditioning* him, adapting him so that he conforms more comfortably to our contemporary theological sensibilities. This we must not do, lest we lose our ability to learn from the mistakes of the past as well as from its successes. The seeds of solid Trinitarian theology *are* present in Wesley's own theology, but they are prohibited from germinating there. One reason Wesley did not *discover* or *recover* a doctrine such as the rich Trinitarian theology of *perichoresis* is that he could not allow himself to go looking for it. And so British Christianity had to wait another two hundred years before the doctrine of Trinity was revived to the level of practical importance. If we can recognize this mistake for what it is and see it as a result of Wesley's failure to live up to his own theological method, then we are in a much better position not to make the same mistake ourselves.

Implications for Contemporary Theology

The danger of foreshortening the arena of experience under the guise of being *practical* is a constant one, particularly among those who are sincerely interested in tangible results—be they evangelists and pastors or ecumenical activists. If we want to employ a theological method that takes experience seriously, then we must be aware of the dangers of taking it seriously in the wrong way. The places in the contemporary theological arena in which that balance is particularly important are in the questions of ecumenical cooperation and in the movement to identify too quickly Christianity with an ethical program.

There are many Christians who are concerned about the problem of the visible unity of the Church. There are many deeply committed Methodists, Roman Catholics, Orthodox and Presbyterian believers who may long to celebrate the Eucharist together but who cannot because of authoritatively enforced doctrinal claims. In such a situation, it would be easy to allow practical concerns to take over, to allow ourselves to become overly pragmatic and to eschew the doctrinal issues we have because they are just not practical.

It did not take long for the Life and Work movement of the early twentieth century to discover that their original formula of "doctrine divides, service unites" was inadequate. It did not take much experience to discover that questions of practice inevitably raise questions of theory, which is one reason why the Life and Work movement and the Faith and Order movement eventually had to coalesce into a more or less unified institution.[23] It is a cautionary tale from recent history for any who might still decry the impracticality of doctrinal reflection in order to advance more practical causes like evangelism, missions or church unity. Here a reflection on Wesley's theological method may be of use.

Wesley's method shows us both the promises and pitfalls of serious theological engagement with experience in dialogue with some traditional source of authority (be that Scripture or Tradition or some combination of the two). *Epistemologically*, he gives us a way to see the distinction between theory and practice as one way of understanding a fundamental tension between authority and experience. *Theologically*, he provides us a way to balance those two in the context of an engaged *and* historically responsible Christian faith. Even in his failure to fully live up to his own way of doing theology, he demonstrates its validity and he warns us that too quick an attention to practical concerns may in the end rob us of some very practical tools.

In addressing the question of ecumenical cooperation, that is a lesson worth bearing in mind. In the quest to find practical solutions to our problems of disunity, Wesley—by his negative example—points out the dangers of allowing practical concerns to have the final say too quickly. True, many Protestants and

Catholics would long to celebrate at a common table, but perhaps the most practical way of making that happen is to spend more time in theological reflection on the issues that yet divide those two communions. To force a practical solution now may foreshorten the possibility of an even more practical solution in the future. Perhaps it would the be equivalent of settling for an inferior practical tool (like a hand saw) because we could not be bothered to think our way through to a better one (like a power saw). So long as we keep our long-term desire for practical application in view and maintain that whatever we do ought eventually to move us in that direction, we can apply our mutual reflections to our mutual experience and allow that experience to guide our future reflections until the day that we can enjoy the level of cooperation that for now is only a dream.

A very similar warning exists for those would may seek to reduce Christianity to a set of practices or to an ethical program. This may be a particularly late-modern temptation, but it is one that Wesley's own experience may be made to address. Again, if Wesley's epistemology is sound, then practice (i.e., experience) is always pre-informed by theory as well as being corrective to it. To reduce Christianity to a system of ethics then is not simply unwise given the long-standing history of the importance the Church has given to theological reflection, it is outright impossible. To reduce Christianity (or any other such complex system) to praxis is merely to cover up one's preconceptions about theory; it never nullifies their role. The very idea of the validity or importance of ethics—as practical as that idea is—is already connected to and informed by ideas we have about the human person and human behavior.

What Wesley's own overly-pragmatic failure teaches us in this case is this. By too quickly cutting off theological reflection on the nature of Trinity, Wesley robbed himself of an opportunity to reflect on an area that would have ultimately strengthened all of his most treasured emphases. A better articulation of the immanent Trinity would have helped him integrate the justification work of the Son with the sanctification work of the Spirit in a way beyond the simple affirmation that they were connected. The ideas that the sanctifying work of the Spirit is designed to make us more Christ-like and that the work of Christ on earth was Spirit-empowered are easier to explain if one has a coherent doctrine of the immanent Trinity. More sustained Trinitarian explorations might have made it easier for Wesley himself to unite his Father-centered theme of *New Creation* with the work of Christ and the Spirit. This is not to say that Wesley's theology in each of those areas is bad—it is actually quite good. What is lacking is the kind of systematic integration that could move these ideas from isolated bits of good theology to a compelling vision of Christianity. The seeds are there, but the integration is not; and if it had been, his theology would have been that much more useful—even by the terms Wesley himself would have dictated. In the same way, Christians who are ultimately concerned about questions of ethics need to be reminded to stay open to the theoretical and doctrinal part of the Christian faith, lest they deprive themselves of important practical tools for addressing the issues that do concern them.

Someone may style himself a *liberal* Christian, one, say, much more concerned with the practical issues of the economically oppressed people of Latin American than with the philosophical niceties of Nicene-Chalcedonian orthodoxy. Nevertheless, if he is willing to allow experience some role in judging and reinforcing his concerns, then he cannot afford to dismiss those philosophical niceties as impractical speculation. After all, he must admit that he has his own theories about economics and anthropology that inform his concerns. To dismiss a priori the economic and anthropological implications of Chalcedonian Christology may be to deprive him of theological resources that could undergird his own concerns even better than his present beliefs. The point is not to make the judgment call one way or the other. The point is that any over-focus on practical issues is eventually detrimental to the very practical issues that one may have originally wanted to protect. This we can see from Wesley's own failure to follow through on the methodological trajectory on which he sets out.

Conclusion to Part Four

In these last chapters, we have traced very briefly just a few implications of following through with Wesley's theological method. On the positive side, we have seen it to be a tool that could ground relational, ecumenical, and interdisciplinary approaches to theology. It can be relational in that it recognizes both the communal context in which theology is done and also the relational ends at which theology ought to be focused. It is ecumenical in that it attempts to balance a concern for orthodoxy and an openness to the beliefs and experience of others by establishing a process of engaging reality in which we judge ourselves by the same terms as we judge others. Finally, it is interdisciplinary in that it recognizes that all deliberate engagement with the breadth of human learning can eventually be brought to bear on theology. Learning about all facets of human life can help in constructing better interpretations of our interaction with the divine and thus open up the possibilities of better relationship to that divinity. Such characteristics for theology are ones that contemporary theology needs to deliberately cultivate, and that makes Wesley's theological method worthy of future investigation.

At the same time, we have seen at least one pitfall of focusing too quickly or too narrowly on experience as the "crucible of life." If Wesley's theological method is to reach is best potential, then it must be allowed to operate in an environment of maximal freedom. Again, Wesley himself seems to have recognized and enforced this, even if he did not always live up to it in his theological practice. In our concern to engage our theological constructions in life, we must not demand that they be engaged immediately, lest we, like Wesley, lose the capacity to develop even better means of engagement than the ones we already posses.

There are other theological implications of Wesley's experiential theology, but these are sufficient to advertize his theological method as one worthy of future exploration and engagement. Wesley's example—both positive and negative—can be used by anyone interested in cultivating an engaged Scriptural theology. And should a Roman Catholic or convinced Calvinist succeed in cultivated such a theology in dialogue with Wesley—even if he or she might never agree with Wesley's own doctrinal conclusions on ordination or predestination—we might well imagine that Wesley himself would be pleased and feel his contribution worthwhile.

Notes

1. Cf. *Journal* 21 February 1784 (*Jackson* 4:266) and "Letter to Miss Bishop" [18 August 1784] (*Jackson* 13:39).

2. So his evaluation of David Hume (cf. Chapter 4) and his general estimate of "minute philosophy" (Cf. Sermon #56 "God's Approbation of His Works" §II.1 [*Jackson* 6:213] and Sermon #15 "The Great Assize" §III.4 [*Jackson* 5:180]).

3. *Journal* 4 January 1768 (*Jackson* 3:311).

4. "Preface" to *Primitive Physic* §8-10 (*Jackson* 14:310-11).

5. This recognition is actually much more consonant with Wesley's own evaluations of the extent of human ignorance and his avowal (noted above) of the importance of "think and let think" than his overly pragmatic approach to medicine (cf. Sermon #70 "The Case of Reason Impartially Considered" [*Jackson* 6:350-60] and *Remarks on the Limits of Human Knowledge* [*Jackson* 13:488-99]). We may thus argue that, in this area, Wesley is not really being true to himself.

6. For Wesley's monophysite leanings, cf. the comments of Maddox, *Responsible Grace*, 114-118.

7. Cf. *Thoughts on the Writings of Baron Swedenborg* §9-12 (*Jackson* 13:429-31)

8. Sermon #55 "On Trinity" §18 (*Jackson* 6:206).

9. Though the contention of Maddox (following Outler) that it was a "favorite topic of his actual preaching" may be overstated (Maddox, *Responsible Grace*, 139). In his note on this sermon, Outler affirms 23 instances of its preaching (cited in Maddox, *Responsible Grace*, 322 n. 158), but even 23 times out of thousands of sermons over more than half a century hardly proves that it was a favorite topic for preaching. If it was a favorite sermon of Wesley's, then it is hard to explain why the sermon only appears in the Second Series of Sermons—not in the First—and why that sermon (Sermon #55) was written, according to Wesley's own prefixed note, hastily and in 1775 (*Jackson* 6:199). If Trinity was one of Wesley's favorite or even highly valued topics to preach on, one wonders why Wesley would make apology for the state of the sermon and why so late a version of it is the only one he published, and that explicitly without a careful editing.

10. The most crucial of these being the extended note on 1 John 5:8 affirming the doctrine, the notes on the conjunction of the activities of the Father, Son and Spirit in Matt 3:17, Hebrews 9:14, and 1 John 5:20, and the Trinitarian reinterpretation of the phrase "baptized in the name of the Lord" in Acts 10:48. See also Matt 6:13, Luke 1:34 and 4:18, Acts 2:38 and Ephesians 4:4.

11. Wesley often approvingly quotes de Renty's statement, "I bear about with me an experimental verity and a plenitude of the presence of the ever-blessed Trinity" as one representing mature Christianity (Cf. Sermon #55 "On the Trinity" §17 (*Jackson* 6:205). He also endorses the *Trinitarian experience* of others (e.g., "Letter to Hester Ann Roe" [11 February 1777] [*Jackson* 13:79]).

12. Which focus Maddox notes approvingly (*Responsible Grace*, 140).

13. "Letter to Miss Bishop" [17 April 1776] (*Jackson* 13:30). Virtually the same sentiments are also expressed in "Letter to a Member of the Society" [3 August 1771] (*Jackson* 11:293) as well as Sermon #55 "On the Trinity" §14 (*Jackson* 6:204).

14. Sermon #55 "On the Trinity" §3 (*Jackson* 6:200).

15. "Letter to Miss Bishop" [17 April 1776] (*Jackson* 13:30).

16. Maddox, *Responsible Grace*, 140.

17. An examination of Geoffery Wainwright's article on Trinity and Scripture in Wesley is interesting in this light (G. Wainwright, "John Wesley's Trinitarian Hermeneutics," *Wesleyan Theological Journal* 36 [2001]: 7-30). Wainwright rightly notes that references to the Trinity are pervasive in Wesley's approach to Scripture, but he does not deal with the fact that all of those references are *economic*, i.e., dealing with the separate and coincident activity of the Father, Son and Holy Spirit toward humankind and not at all with the life of God that immanently unites those diverse activities. The "Trinitarian Hymn" with which he closes the article is fully illustrative of that, in which we have a strong affirmation of the importance of the individual work of the Father, Son and Spirit, and of our response to the "Three-One God," but no hint whatsoever of anything that may be seen to essentially unite those activities. In this article, Wainwright joins with Runyon and Maddox in reading the power of their own (and much more adequate) ideas about Trinity back into Wesley to fill out Wesley's own insufficiencies in this regard.

18. Cf. Jason Vickers, *Invocation and Assent* (Grand Rapids: Eerdmans, 2008); and William S. Babcock, "A Changing of the Christian God. The Doctrine of the Trinity in the Seventeenth Century," *Interpretation* 45 (1991): 133-46.

19. E.g., Miroslav Volf, *Church in the Image of the Trinity*, Grand Rapids: Eerdmans, 1998.

20. As in the Trinitarian approach to election found in Jonathan Edwards (cf. Stephen R. Holmes, *God of Grace and God of Glory. An Account of the Theology of Jonathan Edwards* [Edinburgh: T & T Clark, 2000]; and Amy Plantinga Pauw, *The Supreme Harmony of All. The Trinitarian Theology of Jonathan Edwards* [Grand Rapids: Eerdmans, 2002]) or even Karl Barth (*Church Dogmatics*, Vol. II/2, ed. G. W. Bromiley and T. F. Torrance, trans. G. W. Bromiley et al. [Edinburgh: T & T Clark, 1957]).

21. A notable exception to this is Colin Williams, who finds Wesley's Trinitarian reservations ecumenically responsible (Williams, *Wesley's Theology*, 93-97).

22. Cf. Runyon, *New Creation*, 55, 132; and Maddox, *Responsible Grace*, 136-40.

23. Cf. Robert McAfee Brown, *The Ecumenical Revolution. An Interpretation of the Catholic-Protestant Dialogue* (New York: Doubleday, 1967), 31; W. A. Visser 't Hooft, *The Genesis of the World Council of Churches* (New York: World Council of Churches, 1988); and Nils Ehrenström, "Movements for International Friendship and Life and Work 1925-1948," in *A History of the Ecumenical Movement 1517-1948*, ed. Ruth Rouse and Stephen Charles Neill (New York: World Council of Churches, 1993), 545-96, esp. 559-63 and 570-74.

20

Retrospect and Prospect

We come now to the end of our multi-stage investigation of experience in Wesley's epistemology and theological method. We have moved through both philosophical and theological territory, and we have not always been concerned about keeping the dividing line between those two arenas of thought clear. However, if the results of such an investigation do prove to be useful, perhaps it serves as a validation of the kind of reflection Wesley himself sought to embody, reflection that would use the widest possible range of human thinking tools to get at that reality which ultimately concerns us all. In wrapping up our investigation, we will look back at what we have covered and also look forward to what use these investigations might have in contemporary theology.

Retrospect

We began our investigation in Part One in philosophy, exploring some questions of eighteenth century language use and philosophical background to see how those might guide us in understanding Wesley's approach to experience and how that might eventually inform his theological method. Our linguistic exploration posed some possible questions about the way *experience* was understood in eighteenth century England, and in our philosophical investigation, we saw that Wesley is best understood as an Aristotelian empiricist, not the Lockean empiricist that he is usually portrayed as. His philosophical home in Aristotelian logic and thought integrates well with his fundamentally religious concerns, and it allows him to affirm the practical and devotional benefits of the various strands of British empiricism and rationalism without compromising his own basic position. He believes in experience as the source of knowledge, and so he is an empiricist, but as a good Aristotelian (and therefore a bad Lockean) he will allow his approach to experience to be positively pre-informed by other authorities. His Aristotelian position and his philosophical interactions with other strands of thought give us the proper backdrop against which to read his concerns about knowledge in general and theological knowledge in particular. That

In moving beyond Wesley's explicit interactions with other strands of philosophy to his own explicit and implicit epistemology in Part Two, we explored various features of Wesley's understanding of experience, particularly as it impacted the question of knowledge. We saw that his view of experience is external and public, and therefore not internal and psychological. Experience is, therefore, seen as a broadly accessible arena in which we encounter reality, and not just a creation of our minds. We also saw that experience in Wesley has a very active component, which further mitigates against reading his view of experience in a passive psychological way. We then explored in some detail the way in which his Aristotelian empiricism allows him to give a large and important a priori role to both logic and Scripture in approaching experience. This, finally, led us to a construction of Wesley's implicit epistemology as one of dynamic interplay between reason and experience and Scripture, which we described as a hermeneutical circle and which is helped along by Wesley's articulation of an idea of "spiritual senses."

On the basis of that reconstructed epistemology, we then explored the way in which experience directly functioned to inform Wesley's theological method in Part Three. This, too, we articulated as a hermeneutical circle between Scripture and experience, and we explored the various ways in which knowledge is advanced by both the "first-order move" of acquiring data from experience (which may be pre-informed by Scripture) and the "second-order move" of reapplying interpreted data back to experience. In all of this, we saw how Wesley's idea of theology functions both to provide theological knowledge with a high degree of reliability but also keeps that knowledge directed toward the end of an encounter with the reality that such knowledge seeks to represent. Understanding this dynamic between experience and Scripture also helps us to integrate the other tools (reason and tradition) that Wesley employed in constructing theology, as each of them can be understood as various extensions of his basic Scripture-experience dynamic.

In Part Four, finally, we explored the way in which Wesley's theological method reinforced a theology that can be praised as relational, ecumenical, and interdisciplinary, but which also needs to be critiqued as, at times, overly-pragmatic. These are features which can be understood as rooted the attention that Wesley gives to experience and the way in which he balances experience with Scripture. Looking at these features methodologically also gives us a way to propagate the positive features (and avoid the negative ones) in contemporary theology without requiring substantial content-oriented commitments.

Throughout this exploration of experience in Wesley and its implications, several key ideas have been ever-present and at times seem almost to leap into the foreground. First of all, there is the idea that experience and Scripture only function when they function together. Neither of them are sufficient to serve as independent epistemic criterion for certain knowledge, but in working together they allow the process of knowledge to function in a trustworthy way.

Secondly, we have seen that Wesley's view of theology is consistently engaged. The importance of that engagement cannot be overestimated. For theology to be meaningful, it must be more than speculation about things of God. As Thomas Langford has noted concerning Wesley, "Theology is important as it serves the interest of Christian formation. Theology is never an end, but is always a means for understanding and developing transformed living."[1] In that, Wesley offers a model of theology that is both academic and pastoral, and in which each of those qualities actually reinforces rather than detracts from the other.

Finally, we have seen that Wesley's project of knowledge and theology is capable of being understood in both philosophical and theological terms. We have been able to employ the categories of both philosophy and theology to elucidate Wesley's thought, and although the former is grounded in later, even that can be seen as a question of philosophical contextualization. While Wesley's thought gives us neither a system of philosophy nor a system of theology, it is systemic enough to provide tantalizing hints and possibilities that might prove fruitful through further, more systematic, exploration.

Prospect

Although we have explored a good deal of Wesley's thought and interacted with a broad range of his writing, there is much yet that could be done both in elucidating Wesley's theological method and in tracing the implications that method has for both theology and philosophy—either in Wesley's day or in our own. Before we leave this investigation, it might be beneficial to tentatively point to a number of those areas in which further reflection might be fruitful.

Concerning the functioning of Wesley's theological method and its impact on his own theology, we have already noted that there is a wide open field for exploring the way in which Wesley's thought and experience and reading of Scripture help him to formulate and modify his key doctrines. The history of the development of any particularly important doctrine in Wesley (such as justification by faith or entire sanctification) may be traced and explored as one line of interaction between experience and Scripture. Such explorations may serve to show both the importance of change for Wesley's own theology and also illuminate why Wesley tended to be reluctant to admit change, usually taking the tact of *clarifying* his earlier position rather than admitting that he had changed it. If Wesley saw his later thought as a natural outgrowth of his earlier thought, further refined by the dynamic interplay of Scripture and experience, then we would not expect him to perceive the differences in his early and later thought as *changes*. They are, perhaps, properly articulated (which is essentially what Wesley does) as coming nearer the mark, nearer the reality those ideas represent. It may be the same mark that he was aiming for in 1725 as in 1775, so little change is involved there. But his theological *accuracy* is better in 1775, and so those fifty years do make a qualitative difference in his theology.

In addition to content-oriented issues like these, it might also be worthwhile to explore some form-oriented issues in Wesley. One of the reasons why Wesley was not treated seriously as a theologian is that he did not employ the typical theological forms and write systematic theologies or extended philosophically interactive monographs on various doctrines. His favored forms were the journal, sermons, and tracts. Theologians tended (perhaps still do tend) to write for the theological academy. Wesley wrote primarily for ordinary people. In light of the way in which experience functioned in his theology, it would be interesting to explore the way in which Wesley's theological method influenced the forms he employed to make that theology accessible.

There are other implications for Wesley's method that go beyond simply helping someone better understand Wesley himself. As we have noted throughout this project, his methodological insights may be very fruitful in contemporary theological discussions. Again, we do not have space to lay out all of those possible lines of future investigation, but at least two ought to be considered especially important.

The first of those issues is the epistemological one. Writing and working as he does before the full advent of what we have come to call *modernity*,[2] Wesley's practical wrangling with truth and meaning may have something to offer those of us coming out of the other side of that philosophical project. This is not to say that we are looking for a *pre-critical* understanding of knowledge that would somehow skip over or obviate the work of the Enlightenment. However, as we move away from the kind of foundationalism that modernity sought to enforce and seek other directions, people like Wesley provide us with useful models and examples. The now standard debates between correspondence views of truth (championed by the analytical tradition of philosophy) and coherences views (championed by so called post-moderns) are seen differently when we can look at an epoch in history before they ossified into their present positions. Wesley's functional epistemology acknowledges the absolute dependence of meaning on experience and so on all of those vagaries that color experience. However, he was able to maintain that quest for meaning without abandoning an idea of truth and its "knowability." Even if we find fault with the faith assumptions that initiate the quest for knowledge or do not approve of the way Wesley balances experience and authority, we may still find that we can learn from his work. Perhaps Wesley's contextualization of the project of knowledge into a larger arena of relational encounter offers an even presently relevant way out of that philosophical impasse.

Moving away from philosophy and back to theology, we may also find in Wesley a useful pattern for addressing current issues in methodology. Since the promulgation of *Divino afflante Spiritu* in 1943, many sectors of the Roman Catholic church have struggled to balance the issues of authority and Scripture. Might not Wesley's hermeneutical understanding allow one to balance those concerns much as he balanced the issues of experience and Scripture? In contemporary debates regarding the role of religious experience, Wesley's insights into both the power and limits of experience may still be relevant. If Wesley is right, experience must play a role, but it can never be the driving role if the process of knowledge is to lead to anything resembling truth.[3] The question then is not, "Can religious experience ground inter-religious or ecumenical dialogues?" The question is "How can our understanding of the relationships between experience and authority help us to move those dialogues forward?" If we grant him his faith assumptions here—or even only one or two of them—then Wesley's *pre-critical* method may offer those of us dealing with *post-critical* theology some compelling food for thought.

If we have done nothing else throughout this project, we have hopefully at least presented a view of Wesley as a theologian in the truest sense of that word. Wesley modeled and promoted a way of doing theology which proved to be productive in his own thought and which offers some attractive features to anyone committed to doing theology as more than just personal speculation or a purely academic enterprise. If Wesley's method provides us with one way of cultivating good theology, and that without requiring any a priori changes in our already existing belief structure, then many may find it worthy of further pursuit and investigation. If a dialogue with Wesley challenges us to consider more deeply both the epistemological issues involved in the construction of theological knowledge and the theological issues involved in the application of such knowledge, then he will have served us well—even if we should find ourselves disagreeing with him in the end.

There is, however, a warning that ought to be issued to anyone who does engage Wesley on these terms. Engaging experience in the way that Wesley does could be considered dangerous, in that it opens up the very real possibility that we must change some things that we believe. However, if we affirm, with Wesley, that such changes are really adaptations of our thought to reality, then they can hardly be considered threatening. If we can believe that there is a reality out there to be experienced and if we can believe that our experience of that reality is in some way understandable, then we want the possibility of reality challenging our inadequate conceptions of it—be those ideas of science or understandings of God. We expect that we will learn new things as new understandings open the door to new encounters with reality, which then lead to better understandings. To be Wesleyan in this sense is to be on the same journey of understanding that Wesley was on. Where Wesley discovered truth, we want to be able to reaffirm it and own it for ourselves because it is true, not merely because Wesley said it. And if our own investigations take us further down the road to true understanding than even Wesley himself went, but we found that road through Wesley's mentoring and modeling, then that may be the best use we could make of his legacy and the best legacy we could bequeath to those who come after us.

Notes

1. Thomas A. Langford, *Practical Divinity. Theology in the Wesleyan Tradition* (Nashville: Kingswood, 1983), 20.

2. On the thesis that modernity does not really start in England outside of the intellectual elite until after Wesley's time, cf. Clark, *English Society.*

3. Ironically, here Wesley and Hume are on the same page. Though Wesley's faith in Scripture would not permit him to accept the legitimacy of Hume's skepticism, the two agree implicitly on the problem of knowledge by experience alone.

Works Cited

Primary Sources

Wesley, John. *The Works of John Wesley*, 14 vols. Edited by Thomas Jackson. Kansas City: Beacon Hill Press of Kansas City, 1986.

Wesley, John. *The Letters of the Rev. John Wesley, A.M.*, 8 vols. Edited by John Telford. London: Epworth Press, 1931.

Wesley, John. *The Bicentennial Edition of the Works of John Wesley*. General editors Frank Baker and Richard P. Heitzenrater. Nashville: Abingdon Press, 1976—.

Secondary Sources

Abraham, William J. *Canon and Criterion in Christian Theology*. Oxford: Oxford University Press, 1998.

Babcock, William S. "A Changing of the Christian God. The Doctrine of the Trinity in the Seventeenth Century," *Interpretation* 45 (1991): 133-46.

Baker, Frank. *John Wesley and the Church of England*. Nashville: Abingdon, 1970.

Bangs, Carl. *Arminius: A Study in the Dutch Reformation*. Grand Rapids: Zondervan, 1985.

Barth, Karl. *Church Dogmatics,* 14 vols. Edited by G. W. Bromiley and T. F. Torrance. Translated by G. W. Bromiley et al. Edinburgh: T & T Clark, 1957.

Bett, Henry. *The Spirit of Methodism*. London: Epworth, 1937.

Boshears, Onva K., Jr. "John Wesley, the Bookman: A Study in His Reading Interests in the Eighteenth Century." Ph.D. diss., University of Michigan, 1972.

Brantley, Richard. *Locke, Wesley, and the Method of English Romanticism*. Gainesville, FL: University Presses of Florida, 1984.

Bready, J. Wesley. *This Freedom Whence*. New York: American Tract Society, 1942.

Brooke, John Hedly. "Science and the Fortunes of Natural Theology: Some Historical Perspectives," *Zygon* 24 (1989): 3-22;

Brown, Dale W. "The Wesleyan Revival from a Pietist Perspective," *Wesleyan Theological Journal* 24, (1989): 7-17.

Brown, Robert McAfee. *The Ecumenical Revolution. An Interpretation of the Catholic-Protestant Dialogue*. New York: Doubleday, 1967.

Buckley, Michael J. *At the Origins of Modern Atheism*. New Haven, CT: Yale University Press, 1987.

Burtt, Edwin, ed. *English Philosophers from Bacon to Mill*. New York: The Modern Library, 1939.

Caferro, William and Duncan G. Fisher, eds. *The Unbounded Community: Papers in Christian Ecumenism in Honor of Jaroslav Pelikan*. New York: Garland, 1996.

Calvin, John. *Institutes of the Christian Religion,* 2 vols. Translated by Henry Beveridge. Grand Rapids: Eerdmans, 1953.

Campagnac, E. T., ed. *The Cambridge Platonists*. Oxford: Clarendon, 1901.

Campbell, Ted A. *John Wesley and Christian Antiquity. Religious Vision and Cultural Change*. Nashville: Kingswood, 1991.

Caponigri, Robert. *Philosophy from the Renaissance to the Romantic Age*. Chicago: University of Notre Dame Press, 1963.

Cassirer, Ernst. *The Platonic Renaissance in England*. Translated by James P. Pettegrove. Austin: University of Texas Press, 1953.

Cell, George Croft. *The Rediscovery of John Wesley*. New York: Holt, 1935.

Church, R. W. *A Study in the Philosophy of Malebranche.* London: George Allen and Unwin, 1931.

Clark, J. C. D. *English Society 1660-1832.* Cambridge: Cambridge University Press, 2000.

Collier, Frank W. *John Wesley Among the Scientists.* Nashville: Abingdon, 1928.

Cone, James. *Black Theology and Black Power.* Maryknoll, NY: Orbis, 1997.

Copleston, Frederick. *A History of Philosophy,* 11 vols. London: Search Press, 1959.

Coppedge, Allen. *Shaping the Message: John Wesley in Theological Debate.* Nappanee, IN: Evangel, 1987.

Cragg, Gerald R. *The Church and the Age of Reason 1648-1789.* Pelican History of the Church, vol. 4. Grand Rapids: Eerdmans, 1960.

Cragg, Gerald R., ed. *The Cambridge Platonists.* New York: Oxford University Press, 1968.

Cranefield, Paul F. "On the Origin of the Phrase *Nihil est in intellectu quod non prius fuerit in sensu,*" *Journal of the History of Medicine and Allied Sciences,* 25 (1970): 77-80.

D'Aquili, Eugene and Andrew B. Newberg. *The Mystical Mind.* Minneapolis: Augsburg, 1999.

Daly, Mary. *Beyond God the Father. Toward a Philosophy of Women's Liberation,* 2nd edition. Boston: Beason Press, 1985.

Daniel-Rops, Henri. *The Church in the Eighteenth Century.* Translated by John Warrington. London: Dent, 1964.

Deblaere, Albert. "Christian Mystic Testimony," *Ons Geestelijk Erf* 72 (1998): 129-53.

Dreyer, Frederick. "Faith and Experience in the Thought of John Wesley," *American Historical Review,* 88 (1983): 12-30.

Dunning, H. Ray. *Grace, Faith and Holiness.* Kansas City: Beacon Hill Press of Kansas City, 1988.

Dymond, Sydney G. *The Psychology of the Methodist Revival.* Oxford: Oxford Univ. Press, 1926.

Eayrs, George. *John Wesley: Christian Philosopher and Church Founder.* London: Epworth, 1926.

English, John. "John Wesley's Indebtedness to John Norris," *Church History* 60 (1991): 55-69.

English, John. "The Cambridge Platonists in Wesley's 'Christian Library'," *Proceedings of the Wesley Historical Society* 36 (1968): 161-68.

Frei, Hans. *The Eclipse of Biblical Narrative: A Study in Eighteenth and Nineteenth Century Hermeneutics.* London: Yale University Press, 1974.

Gadamer, Hans Georg. *Truth and Method.* Translated by Joel Weinsheimer and Donald Marshall. New York: Continuum, 2004.

Gaustad, Edwin and Leigh Schmidt. *The Religious History of America: The Heart of the American Story from Colonial Times to Today,* rev. ed. New York: HarperCollins, 2002.

Graves, Frank P. *Peter Ramus and the Educational Reformation of the Sixteenth Century.* Charleston, SC: Bibliobazaar, 2009.

Gray, Wallace. "The Place of Reason in the Theology of John Wesley." Ph.D. diss., Vanderbilt University, 1958.

Green, Vivian H. H. *The Young Mr. Wesley. A Study of John Wesley at Oxford.* London: Edward Arnold, 1961.

Gunter, W. Stephen. *The Limits of 'Love Divine'.* Nashville: Kingswood, 1989.

Haas, J. W. "John Wesley's Views on Science and Christianity: An Examination of the Charge of Antiscience" *Church History* 63 (1994): 378-392.

Heitzenrater, Richard. *John Wesley and the Oxford Methodists.* Ph.D. diss., Duke University, 1972.

Heitzenrater, Richard. *Mirror and Memory: Reflections on Early Methodism.* Nashville: Kingswood, 1989.

Helm, Paul. "Locke on Faith and Knowledge," *Philosophical Quarterly* 23 (1973): 52-66.

Hindley, J. Clifford. "The Philosophy of Enthusiasm: A Study in the Origins of 'Experimental Theology,'" *The London Quarterly and Holborn Review,* 182 (1957): 102-06.

Holmes, Stephen R. *God of Grace and God of Glory. An Account of the Theology of Jonathan Edwards.* Edinburgh: T & T Clark, 2000.

Horst, M. L. "Christian Understanding and the Life of Faith in John Wesley." Ph.D. diss., Yale University, 1985.

Howell, Wilbur S. *Eighteenth Century British Logic and Rhetoric.* Princeton, NJ: Princeton University Press, 1971.

Howell, Wilbur S. *Logic and Rhetoric in England 1500-1700.* Princeton NJ: Princeton University Press, 1956.

Hume, David. *An Enquiry Concerning Human Understanding.* Edited by Tom Beauchamp. Oxford: Oxford University Press, 2000.

Jobling, J'annine and Ian Markham, eds. *Theological Liberalism.* London: SPCK, 2000.

Jones, Scott J. *John Wesley's Conception and Use of Scripture.* Nashville: Kingswood, 1995.

Jones, W. T. *A History of Western Philosophy.* New York: Harcourt, Brace and World, 1952.

Keefer, Luke L. "John Wesley, Disciple of Early Christianity." Ph.D. diss., Temple University, 1982.

Kneale, William and Martha Kneale. *The Development of Logic.* Oxford: Oxford University Press, 1962.

Lakatos, Imre and A. Musgrave, eds. *Criticism and the Growth of Knowledge.* Cambridge: Cambridge University Press, 1976.

Langford, Thomas A. *Practical Divinity. Theology in the Wesleyan Tradition.* Nashville: Kingswood, 1983.

Lawton, George. *John Wesley's English. A Study of His Literary Style.* London: Allen and Unwin, 1962.

Lee, Umphrey. *John Wesley and Modern Religion.* Nashville: Cokesbury, 1936.

Leger, J. Augustin. "Wesley's Place in Catholic Thought," *Constructive Quarterly* 2 (1914): 329-60.

Lindstrom, Harald. *Wesley and Sanctification: A Study in the Doctrine of Salvation.* Grand Rapids, MI: Zondervan, 1980.

Lodahl, Michael. *The Story of God.* Kansas City: Beacon Hill Press of Kansas City, 1994.

Louth, Andrew. *Discerning the Mystery. An Essay on the Nature of Theology.* Oxford: Oxford University Press, 1984.

Luby, Daniel J. "The Perceptibility of Grace in the Theology of John Wesley: A Roman Catholic Consideration." Ph.D. diss., Pontifical University of Thomas Aquinas in Urbe, 1984.

Luther, Martin. *Luther's Works.* Edited by Jaroslav Pelikan and Helmut T. Lehman. St. Louis: Concordia, 1955-1986.

Maddox, Randy. *Responsible Grace.* Nashville: Kingswood, 1994.

Maddox, Randy, ed. *Aldersgate Reconsidered.* Nashville: Abingdon Press, 1990.

Malebranche, Nicolas. *The Search After Truth.* Translated and edited by Thomas M. Lennon and Paul J. Olscamp. Cambridge: Cambridge University Press, 1997.

Matthews, Rex Dale. "'Reason and Religion Joined': A Study in the Theology of John

Wesley." Th.D. diss., Harvard University, 1986.

McCraken, Charles J. *Malebranche and British Philosophy.* Oxford: Oxford University Press, 1983.

McGiffert, Arthur C. *Protestant Thought before Kant.* London: Charles Scribner's Sons, 1919.

McIntire, Carl. *Servants of Apostasy.* New York: Christian Beacon Press, 1954.

Mercer, Jerry L. "Toward a Wesleyan Understanding of Christian Experience," *Wesleyan Theological Journal* 20 (1985): 78-93.

Meyers, Arthur C., Jr. "John Wesley and the Church Fathers." Ph.D. diss., St. Louis University, 1985.

Montecheuil, Yves de. *Malebranche et le quietisme.* Paris: Aubier, 1946.

Morawetz, Bruno. "The Epistemology of John Norris." Ph.D. diss., Ontario University, 1963.

Müller, Richard. *God, Creation, and Providence in the Thought of Jacob Arminius.* Grand Rapids: Baker, 1991.

Nadler, Steven. *Malebranche and Ideas.* Oxford: Oxford University Press, 1992.

Nelson, Norman E. *Peter Ramus and the Confusion of Logic, Rhetoric and Poetry,* Contributions in Modern Philology #2. Ann Arbor MI: University of Michigan Press, 1947.

Newton, John A. "The Ecumenical Wesley," *Ecumenical Review* 24 (1972):160-75.

Nielsen, Kai. "Wittgensteinian Fideism," *Philosophy* 42 (1967) 191-209.

Noro, Yoshio. "Wesley's Theological Epistemology," *Iliff Review* 28 (1971): 59-76.

Oden, Thomas. *John Wesley's Scriptural Christianity: A Plain Exposition of His Teaching on Christian Doctrine.* Grand Rapids: Zondervan, 1994.

Ong, Walter J. *Ramus. Method, and the Decay of Dialogue.* Chicago: University of Chicago Press, 1958.

Ott, Philip W. "John Wesley and the Non-Naturals," *Preventive Medicine* 9 (1980): 578-84.

Ott, Philip W. "John Wesley on Health as Wholeness," *Journal of Religion and Health* 30 (1991): 43-57.

Ott, Philip W. "John Wesley on Health. A Word for Sensible Regime," *Methodist History* 18 (1980):193-304.

Ott, Philip W. "John Wesley on Mind and Body. Toward and Understanding of Health as Wholeness," *Methodist History* 27 (1989): 61-72.

Outler, Albert C. "The Wesleyan Quadrilateral in Wesley," *Wesleyan Theological Journal* 20 (1985): 7-18.

Pauw, Amy Plantinga. *The Supreme Harmony of All. The Trinitarian Theology of Jonathan Edwards.* Grand Rapids: Eerdmans, 2002.

Powicke, Frederick J. *The Cambridge Platonists. A Study.* London: Dent, 1926.

Rattenbury, John E. *Wesley's Legacy to the World: Six Studies in the Permanent Values of the Evangelical Revival.* Nashville: Cokesbury, 1928.

Redwood, John. *Reason, Ridicule and Religion: The Age of Enlightenment in England 1660-1750.* Cambridge, MA: Harvard University Press, 1976.

Reist, Irwin W. "John Wesley and George Whitefield: A Study in the Integrity of Two Theologies of Grace," *Evangelical Quarterly* 47 (1975): 26-40.

Rivers, Isabel. *Reason, Grace and Sentiment. A Study of the Language of Religion and Ethics in England 1660-1780,* 2 vols. Cambridge: Cambridge University Press, 1991.

Rome, Beatrice K. *The Philosophy of Malebranche. A Study of his Integration of Faith, Reason, and Experimental Observation.* Chicago: Henry Regnery, 1963.

Rouse, Ruth and Stephen Charles Neill, eds. *A History of the Ecumenical Movement 1517-1948.* New York: World Council of Churches, 1993.

Runyon, Theodore. *The New Creation.* Nashville: Abingdon, 1998.

Russell, Bertrand. *History of Western Philosophy and its Connection with Political and Social Circumstances from the Earliest Times to the Present Day.* London: George Allen and Unwin, 1946.

Shelton, R. Larry. "The Trajectory of Wesleyan Theology," *Wesleyan Theological Journal* 21 (1986): 159-75.

Shimuzu, Mitsuo. "Epistemology in the Thought of John Wesley." Ph.D. diss., Drew University, 1980.

Smith, David L. *A Handbook of Contemporary Theology.* Grand Rapids: Baker, 1992.

Stacey, John, ed. *John Wesley: Contemporary Perspectives.* London: Epworth, 1988.

Starkey, Lycurgus M. *The Work of the Holy Spirit: A Study in Wesleyan Theology.* New York: Abingdon, 1962.

Stephen, Leslie *History of English Thought in the Eighteenth Century,* 2 vols. Boston: Adamant Media Corporation, 2007.

Thompson, Edward P. *The Making of the English Working Class.* New York: Pantheon, 1966.

Thorsen, Donald A. D. *The Wesleyan Quadrilateral.* Lexington, KY: Emeth, 1990.

Todd, John M. *John Wesley and the Catholic Church.* London: Hodder and Stoughton, 1958.

Townsend, William, Herbert B. Workman, and George Eayrs, eds. *A New History of Methodism,* vol. 1. London: Hodder and Stoughten, 1909.

Turner, George Allen. *The More Excellent Way: The Scriptural Basis of the Wesleyan Message.* Winona Lake, IN: Light and Life, 1952.

Tuttle, Robert. *John Wesley: His Life and Theology.* Grand Rapids: Zondervan, 1978.

Vickers, Jason. *Invocation and Assent.* Grand Rapids: Eerdmans, 2008.

Vidgrain, Joseph. *Le christianisme dans la philosophie de Malebranche.* Paris: Alcan, 1923.

Visser 't Hooft, W. A. *The Genesis of the World Council of Churches.* New York: World Council of Churches, 1988.

Volf, Miroslav. *Church in the Image of the Trinity.* Grand Rapids: Eerdmans, 1998.

Von Balthasar, Hans Urs. *Word and Redemption. Essays in Theology,* 2 vols. Translated by A. V. Littledale in cooperation with Alexander Dru. New York: Herder and Herder, 1965.

Wainwright, Geoffery. "John Wesley's Trinitarian Hermeneutics," *Wesleyan Theological Journal* 36 (2001): 7-30.

Walls, Jerry L. "The Free Will Defense, Calvinism and Wesley, and the Goodness of God," *Christian Scholar's Review* 13 (1983): 19-33.

Williams, Colin W. *John Wesley's Theology Today.* Nashville: Abingdon, 1960.

Winnett, Arthur R. *Peter Browne. Provost, Bishop, Metaphysician.* London: S. P. C. K., 1974.

Wood, Laurence. "Wesley's Epistemology," *Wesleyan Theological Journal* 10 (1975): 48-59.

Wright, John W. and J. Douglas Harrison. "The Ecclesial Practice of Reconciliation and the End of the 'Wesleyan'," *Wesleyan Theological Journal* 37 (2002): 212-214.

Wynkoop, Mildred Bangs. *A Theology of Love.* Kansas City: Beacon Hill Press of Kansas City, 1972.

Yates, Arthur. *The Doctrine of Assurance with Special Reference to John Wesley.* London: Epworth, 1952.

Index

A

Act of Toleration, 31
Address to the Clergy, 30, 33–35, 44, 65, 66, 70, 90, 95, 98, 111, 113, 244, 246
Age of Reason, 25, 26, 67
agnosticism, 50, 56
Aldersgate, 59, 77, 80, 86, 136, 137, 150, 151, 153, 155, 175–79, 182
Aldrich, Henry, 27, 30, 52, 59
antinomianism, 171, 233
antiquity, 96, 205–07
apprehension, 27, 28, 30, 52, 53, 58, 79, 84, 90, 94, 130, 132, 146, 163, 172, 193
Aristotle, 38, 39, 54, 61
    empiricism, 11, 16, 42, 51, 56, 57, 68, 76, 84, 89, 94, 115, 117, 119–21, 123, 135, 142,
        158, 204, 259, 260
    logic, 25, 27–33, 37, 47, 52, 53, 89, 91, 105, 116
Arminian Magazine, 24, 51
Arminianism, 91, 158, 164, 216
Arminius, Jacob, 28, 159
Arndt, John, 197
assent, 47, 49, 51, 59, 131, 132, 134, 155, 156, 177
Atheism, 42, 107

B

Bacon, Francis, 25, 30, 37–49, 53, 54, 57, 61–63, 65, 116, 118
Beattie, James, 56
belief, 32, 40, 49, 97, 102, 109, 117, 125, 143, 148, 155, 160, 165, 187–89, 191, 235, 239,
    249, 263
Bell, George, 106, 221
Berkeley, George, 25, 45, 57
Bible. *See* Scripture
biography, 186, 190, 195–98
Boehme, Jacob, 113, 220, 221
Böhler, Peter, 80, 108, 150, 151, 175–78
Britain, 21, 22, 33, 37, 39, 63, 216

British Empiricism, 16, 25, 28, 42, 45–57, 80
Browne, Peter, 16, 45, 46, 48–50, 53, 55, 56, 58, 59, 66, 81, 82, 120

C

Calvin, Jean, 65, 158, 159, 162, 164, 166, 181, 201, 216, 233, 256
Cambridge Platonists, 25, 61–67, 125
Campbell, George, 17, 56, 211
Case of Reason Impartially Considered, The, 110, 146
categories (philosophical), 30, 53
Catholic Spirit, 78, 231, 233, 235
Cell, George Croft, 17, 76, 126, 136, 155, 180, 181
Cheyne, George, 37, 39, 40
Christ, 40, 81, 99, 108, 110, 118, 125, 130, 132, 137, 150, 156, 161, 162, 165, 166, 170,
    176–78, 186, 188, 189, 194, 196–98, 205, 206, 211, 233, 234, 236, 241, 254
Christian Library, 65, 205
Christianity, 15, 39, 43, 62, 79, 80, 96, 97, 129, 134, 161, 177, 178, 189, 196, 197, 211,
    217, 218, 225, 228, 231–33, 237, 246, 248, 249, 251–54, 256
Christology, 249, 251, 252, 255
    monophysitism, 249, 256
Church of England, 15, 29, 155, 205, 207, 208, 212
Clark, J. C. D., 46
Clarke, James, 233
Clarke, Samuel, 144
community, 185, 196, 212, 221, 222, 225, 226, 227, 228
conversion, 78, 80, 191–93, 195, 237, 238
Cudworth, Ralph, 61–63, 65

D

Deism, 42, 49, 107, 108, 233
demons, 93, 150, 156
Descartes, Rene, 47, 62–64, 119
Desideratum, The, 41
Devil. *See* Satan
double truth, 38

E

Earnest Appeal to Men of Reason and Religion, 79, 125, 131, 146
Eayrs, George, 17, 76
ecumenism, 217, 218, 231, 232, 235, 237, 238, 240, 241, 253, 255, 260, 262
election, 91, 158–66, 257
electricity, 39, 40, 43, 248
England, 15, 16, 22, 25, 30, 33, 43, 45, 46, 49, 50, 61, 68, 69, 77, 82, 85, 103, 109, 113,
    114, 124, 159, 167, 186, 190, 205–09, 211, 259, 263
English (language), 9, 17, 22, 23, 25, 26, 43, 57, 58, 59, 61, 64, 69, 70, 97, 107, 111, 129,
    137, 218, 263

English, John, 65
Enlightenment, The, 42, 43, 45, 107, 111, 112, 262
enthusiasm, 15, 32, 47, 55, 71, 81, 94, 104–08, 110, 125, 127, 128, 137, 158, 168, 171, 174, 180, 187, 199, 221
episcopacy, 206
epistemology, 11, 16, 28, 39, 40, 45, 47, 49, 51, 55, 57, 66, 67, 68, 70, 75, 76, 82, 84, 85, 95, 110, 116, 123, 125, 126, 135, 138, 142, 143, 174, 175, 178, 204, 224, 246, 254, 259, 260, 262
    religious, 16, 17, 21, 22, 69, 75, 89, 237
Evangelical Revival, 17, 159, 192
experience
    and reason, 115–17
    and Scripture, 145–51
    as active concern, 82–85
    as communal, 189–99
    as hermeneutical circle, 119–20
    as public appeal, 77–82
    cultural background of the word, 22–24
    individual religious, 186–89
    philosophical background, 24–25
experimental religion, 26, 118, 155, 174, 180

F

faith, 18, 31, 33, 35, 38, 40, 41, 47, 48, 51, 57–59, 63, 65, 67–69, 76, 78–80, 86, 89, 91–95, 97, 102, 103, 108, 110, 111, 113, 115–37, 142, 146–56, 161, 162, 164, 165, 171, 175–82, 186, 187, 192–96, 204, 207, 215, 217, 223–25, 228, 232, 234, 236–41, 244, 250, 251, 253, 254, 261, 262, 263
Farther Appeal To Men of Reason and Religion, 31, 80, 92, 143, 188
Fiddes,Richard, 51
fideism, 119, 246
field-preaching, 31, 207, 211, 240
Fletcher, John, 195, 196, 201
Free Grace, 159, 162

G

Georgia, 29, 41, 81, 150, 178, 186, 190
Gospel, 61, 99, 112, 132, 205, 223, 228, 235
grace, 105, 124, 150, 152, 158, 161–66, 176, 179, 199, 216, 232
Guyon (Guion), Madam, 101, 197–99

H

Hartley, David, 37, 39, 40
heaven, 53, 107, 137, 143, 146, 160, 201, 232, 234
hermeneutical circle, 119–23, 125, 131, 134, 135, 141–51, 153, 156, 158, 177, 180, 208, 215, 217, 219, 221, 223–25, 232, 235, 236, 240, 243, 249, 252, 260

history, 48, 64, 78, 89, 90, 95, 101, 102, 122, 159, 175, 180, 197, 205, 208, 221, 243, 246, 248, 253, 254, 261, 262
Hobbes, Thomas, 25, 37–41, 43, 45–49, 61–63, 118
holiness, 32, 99, 133, 150, 151, 160, 164, 165, 196, 198, 224
Holy Spirit, 129, 132, 133, 147, 182, 185, 188, 189, 205, 228, 241, 257
Hume, David, 25, 29, 45, 47–50, 56, 57, 63, 66, 68, 82, 84, 86, 116, 256, 263
Hutchinson, John, 98, 112, 113

I

Ignatius, 197, 205
interdisciplinary theology, 217, 218, 243, 244, 255, 260
inter-religious dialogue, 237, 239, 262
intuition, 49, 110, 126, 137, 204
inward feelings, 129, 130, 133, 186–89

J

Jesus, 81, 91, 99, 110, 118, 125, 131, 150, 162, 165, 166, 170, 189, 197, 198
Johnson, Samuel, 23, 24, 26
Jones, Scott, 77
Jones, William, 250
Journal, 9, 18, 26, 33–35, 41–44, 59, 78, 81, 82, 85, 86, 91, 92, 95, 96, 106–08, 111–13, 118, 122–24, 130, 132, 136–38, 147, 150–53, 158, 165, 177, 179–82, 186–96, 199–201, 206, 211, 218, 227, 228, 236, 241, 248, 256, 257
judgment, 27, 29, 40, 52, 70, 84, 89, 97, 104, 120, 128, 144, 198, 206, 220, 232, 233, 234, 237, 255
justification, 31, 35, 86, 94, 95, 113, 161, 174, 176, 181, 207, 246, 250, 251, 254, 261

K

Kant, Immanuel, 17, 30
King, Lord Peter, 206, 207
Kingswood School, 30, 51

L

latitudinarianism, 234
Lavington, Bishop George, 26, 35, 86, 110, 114, 187, 199, 241
Lewin, Margaret, 30, 34, 35, 51, 59, 70, 96, 112, 244, 246
Liberation theology, 226
Locke, John, 11, 16, 25, 28–30, 33, 45–59, 62–68, 82, 84, 86, 91, 95, 101, 112, 116, 119, 123, 126, 135, 259
logic. *See* Aristotle, logic
Luther, Martin, 116, 176, 181

M

Macarius, 197

Maddox, Randy, 18, 44, 85, 109, 111, 113, 136, 137, 144, 152, 153, 158, 159, 181, 182, 199, 211, 218, 252, 256, 257

Malebranche, Nicolas, 25, 61, 63–70

Markham, Ian, 239, 242

martyrs, 28, 197, 201

materialism, 25, 37, 38, 42, 54, 107, 118

Matthews, Rex, 17, 25, 26, 33, 34, 70, 71, 85, 95, 124, 126, 136, 180

metaphysics, 27–34, 37, 38, 41, 45, 47, 51–53, 55–57, 61, 65, 66, 68, 75, 89–91, 94, 126, 217, 243

Methodism, 12, 15, 17, 34, 35, 43, 44, 82, 96, 111, 122, 123, 159, 180, 187, 191, 206, 207, 212, 216, 218, 222, 224, 227, 233, 236, 241, 253

Middleton, Conyers, 80, 86, 113

ministry, 15, 29, 30, 90, 151, 196, 206, 221, 232, 244, 245

miracles, 42, 92, 93

missions, 253

Montesquieu, Barren Charles- Louis de Secondat, 51, 56, 59

Moravians, 175, 178, 193

mysticism, 65, 70, 100, 104, 106, 182, 185, 190, 198, 233

N

natural philosophy, 34, 38, 42, 43, 55, 98, 102, 111, 112

natural theology, 143–45

Newton, Sir Isaac, 98, 240

Norris, John, 25, 61–70, 137

O

omniscience, 223

ordination, 29, 206, 207, 240, 256

orthodoxy, 15, 175, 216, 232–37, 255

Outler, Albert, 34, 137, 256

overly pragmatic theology, 247–53

Oxford, 17, 25–29, 33, 34, 45, 48, 50, 51, 55, 57, 58, 61, 65, 69, 70, 86, 150, 155, 228, 232

P

Palau, 40, 102, 103

Parliament, 84

Patrick, Simon, 65

Pelew. *See* Palau

perichoresis, 252

philosophy, 28, 37, 38, 42, 44, 45, 48–50, 58, 61–68, 85, 97, 98, 101, 102, 123, 127, 221, 243, 248, 256, 259, 261, 262

physicians, 41, 44, 248
piety, 95, 205
Plain Account of Christian Perfection, 99, 109, 111–13, 166, 182, 233, 242
Plato, 27, 61
Plotinus, 61
pluralism, 231, 237
Pneumatology, 251, 252
Polycarp, 197, 205
post-modernity, 22, 57, 224, 262
praxis, 254
prayer, 99, 103, 147, 176, 194
predestination, 91, 159, 160, 164, 165, 252, 256
Predestination Calmly Considered, 79, 86, 159, 161, 181
Priestly, Josephy, 39
Primitive Physic, 41, 43, 44, 119, 248, 256
Protestants, 17, 28, 69, 158, 159, 162, 253, 257
Providence, 107
psychology, 22, 24, 39, 68, 77, 81, 157, 174, 175, 180, 186, 246, 260
Puritans, 28, 195, 196

Q

Quakers, 127, 128, 129, 137, 232, 233, 241
quietism, 104

R

Radical Orthodoxy, 217
Ramsay, Andrew, 104, 144, 145
Ramus, Peter, 28, 34
Rationalism, 25, 27, 28, 46, 62, 64, 65, 259
reason, 11, 15–18, 25–35, 38, 39, 43, 46–48, 51, 58, 61–71, 77, 81, 84, 85, 89, 90, 93–99
    102, 104, 105, 108–37, 141–58, 162, 166, 169, 171, 179, 180, 183, 188–91, 193, 194,
    197, 198, 203–08, 210, 220–22, 227, 235, 236, 238, 241, 250–53, 256, 260
Reid, Thomas, 56
relational theology, 219, 222
religious experience, 50, 76, 85, 89, 98, 100, 101, 105, 141, 180, 185, 186, 190, 191, 195,
    199, 220, 249, 262
Renty, Marquis de, 24, 249, 256
reprobation, 159, 162, 164
revelation, 15, 16, 41, 47–49, 52, 55, 56, 64, 68, 103, 104, 118, 129, 130, 142–45, 152,
    180, 208, 210
Roman Catholicism, 105, 106, 132, 187, 199, 212, 231, 233, 241, 245, 253, 256, 262
Rousseau, Jean-Jacques, 56, 98
Rutherforth, Thomas, 70, 133, 138, 189, 199

S

salvation, 31, 91, 92, 108, 132, 160–64, 176–79, 192, 194, 198, 200, 232, 234, 249, 251
sanctification, 94, 99, 109, 176, 183, 216, 251, 254, 261
Sanderson, Robert, 27, 28
Satan, 31, 93, 103, 148, 164, 165, 170, 171, 228, 232, 233
scholasticism, 38, 39, 61
science, 16, 21–26, 30, 32, 34, 37–42, 54, 57, 63–65, 68, 89, 90, 98, 101–03, 106, 107, 112, 138, 144, 147, 152, 156, 158, 238, 245, 246, 249, 263
Scripture, 11, 15–17, 21, 29, 31, 40, 42, 44, 53, 54, 64, 66, 68, 77, 81, 86, 89–115, 120–37, 141–85, 188–212, 215–26, 233–40, 243–53, 257, 260–63
    and reason, 109–11
    and religious experience, 103–05
    and science, 101–03
    improper interpretation of, 105–09
    in relation to experience, 120–23
sermons, 9, 24, 33, 67, 112, 113, 122, 123, 137, 144, 156, 168, 174, 186, 195–201, 223, 227, 228, 236, 250, 256, 261
Shimizu, Mitsuo, 70, 126
sin, 24, 40, 41, 92, 94, 99, 102, 106, 109, 124, 133, 145, 148–50, 153, 162, 167, 170, 173, 176, 177, 192, 204, 234
    Original, 9, 26, 43, 85, 86, 123, 148, 152, 228
skepticism, 28, 49, 63, 82, 98, 263
Smith, John (Anonymous Correspondent), 156, 188, 232
Smith, John (Cambridge Platonist), 61–65
Socrates, 51
Soteriology, 250
spiritual senses, 17, 56, 63, 68, 75, 84, 123, 125–37, 145, 146, 171, 172, 260
Stillingfleet, Bishop Edward, 206, 211
Survey of the Wisdom of God in Creation, 42, 98, 102
Swedenborg, Baron Emanuel, 100, 220, 227, 249, 256
syllogism, 30–35, 53, 54

T

tabula rasa, 57
Taylor, Jeremy, 148, 149, 190
testimony, 46, 47, 78, 80, 93, 100, 102–04, 107, 112, 129, 151, 169–74, 177, 185, 186, 191–96, 200, 208, 210
theological method, 16, 17, 21, 68, 76, 89, 94, 115, 120, 135, 136, 141, 149, 151, 157, 158, 167, 168, 173–75, 178, 180, 203, 205, 207, 208, 210, 215–45, 250, 253, 255, 259–62
theology, 11, 12, 15–17, 21, 24–26, 40, 41, 65, 70, 76, 77, 85, 97, 109, 135, 141–45, 151, 152, 155–57, 167, 173–75, 179, 182–87, 190, 191, 203–212, 215–39, 243–55, 259–63
    at a university, 244–46
Thorsen, Donald, 18, 26, 85, 109, 111, 113, 136, 152, 153, 181, 211
Thoughts Upon Necessity, 83

tradition, 11, 16, 18, 25–30, 33, 38, 45, 50, 54, 55, 59, 61, 64, 65, 89, 106, 110, 142, 152, 162, 182, 185, 203–212, 221, 240, 260, 262

trans-sensory reality, 62, 63, 121, 130–35, 142, 145, 158, 164, 179, 185, 193, 195, 208, 215

Trinity, 9, 24, 26, 144, 181, 234, 241, 247–57

truth, 15, 28–33, 37–40, 44, 46, 47, 53, 56, 61–64, 77, 80–84, 90, 97–100, 103, 108, 114, 118, 119, 129, 130, 132, 134, 137, 138, 145–53, 156, 157, 163, 165, 167, 170–73, 177–79, 186, 193, 195, 205, 210, 215, 217, 221–28, 231–38, 247, 249, 262, 263

U

unbelief, 186, 187, 249

V

Voltaire, 56, 97, 101

W

Wallis, John, 30
Wesley, John
    and British Empiricism, 45–57
    as Aristotelian logician, 27–33
    as Arminian, 158–66
    as pragmatic empiricist, 117–19, 263
    as Rational Devotionalist, 65–67
    as scientist, 39–42
    experience at Aldersgate, 175–79
    implicit epistemology of, 75–76
    reaction to David Hume, 56
    reaction to John Locke, 50–55
    reaction to Peter Browne, 55–56
Wesleyan Quadrilateral, 18, 26, 34, 85, 111, 113, 136, 142, 152, 153, 181, 203, 210, 211
Whichcote, Benjamin, 61–65, 69, 124
Whitefield, George, 159–61, 181, 195, 196, 201, 241
Williams, Colin, 18, 111, 113, 138, 152, 157, 181, 190, 240, 241, 257
Wilson, Henry, 40, 102, 103
witchcraft, 42, 107, 108
witness of the spirit
    sermon, 79, 84, 99, 168
    theological concept, 68, 99, 160, 168, 171, 172, 174, 175
Wittgenstein, Ludwig, 246
worldview, 37–43, 62, 107, 108, 115, 117, 136, 147
worship, 31, 103, 105, 122, 179, 194, 200, 236

Z

Zinzendorf, Count Ludwig, 130

CPSIA information can be obtained
at www.ICGtesting.com
Printed in the USA
LVOW10s1557121216
516922LV00003B/763/P